Exploring the Scottish Past

EXPLORING THE SCOTTISH PAST

Themes in the History of Scottish Society

T. M. Devine

TUCKWELL PRESS

First published in 1995 by Tuckwell Press Ltd
The Mill House
Phantassie
East Linton
East Lothian EH40 3DG
Scotland

Reprinted in 1996 and 1998

British Library Cataloguing in Publication Data

A catalogue record for this book is available from the British Library

ISBN 1 898410 38 0

The Publishers acknowledge subsidy from the Scottish Arts Council
towards the publication of this volume

Typeset by Hewer Text Composition Services, Edinburgh
Printed by Athenæum Press Ltd

For Catherine

CONTENTS

PREFACE

This volume reprints a selection of the essays which I have published on seventeenth-, eighteenth- and nineteenth-century Scottish history over the last two decades in a variety of books and learned journals. The essays are presented as they first appeared. No attempt has been made to include revisions in the light of more recent work. I have, however, tried to give some overall shape to the book by setting out the chapters within a chronological and thematic framework. The essays range in type from detailed pieces of original research to general interpretations of some key topics in modern Scottish history.

By collecting together varied pieces on a number of themes, I hope to reveal something of my own approach to Scottish historical studies. I regard the subject as both important and exciting not only in promoting an understanding of the Scottish present but because the Scottish past of the last three centuries poses enormous intellectual challenges to the historian. Few societies in Europe experienced such radical and rapid social and economic changes as Scotland from the later seventeenth century. The Scottish past presents remarkable opportunities to study such seminal historical issues as industrialisation, urbanisation, emigration, migration, the modernisation of rural society and a host of other themes.

By analysing Scottish history in this way, scholars can seek to integrate the subject into the mainstream of European historical studies. To do this in a satisfactory manner, however, at least two steps are vital. First, Scottish studies must be set in a comparative context. We cannot know what is distinctive about Scottish society unless we compare and contrast it with other areas of Britain or Europe. Second, Scottish historians should be aware of the general historiographical agenda and attempt to link their detailed work with the broader issues and controversies being addressed by scholars outside Scotland. If they do so they will not only avoid any tendency towards parochialism and antiquarianism but will also ensure that Scottish historical studies take their rightful place on the British and European scene.

The topics addressed in this book reflect some of the historical issues which have intrigued me over the past twenty years. They do not represent any clearly formulated research agenda systematically pursued over time. My approach to Scottish historical scholarship has been to address problems which have puzzled and fascinated me, whatever their period and subject. This helps to account for the eclectic nature and chronological range of this collection. The essays I wrote in the 1970s had a primarily 'economic' emphasis; those from the 1980s and early 1990s mainly focused on 'social' issues. However, the approach I have adopted in all my work has been to try to integrate political, economic, social and cultural explanation in an overall interpretation.

T. M. Devine

ACKNOWLEDGEMENTS

I am grateful in particular to the many teachers, academic colleagues and friends who have helped to shape my understanding and interpretation of Scottish history over the last two decades. A special debt is owed to my undergraduate and postgraduate students, past and present, at Strathclyde University who have been a constant source of both stimulus and criticism and who in several cases by their curiosity have inspired me to address some of the themes considered in this book.

Thanks are also due to Mrs. Jean Fraser, former secretary in the Department of History, University of Strathclyde, who assisted with the preparation of the material.

It is also very pleasant to acknowledge publicly, with deep gratitude, the enormous support give me in my research by Catherine, and my sons and daughters over the years. Their patience and tolerance should also be recorded!

The chapters of this book first appeared in the following and thanks are due to both publishers and editors for permission to allow publication in this form. Original conventions of referencing and citation have been retained:

1. J. Butt and J. T. Ward, eds., *Scottish Themes* (Scottish Academic Press, 1976), pp. 1–16.
2. G. Gordon and B. Dicks, eds., *Scottish Urban History* (Aberdeen University Press, 1983), pp. 92–111.
3. *Scottish Economic and Social History*, 5 (1985), pp. 23–40.
4. T. M. Devine and D. Dickson, eds., *Ireland and Scotland 1600–1850* (John Donald Publishers, 1983), pp. 12–30.
5. *Scottish Historical Review*, LII, 1: No. 153 (1973), pp. 50–71.
6. O. D. Edwards and G. Shepperson, eds., *Scotland, Europe and the American Revolution* (Edinburgh University Student Publications, 1976), pp. 61–5.
7. R. Mitchison, ed., *Why Scottish History Matters* (Saltire Society, 1991), pp. 59–67.
8. T. M. Devine and R. Mitchison, eds., *People and Society in Scotland, I, 1760–1830* (John Donald Publishers, 1988), pp. 27–52.
9. A. Digby and C. Feinstein, eds., *New Directions in Economic and Social History* (Macmillan Education, 1989), pp. 35–52.
10. *Economic History Review*, 2nd series, Vol. XXXII (1979), pp. 344–59.
11. L. Leneman, ed., *Perspectives in Scottish Social History* (Aberdeen University Press, 1988), pp. 141–162.

ACKNOWLEDGEMENTS

12. R. Mitchison and P. Roebuck, eds., *Economy and Society in Scotland and Ireland. 1500–1939* (John Donald Publishers, 1988), pp. 126–139.
13. *Social History*, Vol. 3(3) (1978), pp. 331–346.
14. T. M. Devine, ed., *Farm Servants and Labour in Lowland Scotland, 1770–1914* (John Donald Publishers, 1984), pp. 98–123.
15. T. M. Devine, ed., *Scottish Emigration and Scottish Society* (John Donald Publishers, 1992), pp. 1–15.

1

THE CROMWELLIAN UNION AND THE SCOTTISH BURGHS: THE CASE OF ABERDEEN AND GLASGOW, 1652–60

The Parliamentary Union of 1707 was a unique constitutional watershed in Scottish history. Yet in itself union between England and Scotland was no novelty. Half a century before, the army in the south had effected a conquest of Scotland which had resulted in the so-called 'Cromwellian union' of 1652–60. 'Unity' in this context was a response to English military diktat rather than an expression of Scottish aspirations. Inevitably therefore, the conditions of the new relationship reflected the southern government's desire to bring stability and security to its northern frontier.[1]

Much is already known about this brief period when Scotland was annexed to England. A series of volumes issued by the *Scottish History Society* and a variety of other publications enable the interested student to acquire a fairly clear impression of political and religious life at the time.[2] Unfortunately, however, the economic historian has not been as well served. Recently, the economy of the first quarter and last forty years of the seventeenth century has been described in some detail but the middle decades remain 'an obscure period'.[3] Yet the known and massive gaps in data have not inhibited several writers from judging Scottish economic experience although some of this work is reduced in value by a tendency to *a priori* reasoning and to bold generalisation based on a series of literary sources and diary accounts likely to be biased. This criticism may indeed be most pertinently directed at an important article written by Theodora Keith, the pioneering historian of Scottish trade, published as long ago as 1908, but whose viewpoint has influenced most writers to the present day.[4]

Keith was concerned to repudiate vigorously any suggestion that Scotland had benefited from the union. She admitted that the end of the civil wars re-established a secure context for commercial activity and that the Scots were allowed to trade freely both in England and her transatlantic colonies for the first time. But, in her opinion, these advantages were illusory and were more than counter-balanced by higher customs duties, heavy taxation by the commonwealth government and commercial legislation designed to suit English but not Scottish interests. Thus, the export of skins, hides and wool, traditional Scottish staples, was banned. Furthermore, in her opinion, the Anglo-Dutch war of 1652–4, a conflict with one of England's greatest rivals but one of Scotland's best customers, confirmed the malaise in overseas trade which had developed in the 1640s. As Keith concluded:

> On the whole, therefore, it does not seem that the country benefited materially during the Interregnum. Poverty was great, manufactures could not be set up. Trade, both inland and foreign, decayed, and showed little sign of recovery, and the bankruptcy of the country contributed towards the bankruptcy of the whole government and the downfall of the Protectorate.[5]

This assessment was based partly on the apparently obvious fact that Scotland was exhausted after the civil wars and that the negative legislation of 1652–60 could not possibly have accomplished anything but the prolonging of distress. Miss Keith then supported this assumption by citing evidence from such sources as were available to her at the time. Inevitably the historian of the Convention of Royal Burghs made full use of that body's records. However, while petitions to government from the Convention are informative about its desire to ameliorate the lot of its members and cut tax assessment, they are of more limited value, unless used very carefully, concerning the true nature of burghal conditions.

In this short essay a modest attempt will be made to test Keith's arguments against the commercial history of two leading Scottish burghs during the Cromwellian Union. In the 1650s, according to the tax roll of the Convention of Royal Burghs, Aberdeen and Glasgow were ranked the third and fourth towns respectively in Scotland in terms of wealth and commercial influence. Both served regional economies in the north-east and west-central parts of the country. Each was taxed according to its position in the burghal tax roll by the governments of the protectorate.[6] There is no obvious evidence that either was fortunate enough to escape the privation or the effects of the civil wars and their aftermath.

In September, 1644, for instance, Aberdeen had been sacked by the Earl of Montrose's levies after the battle of Justice Mills. A graphic account described how:

> Montrose followis the chaiss in to Aberdeen, his men hewing and cutting down all maner of men they could overtak within the towne, upone the streitis or in thair housses, and round about the towne as oure men wes fleing with brode swerdes but mercy or remeid. Thir cruell Irishis, seing a man weill clad, wold first tyr him and souf the clothis onspoyllet, syne kill the man. We lost thrie piece of cannon with muche armour besydes the plundering of oure toune housses, merchand butthis, and all, which wes pitifull to sie . . . the Irishis killing, robbing and plundering of this toune at thair plesour and

2

nothing hard bot houling, crying weiping, murning throw all the streittis.[7]

Three years later, in the autumn of 1647, a severe plague struck the burgh, killing 1,600 persons on one estimate, and temporarily depopulating the town.[8] Over the period 1639–48, the town council calculated that thirty-two merchant vessels had been lost and nearly £164,000 Scots spent on town defence, quarterings and acquisition of weapons.[9] Glasgow fared little better in the era of war before the union although, unlike Aberdeen, it was not plundered by enemy troops.[10] Nevertheless, in 1652, a crisis of even greater magnitude overtook the burgh when a major fire destroyed eighty closes and rendered 1,000 families homeless.[11]

The experience of these two towns during the Cromwellian Union will be considered principally on the basis of data relating to their seaborne commerce. Unfortunately in the case of both Aberdeen and Glasgow, centrally administered customs accounts, the historian's favourite tool for trade studies, are not available for the relevant years. Alternative materials were therefore employed. For Aberdeen the major source was the *Shore Work Accounts*. These were compiled as a result of a decision by James VI in 1596 to grant Aberdeen the privilege of collecting levies on vessels using the town's harbour, the sum accruing to be used for maintenance and extension to the quay. Through good fortune, a record of receipts from this impost, which incorporates details on the volume of commerce and shipping using the port, has survived in an almost continuous series from 1596 to 1810.[12]

Despite their obvious value, the *Accounts* must be treated with caution. It is difficult, for instance, to say anything with much confidence about the precise changes in the *value* of commodity trade over time. Contemporary weights and measures varied both in description and meaning and this renders conversion to uniform measurement well-nigh impossible.[13] Moreover, it is apparent that the administrative competence of those charged with the collection of the levy also varied, though perhaps not to such an extent as to invalidate the value of the source altogether. It might be added that since the records relate to a harbour rather than a port as administratively defined, a small proportion of goods could have passed through the town and not been registered in the *Accounts*.[14] This criticism, on the other hand, is less likely to relate to the burgh's foreign commerce.

In order to circumvent these problems, the aim here will simply be to aggregate the annual arrivals and departures of merchant vessels. This exercise can provide a crude index of trading activity and at the same time is less likely to be distorted by some of the flaws in the *Accounts* described above. As Professor Smout has said, from the point of view of the contemporary customs official, 'The coming and going of boats in themselves are easy to see and easy to count'.[15]

The main source of information for Glasgow's trade was the *Register of Ship Entries* at Dumbarton from 1595 to 1658. This is preserved in the

Dumbarton burgh archives and lists ships arriving in the Clyde from ports furth of Scotland.[16] In fact, almost all this trade seems to have been on Glasgow's account. Two local historians, Dr Macphail and Mr Roberts, have assessed the value of the *Register* as an indicator of the Clyde's foreign commerce by checking entries in it against three contemporary analyses: a list of ships engaged in the wine trade in April–May 1597, the return of the Collector of Customs in Glasgow for the period November 1626–November 1627 and the report of the English customs commissioner, Thomas Tucker, in 1655. Their conclusions suggest that when the *Register* is supplemented by additional information extracted from the *Dumbarton Common Good Accounts* it offers 'a fairly accurate picture' of seaborne commerce on the Clyde.[17] Some qualifications, however, must be borne in mind. There is evidence that before about 1620 the level of the timber trade may have been underestimated and the sources only describe the import side of foreign commerce while giving no information concerning the volume of coastal trade carried on in small boats. Because of these gaps, material from the Glasgow burgh records and the burgess register was also employed in this essay. As recent work has shown, changing levels of registration of merchant and craftsmen burgesses can provide an approximate guide to the economic fortunes of a Scottish burghal community.[18]

In April 1654, the Town Council of Aberdeen petititioned government that as a result of war and taxes, '. . . this place is become so miserable that almost there is none in it than can subsist or have any liveing'.[19] The suspicion that this statement was an example of special pleading is fully borne out by the evidence of trade data. One year before the declaration was made, the total number of entries and departures at the burgh's harbour reached 154, the highest figure for the entire period, 1596 to 1670.[20] Nor was this a fluke year. The depression in trade of the later 1640s seems to have ended in the following decade. As Figure 1 illustrates [p 5], the commerce of Aberdeen had been quite obviously affected by war and pestilence in the earlier period. The plague year, 1647, for example, stands out clearly as one of depression with entries falling to 37. However, this trend was reversed from 1652 and the level of activity suggested in the following eight years was more comparable with the 1620s and 1630s than with the era of the Bishops Wars and English invasions.

Further, despite the conflict between England and Holland from 1652–4, the Spanish War of 1657, and prohibition of export of skins, wools and hides, the foreign trade of Aberdeen did not stagnate during the union. Total foreign entries which reached a low of five in 1652, after three previous years of depression, recovered in the subsequent period (see Table 1). Two major sectors of overseas commerce, crucial to the prosperity of Aberdeen, were both particularly active after the malaise of 1647–52 (see Table 1). The renewal of the timber trade from Norway may perhaps indicate revival in the urban economy. Wood at this time was the universal packaging material, especially relevant to the Aberdeen fish trade, as well as

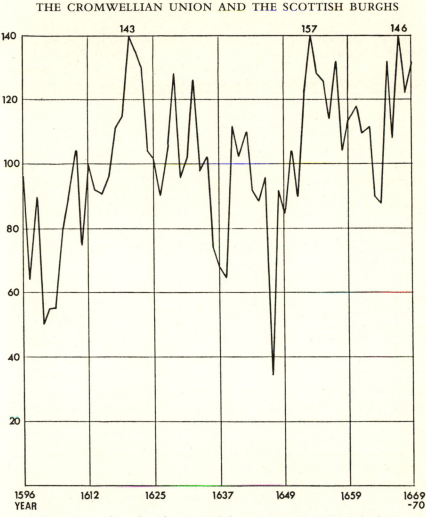

Figure 1 Total number of entries and departures, 1596–1669 (Aberdeen)

being vital in building and construction.[21] Significantly too, commercial relationships with Holland and Flanders seem to have deteriorated during 1652–3, coincident with the Anglo-Dutch War. But, as Table 1 shows, this was only a temporary disruption. The Dutch market was particularly important before the union as a source of demand for salmon and plaiding, the two great exports of Aberdeen. Export figures for the latter correlate with evidence already presented of a generally higher level of business activity in the 1650s than had characterised the previous decade. From 3 fardels of plaiding in 1650–1, total volume rose to 14 in 1652–3, 92 in 1654–5, 92 in 1655–6, fell to 44 in 1657–8 and increased again to 98 in 1659–60. In 1645–6 there was only one reference to plaiding exports and none in 1647–8.[22] While assessment over longer periods is made difficult by changing nomenclature of weights and measures, it would appear on the

5

evidence available, that 1652–60 does compare favourably with the period 1610–30, and with the 1660s.[23]

Table 1 'Foreign' Ship Entries at Aberdeen, 1640–65

Year	Norway	Holland/ Flanders	France	Baltic	Total
1640–1	7	12	2	9	30
1641–2	9	8	2	7	26
1642–3	5	15	3	5	28
1643–4	4	6	3	—	13
1644–5	3	9	1	3	16
1645–6	4	5	3	1	13
1647	1	2	2	—	5
1648–9	7	5	—	6	18
1649–50	4	6	1	—	11
1650–1	1	7	2	3	13
1651–2	2	5	2	2	11
1652–3	2	—	2	1	5
1653–4	3	3	3	6	15
1654–5	10	13	4	10	37
1655–6	6	8	3	—	17
1656–7	10	6	5	3	24
1657–8	6	4	3	14	
1658–9	4	11	1	1	17
1659–60	4	2	4	3	13
1660–1	6	10	2	1	19
1661–2	7	9	—	3	19
1662–3	9	6	6	1	22
1663–4	5	6	8	3	22
1664–5	3	2	1	—	6

Source: Aberdeen Accounts, 1640–65

This well documented revival in commercial fortunes was reflected too in the extension and improvement of the burgh's harbour. When Tucker visited Aberdeen in 1655 he was very favourably impressed by the work being carried out there.[24] Since financial support accrued from the levy on vessels using the port, this construction work can be regarded as both a cause and effect of the town's recovery.

While therefore there is substantial support for the proposition that Aberdeen achieved a return to 'normal' levels of commerce during the union there are fewer indications that free trade permitted the growth of a vigorous new relationship either with England or her colonies. Most entries in the *Accounts* continued to relate to coastal trade with other north-east ports or Dundee and Leith to the south; 'foreign' trade was almost exclusively with traditional customers in Norway, Holland, France and, to a lesser extent, the Baltic. Between 1652–60 only eleven ships either from English ports or owned by English merchants visited Aberdeen. Five of these were freighted, however, by Scottish merchants and only two carried manufactured goods; most shipped salt and lime.[25] Clearly here there is no basis for a recent assertion that 'free trade allowed the import to Scotland of English manufactured goods, more cheaply produced than those of Scotland, and they went a long way to drive Scottish manufactures off the market'.[26] Furthermore, the Aberdeen men showed little apparent inclination to move into the English or colonial market. Seventeenth century commercial relationships functioned on a foundation of trust and personal acquaintance developed over generations by merchant families in an epoch of high risk and insecure markets. War and political change, especially if only of short duration, did not seriously disturb these established business networks, and, in addition, paucity of capital resources often inhibited diversification as effectively as 'conservatism'.

The foreign trade pattern of Glasgow, the most rapidly growing burgh in Scotland, differed somewhat from Aberdeen. As the focus of the Clyde region it specialised in the importation of salt and wine from France and the export of salted fish. Yet, its commercial history during the middle decades of the seventeenth century was remarkably similar to that of the northern burgh. Both towns seem to have experienced difficulty in the years 1646–51 and each achieved a higher level of activity thereafter. If anything, perhaps, the data suggest that the rate of recovery was more spectacular on the Clyde than on the Dee. Between 1654 and 1657 entries at Dumbarton of vessels from ports outside Scotland were greater than at any period since 1620.[27] [see Figure 2, p. 8]. The average number of entries between 1658 and 1658 (when the *Register of Ship Entries* ends) was 15.3 per annum, compared with 8.3 from 1600–10, 8.6 from 1620–30, 6.3 from 1631–40 and 7.8 from 1641–50.[28]

Alternative measurements of Glasgow's economic condition give a similar impression of sustained recovery. Registration of craftsmen and merchant burgesses show an interesting correlation over time with the level of ship entries in the Clyde.[29] This may indicate that the guilds regulated the number of new burgesses at least partly according to the level of business activity. For instance, both burgess and ship registers show falls in the early 1620s, early and late 1630s and early 1650s together with substantial gains in the early 1640s and mid 1650s [See Figures 2 and 3]. Just as significantly there was a fairly marked correlation between merchant and craftsmen enrolments over the same period. As Figure 3 reveals, the number of new burgesses registered between 1654–8 was high and can be compared with other years of peak enrolment throughout the century.[30]

In the later 1640s and early 1650s there was considerable emphasis in the Glasgow burgh records on the ill effects of war and taxation on the town's economy.[31] The absence of such complaints thereafter is perhaps in itself eloquent testimony of better times. Yet, in addition, positive indicators of a more prosperous burghal economy emerged. In 1659, the Convention of Royal Burghs pointed out that the coal trade, in which Glasgow had an interest, was doing well.[32] Four years before this a new coal work had been

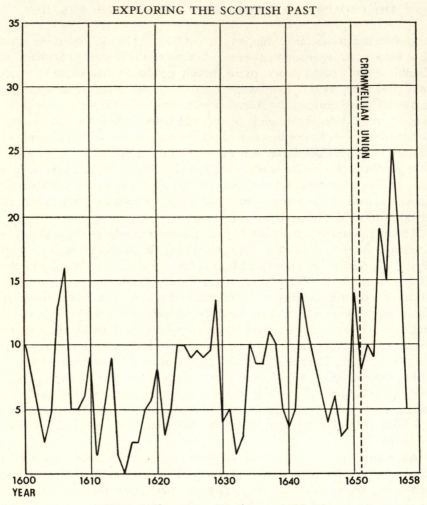

CROMWELLIAN UNION

Figure 2 Ship entries: Dumbarton, 1600–58

set up in the burgh and the town council had advanced 2,000 Scots merks to encourage it. In the same year £ 600 Scots were employed to extend the College.[33] Even the great fire of 1652 does not appear to have unduly disturbed the return to normality. £ 1,000 sterling were paid out by the Commander-in-Chief, Scotland from 'the treasury of the sequestrations' to aid the rebuilding programme.[34] Several Scottish burghs also gave subsidies and in July 1654, by ordinance of the Lord Protector, the town's contribution to the monthly cess was suspended because of the material damage it had sustained as a result of the fire.[35] In the aftermath of the disaster economic activity was stimulated by the development of employment opportunities. Wrights, masons and others were recruited, 'quherever they can get them, in the countrey or ellis quhair'.[36] Certainly Thomas Tucker, who visited Glasgow three years after the fire, made no comment about its ill effects in his praise of the burgh's success:

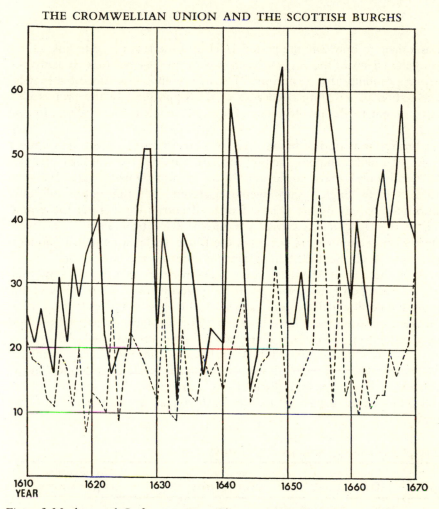

Figure 3 Merchant and Craftsman entries, Glasgow, 1610–70; M = - - - -; C = ——

This towne . . . handsomely built in forme of a crosse, is one of the most considerablest burghs in Scotland, as well for the structure as trade of it . . . the situation of this towne in a plentifull land, and the mercantile genius of the people are strong signs of her increase and groweth.[37]

Her 'increase and growth' during the Comwellian Union was indeed substantial if the Dumbarton registers are any guide. Between 1600–50, the major proportion of Glasgow's foreign trade was handled by foreign-owned vessels freighted by Glasgow merchants. From 1651, however, this pattern was apparently altered with, as Table 2 demonstrates, a considerable expansion in the number of Glasgow-owned ships. At the same time, this development was paralleled by an apparent fall in the number of Dutch-owned vessels. From a total of 48 such entries between 1642 and 1650, there

9

was a drop to only 2 in the period 1651–8. One is tempted to link all this with the effects of the Anglo-Dutch war of 1652–4 but there remains the strong possibility that a continued Dutch presence was concealed by false registration papers, forged because of the opposition of the protectorate government to the involvement of foreign vessels in the British carrying trade.[38]

During the period of union there was an extension, albeit on a limited scale, of English shipping activity on the Clyde. Over the half century, 1600–50, only twelve entries related to English-owned vessels. Between 1652–8 eight English ships were registered. Yet this figure still only amounted to just over 8 per cent of total entries throughout the union. Six of the eight vessels carried salt and/or wine from France, and were clearly being employed as carriers in the Biscay trade rather than as pioneers in a new Anglo-Scottish trading development up the west coast.[39]

As in the case of Aberdeen, there is no evidence that the Glasgow men took advantage of the access given by government to trade freely in the English colonies. Tobacco does appear in the *Register of Ship Entries* but on only one occasion was it listed between 1652–8 when a cargo was imported by a vessel from Rotterdam. Five years before union, in 1648, the *Antelope* of Glasgow shipped 20,000 lb of tobacco from the French island of Martinique. In this sector, however, financial weakness inhibited steady expansion; long voyages to distant lands on an annual basis would still have called for greater resources than those of the typical Scottish merchant of the time.

Table 2 Ship Entries at Dumbarton, 1595–1658

Date	Total entries	No of entries Glasgow owned
1595–1600	70	14
1601–10	43	36
1611–20	39	6
1621–30	77	21
1631–40	64	11
1641–50	75	2
1651–8	104	43

Source: Fergus Roberts and I. M. M. Macphail (eds), *Dumbarton Common Good Accounts, 1614–1660* (Dumbarton, 1972), 264

It seems plain that the Cromwellian Union was not disastrous for the two leading burghs considered in this study. While few new exciting developments took place, both towns seem to have fairly quickly re-established the level of commercial operations which prevailed before the civil wars. It would be dangerous, on the other hand, to assert that their experience was typical of other burghs, or, indeed, of Scotland as a whole. The 'Scottish economy' in the seventeenth century was in essence the aggregate of a series of local and regional economies which often displayed independent characteristics. It would seem, for example, on the basis of the available evidence, that Dundee, the second largest burgh in the land, continued a decline, which had begun before 1652, but which was probably exacerbated by the plundering of General Monck's army in 1651.[40] For three consecutive years thereafter not a single Dundee ship moved into the Baltic.[41]

Table 3 Total No of Vessels, with Scottish Domicile Passing Eastwards To Baltic, 1635–57

Year	No of vessels
1635	93
1637	69
1638	47
1639	27
1640	43
1641	53
1642	59
1643	47
1644	21
1645	35
1647	17
1648	17
1649	20
1650	11
1651	5
1652	11
1653	—
1654	9
1656	9
1657	12

Source: N. E. Bang (ed), *Tabeller over Skibsfart og Varetransport gennem Øresund, 1497–1660 (Copenhagen, 1906 and 1922)*

Indeed, Scottish commerce to the Baltic as a whole apparently did not experience the resilience characteristic elsewhere and while the *Sound Toll Registers*, the major historical source for Baltic trade, are open to criticism and possibly understate the extent of Scottish shipping activity, there is no doubting the general downward trend which they reveal (see Table 3).[42] It is true that the general level of commercial activity in the Baltic did falter as a result of the Dutch War. Nevertheless, the Scottish share fell disproportionately from 3.7 per cent of total ships, 1630–9, to 2.3 per cent in 1640–9 and 0.7 per cent, 1650–7.[43] This may reflect the fact that those burghs which specialised in Baltic trade, notably the south-east congerie of Leith, Dundee, St Andrews and Anstruther, had a markedly worse experience at this time than Aberdeen and Glasgow (see Table 4). Most of them had suffered heavily in the troubles of the 1640s. As Professor Lythe has remarked, 'Dysart's experience was probably typical: it was, so its representative said, "an antient

11

and flourishing burgh royall . . . till the year of God 1644 and 1645 it came to decay by the intestine and unnatural war against Montrose, where the most pairt of the skippers and traffiquers were killed and destroyed".[44] Because it was the political and administrative heart of Scotland, this region was always likely to be particularly affected in a period of civil war.

Table 4 Distribution of Scottish Ships Entering the Baltic, Distinguished by Home Port, 1565–1655

Year	Total	Aberdeen	St Andrews	Anstruther	Dundee	Leith	Montrose	Others
1565	18	3	0	0	5	7	1	2
1575	87	3	12	4	22	21	3	22 (1)
1585	29	3	6	4	3	7	0	6
1595	72	6	7	10	15	20	2	12 (2)
1605	51	2	3	2	11	9	4	20 (3)
1615	53	2	4	11	13	12	2	9 (4)
1625	73	1	6	10	15	14	9	18 (5)
1635	74	6	5	10	6	8	4	35 (6)
1645	40	3	2	5	1	3	1	25 (7)
1655	30	5	3	0	5	5	4	8 (8)

1. Notably Dysart (7), Kinghorn, Kirkcaldy, St Monance and Pittenweem (3 each).
2. Notably Craill (3), Dysart and Kinghorn (3 each).
3. Notably Burntisland (4), Kirkcaldy (3), Pittenweem, Craill and Ayr (2 each).
4. Notably Burntisland (3), Kirkcaldy (3).
5. Notably Kirkcaldy (4), Craill (3), Bo'ness and Queensferry (2 each).
6. Notably Pittenweem (7), Burntisland (5), Bo'ness and Queensferry (4 each), Kirkcaldy (3).
7. Notably Pittenweem (4), Queensferry (4), Glasgow (3), Burntisland and Kirkcaldy (2 each).
8. Notably Burntisland (3).

Source: S. G. E. Lythe, 'Scottish Trade with the Baltic, 1550–1650', in J. K. Eastham (ed), *Economic Essays in Commemoration of the Dundee School of Economics* (Dundee, 1955), 69 after the *Sound Toll Registers*.

Nevertheless, if the Aberdeen and Glasgow data do reflect conditions in their respective hinterlands, it can be tentatively concluded that the north-east and west-central areas were more fortunate. It is not easy to explain why this should be. The nature of economic activity at the time may have helped. An agricultural economy with a limited commercial sector functioning mainly on the exchange of food and raw materials is less vulnerable to the adverse long-term effects of war than the sophisticated industrial states of modern times. In the Scottish economy of the seventeenth century the crucial determinant of business activity was not war but the yield of the harvest, although occasionally one obviously affected the other. The limited evidence for the north-east and Clyde regions suggests very high grain prices in the period 1648–52 but thereafter a drastic fall in most years until the Restoration. For instance, the average annual fiars prices for 'ferme bear' in Aberdeenshire was £7 15s od per boll from 1648–52 and

£4 6s 8d from 1654–8 which was as low as any point in the century. The same trend was displayed in prices for small oats and malting barley.[45] While fiars returns are not extant for the Glasgow area, other data also indicate a drop in grain prices as a consequence of better harvest conditions. In March 1654 the Town Council drew attention to the fact that 'victuall is become so cheipe'.[46] Significantly too, burghal price control of food products, which occurred regularly in the 1640s, seems to have been abandoned from 1651.[47] Moreover, there is no trace of grain imports from Ireland or elsewhere in the *Register of Ship Entries* such as tended to be common during years of food shortage. It may be suggested, therefore, that harvests in these parts of Scotland were adequate during these years.[48] The country's 'emergency granary' in the south Baltic was hardly utilised between 1652–7 whereas recourse to it had been frequent throughout the later 1630s and 1640s (see Table 5). As Professor Lythe has argued, high grain prices often meant the diversion of scarce currency to the buying of food overseas, a consequent fall in demand for other goods and the sapping of business initiative.[49] Therefore, it could be that stabilisation of domestic food supply at least created the opportunity and the context for commercial recovery. It may well be too that the deleterious impact of war on the

Table 5 Scottish Grain Imports from the Baltic, 1635–57

Year	Rye (Lasts)	Wheat (Lasts)	Barley (Lasts)	Oats (Lasts)	Flour (Lasts)
1635	54	6	0	0	29
1636	1,382	28	158	37	0
1637	146	6	73	0	2
1638	77	15	70	0	0
1639	4	0	0	0	0
1640	304	48	0	0	0
1641	324	103	23	0	0
1642	489	10	36	16	5
1643	772	115	12	49	2
1644	81	6	0	0	0
1645	94	0	0	0	65
1646	0	0	0	0	0
1647	80	0	0	0	0
1648	15	0	0	0	0
1649	172	0	126	60	2
1650	14	0	0	0	0
1651	0	0	0	0	0
1652	0	0	0	0	0
1653	0	0	0	0	0
1654	0	0	0	0	0
1655	0	3	0	0	0
1656	0	0	0	0	0
1657	0	0	0	0	0

Source: N. E. Bang (ed), *Tabeller over Skibsfart Og Varetransport gennem Øresund, 1497–1660* (Copenhagen, 1906 and 1922)

merchant marine of *some* burghs has been exaggerated. In a 'Compt of losses be sea sustainst be the inhabitants of Aberdeen', it was reported that 32 vessels had been lost between 1639–48. Although these losses were sustained during war, however, not all were the result of war. For a start, twelve of the ships belonged to other ports and were merely freighted by Aberdeen merchants. Goods, if lost as a result of pirate or privateer action, could be ransomed. Furthermore, on the calculation of the Town Council itself, only eight vessels disappeared because of the action of pirates or enemy ships. Thus, the merchants of Aberdeen lost, on average, less than one vessel per annum as a result of hostilities to 1648.[50] Even during the Anglo-Dutch war of 1652–4, the Lords of the Admiralty of Zeland gave convoy to Scots vessels as far as Newcastle and also issued safe conducts 'by which they passed freely home to Scotland, without any hinderance of men of warre or private freebooters that had letters of retortion from the States Generall'.[51] During the Spanish War of 1659 Scottish merchants continued to venture abroad:

> but under the covert and pretext of being Dutch, in whose ports they enter theyr shippes and sayle with Dutch passes and mariners or els bring home theyr goods in Dutch bottomes, which are made over by bill of sale, and so become the shipps of the natives when they arrive there but once unladen, they depart, and are then Dutch bottomes again.[52]

The fact that maritime hostilities increased risk and diverted commerce for short periods from accustomed routes is beyond doubt. Equally, however, their longer term effects should be kept firmly in perspective.

NOTES

1. The origins of the union have been studied in most detail by Gordon Donaldson, *James V to James VII* (Edinburgh and London, 1965), 343–57. Relevant documents have been printed in C. H. Firth (ed), *Scotland and the Protectorate, 1654–9* (Scottish History Society, 1899), *Scotland and the Commonwealth* (Scottish History Society, 1895) and C. S. Terry (ed), *The Cromwellian Union* (Scottish History Society, 1902). Although union was effective from 1652, a number of obstacles prevented it being formally established by act of parliament until April 1657.

2. Ibid. For detailed references to publications on the subject see Donaldson, op cit, 418–9.

3. The phrase is Prof T. C. Smout's. See *Northern Scotland*, 1 (1973), 235. The works referred to are S. G. E. Lythe, *The Economy of Scotland in its European Setting, 1550–1625* (Edinburgh and London, 1963), and T. C. Smout, *Scottish Trade on the Eve of Union, 1660–1707* (Edinburgh and London, 1963).

4. Economic Conditions under the Commonwealth and Protectorate', *Scott Hist Rev*, V (1908), 274–84. Recent writers broadly agree with Keith's assessment. Prof Donaldson concludes that 'economic conditions were such that no section of the community had much opportunity to prosper during the brief period of commonwealth rule' (op cit, 351). To Professor Smout, 'the arrival of the Cromwellian Union after years of anarchy did nothing to restore prosperity:

Scotland was too enfeebled to take much advantage of the opportunities it offered' (op cit, 195, citing Keith's article).

5. Keith, loc cit, 17.
6. Although Glasgow's assessment was temporarily suspended because of the fire in the town in 1651. For histories of the two burghs at this time see W. Kennedy, *Annals of Aberdeen* (1818); T. C. Smout, 'The Glasgow Merchant Community in the seventeenth century', *Scott Hist Rev, XLVII (1968);* 'The Development and Enterprise of Glasgow, 1550–1707', *Scott Journ of Political Economy*, VII (1960).
7. John Spalding, *Memorialls of the Trubles in Scotland and in England 1624–1645*.
8. 'Aberdeen Burgess Register, 1631–1700', *The Miscellany of the Third Spalding Club*, II (1906).
9. Louise B. Taylor (ed), *Aberdeen Council Letters*, III (London, 1952), 68–169 (hereafter cited as *Aberdeen Council Letters*). At this time £1 Scots equalled 8d sterling.
10. See, for instance, references to taxation and quarterings in J. D. Marwick (ed), *Extracts from the Records of the Burgh of Glasgow, 1630–1662* (Glasgow, 1882) (hereafter cited as *Glasgow Burgh Records*).
11. Ibid, 229–30.
12. These are housed in the Charter Room in Aberdeen Town House and are hereafter referred to as *Aberdeen Accounts*. Those for the period 1596–1670 have recently been edited and published in Louise B. Taylor (ed), *Aberdeen Shore Work Accounts, 1596–1670* (Aberdeen, 1972).
13. In a review of Miss Taylor's edition, T. C. Smout has shown the massive variety in contemporary measures of apparent uniformity. See *Northern Scotland*, I (1973), 236.
14. A point made in Robin Craig's review of the *Accounts, Economic History Review*, 2nd ser, XXVIII (1975).
15. *Northern Scotland*, I (1973), 236.
16. A summary of this material appears in 'Abstract of Ship Entries at Dumbarton', in Fergus Roberts and I. M. M. Macphail (eds), *Dumbarton Common Good Accounts 1614–1660* (Dumbarton, 1972), 260–73 (hereafter cited as *Dumbarton Register*).
17. Ibid, 262.
18. Smout, loc cit (1968); T. M. Devine, 'Glasgow Merchants in Colonial Trade, 1770–1815' (unpublished PhD thesis, University of Strathclyde, 1971), I, 16–7.
19. *Aberdeen Council Letters*, April 1654, 228.
20. *Aberdeen Accounts*: All references in subsequent paragraphs unless otherwise stated are to this source.
21. Lythe, op cit, 144–5; Smout, op cit, 154–5.
22. In the 1640s–60s a fardel measured between 400–700 ells.
23. *Northern Scotland*, I (1973), 237.
24. 'Report by Thomas Tucker upon the settlement of the Revenues of Excise and Customs in Scotland A.D. MDCLVT', *Miscellany of the Scottish Burgh Records Society* (1881) (henceforth cited as *Tucker's Report*).
25. *Aberdeen Accounts*.
26. Donaldson, op cit, 352.
27. *Dumbarton Register*.
28. Ibid.
29. J. R. Anderson (ed), *The Burgesses and Guild Brethren of Glasgow 1573 – 1750* (Edinburgh, 1925).
30. Ibid.
31. *Glasgow Burgh Records*, 197, 199, 209, 209.
32. J. D. Marwick (ed), *Extracts from the Records of the Convention of the Royal Burghs of Scotland, 1615–76* (Edinburgh, 1878), 475.

33. *Glasgow Burgh Records*, 308, 316.
34. Ibid, 255, 7 and 17 September 1652.
35. Ibid, 291, 11 July 1654. This monthly abatement was partly a reflection of the protectorate's policy of appeasing the middle and lower classes with the aim of reconciling them to the union and breaking the influence of the clergy and aristocracy. General Monck asked for tax relief for the burghs in 1654 because 'they are generally the most faithful to us of any people in this Nacion'. The inhabitants of Glasgow, in particular, 'being a good people' he was anxious that they have abatements. See C. H. Firth (ed), *Scotland and the Protectorate, 1654–9* (Scottish History Society, 1899), 162.
36. *Glasgow Burgh Records*, 3 July 1652.
37. *Tucker's Report*, 26.
38. *Dumbarton Register*.
39. See also P. McGrath, *Merchants and Merchandise in Seventeenth Century Bristol* (Bristol Record Society, 1955), 278–81.
40 *Tucker's Report*, 26; Smout, op cit, 140; S. G. E. Lythe, *Life and Labour in Dundee from the Reformation to the Civil War* (Dundee, 1958), 27–30.
41 N. Bang (ed), *Tabeller over Skibsfart og Varetransport gennen Øresund, 1497–1660* (Copenhagen, 1906 and 1922) (henceforth cited as *Sound Toll Registers*).
42 For the weaknesses of the *Sound Toll Registers* see J. Dow, 'A comparative note on the Sound Toll Registers, Stockholm Customs Accounts and Dundee Shipping Lists, 1613–22', *Standinavian Econ Hist Rev*, XII (1964), 79; T. M. Devine and S. G. E. Lythe, 'The economy of Scotland under James VI: a Revision Article', *Scottish Historical Review*, L (1971), 101.
43 *Sound Toll Registers*.
44. S. G. E. Lythe, 'Scottish Trade with the Baltic 1550–1650' in J. K. Eastham (ed). *Economic Essays in Commemoration of the Dundee School of Economics, 1931–1955* (Dundee, 1955), 70.
45. 'Fiars Prices in Aberdeenshire' in *Miscellany of the Third Spalding Club II* (1906). For the value of fiars prices as a crude indicator of market trends see Rosalind Mitchison, 'The Movement of Scottish Corn Prices in the Seventeenth and Eighteenth Centuries', *Economic Hist Rev*, 2nd ser, XVIII (1965).
46. *Glasgow Burgh Records*, 283, 4 March 1654.
47. Ibid.
48. East Lothian apparently had a different experience. See Mitchison, loc cit, 281.
49. Lythe, op cit, 28.
50. *Aberdeen Council Letters*, 124.
51. Elinor J. Courthope (ed), *The Journal of Thomas Cuningham of Campver, 1640–1654* (Scottish History Society, 1928), 245–6.
52. *Tucker's Report*, 30.

2

THE MERCHANT CLASS OF THE LARGER SCOTTISH TOWNS IN THE LATER SEVENTEENTH AND EARLY EIGHTEENTH CENTURIES

Recent work in Scottish agrarian history has prompted a new assessment of the pace and pattern of economic change in rural society before 1750. The period before the 'Agricultural Revolution' of the later eighteenth century has been shown to be one of continuous development which seems to have visibly accelerated in the decades before the Union of 1707 thus establishing a firm base for the more radical alterations of later times.[1] The new awareness that rural society was far from static has, however, partly helped to confirm the conventional view that the towns were the conservative sector in the early modern Scottish economy. A powerful case can be advanced to demonstrate that they were more concerned with privilege than progress and attached to an older world of guild restrictionism and monopoly increasingly irrelevant in the new age of widening commercial opportunity.[2] On the other hand, the roots of economic advance can be identified in the Scottish countryside where landowners were establishing salt and coal industries outside the control of reactionary town oligarchies and founding 'burghs of barony' where the spirit of free enterprise could flourish. Thus, one agrarian historian asserts in a recent volume of essays that the landed classes were the pioneers in Scottish economic and social development before 1760 and that 'the towns rarely threw up men of any real stature . . . for the most part the burghs were rather sad places whose leaders wallowed in their own corruption'.[3] My purpose is to suggest that the contrast between country and town in Scotland between 1660 and 1740 has been overdrawn and that whatever the relative importance of landowners and townsmen the contribution of the latter cannot be ignored. Through a consideration of the merchant classes of the larger Scottish burghs it is hoped to demonstrate that they did not remain immune from the wider economic changes of the period and that their 'conservatism' has been exaggerated.

The focus of this study is restricted to the merchants of the larger burghs of Edinburgh, Glasgow, Aberdeen and Dundee. These were by far the most significant towns in Scotland, accounting in 1705 for about 64 per cent of total burghal taxation as measured by the stent rolls of the Convention of Royal Burghs.[4] Edinburgh and Glasgow alone contributed 35 per cent and 20 per cent respectively. Moreover, the dominance of these two major towns in Scottish commerce was further enhanced by the control which some of their leading merchants had over the trade of smaller and superficially independent centres in the eastern and western lowlands. The differences between the four towns in size, geographical location, trade connection and historical tradition is also significant because the danger of generalising from unrepresentative experience is at least mini-mised. In this period, as is well known, Glasgow grew rapidly and forged important transatlantic links with the tobacco and sugar colonies. Dundee, on the other hand, took a long time to recover from the Civil War of the mid-seventeenth century and retained her old connections with Europe. Edinburgh, despite the pace of Glasgow's development, remained the premier seat of commerce in Scotland with the largest and most opulent merchant community, while Aberdeen was an important centre of regional significance.

THE INSTITUTIONAL FRAMEWORK OF MERCANTILE ACTIVITY

It is part of the conventional wisdom of Scottish economic history that town merchants in the seventeenth century functioned within an elaborate structure of protectionism.[5] Only royal burghs had the legal right to trade overseas. Commerce in the 'liberty' of the burghs was reserved for official burgesses of the town. Entry to this class and in particular to the merchant guild, the élite of the business community, was jealously guarded to favour the kinsmen of established families. Both admission fees to full burgess-ship and the mandatory period of apprenticeship were markedly less onerous for those of burgess stock. Moreover, since the burghs pursued a policy of establishing limitations on prices and controls on marketing it is possible to argue that their public face was set firmly against competition and free enterprise. Yet, it is unclear how far these restrictions were always effective in reality or, if effective, the extent to which they inhibited Scottish development. Protectionism can be regarded as a response to rather than a basic cause of economic difficulties. On this reckoning, controls on competition are to be seen more as symptoms of chronic economic insecurity rather than in themselves the basic influence on distress. Equally, if this view is correct, a reduction in the force of protectionist legislation might be anticipated when better times developed after the crisis of the middle decades of the seventeenth century. In the forty years between 1660 and 1770 harvest failure became uncommon, *pace* the 'Seven Lean Years', and trade recovered.

At first glance some of the evidence is against such an interpretation. The

18

royal burghs did lose their monopoly of foreign trade in the famous act of the Scottish Parliament in 1672 but this can be interpreted as evidence that the landed classes imposed a more realistic régime on the conservative towns. Moreover, throughout the later seventeenth century, the records of the Convention of Royal Burghs still abound with attempts to preserve the rights of 'free' burgesses, limit the pretensions of 'unfree' towns and maintain the exclusive nature of the merchant classes by supporting rigorous enforcement of apprenticeship regulations.[6] Yet the Convention records, on which so many generalisations about the burghs have been based, are only a partial guide to real practice within the Scottish merchant community and may simply reflect the vested interests of those royal burghs which were adversely affected by changing patterns of trade. Significantly, for example, the distinction between privileged royal burghs and 'unfree towns' which the Convention sought to preserve, had been effectively undermined by the merchants of the larger towns who were exploiting these smaller centres for their own benefit. In 1691 the Convention itself acknowledged that the traders of those towns who supposedly benefited from the old monopolies were in actuality contributing vigorously to their rapid decay: 'It is resolved no longer to suffer the rights of royal burghs to be abused and encroached upon by there owne burgesses, whoe be joining stocks with un-freemen inhabitants in the burghs of regalities and baronies and other unfree places bothe in point of trade and shipping'.[7] A year after this resolution was passed the royal burgh of Dundee admitted that it had trading links with at least fifteen 'unfree' towns and villages.[8] Moreover, Glasgow's commercial position was vitally dependent on her satellite towns of Greenock on the Clyde and Bo'ness on the Forth: 'as to trade with unfreemen or unfree burghs there is ordinarily bought of the herrings exported by the merchants of Glasgow, about two hundred last from Greenock men as also the far greater pairt of Hollands commodities brought to this towne from skippers, seamen and others living at Barrowstowness and other places upon that coast.'[9] These smaller centres were complementary to the larger towns and in some cases their development reflected the marketing policies of the merchant class of the bigger burghs who were the main organising force behind the changing currents of trade. The royal burghs which complained so vociferously in 1692 about competition from burghs of barony and the like were not Glasgow and Edinburgh but smaller towns such as Linlithgow and Haddington.[10]

The erosion of legal impediment to free trade between towns was paralleled by the relaxation of burgess and guild controls within the burghs. From 1681, non-burgesses of the inland town of Stirling were permitted to carry on business within the burgh without the need to gain formal admission as burgesses. Instead, they were permitted to conduct trade upon making a small annual payment to town funds.[11] Here was a clear acknowledgement of the futility of attempting to impose traditional monopolies in a period of more vigorous commercial activity. Similarly, the Dundee guildry in 1696 agreed to admit new members on payment of a fee of £12 Scots rather than £60 as formerly and after a three year rather than the traditional five to seven year apprenticeship. It is evident from the guildry minutes that this change in policy reflected the difficulties recently encountered in administering the more rigorous controls.[12] The same trend was apparent in Aberdeen and Glasgow because by the 1720s, in both towns, burgess-ship seems to have become regarded as a mark of social distinction rather than a necessary qualification for the prosecution of trade.[13] The extent of the breakdown of the burgess-ship system became clearly apparent in Glasgow several decades later. In 1784 the Merchants House estimated that there were at least 135 merchants trading in the city who were not burgesses and guild brothers of the burgh, and among them were members of such well-known mercantile dynasties as the Buchanans, Speirs, Alstons and Bogles.[14] The growing irrelevance of legal controls is further illustrated by the inadequacy of disciplinary procedures against those who broke the law. Between 1715 and 1740 Aberdeen failed to prosecute anyone for trading while not a member of the guild, while Dundee fined only one person, Thomas Webster, 'Shipmaster of North Ferry of Dundee', £1 sterling for this offence in 1737.[15] Yet this leniency should not be taken as evidence that an 'unofficial' sector of trade did not exist or was so insignificant as not to merit serious attention; on the contrary, it occurred in a period when 'unfree' commerce was almost certainly expanding.[16]

The apprenticeship system had been a traditional constraint on entry to the merchant class both because of the lengthy duration of apprenticeship, the burden of fees which it imposed and the power it bestowed on established merchants to select recruits to the next generation. However, two changes in apprenticeship can be identified in the later seventeenth and early eighteenth centuries. First, there seems to have been a decline in the length of apprenticeships from seven years, apparently the common period in the middle decades of the seventeenth century for aspiring overseas merchants, to between three and five years by the early eighteenth century. Indeed, by the 1720s, three-year apprenticeships had become the norm in both Dundee and Aberdeen.[17] Second, in some towns, the total number of apprenticeships declined both in absolute terms and as a proportion of the total of new merchant burgesses. Between 1666 and 1700, 910 boys were apprenticed to Edinburgh merchants but, from 1701 to 1740, this figure fell to 279 although there is no evidence of a similar dramatic reduction in the number of merchant burgesses entered in the city in this period.[18] An annual average of 29 merchant burgesses were registered at Glasgow between 1715 and 1740 but only 2 per annum did so as a consequence of completing a formal apprenticeship.[19] Nor is it likely that these merchants had actually undergone a formal apprenticeship and then been admitted as burgesses on a different basis. The evidence of burgess admissions for Glasgow can be checked against the Merchants House Register of Apprentices. This confirms that only a total of 35 merchant apprentices were 'book'd' between 1715 to 1740, a figure which is remarkably close to the figure derived from the burgess register above.[20] A real decline in the number of apprenticeships seems to have occurred from earlier times. Between 1680 and 1715 the average annual number of new Glasgow merchant burgesses was 18 while the number of those obtaining burgess-ship by apprenticeship was 4 per annum. Judged by both absolute and relative criteria more merchants seem to have undertaken formal apprenticeships in Glasgow in the later seventeenth century compared with the first few decades of the eighteenth.

In essence, mercantile training in this period seems to have become less burdened by the strict letter of burghal law. It is tempting, for example, to see a connection between the apparent decline of formal apprenticeship in some towns and the rise of alternative modes of mercantile education. In the later seventeenth century Scots enrolled in mercantile 'schools' in the great Dutch commercial centres of Amsterdam, Rotterdam and Dort where the arts of cyphering, accounting and languages were taught. When William Dunlop of Glasgow was in Dort in 1681 there were five fellow Scots from Edinburgh in his class and a much larger number under instruction in Rotterdam.[21] In the same way as Scots lawyers and divines went to the continent for advanced education in universities so Scottish merchants sought to develop their expertise in these commercial schools. In addition, from the 1690s, similar institutions were established in Scotland.[22] Glasgow employed a teacher in 'the airt of navigation, book-keeping, arithmetic and wryting' from 1695. Edinburgh appointed its burghal accountant, once a merchant, 'Professor of Book-keeping' to the city in 1705. Ayr and Dunbar also provided teaching in navigation and book-keeping from 1721 and these subjects became integrated into the curricula of the grammar schools in the smaller burghs of Stirling in 1728 and Perth in 1729.

There does seem to be sufficient evidence to suggest significant changes in the institutional framework of mercantile activity in this period. The ethic of the guild was arguably less influential than before and legal constraint on competition was rapidly becoming redundant. This development was partly cause and effect of wider advances in the Scottish economy. From the middle decades of the seventeenth century the supply of food markedly improved and this was the crucial regulator of everything from demand for merchant goods to the balance of payments. The 'Seven Lean Years' can be regarded in the long perspective as an abnormal phase, the result of exceptionally severe but ephemeral climatic conditions. Increasingly the problem for many Scottish farmers and landlords between 1660 and 1730 became one of food surpluses rather than grain deficiency. Moreover, the old rigidities of the domestic economy began to recede from the later seventeenth century. The physical size of the larger towns grew. Burghs of barony, villages and fairs proliferated. Commodity exchange increased, as demonstrated by the conversion of rentals in kind to rentals in money in both highland and lowland Scotland. Similar trends are suggested in the evidence of decline in regional price differentials for grain and in the vigour of the coastal trade in meal, salt and coal, demonstrated, for instance, in the Dundee shipping registers for the early eighteenth century.[23]

The greater velocity of exchange demanded quicker and more effective methods of settling credits and debits and this led to a more sophisticated use of the bill of exchange. In the mid-seventeenth century Scottish merchants had already become familiar with the bill of exchange as a credit instrument. Its use, however, was still restricted because of a lingering prejudice in some branches of foreign trade in favour of specie and the preference of many domestic merchants for coin.[24] Yet, a survey of eleven sets of mercantile papers for the 1720s and 1730s shows that those concerned in overseas trade by the early eighteenth century always used bills in their transactions and that these instruments were also widely employed by a wide range of smaller merchants, retailers, packmen and cattle drovers.[25] By the 1720s the bill of exchange had begun to serve the purpose of a cash medium, circulating for much longer periods than before and used to cover very small sums and transactions.

All this is indicative of an economy in which the commercial enclave was becoming stronger. In such a context, the old institutional structure which had governed mercantile practice in the Scottish towns was likely to become increasingly inappropriate. Greater economic maturity at once rendered protectionism less necessary and, at the same time, more difficult to enforce. Legal controls had developed to suit the requirements of a society with a small, vulnerable and insecure commercial sector. Manifestly, they were unsuited to the needs of a new era.

THE SOCIAL COMPOSITION OF THE MERCHANT CLASS

It is important to recognise at the beginning of this section that the Scottish merchant class was far from homogeneous. The point is immediately obvious if the meaning of the term 'merchant' in burghal tradition and practice is considered. As John Gibson, himself a merchant, noted in his *History of Glasgow* published in 1777, 'by merchants are to be understood all those who buy and sell'.[26] He implied therefore a most complex and diverse grouping which included at one extreme the petty shopkeeper and packman, at the other the opulent merchant prince and between a myriad army of men of varied social and material standing. Only by simplifying these complexities is it possible to carry the discussion beyond the level of description and impression. Three major categories within the merchant class can be identified. First, there were those involved in trade who were not registered burgesses of a Scottish town. As has been shown, this 'unofficial' sector of commerce had always existed and seems to have become active in the later seventeenth century to such an extent that some towns acknowledged its growth by adjusting existing legal restrictions on permission to trade. Unfortunately, however, members of this group are inevitably poorly documented in town records and it is impossible therefore to examine them in any systematic fashion. It is tolerably clear, nonetheless, from the scattered references to them, that they were mainly men and women of relatively low status in the urban hierarchy because even if burgess-ship was becoming less important in strictly economic terms it still retained its value as a mark of social distinction. Normally, they seem to have plied the trades of small shopkeeper, pedlar, hawker and packman and were concerned with retail services in the towns or in the buying up of goods from greater wholesale merchants for distribution in the surrounding countryside.[27] A typical reference to their activities is to be found in the Edinburgh council minutes of 1692 where there was noted the existence of, '. . . several persons who have taken up the trade of ale-selling and stableing albeit they have no title which is an incroachment on the burgess-rights . . . and a great many women, servants and others who turning wearie of their services, have, out of a principle of avarice and laziness, taken up little shops which is evidently hurtful to the trading burgesses who bear the publick burdens of the place'.[28] The importance of this sector lay in the fact that it permitted people of humble background and modest means to become involved in buying and selling to some extent though it is doubtful if many of them managed to move up very far in the urban hierarchy during their own lifetimes.

The second and third groupings both consisted of registered burgesses of the four towns considered in this study. For analytical purposes, however, they are distinguished by the extent of their participation in either domestic or foreign trade. In practice, of course, this distinction is to some degree an artificial one. Individuals who imported wine, such as John Innes and William Caldwell of Edinburgh in the 1720s, were also involved in marketing it throughout Scotland.[29] Similarly, merchants such as John Steuart of Inverness and Walter Gibson of Glasgow had interests in the domestic fisheries, exported fish to Europe and the New World and imported foreign commodities in return.[30] Examples such as these could be multiplied but they ought not to obscure the crucial point that only a relatively small number of merchants were regularly involved in overseas trade. At Glasgow in the later seventeenth century there was a merchant community of 400–500 strong in a town of about 12,000 in total population. Yet only about 20 to 25 per cent of all merchants were committed to foreign trade and invariably they were among the wealthier elements of town society.[31] The position in Glasgow reflected the economy of a burgh with important and growing overseas connections. At Dundee, in the same period, where foreign trade was in the doldrums but coastal commerce very active, the proportion of overseas merchants was probably even less than at Glasgow.[32] Only a minority, then, had the finance, experience and contacts to pursue foreign trade on a consistent basis: a distinction therefore tended to develop and became recognised in contemporary parlance between ordinary merchants and those who traded abroad, the 'merchant adventurers' or 'sea adventurers' as they were described.[33] It was embodied also in burghal law and tradition by the old regulation that, while all burgesses had the right to trade, only members of the merchant guild, for which entry fees were higher and social obstacles to membership greater, had the legal right to trade abroad.

The possibility of the existence of an élite group of merchants within the general merchant class is confirmed when the poll tax records for the 1690s are examined. In Aberdeen a small group of 27 men can be identified among the larger community of 239 merchant burgesses. Members of this inner circle possessed stock valued at 10,000 merks Scots (or about £530 sterling) and above. Seven possessed country properties in the vicinity of the burgh though ownership of land outside the environs of the town was relatively uncommon among the merchant class as a whole. The provost, dean of guild and magistrates of Aberdeen were recruited exclusively from the ranks of this élite. At the other end of the social scale, 62 merchants were reckoned to have stock valued at less than £27 sterling while the remaining 150 of middling status were assessed at between £27 and £260 sterling.[34]

In the two inner parishes of Edinburgh a similar pyramid-type structure existed though in the capital the number of opulent merchants was much greater than in Aberdeen and their individual stock more substantial.[35] In Tolbooth parish, 25 merchants, or almost one-third of the total resident there, had assets valued at 10,000 merks, or about £530 sterling, and above. Five, however, were worth 30,000 merks, a figure which no Aberdonian merchant could approach. In the same parish only two were estimated to own stock of less than 500 merks while 38 of the total resident merchant population were men of middling rank assessed at between 1000 and 10,000 merks. In the adjacent Old Kirk parish there was an even greater concentration of well-to-do merchants. Twenty-six of a community of 51 were reckoned worth 10,000 merks or above with five individuals valued at three to four times that amount. It follows from this that a satisfactory assessment of the social composition of the merchant class depends on the completion of two different but complementary tasks. First, one has to determine how easy or difficult it was to attain merchant burgess status in this period and, second, to focus specifically on the business élites of the towns and discover whether they were closed oligarchies or refreshed themselves through the recruitment of newcomers drawn from outside their own ranks.

On superficial examination major barriers did exist to prevent easy entry into the official merchant community of the Scottish towns. Legal restrictions were in decline but the main obstacles were not rooted in law but in the nature of economic and social relationships at the time. Merchant fathers commonly laid aside cash sums to enable their sons to set up business on their own account on attainment of their majority. Substantial amounts were often involved as when James Dunlop of Garnkirk, merchant of Glasgow, wrote a bond of provision in 1716 in favour of his son, John, for £175 sterling 'on his taking up a lawful trade'.[36] Such inheritance practices were a way of perpetuating the commercial prominence of many established families into the next and succeeding generations. The character of business life in the period tended also to benefit those with existing ties and contacts. To a considerable extent, especially in foreign trade, commerce functioned through a network of kin and personal connections. This was an era of developing but still unreliable communications, high risks and unsophisticated commercial law. The business world was thus a tight nexus in which a merchant's reputation and that of his family was his most precious asset: to deal with kin and trusted acquaintances was not simply understandable but justifiable. Nepotism had a basic commercial rationale.

In the light of this it is hardly surprising that merchants' sons formed the largest single category of new merchant burgesses admitted during the period covered by this study. From 1710 to 1730, 46 per cent of Edinburgh merchants gained entry to burgess status by right of their fathers while at Dundee 48 per cent did so between 1705 and 1740 and 30 per cent at Aberdeen from 1707 to 1740.[37] But these data also reveal that the majority of new entrants in each of these towns was born outside established families and gained burgess rank by marriage, apprenticeship, purchase or by some other means. Nor was this pattern unique to the *later* seventeenth century for the Edinburgh burgess register, which has been analysed for the whole of the century, suggests that numbers admitted through marriage or apprenticeship were consistently greater than those enrolled by right of a father. Moreover, if anything, the data underestimate the proportion of new men. One can only speculate on the number of merchants' sons who were simply awarded burgess status in a formal sense—because the cost of entry fees for them was entirely nominal—but who never went on to practice as professional traders.   It is appropriate now to ask whether there is similar evidence of movement among the inner élite of the merchant class. Here the barriers to mobility were more formidable than those limiting access to the merchant community as a whole. The most obvious one was financial. Membership of the socially prestigious merchant guild was probably almost a prerequisite for membership of the élite but to be accepted into this body required good connections and considerable means. The Guildry Court at Aberdeen resolved in 1751 that, 'When any persons apply to the Court for admission they resolved that none be found qualified unless they depon that they are worth one hundred and fifty pounds sterling of free stock and that they produce a certificate signed by two creditable burgesses attesting that the petitioner is of good character . . .'[38] At Glasgow, fifty years earlier, the property qualification for a guild brother was about 3½ times that for a mere burgess.[39] Again, the greater merchants, as will be shown in more detail later, tended to diversify their assets and so, by minimising the insecurities of trade, endeavoured to preserve the integrity of the family fortune for future generations.[40]

To determine whether these influences were sufficient to stabilise the composition of the dominant merchant families in the Scottish towns the names and social backgrounds of those who controlled the institutions of civic authority were scrutinised, because membership of town council, burgh offices and the guildry courts offers a rough guide to the membership of the business élite. A comparison of the leading families of late seventeenth century Glasgow with those of the mid eighteenth century reveals a remarkably fluid pattern. Several families did manage to maintain their position. The Bogles, Dunlops, Corbetts, Murdochs and Buchanans were all noted commercial dynasties in the 1670s and 1680s and still of considerable eminence a century later.[41] Others, however, had disappeared while the continuing distinction of some was not inconsistent with the emergence of new elements within the very highest echelons of the merchant class. The great figures of the golden era of Glasgow's Atlantic trades, Glassford, Speirs, Cunninghame, Oswald and McDowall, were not only born outside the established circle but outside Glasgow itself. John Glassford's father was a merchant burgess of the nearby town of Paisley;[42] Alexander Speirs was the son of an Edinburgh merchant;[43] William Cunninghame's father was a trader in Kilmarnock who belonged to a cadet branch of the Cunninghames of Caprington, lairds in Ayrshire.[44] The Oswalds were from clerical stock in Caithness[45], while the McDowalls, major partners in the giant West India house of Alexander Houston and Co., were the offspring of a Scots soldier who had made good in the Caribbean but could trace his lineage back to landed stock in Wigtownshire.[46]

The evidence of a turnover in the Glasgow mercantile élite, though significant, must however be treated with caution. The town's rate of growth in the eighteenth century was exceptional and so also, it might be argued, was movement within the higher echelons of the business class. An examination of the ruling families in Dundee and Aberdeen, two burghs with a less dramatic economic history than that of Glasgow, might determine how representative the position in Glasgow was. In both cases a similar steady movement among the élite can be identified. In the 1690s, Aberdeen was ruled by the Mitchells, Skenes, Johnstones, Robertsons and Gordons but, by the 1750s, little trace remained of any of these names in council and guildry records. Instead, a new grouping built around the Youngs, Brebners, Auldjos, Mores and Leys, had emerged to dominate the political and economic life of the burgh.[47] It is true that a simple turnover in names may not necessarily reflect changes in *family* status and position which could have been perpetuated through the female rather than the male line. On the other hand, the evidence of new surnames is at least an indicator of the steady recruitment of new men to the élite. Such a pattern also existed in Dundee. Between 1683 and 1720, membership of the Guildry Court, the body concerned with the maintenance and defence of the privileges of the greater merchants, fluctuated between 15 and 18. In 1689, 7 of the families present in 1683 were still represented. By 1702 the number had dwindled to

4 and all of the individuals concerned were the sons of the leading figures of the early 1680s. In 1708 only 2 names survived of the original membership and by 1715 there was no trace of any of the families who had served on the court three decades before.[48] The Glasgow experience therefore does not appear to have been untypical. The personnel of the élites was not obviously more stable than that of the merchant class as a whole.

Some reasons can be advanced for this social movement within the merchant community. Occasionally some members of the élite were lost to commerce by moving into landownership. Such was the case with the Skenes of Rubislaw in Aberdeen in the later seventeenth century and the Campbells of Shawfield in Glasgow in the early eighteenth.[49] But the evidence suggests that this was not a central influence on the changing social composition of the merchant class. First, as will be discussed in more detail below, only a small minority of successful merchants bought estates in this period.[50] Second, when land was acquired it was not often secured in sufficient quantity to permit families to completely sever their links with commerce. If the investment strategies of Glasgow and Aberdeen merchants are typical most trading families who became landowners retained their commercial interests over several generations.[51] It might indeed be argued that the buying of land gave mercantile families more security and so enabled them to perpetuate their position rather than cede it to newcomers.

A much more powerful agency of change was the growth in internal and external commerce which characterised the period 1660 to 1750. Most obviously this tended to widen and deepen the opportunities for men of commerce particularly as legal controls and restrictions diminished. Equally, however, a period of growth was also a period of commercial risk especially in some of the new and more lucrative branches of international trade. The expansion of Scottish North American and Caribbean commerce was punctuated by a series of spectacular bankruptcies in Glasgow which helped to limit the possibility of a self-perpetuating monopoly among a handful of rich families. Such commercial dynasties as the Buchanans, Dunlops, Dunmores, McDowalls and Houstons were all affected by financial disaster.[52] In other towns the incidence of financial failure can best be studied in the records of the merchant guilds. These institutions had the responsibility of providing support for those members who had fallen on hard times and their minutes are often a poignant guide to the fragility of contemporary business fortunes. So in Aberdeen in 1736, the pressures on the guild's finances because of the misfortunes that had overtaken some of its members were such that '. . . the monies belonging to the Guild Box is not in a condition to support the poor decayed brethern of guild of this burgh and their widows and children'.[53] In 1730, the funds of the Dundee guildry were deemed insufficient to meet the needs of families of insolvent members with the result that entry fees were raised to provide for these unfortunates.[54]

Moreover, high mortality rates in the seventeenth and early eighteenth centuries together with the desire of some sons to opt for careers outside commerce doubtless brought some families to an end in the male line. This process, however, left daughters and widows to provide opportunities for social movement through marriage and re-marriage. In all the towns studied, entry to burgess-ship by right of marriage was second only to paternity as the most common means of registration. Thus, of the 110 new merchant burgesses admitted at Dundee between 1705 and 1740, 47 obtained entry by right of a father, 27 by marriage, 25 by purchase and 12 by apprenticeship.[55] At Edinburgh from 1710 to 1720, 59 achieved burgess-ship by right of their fathers, 40 by marriage, 31 by apprenticeship and 24 by purchase.[56]

It is more difficult to determine whether the turnover in the composition of the merchant class also implied substantial social mobility within the hierarchy of the towns because the evidence on the social origins of new merchants is too incomplete to permit a systematic analysis. Nevertheless, extant data on the social background of Aberdeen and Edinburgh merchant apprentices do allow some tentative conclusions to be made though, since only a proportion of all merchants undertook a formal apprenticeship in the period, this evidence is only a very partial guide to the origins of the merchant community as a whole. Both the Edinburgh and the Aberdeen material suggest that when merchant apprentices were not sons of merchants they invariably came from similar social backgrounds to those who were. Overwhelmingly they were recruited from the middle strata of Scottish society. Of 27 Aberdeen apprentices in the period 1709 to 1740, 8 were sons of tenant farmers, 4 of ministers of the Church, 2 were sons of small landowners, 2 of craftsmen, 2 of lawyers and 1 was the son of a school-master. The occupations of the remaining 8 fathers was unknown.[57] 279 persons were admitted to merchant apprenticeship in Edinburgh between 1701 and 1730. Of these, 84 were the sons of lairds, 42 were recruited from professional families with backgrounds in the law, the ministry and education, 30 were the sons of merchants in other Scottish towns, 37 of craftsmen burgesses (mainly from Edinburgh) and the occupation of 48 fathers was unknown. Aberdeen and Edinburgh did, however, differ in two respects. Almost all Aberdeen apprentices were born in the burgh itself or in its rural hinterland whereas a substantial minority of Edinburgh apprentices came from outside the capital and the south eastern region. Secondly, the social status of Edinburgh apprentices tended to be somewhat higher than that of the Aberdeen men. The number of Edinburgh merchant apprentices recruited from landed and professional backgrounds is especially significant.

Entry to the more lucrative types of merchanting was probably restricted to men of middle rank and above not because of legal restriction but through the system of patronage. The world of eighteenth-century commerce was little different from that of politics and the professions in this respect. Places were obtained through an informal but powerful network of clientage, connection and recommendation. Success in overseas trade required not simply business acumen and skill but introduction to a world where personal contacts were vital in the establishment of trust between merchants. Commonly, therefore, established merchants were approached by close and distant kinsmen, friends and associates who sought to find an opening in trade for their offspring. Adam Montgomery, a Glasgow factor in Stockholm in the early eighteenth century, took on several young Scots as apprentices but his letterbook shows that they were invariably his own kinsman or sons of his personal friends.[59] Similarly, Alexander Shairp, an Edinburgh merchant resident in Amsterdam in 1717, supervised the education of a number of the sons of his Scottish friends in the arts of book-keeping, ciphering and foreign languages.[60] These connections, however, were not unique to the European commercial context. Young men who sought positions in Scottish-owned plantations in the Caribbean or in Glasgow stores in Virginia and Maryland were placed in exactly[61] the same manner. This meant that despite the decline of legal controls access to the lucrative branches of trade still depended to a very large extent on the influence and power of those with an existing stake in them.

PATTERNS OF INVESTMENT AMONG THE GREATER MERCHANTS

The distribution of profits earned by merchants in the course of trade is, of course, a key aspect of the more general issue of the impact of the merchant class on the Scottish economy. It is vital to determine whether they tended to invest in 'productive' assets, for instance, in further expansion of commercial ventures or industrial concerns or in 'non-productive' assets, for example, in household furnishings, personal clothing and land. Yet, clearly, no precise indication of the distribution of merchant profits can be given because of the great variety both between merchants and over time in investment practice. Here it is intended merely to provide a general and tentative evaluation of the investment patterns of those merchants engaged in foreign trade because they were invariably the ones with the surplus resources to deploy elsewhere.

Some contemporaries did argue that mercantile profits tended to be dissipated in the purchase of landed estates or in other forms of conspicuous consumption. So William Seton, writing in 1700, complained that, 'So soon as a Merchant hath scraped together a piece of money, perhaps to the value of 4000 or 5000 lib. sterling instead of employing it for promoting Trade or by projecting any new thing that may be serviceable to his country, and to the augmenting of his stock, nothing will satisfy him but the laying of it out upon a land Estate, for having the Honour to make his son a Laird, that is, an idle person, who can find out as many methods in spending his Father's Money, as he had of gaining it'.[62] That some merchants managed to buy their way into land is beyond question. Land was both a sound investment and a route to an enhanced and enduring social position for a merchant's family. There are therefore several examples of successful traders, buying estates scattered throughout the secondary literature.[63] Yet, almost certainly, Seton both exaggerated the extent of this practice and the adverse economic effects which, in his view, it inevitably caused.

Two sources of data demonstrate that merchants had only a limited impact on the land market before 1740. Firstly, land transactions recorded in the Register of the Great Seal were analysed for the years 1660–8.[64] These reveal that merchants only accounted for 5.7 per cent of all transactions and that only rarely did merchant involvement in the land market imply the purchase of a landed estate. Those merchants who obtained land did so commonly in relatively small quantities of less than fifty acres not as a means of enhancing their social position but rather in satisfaction of debts for which land had been employed as security. Thus, of 984 transactions recorded in the Register of the Great Seal over the longer period 1593 to 1660 involving non-landed groups, 300 were carried out as 'apprisings' by which the heritable rights of the debtor were sold for payment of the debt due to the appriser. The largest number of apprisings, about 68 per cent, was carried out by merchants.[65] It would appear that ownership of land within the merchant community can be regarded as an integral feature of the commercial regime rather than a means of withdrawing from trade. Secondly, the Valuation Rolls for Lanark, Renfrew, Stirling, Berwick and Midlothian were scrutinised for the eighteenth century because it was assumed that landownership patterns in these central lowland counties might reflect the estate purchases of the merchants of the larger towns. No significant penetration, however, was detected until after c. 1750. The main trend revealed in the earlier period was the steady increase in the size of the properties of the bigger landowners at the expense of the smaller lairds, although this development was notably less marked in the western counties than in the eastern lowlands. This would suggest that the pattern over the entire period 1660 to 1740 was relatively stable. Both the Great Seal data and the Valuation Rolls tend to indicate that the typical purchaser of land was the great aristocrat rather than the town merchant.

Merchants who did manage to acquire estates were very much in the minority. Landownership was the mark of the especially successful trader if only because few at this time had the resources to embark on substantial purchases of territory. Daniel Campbell, the well-known Glasgow merchant, had to pay out £4000 for the estate of Shawfield near Glasgow in the early eighteenth century but as the poll tax data for the 1690s revealed only a handful of members of the Scottish business community could have afforded such an outlay.[67] Only 7 of the 239 merchants listed in the Aberdeen poll tax records owned a country estate and all of them were among the two dozen wealthiest men in the burgh.[68] Not surprisingly the merchants of the most prosperous and largest towns were the most active in the land market. Edinburgh merchants were pre-eminent in the later seventeenth century.

30

Between 1660 and 1668 they accounted for about 61 per cent of all transactions involving merchants recorded in the Register of the Great Seal with Glasgow and Aberdeen men together accounting for a further 20 per cent. Nevertheless, this evidence in itself does not necessarily imply a haemorrhage of capital from trade to land. Only two examples have been uncovered so far of trading families who built up their estates to such an extent that they were able to sever their links with commerce. These were the Skenes of Rubislaw from Aberdeen and the Campbells of Shawfield from Glasgow. Recent analyses of the eighteenth century merchant class of both towns have shown that it was more common for families to retain links with *both* commerce and land over successive generations.[70]

In fact, the specific pattern of mercantile investment in land merely reflected the general business strategy of the greater merchants. No one activity was necessarily favoured at the expense of others and surpluses were distributed widely both to provide security against misfortune and maximise returns. There is very little indication of rash dissipation in current consumption or in extensive land purchases but much evidence of careful investment in a range of activities intended to generate continued profit. When funds were not absorbed in trade itself they tended to be deployed in the building and leasing of urban property, in the provision of long-term credit and in industrial investment. Local registers of deeds and sasines reveal a most active market in the buying and selling of small plots of land and tenement properties in which the merchant class was much involved.[71] Again, virtually every will and testament of overseas merchants showed the popularity of lending out surplus funds on personal or heritable bond.[72] The creditor received an annual 'rent' or interest and a 'liquidate penalty' or additional sum levied if the loan was not liquidated within the period of time specified in the original bond. Such loans could be maintained over a number of years and were increased or reduced as circumstances warranted. Some merchants became involved in a major way in the provision of these primitive 'overdraft' facilities. The 1715 testament of Henry Eccles, merchant of Dundee, documents his bonded loans to 24 individuals, including the Earls of Strathmore and Haddington. A total of £700 sterling had been distributed in sums varying from £8 to £100. On one of his loans, moreover, Eccles had been drawing interest since 1691 and on most of the other loans for periods of five to ten years.[73] Some Glasgow merchants, such as Peter Murdoch, Andrew Cochrane and Robert Robertson, became so committed to lending on bond that they can be regarded as proto-bankers and when they helped to establish banking companies in the city in the 1750s they were simply formalising and extending a business in which they had long been engaged.[74]

The provision of finance for industry was an increasingly common feature of the investment strategies of the greater merchants in the later seventeenth century. Throughout the period of the present study 'industry' was more typical of the country than the towns because it was obviously in the rural areas that coal-mining, salt-burning and textile production was concentrated. Yet, after 1660, the number of processing plants in the larger burghs rose significantly in the wake of expansion in internal and external trade. The protectionist policy of the Scottish Parliament was also partly responsible for this development as a determined effort was made to reduce the importation of foreign manufactures and the export of Scottish raw materials through exempting Scottish native manufactories from custom duties and taxation. Between 1660 and 1710 about 52 industrial ventures were established in the towns and, according to the sources consulted, survived after their inception for a minimum period of three years.[75] They were concerned with the production of a range of different commodities: sugar, wool, glass, soap, paper, leather, lead, pins, rope, linen, sailcloth, gunpowder, salt, hardware and spirits. Equally they varied enormously in size and significance. In 1675 the Glasgow Easter Sugar House had a capital stock of £5555 and in 1680, the Leith Glassworks had a first issue of stock totalling almost £17,000 but these were exceptionally large by the standards of the majority. The majority attracted capital sums of less than £500.

What, however, is more pertinent to this analysis is not so much the nature of the manufactory movement as such as the extent of merchant participation in it both in terms of enterprise and finance. It is possible to identify the origins of capital in 49 of the 52 ventures. Thirty-eight manufactories attracted merchant investment in combination with landed and professional groups while merchants were the sole source of capital in 34 cases. Landowners were the next most significant group with interests in 10 firms. Merchant capital was, however, decisive and was usually contributed in the form of joint-stock enterprise involving 5 to 10 individual partners. As in landed investment most capital derived from the merchant communities of Edinburgh and Glasgow. Edinburgh men were responsible for the creation of 19 establishments and Glasgow merchants for 16. The merchant classes of the other Scottish towns had only a minor role: Aberdeen traders helped to organise and finance 4 ventures and Ayr burgesses 1. In the second half of the eighteenth century, merchant capital was a major factor in industrial expansion but this was a development which had significant, though much more modest origins, in earlier times.

CONCLUSION

The Scottish achievement of industrialisation in the later eighteenth century was based upon a vigorous national response to emerging markets and technical advance. Whether or not these possibilities were exploited depended in the final analysis on the quality of Scottish business talent and initiative. It was therefore of importance that before the period of substantial growth, a vigorous mercantile class had already evolved in lowland Scotland and had begun to demonstrate the skills of careful investment and willingness to take advantage of new commercial opportunity. The old institutional structure of mercantile controls which had developed to service the needs of a more stagnant economic system was rapidly being abandoned in the later seventeenth and early eighteenth centuries. The extent of social movement within the merchant communities of the larger towns implied the evaluation of a setting conducive to enterprise, of a milieu in which status depended on commercial ability as well as inherited rank. Above all, the investment patterns of the greater merchant class reveal a marked tendency to fund productive assets which were geared to further profit growth and diversification. All this helps to explain why, when markets expanded rapidly after 1750, the Scottish business class of that era, which had been formed in the urban world of the early eighteenth century, responded in an efficient and positive fashion.

REFERENCES

1. See *inter alia*, R. A. Dodgshon, 'The Removal of Runrig in Roxburghshire and Berwickshire 1680–1708', *Scottish Studies*, 16 (1972); M. L. Parry and T. R. Slater (eds.), *The Making of the Scottish Countryside* (London, 1980); I. D. Whyte, *Agriculture and Society in Seventeenth Century Scotland* (Edinburgh, 1979); John Di Folco, 'The Hopes of Craighall and Investment in Land in the Seventeenth Century', in T. M. Devine (ed.), *Lairds and Improvement in the Scotland of the Enlightenment* (Dundee, 1979), pp. 1–10.
2. T. C. Smout, *A History of the Scottish People, 1560–1830* (London, 1969), p. 161.
3. I. H. Adams, 'The Agents of Agricultural Change', in Parry and Slater, op. cit. p. 157.
4. J. D. Marwick (ed.), *Extracts from the Records of the Convention of the Royal Burghs of Scotland, 1677 1711* (Edinburgh, 1880). Hereafter referred to as *Convention Records*.
5. The standard descriptions of the institutional framework of merchant activity are: W. M. Mackenzie, *The Scottish Burghs* (Edinburgh, 1949); David Murray, *Early Burgh Organisation in Scotland* (Glasgow, 1924); A. J. Warden, *Burgh Laws of Dundee* (London, 1872).
6. *Convention Records*, pp. 24, 26, 44, 46, 133, 209.
7. Ibid. p. 133.
8. 'Register containing the state and Condition of every burgh within the Kingdome of Scotland in the year 1692', *Miscellany of the Scottish Burgh Records Society* (Edinburgh, 1881), p. 75.
9. Ibid. p. 81.
10. Ibid.
11. David B Morris, *The Stirling Merchant Gild and the Life of John Cowane* (Stirling, 1919), p. 73.
12. Dundee City Archive and Record Centre (DCARC), Dundee Guildry Book, GD/GRW/G1/1, 1570–1696.
13. Strathclyde Regional Archives (SRA), T-MH/2, Minute Book of the Merchants House of Glasgow, vol. 2, 1711–54; T. Donnelly, 'The Economic Activities of the Aberdeen Merchant Guild, 1750–1799', *Scottish Economic and Social History*, **1** (1981), 27.
14. SRA, T-MH 13, List of Persons carrying on or concerned in Trade in the city of Glasgow, 4 Oct. 1784, but whose names do not appear in the Register of Freemen kept by the Town Clerks.

15. Aberdeen Charter Room, Town House, Aberdeen (ACR), A25/1, Aberdeen Guildry Minute Books; DCARC, GD/GRW/G1/2, Sederunt Book of Dundee Guild Court; GD/GRW/G3/1, Guildry Incorporation Account Book, 1696–1751.

16. J. D. Marwick, *Edinburgh Guilds and Crafts* (Edinburgh, 1910), pp. 182, 192, 204–5, 207; Helen Armet (ed.), *Extracts from the Records of the Burgh of Edinburgh, 1689 to 1701* (Edinburgh, 1962), pp. 121–2; DCARC, GD/GRW/G1/2, Dundee Guild Court Sederunt Book, 6 July 1728; ACR, A25/1, Aberdeen Guildry Minute Book, 12 Mar. 1736.

17. DCARC, Guildry Incorporation Account Book, 1696–1751; ACR, Aberdeen Registered Deeds, A.32.

18. CBB Watson (ed.), *Register of Edinburgh Apprentices, 1660–1700* (Edinburgh, 1929); *Register of Edinburgh Apprentices, 1701–1755* (Edinburgh, 1929).

19. J. R. Anderson (ed.), *The Burgesses and Guild Brethren of Glasgow, 1573–1750* (Edinburgh, 1925).

20. SRA, T-MH/2, Minute Book of Merchants House of Glasgow, 1711–54, Register of Apprentices Book'd.

21. Mitchell Library, Glasgow (ML), Dunlop Papers, D24/2a, William Dunlop to James Dunlop, n.d., *c.* 1681.

22. Donald J. Withrington, 'Education and Society in the Eighteenth Century', in N. T. Phillipson and R. Mitchison (eds.), *Scotland in the Age of Improvement* (Edinburgh, 1970), p. 170.

23. These trends are outlined in the following: Whyte, op. cit. pp. 222–45; R. Mitchison, 'The Movement of Scottish Corn Prices in the Seventeenth and Eighteenth Centuries', *Econ. Hist. Rev.* (2nd ser.), **18** (1965); C. L. Horricks, 'Economic and Social Change in the Isle of Harris, 1680–1754' (unpublished PhD thesis, Edinburgh University, 1974); DCARC, Register of Ships of Dundee, 1701–13.

24. T. C. Smout, *Scottish Trade on the Eve of Union, 1660–1707* (Edinburgh, 1963), pp. 116–30.

25. Scottish Record Office (SRO), RH15/147, Papers of John Innes, merchant in Edinburgh; RH15/139, Accounts and Papers of William Nicoll, merchant in Edinburgh; RH15/186, Papers of William Cleghorn; RH15/54, Accounts and Papers of Edward Burd; W Mackay (ed.), *The Letter-Book of Baillie John Steuart of Inverness, 1715–1752* (Edinburgh, 1915); SRO, CC/8/85, Testaments of Robert Young, William Blair, Uthred McDowall; ML, B.325799, Copy Book of Letters of Adam Montgomery, 1700–1702 and Campbell of Shawfield Papers; National Library of Scotland (NLS), MS 1884, Letterbook of Alexander Shairp, 1712–19.

26. John Gibson, *The History of Glasgow from the Earliest Accounts to the Present Time* (Glasgow, 1777), p. 113.

27. *Convention Records*, pp. 133, 209, 212; Marwick, op. cit. pp. 182, 192, 204–5, 207; *Miscellany of the Scottish Burgh Records Society* (Edinburgh, 1881), pp. 75, 81; DCARC, Dundee Guild Court Sederunt Book, 6 July 1728; ACR, A.25/1, Aberdeen Guildry Minute Book, 12 Mar. 1736.

28. Marwick, op. cit. pp. 204–5.

29. SRO, RH15/147, Papers of John Innes, merchant in Edinburgh; RH15/126/1, Letters and other papers pertaining to William Caldwell, merchant, Leith *c.* 1720–34.

30. W. Mackay (ed.), *The Letterbook of Ballie John Stewart of Intverness, 1715 1752* (Edinburgh, 1915); John McCure. *A View of the City of Glasgow* (Glasgow, 1736), p. 169.

31. T. C. Smout, 'The Glasgow Merchant Community in the Seventeenth Century', *Scottish Historical Review*, 47 (1968), 53-68.

32. For the relatively sluggish condition of overseas commerce in the early eighteenth-century Dundee *see* DARC, TC/TS/3–4, Dundee Register of Ships, 1701–13.

33. McCure, op. cit. p. 170; Robert Chambers, *Edinburgh Merchants and Merchandise in Old Times* (Edinburgh, 1899). p. 5.

34. J Stuart (ed.), *List of Pollable Persons within the Shire of Aberdeen in 1694* (Aberdeen, 1844). Hereafter referred to as *Aberdeen Poll List, 1694.*

35. Marguerite Wood (ed.). *Edinburgh Poll Tax Returns for 1694* (Edinburgh, 1951).

36. ML, MS 120, Dunlop Papers, Bond of Provision for James Dunlop, 1 Sept. 1716.

37. C. B. B. Watson (ed.). *Roll of Edinburgh Burgesses and Guild Brethren 1701 1760* (Edinburgh, 1930). Hereafter referred to as *Edinburgh Burgess Roll*; DCARC, Lockit Book of Burgesses of Dundee, 1513 1973; ACR, Aberdeen Burgess Book, 1694 1760. These calculations exclude honorary and 'gratis' burgesses of which there were many.

38. ACR, A. 25/1, Aberdeen Guildry Minute Book, 29 June 1751.

39. McCure, op. cit. pp. 166 ff.

40. See above, pp. 29–32.

41. Smout, loc. cit.; T. M. Devine, *The Tobacco Lords* (Edinburgh, 1975); 'An Eighteenth Century Business Elite; Glasgow West India Merchants, *c.* 1750 1815', *Scottish Historical Review* 57 (1978), 40–67.

42. James Gourlay, *A Glasgow Miscellany* (privately printed, n.d.), p. 43.

43. SRA, Register of Deeds, B. 10/15/8435, Settlement of Alexander Speirs.

44. SRO, GD 247/10, Answers for William Cunninghame . . . 1.

45. W. St Robinson jun., 'Richard Oswald the Peacemaker', *Ayrshire Collections,* 1950–4 (2nd set.) III (1955).

46. P A Ramsay, *Views in Renfrewshire with Historical and Descriptive Notices* (Edinburgh, 1839), 163; SRO, GD 237/139, Minutes of Agreement between W McDowall and J Gordon, St Kitts, 28 Dec. 1723. For the position of those families which had retained their position from the later seventeenth century see M L Bogle MSS, Geneology of the Bogle family; A Dunlop, *Memorabilia of the family of Dunlop* (privately printed, n. d.); Anon, *Old Country Houses of the Old Glasgow Gentry* (Glasgow, 1870); R M Buchanan, *Notes on Members of the Buchanan Society, 1725– 1829* (Glasgow, 1931).

47. *Aberdeen Poll List, 1694*; A Munro, *Memorials of the Aldermen, Provosts and Lord Provosts of Aberdeen* (Aberdeen, 1897), pp. 244–62; ACR, A. 5–6, Aberdeen Council Register, 1690–1750; Donnelly, loc. cit. pp. 25–41.

48. DCARC, GD/GRW/G1/1–2, Dundee Guildry Book, 1683–1720.

49. ML, Campbell of Shawfield Papers, 1/576, Robert Campbell to Daniel Campbell, 10 June 1712; W F Skene, *Memorials of the Family of Skene of Skene* (Aberdeen, 1881), p. 131.

50. See above, pp. 29–32.

51. For Glasgow see Devine, op. cit. pp. 25–7; for Aberdeen, Munro, op. cit. pp. 244– 62.

52. Devine, op. cit., pp. 7–8.

53. ACR, A.25/1, Aberdeen Guildry Minute Book, 19 Feb. 1736.

54. DCARC, GD/GRW/G1/2, Sederunt Book of Dundee Guild Court, 30 Jan. 1730.

55. Ibid. Lockit Book of Burgesses of Dundee, 1513–1973.

56. *Edinburgh Burgess Roll,* 1710–20.

57. ACR, A.21, Aberdeen Register of Indentures, 1622–1798.

58. *Register of Edinburgh Apprentices,* 1701–55.

59. ML, B.325799, Adam Montgomery Letterbook, 1700–2.

60. NLS, MS 1884, Letterbook of Alexander Shairp, merchant in Edinburgh, 1712– 19.

61. Devine, op. cit. pp. 9–10, 83–4; loc. cit. p. 51.
62. William Seton, *The Interest of Scotland* (1700), p. 75.
63. See, for example, Smout, op. cit. (1963), pp. 78–9.
64. J H Stevenson (ed.), *The Register of the Great Seal of Scotland*, 1660–1668 (Edinburgh, 1914). Hereafter referred to as *Register of the Great Seal*.
65. See the calculations in J di Folco's essay in T M Devine (ed.), *Lairds and Improvement in the Scotland of the Enlightenment* (Dundee, 1979), pp. 1–10.
66. SRO, County Valuation Rolls E/106. See also L Timperley, 'The Pattern of Landholding in Eighteenth Century Scotland', in Parry and Slater, op.cit. pp. 137–54.
67. ML, Campbell of Shawfield Papers, 1/576, Robert Campbell to Daniel Campbell, 10 June 1712.
68. *Aberdeen Poll List, 1694.*
69. *Register of the Great Seal, 1660–1668.*
70. Devine, op. cit. pp. 18–33; Donnelly, loc. cit.
71. See, for example, Edinburgh City Archives (ECA), Inventory of Miscellaneous Papers called Moses' Bundles; ACR, Burgh Court Deeds Recorded, 1736–40.
72. Many of the generalisations which follow are based on an analysis of approximately sixty merchant testaments for the period 1680–1740 in the Edinburgh and Glasgow commissary court records. See SRO, CC8/8 (Edinburgh) and CC9/7 (Glasgow).
73. SRO, CC 8/8/86.
74. SRA, B.10/15/5402, Disposition and Assignation, Robert Robinson to his Creditors, 1740; S G Checkland, *Scottish Banking: a History, 1695–1973* (Glasgow, 1975), p. 69.
75. The assessment of the number and capital structure of the town manufactories which follows is based on: SRA, B.10/15, Glasgow Register of Deeds; ECA, Inventory of Moses Bundles; ACR, Aberdeen Registered Deeds, A31–32; *The Acts of the Parliament of Scotland; The Register of the Privy Council of Scotland*; W R Scott, *The Constitution and Finance of English, Scottish and Irish Joint-Stock Companies to 1720* (Cambridge, 1910–12); T C Smout, 'The Early Scottish Sugar Houses, 1660–1720', *Econ. Hist. Rev.* (2nd ser.), 1961; A G Thomson, *The Paper Industry in Scotland, 1590–1861* (Edinburgh, 1974).

3

THE UNION OF 1707 AND SCOTTISH DEVELOPMENT

An impressive intellectual case can be made that the Scottish achievement of rapid economic growth from the later decades of the eighteenth century rested ultimately on the political framework of Union with England.[1] Several clauses of the Treaty of 1707 were devoted to economic matters, but the two of vital consequence in the view of most historians were Articles 4 and 5. The former provided for free Scottish entry, without payment of customs duties, to both the English domestic and the jealously guarded colonial markets. The latter allowed all Scottish-owned merchant vessels to rank as ships of Great Britain from 1707. Scottish merchantmen were thus to be afforded both the privileges and protection of inclusion within the Navigation Acts.

These political arrangements created the largest and richest common market in western Europe at the time, and gained even greater importance from the Scottish perspective because of the crisis in Scotland in the years before the passage of the Union legislation. Economic difficulties in the 1690s were brought on by a series of harvest failures, the collapse of Scottish colonial aspirations with the bankruptcy of the Darien Company and the twin effects of continental war and aggressive economic nationalism in Europe. The poor and relatively underdeveloped Scottish economy had become vulnerable, according to some writers, in a world of rising tariffs and state mercantilism.[2] The Scots needed much in the international market but had little to offer in return. They were, therefore, in a peculiarly weak position at a time when state military and economic aggrandisement was ruthlessly pursued by the great powers of Europe. It might plausibly be argued, therefore, that for protection, in a more dangerous political and economic environment, Scotland needed access to English markets and the naval support of her southern neighbour.

Those who argue for a positive and inevitable connection between the Union of 1707 and Scottish economic development, support their case with at least four additional propositions: (1) Political stability was enhanced because 1707 diminished the potential danger of Anglo-Scottish conflict rooted in the Jacobite threat, and helped to provide further enduring support for the political and religious settlement achieved in the so-called 'Glorious Revolution' of 1688/9. In this view, a secure political structure, partly at least derived from 1707, produced the long-term basis in the 18th century for economic advance. (2) Closer political association between England and Scotland permitted the easier flow of both factors of production, such as capital and labour, and ideas, such as new techniques and processes, between the two economies. In particular, the political bond accelerated the movement north in the long-run of southern capital, technology and skills there to combine with Scottish mineral resources and cheap labour to stimulate economic change.[3] (3) With the avenues to political influence and activity mainly closed after 1707, because of the disappearance of the Scottish parliament, the Scottish governing class, consisting mainly of the greater landowners and their close kinsmen in the higher echelons of the legal profession, turned their energies directly to economic improvement.[4] (4) Finally, it is suggested that the union added to this psychological response in another way by bringing influential Scots into closer and more frequent contact with a more advanced English civilisation, thus heightening their awareness of Scottish inferiority and contributing to their desire to fashion a new Scotland through systematic and rational improvement in the spheres of both material and cultural life.[5]

This, I would argue, is the bare bones of what can be termed the 'optimistic' thesis on the economic impact of the Union. It was this view, in much simpler form, which was favoured by Victorian writers who assumed that Scotland had been rescued from poverty by the new political association with England. They were in no doubt that the ensuing prosperity of the two nations ultimately depended upon the link forged in 1707 and this assumption in turn became the cornerstone of the enduring political connection.[6] In the twentieth century, the 'optimistic' thesis has been added to and even criticised. Only, however, in the 1950s and early 1960s did economic historians seek to clarify and comment in detail on the issues in the light of modern historical research.[7] But since A. M. Carstairs wrote in the early 1950s and R. H. Campbell in the early 1960s, there has been a rapid increase in the publication of important new work in Scottish economic and social history, much of it pertaining in a direct or indirect sense, to the economic consequences of the Union.[8] The time, therefore, does seem appropriate for an attempt at a fresh examination of the historiography of the Union and the Scottish economy which would seek, in particular, to determine the validity of the 'optimistic' view and the extent to which it might be qualified and refined. What follows, then, is my attempt to interpret the economic effect of 1707 in the light of recent research findings. The analysis will be structured in four parts: (I) the economic and social background of the later seventeenth century and its relevance to the Union of 1707; (II) the Union and the Scottish economy in the short-run to c.1740; (III) the Union and the Scottish economy in the long-run to c.1800: (IV) the Union and the Scottish economy in perspective.

I

In a paper published in 1967, the former Hugh Trevor-Roper, now Lord Dacre, asserted that 'at the end of the seventeenth century, Scotland was a by-word for irredeemable poverty, social backwardness, (and) political faction . . .' a society released from its material and intellectual shackles only by the stimulating effects of closer association with England in the Union.[9] Now, as indicated earlier, Scottish economic experience in the 1690s lends some support to this contention. There was indeed a series of economic difficulties in the last decade of the seventeenth century but it is less certain how permanent the crisis was and, equally, how representative of Scottish economic experience between 1660 and 1707 were the middle years of the 1690s. The evidence now available would tend to suggest that the difficulties of that time were essentially temporary and not necessarily the prelude to a final collapse of the Scottish economic system which could only be avoided by achieving full union with the south.

The critical factor in this whole matter was the viability of Scottish agriculture. At least nine out of ten Scots in 1700 lived on the land. The produce of rural society formed the mix of commodities which was traded overland to England and by sea to Europe. Good harvests were vital to the maintenance of a healthy balance of trade. The accummulation of food and raw material surpluses was the basic precondition for later social diversification, urban expansion and increases in capital. In relation to the overwhelming importance of agriculture, Scottish overseas trade before 1707, though relatively well-documented and studied, fades somewhat in significance.

Judged over the period c.1652 to 1740 Scottish agriculture was remarkably effective in feeding the population of Scotland in most years and, in some, producing a surplus for export. Between 1660 and 1700, there were significant harvest failures and shortages only in 1674 and 1693–7. From 1700, there were difficult years, but not subsistence crises, in 1709, 1724–5 and 1740–1.[10] This is to be compared with the later sixteenth century when, between 1560 and 1600, an estimated one third of the period saw significant food shortage in some parts of Scotland.[11] The so-called 'Lean Years' of the 1690s, therefore, though having savage demographic effects in some regions, were an aberration, a reflection of an especially severe but essentially short-lived spell of climatic deterioration.[12] The fact, for instance, that government policy after the Restoration moved away from protecting grain consumers by forbidding grain exports, to encouraging the grain trade by export bounties, was a telling indicator of changing times. Increasingly, in many years, the problem was seen as one of surplus rather than the recurrent danger of deficiency. It is important, of course, not to exaggerate the scale of change. The late seventeenth century crisis may have been ephemeral but the fact that it happened nonetheless reflected a society in which the market sector was still weak and the subsistence system dominant. Yet, the long-run improvement in food supply also requires emphasis.

Why improvement occurred cannot yet be determined in precise terms. Whether the decisive influence was climatic change, a reflection of slackening demographic pressure after the mortality crises of the later 1640s, greater efficiency, improved marketing or a combination of all four is impossible to say. Nonetheless, thanks to the pioneering researches of such historical geographers as Ian Whyte and Robert Dodgshon we now know that the years before the Union did witness significant alterations *within* the rural economic and social system which may have had a direct connection to the transformation in structure of the second half of the eighteenth century.[13] These movements within the existing order may be summarised as follows:-

(1) Changes in farm organisation involving a movement in several areas of the Lowlands to single and larger tenancies—detected in the Borders and south-east/east central Lowlands.
(2) Alterations in tenure as a result of an expansion in the number and duration of written leases implying that farming competence rather than tradition or kin associations was, on several estates, becoming the test of entry to farms.
(3) An erosion of subsistence agriculture as demonstrated by conversion of rentals in kind to a money basis, expansion of rural market centres and more attention paid to the marketing of grains, stock and raw materials.
(4) Limited advances in productivity and increases in yields through the widespread use of lime and the partial introduction of enclosures and improved rotations.

These findings of recent research would hardly suggest that *structural* change occurred in Scottish farming between 1660 and 1700. On the other hand, the agrarian system before the Union was clearly neither inert nor incapable of change without the civilising influence of southern example. The 'improvers' of the eighteenth century did exploit 'English methods' (and also Dutch examples) but it would now appear that they were also building on an established indigenous tradition. What is striking indeed, is the slow, continuous and piecemeal nature of agrarian change, developing organically below the surface, both before and after 1707, but apparently little affected, in any obvious fashion, by the ebb and flow of great political events.

In other ways, too, the period 1660 to 1700 may be seen as one of transition rather than stagnation, in which the origin of significant later developments can be identified. The pattern and geographical direction of Scottish external trade was already changing from old connections with Europe to newer and more dynamic links with England in cattle, coal, salt and linen. In 1700, an estimated half of Scottish commerce by value was

reckoned already to be done with England.[14] Moreover, a new sophistication among the Scottish merchant-class has recently been described. The
protectionist system based on the privileges of the royal burghs, the burgess
system and the elaborate regulation of the guilds was in rapid decay.
Merchants in some towns seem to have become more prosperous,
developed new connections (as with the plantation colonies from the
1660s), become accustomed to employ new financial devices such as the
bill of exchange more widely in their transactions in both home and foreign
trade and widened and deepened their investments in urban industry.[15] This
era of increasing mercantile sophistication was relevant to success in the
eighteenth the century when the business classes of Scotland were able to
turn the opportunities of Union to their own advantage. In this period,
however, it also reflected a momentous change in Scotland's position in
international trade. As the axis of European trade moved from the
Mediterranean to the Atlantic world so Scottish merchants, from being
at the periphery now came closer to the centre of activity.

Finally, 1660 to 1700 also witnessed an evolution in attitude among the
Scottish governing classes. It used to be assumed that only in the eighteenth
century, after Union, did Scottish landowners become interested in
encouraging the economy. Only then, we believed, did they commit
themselves, through both public bodies, such as the Society of Improvers
and the Board of Trustees for Manufactures and Fisheries, and private
example, to national economic improvement. But, again, there were
important lines of continuity which hardly seem in the short-run to be
dramatically modified by the new political connection with England. The
same mercantilist urge to improve the Scottish economy can be seen in the
activities of both Privy Council and Parliament in their assorted policies of
aid to trade, industry and agriculture in the 1670s, 1680s and 1690s. For the
first time, between 1660 and 1700, an increase in national economic power
became the aim of both Scottish government and the landed élites which it
represented.[16] It mattered little that most of these policies were ineffective;
what was crucial was the change in attitude and expectation which they
implied. The process by which the landed estate was viewed more as a
source of revenue and less a source of power was far advanced in lowland
Scotland by 1700. In this sense, the Board of Trustees and the other
eighteenth century public bodies were not a new beginning but rather a
logical continuation of the policy of economic reform first evolved in the
Scottish parliament before Union. There can be little doubt, of course, that
'improvement' in the eighteenth century was practised more widely and
systematically than before. Equally, however, the theory that the Scots élites
were jolted out of inertia by the stimulating consequences of closer
association with England is, at best, an over-simplification and, at worst,
erroneous. The evidence seems rather to suggest a governing class which
was perpetuating, widening and adapting policies ultimately derived from
an earlier era, within the new political context of the Union.

II

In any consideration of the short-run economic results of the Union to c.1740 two obvious questions must be confronted: (a) how far did the Scottish economy gain in these years from the political change; (b) to what extent did the Union harm Scottish economic interests?

(a) The three main economic activities which were most likely to derive immediate benefit from free entry to the English home and colonial markets were the linen manufacture, the trade in sheep and cattle and the importation of tobacco from North America. For the first three to four decades after 1707 there is little evidence of sustained and significant advance in any of these sectors though there was modest expansion together with cyclical fluctuation in all of them before 1740. Nonetheless, the pro-Unionist argument that a Scottish economic miracle would be achieved once the new connection was forged was quickly revealed as a hopelessly inaccurate prognosis. Nor, with the historian's key advantage of hindsight, can it be said that this was surprising. Despite the important advances in the period after 1660 already described, the Scottish economy before 1730 was still based on the countryside, with large pockets of subsistence production and hardly yet capable of speedy adjustment. Moreover, any stimulus from the English market before 1740 was unlikely to be significant because the southern economy itself experienced accelerated growth only in the second half of the eighteenth century. Even if it is conceded that the English economic system in the long-run was the vital motor of Scottish development, it could not perform that function in the early eighteenth century.

Indeed, it is clear that the Scottish economic experience in the first two to three decades after 1707 exposed two major fallacies in the economic case for union which had emerged in the parliamentary debates of 1705–6. First, the fact was that Union offered *risks* as well as *opportunities* in almost equal measure. Integration could have meant Scotland's reduction to the status of an English economic satellite, a supplier of foods, raw materials and labour for the English economy, but with little possibility of pronounced economic diversification in her own right. This is roughly what happened to Ireland in the eighteenth century and was analogous also to the economic relationship between highland and lowland Scotland in the period after 1780.[17] To use Andre Gunder Frank's well-known phrase, Union could easily have been the political prelude to 'the development of underdevelopment' in the Scottish economy.[18] Second, and more optimistically, the Union was a factor which could neither cause growth or ensure that growth would be inhibited. The settlement merely offered a context, with both opportunities and risks. Ultimately what mattered, therefore, was the Scottish reaction in the new context and the influences which conditioned this response.

(b) The evidence now available also suggests that publicists at the time and some later historians have exaggerated the harm caused by the Union to the

Scottish economy before 1740. Taxation certainly rose after 1707, most notoriously with the salt and linen taxes of 1711 and the malt tax of 1725. These were politically offensive, against both the spirit and letter of the treaty and may have caused short-term difficulties for some groups. On the other hand, taxation hardly drained Scotland dry; according to Atholl Murray's calculation only about 15 to 20 per cent of tax revenue in the fifty years after Union actually left the country.[19]

The fears of English industrial competition were more solidly based, but Drs. Gulvin and Durie, in their work on wool and linen respectively, have described how the English impact was, at worst, a marginal one.[20] The small fine woollen sector was disrupted by free trade but the harsh winds of competition crushed a manufacture which was already ailing before 1707. More significantly, the important coarse sector survived and in the medium-term was able to take advantage of colonial demand for cheap woollens in the Caribbean and North America. Dr. Christopher Whatley's recent work on salt has added to those findings by demonstrating that the traditional claim that this manufacture was hit badly by the union and the new fiscal system is also erroneous.

We now also have a clearer impression of the response of the Scottish governing classes in the aftermath of the Union. The complaint made in 1733 by James Erskine of Grange that, 'This country now and for some years past, has look on it self as deserted, not only by the courtiers, but by the principall (sic.) part of its nobility and gentry' has been substantially confirmed by the researches of John Shaw.[22] The magnates and even some of the greater lairds did seek position, fortune and influence on the wider stage of London but, as Julia Buckroyd and Patrick Riley demonstrate in their work on the pre-1707 political structure, this represented the acceleration of a social trend which had already begun before 1707.[23]

It is difficult to be certain whether Scotland lost or gained from this migration in material terms. It could be represented as a haemorrhage of scarce capital through remittances to the south. On the other hand, the resources required to live in southern style fuelled demand for higher rents in the north. As Montrose complained in 1708 in an oft-quoted comment, 'London journeys dont verie well agree with Scots estaites'.[24] Absenteeism and improvement were of necessity closely inter-related. As the late Eric Cregeen has shown, in the most ambitious study yet attempted of the management of a large Scottish Highland estate at this time, absenteeism and its costs were indeed one of the most powerful determinants of agrarian change in the early and mid eighteenth century, a period when grain and cattle prices were still relatively stable and the market incentive to introduce efficient practices relatively weak.[25] Agrarian reorganisation at this time was a response to the crushing cost pressures of competitive display rather than to the stimuli of rapid increases in demand.

The obvious question remains, however, *why* did the Scots get off so lightly in the first few decades of full union with England? The dangers of both political and economic dependency were clearly present. The most recent work on Scottish political history in the early eighteenth century has argued that 'fundamentally, power over Scotland's destiny resided after 1707 in the economic-political centre, London'.[2] The Scottish governing class after 1707 was firmly tied to southern sources of patronage and in political circles in London quickly acquired a reputation for venality and corruption. Moreover, there were now no tariffs on the Border to protect the slender Scottish manufacturing sector from competition from the most advanced economic system in Europe. Dependency in political terms was a reality and the scenario for a colonial relationship of the classic type obviously existed. Why did one not develop in these years?

One possible explanation lies in the English motivation for Union. Westminster wanted parliamentary Union with the Scots for reasons of military and political security and had no economic ambitions north of the Border.[27] Scottish commercial links with the south were indeed expanding but as late as 1700 most Scottish external trade was carried on with non-English markets. The market structure which could have sustained speedy dominance of the Scottish economy was only in the process of growth. Here Scotland's relative backwardness was a decided advantage because her limited market sector and poor internal communications were more effective sources of protection against English industry than Border tariffs. The Scottish position contrasts vividly at this point with that of Ireland where in 1700 between 75% and 80% of external trade was already carried on with England, the main market for Irish cattle, grain and wool and the chief source of supply of imported manufactured goods and essential raw materials.[28]

The London government, therefore, merely wanted tranquility and order in Scotland, and when this existed, as it tended to do most of the time, Westminster was broadly indifferent to the Scottish situation. (Thus between 1727 and 1745 only nine Acts of Parliament dealt specifically with Scotland, seven of them of little consequence.) But since the main concern was to ensure stable government, positive intervention in the Scottish economy could occur as part of a wider policy of defusing discontent at times of instability. So the Malt Tax riots resulted in the establishment of the Board of Trustees for Manufactures in 1727 which, as recent work has shown, came about as the result of decisions made by *central* government in London.[29] Most of the time, however, Westminster was apathetic and Scottish matters tended to be left in the hands of the Scottish political 'manager', of the day, of whom the most remarkable in the post-union years was Archibald Campbell, Earl of Islay, who became 3rd Duke of Argyll in 1743 and from 1725 to 1761 was the dominant figure in Scottish politics. His great agent in Scotland, Lord Milton, had a real interest in the economic progress of Scotland and was able to use his considerable influence to found the British Linen Company, later the British Linen Bank, and the Commission for Annexed Forfeited Estates.[30] The political structure in the decades after 1707 may, therefore, not have contributed to a Scottish economic renaissance; neither, however, did it convert Scotland into a colonial appendage of the southern economy.

III

I now want to move on to the third part of my paper and consider how far economic change from the 1740s to the end of the eighteenth century was dependent on the Union connection. To do so, I wish again to return to cattle, tobacco and linen in order to determine what light they each shed on this central issue.

The cattle trade to England had first developed before 1707 and, despite rising English duties against Scottish stock, had expanded because of the consumer demands of London and the salt beef requirements of the Royal Navy. Its history after 1707 suggests that mere absence of tariffs was not sufficient to stimulate significant development. Ultimately the major variables were those of price, weather and market behaviour. One must be careful also not to exaggerate the economic impact of the cattle trade on Scotland.[31] True, it made money for some landlords in the Highlands and in the south–western lowlands centred on Galloway but neither of these areas were in the van of agrarian progress. The cattle trade had limited multiplier effects because it was based on cattle-rearing, not fattening, and because stock went on the hoof to market along the drove roads, thus providing little impetus for basic change in the existing economic infra-structure. The cattle trade undoubtedly made some Scotsmen rich but Adam Smith exaggerated when he asserted in the *Wealth of Nations* that 'of all the commercial advantages which Scotland derived from the union with England, this rise in the price of cattle is, perhaps, the greatest.'[32] The sale of cattle helped the Highland landed classes to afford a higher lifestyle and allowed northern society to import much needed grain supplies but could hardly be described as a strategic presence in the Scottish economy as a whole.[33]

The remarkably successful Scottish tobacco trade was securely based on the Union which allowed the Scots to trade freely within the colonial system. Legitimacy was probably vital because, although Scots merchants were already engaged in commerce with the American colonies before 1707, no English government would have permitted the enormous growth in Scottish tobacco imports which characterised the middle decades of the eighteenth century. Smuggling had its limitations: the Union was necessary for Scottish success in American trade. On the other hand, the Union did not *cause* the growth of the tobacco trade. That came about because Scots merchants adopted more efficient commercial practices than their rivals and competed successfully in the international market for business.[34] The tobacco example is an important one: it provides a further illustration of my main point that Union provided a series of risks and an array of opportunities. Ultimately what mattered, however, was the Scottish response to these stimuli.

Finally, the linen industry merits analysis. Its importance in the eighteenth century was three-fold. First, it was Scotland's biggest manufacturing industry; second, it experienced rapid growth between 1740 and 1780; third, it was an important source of capital, labour an entrepreneurship for the development of the Scottish cotton industry after 1780. The English and colonial markets were the keys to growth, taking in the 1760s, on one estimate, about two-thirds of Scottish output produced for public sale.[35] But for Union, this industry might have been confronted with an English tariff wall in competition with more efficient Dutch and German rivals. Within the British common market, Scots linen producers received both tariff protection from these competitors and export bounties; these two factors, according to Dr. Durie, were more decisive in the growth process than native initiative in improving efficiency.[36] The relationship between the successful linen manufacture and Union is, then, a particularly close one. Again, however, we must beware of simple economic determinism. Ireland, in the eighteenth century, had an even larger and more successful linen industry than Scotland but this wholly failed to propel the Irish economy into the industrial age. Indeed, the current view of linen in Ireland would see it as having an essentially damaging long-term effect on the rural social structure by producing fragmentation of land units much in the fashion of kelping and illicit whisky-making in highland Scotland.[37] The linen manufacture brought prosperity to Scotland in the old economic order; it could not guarantee that the Scots would achieve the break-through to a new type of structure altogether.

IV

This brief examination of three important sectors of the Scottish economy and their relation to Union suggests that 1707 was relevant but not in itself decisive. It can be plausibly argued, for instance, that Scottish external trade in particular rested on the protection of the Navigation System. But that protection mainly disintegrated after 1783, with the emergence of an independent United States, precisely at the time when the Scottish industrial economy began to emerge in a significant way. There could be no clearer proof that Scotland had become *less* dependent on the Union connection by that time. After 1783, Scots merchants re-established the American link, pioneered new trades to the Caribbean, Europe and, eventually in the early nineteenth century, to Latin America and the East Indies. What need to be considered finally, therefore, are those factors which enabled the Scots not only to gain from the Union, when they might equally well have lost, after 1780 to achieve growth independently of the protection of the Navigation System and the political connection on which it was based.

First, Scotland had a political and social élite which was committed to economic improvement. The first signs of this tendency emerged in the second half of the seventeenth century but only in the eighteenth, through both private initiative and public encouragement, did the governing classes aspire to economic growth as a goal. They contributed powerfully to Scottish modernisation by lending status and prestige to the business of economic reform; they directed the course of agrarian improvement. Through political pressures, important tariff and bounty concessions were won from Westminster for such key Scottish industries as the linen manufacture.

Second, Scotland had appropriate geological resources of coal and iron in the central Lowlands close to both water transport and urban development. One must be careful, however, not to substitute for a discredited economic determinism the superficial attractions of an equally simplistic geological determinism. Self-evidently, geological resources were useless in the absence of an appropriate technical, social and economic context. It is the case, also, that though central Scotland had a favoured combination of both abundant coal and iron ore reserves, these were less significant in the eighteenth century than in the nineteenth. Water remained the major source of power long after 1800, and the Scottish iron industry did not experience rapid expansion until after 1830. Scottish geological advantage was, therefore, very relevant to the *sustained* growth of the Scottish economy in the nineteenth century but was inevitably of more marginal consequence in the last quarter of the eighteenth century.

Third, Scottish scientific and technical ingenuity merits attention. To some extent, in cotton technology, coal-mining and agricultural methods the Scots simply borrowed from their more advanced English neighbours. On the other hand, however, Scottish craftsmen and inventors, as B. F. Duckham and J. Butt have shown, quickly improved on southern models and also made their own important contributions to improved technology. The list of achievement in this regard is a formidable one: William Kelly of New Lanark was the first to apply power to Samuel Crompton's cotton mule; James Watt was the first to perfect the separate condenser for the steam engine which revolutionised the source of power for industrial production; in agriculture, James Small's plough and Andrew Meikle's threshing machine were notable instances of Scottish ingenuity; 'Lothians' husbandry' in the early nineteenth century became world famous as a model of efficiency and improved organisation. In banking, the Scots were also world leaders and attracted widespread international recognition and imitation. Bell's *Comet* of 1812 was the second commercial steamship in the world. J. B. Neilson revolutionised iron-manufacture with his 'hot-blast' process of 1829. The list is not exhaustive but the examples are sufficient to emphasise the point that the Scots did not simply adopt southern methods. They made striking and original contributions of their own to the technology of the Industrial Revolution. These achievements in turn, reflected the cultural and social values of Scotland and, in particular, the effects of Scottish educational and religious traditions. These tended to place more emphasis on the practical than the imaginative world, encouraged practices of 'rationalism' and stimulated the examination of alternatives.[33] They were indigenous developments influenced, but not derived from, the effects of a closer connection with England.

Fourth, the Scots had a native business class sufficiently enterprising and developed by the 1740s to take advantage of opportunities within the new political context. Here again relevant comparisons can be made with the Irish merchant community. Commercial institutions and structures were much less developed in Ireland. Only a relatively small proportion of Irish shipping, under 10% according to Lewis Cullen was actually owned in Ireland in 1800.[39] But Christopher Smout's work suggests that already, around 1700, Scottish external trade was mainly carried on in Scottish bottoms.[40] The Irish marine insurance business was under-developed and its dependency on London virtually complete. The Scots also used London but there was considerable local under-writing activity. Similarly, estimates suggest that the Scottish note circulation in the 1770s was between four and six times that of Ireland.[41] A comparison of Dickson's history of Cork merchants, Mannion's study of Waterford merchants and Camble's examination of Belfast traders with my work on the business communities of the four main Scottish towns between 1660 and 1740 suggests that the Irish had lower levels of capitalisation, smaller partnerships, a narrower investment portfolio and recruited from a narrower social base than the Scots.[42]

These differences were both in major part cause and effect of the contrasts in economic relationships with England. Already in 1700 between two-thirds to three-quarters of Irish external trade was done with England and, as the century proceeded, Ireland became yoked to the English economy as a specialist supplier of raw materials and foods. Inevitably, the wealthier and more powerful English merchant community asserted a decisive influence on this trade. The greater part of Anglo-Irish trade was transacted on the account of English merchants and Irish merchants, therefore, tended to rely heavily on English insurance, banking and credit institutions. Many, indeed, were but the agents of more powerful houses across the Irish sea and their real position was analogous to that of the factors of British merchants in the colonial world.[43] The Scots operated in a different environment and had a different business history. They never became as dependent on English trade. Contacts with the new world through Glasgow stimulated the rise of an independent merchant class based on the direct purchase system and they retained their European connections much longer than the Irish.[44]

It is, however, unlikely that even this list of favourable influences, important as they are, comes to the heart of the matter. Comparative economic and social history suggests that the composition and structure of rural society in pre-industrial economies is often decisive in explaining balanced growth and diversification.[45] This is likely also to be so in the case of Scotland: the Lowlands had evolved a social formation by the later eighteenth century which was able to facilitate and sustain the growth of wealth in a society which was also experiencing an increase in population.

The growth in lowland population first merits attention because, as Michael Anderson has suggested, it seems to have been relatively slow certainly by Irish, but even by English standards between 1750 and 1800, which were the crucial decades for the beginnings of change in economic structure.[46] This meant that pressure on capital resources and food supply was eased and that economic expansion was able to gather pace without being overwhelmed by too many extra numbers. Yet at the same time, the alternative danger of labour scarcity was also avoided by the changing shape of rural society. The central Lowlands were fortunate because the region was surrounded by three areas which were shedding labour after 1750: the southern uplands, the southern Highlands and Ireland. Population was being expelled from the first two areas by commercial pastoralism and from Ireland by mounting demographic pressure only partially relieved by extensions to potato cultivation and linen manufacture.[47] The Scottish economy, therefore, in its first phase of precocious expansion had, in a sense, the best of both worlds: a moderate range of aggregate population growth but linked with this the key advantage of labour mobility in certain localities which helped to service the needs of the growing towns and the burgeoning industries.

The structure of rural society was also relevant in a wider sense to the process of balanced growth. By and large, land in Scotland was not owned by working farmers or peasants but was divided into medium—or large-sized—estates, each controlled by individual landlords. In the early nineteenth century there were about 7,600 landed proprietors in Scotland, a handful of them peers of the realm with estates running into several thousand acres, but the overwhelming majority, smaller proprietors, or lairds, owning more modest properties. The vital point about this group was that they were an indigenous and hereditary elite whose families had held the same estates over many generations. Recent work on the structure of landownership by Loretta Timperley has shown how sluggish the Scottish market in land was until after c.1750.[48] This was a peculiar advantage because the landowners, as we have seen, were also an innovative class and thus were able to use their inherited authority and wide administrative and legal powers to gain social acceptance for agrarian change. The social influence which inevitably flowed from their long tenure of hegemony legitimised the movement towards capitalist farming and was one reason why the old order passed away with hardly any dissent or protest in the lowlands.[49]

Below landlord level the tendency in the Lowlands long before 1750 was to enlarge the size of individual farms, ruthlessly limit fragmentation or sub-division and increasingly reduce access to land. Even on the island of Arran, a district not in the forefront of agrarian change, the Duke of Hamilton's factor could assert in 1766 'All subsetts to be Totally excluded without liberty of the Duke or his tutors asked and obtained'.[50] This long-run development of single and larger tenancies stretching back into the seventeenth century, ensured that when grain prices rose markedly after c.1780 there was a pool of farmers able to respond in a vigorous fashion to widening markets. But the same trend also helped lowland society to maintain a broadly favourable balance of resources and population. Controls on access to land encouraged mobility of labour off the land and this was regulated anyway by the Scottish system of hiring farm servants which limited employment and accommodation in accordance with the specific needs of farmers for workers over periods of six months to one year.[51] In addition, the linen industry could develop for long-term benefit, not simply as a peasant bi-employment, a system which might have restricted such migration and ultimately pushed rural society towards diminishing returns through fragmentation of holdings in a context of demographic expansion, as happened in Ulster and the Highlands. Instead, tenant consolidation and limitations on sub-letting meant that linen manufacture and farming gradually became separate activities, the former concentrating in villages and small towns rather than farm steadings. Its workers, therefore, began to form a quasi-proletariat which found little difficulty in adapting to the age of greater specialisation and more rapid growth in textiles after c.1780.

I have tried to argue in this paper that the optimistic thesis concerning the positive effects of the Union on the Scottish economy requires both modification and qualification. In the short-run, the impact of the new political connection was marginal: in the longer-term, it could be regarded as a basic influence on growth only because Scottish society managed to turn the arrangement to its own advantage. The fundamental causes of modernisation lay, however, deeper within the texture of society, the institutional and social inheritance of the period before 1707, and the particular response to external market forces. In the long-run, the structures of society were more decisive than key political events and merit greater attention than they have so far received in Scottish historiography. There is no doubt that the Union conferred benefits over the key period c.1740 to c.1780 when Scotland moved steadily towards the threshold of industrialisation. In a longer-term perspective, however, 1707 was but one of a series of favourable influences which were eventually to revolutionise the Scottish economic structure and transform the nature of Scottish society.

REFERENCES

1. For a recent elaboration of this argument see Tony Dickson (ed.): *Scottish Capitalism: Class, State and Nation from before the Union to the Present* (London, 1980, pp. 89–136. Versions of this paper have been given to the Scottish History Graduate Studies Seminar in the Department of History, University of Guelph, Canada, September 1983, and the Winter Conference of the Economic and Social History Society of Scotland, University of Edinburgh, December 1983. I am

grateful to participants in both Canada and Scotland for several helpful comments and criticisms. A shorter, modified version was delivered as a lecture at the Annual Conference of Scottish Studies, Old Dominion University, Norfolk, Virginia, USA, and will appear in a forthcoming volume of *Scotia: American Canadian Journal of Scottish Studies*.

2. For example, T. C. Smout: *Scottish Trade on the Eve of the Union, 1660–1707* (Edinburgh, 1963) and his 'The Anglo-Scottish Union of 1707: the Economic Background', *Economic History Review*, 2nd series, XVI (1964).

3. S. G. E. Lythe and J. Butt: *An Economic History of Scotland 1100–1939* (Glasgow, 1975), pp. 136–175.

4. N. T. Phillipson: 'Lawyers, Landowners and the Civic Leadership of Post-Union Scotland', *Juridical Review*, Part 3 (August, 1976), pp. 110–111.

5. John Clive: 'The Social Background of the Scottish Renaissance', in N. T. Phillipson and Rosalind Mitchison (eds.): *Scotland in the Age of Improvement* (Edinburgh, 1970), pp. 225–244.

6. For an example of this response see the works of the late nineteenth century Glasgow antiquarian and hagiographer, George Stewart, especially in his *The Progress of Glasgow* (Glasgow, 1883), p. 23.

7. See A. M. Carstairs: 'Some Economic Aspects of the Union of the Parliaments', *Scottish Journal of Political Economy*, II (1955); R. H. Campbell: 'The Anglo-Scottish Union of 1707: II the Economic Consequences', *Economic History Review*, 2nd series, XVI (1964), and 'The Union and Economic Growth' in T. I. Rae (ed.): *The Union of 1707* (Glasgow, 1974).

8. Industrial development is considered in J. Butt: 'The Scottish Cotton Industry during the Industrial Revolution, 1780–1840', in L. M. Cullen and T. C. Smout (eds.): *Comparative Aspects of Scottish and Irish Economic and Social History 1600–1900* (Edinburgh, 1977), pp. 116–128; Alastair J. Durie: *The Scottish Linen Industry in the Eighteenth Century* (Edinburgh, 1979); C. Gulvin: *The Tweedmakers: a History of the Scottish Fancy Woollen Industry* (Newton Abbot, 1973); B. F. Duckham: *A History of the Scottish Coal Industry 1700–1815* (Newton Abbot, 1970); Ian L. Donnachie: *A History of the Brewing Industry in Scotland* (Edinburgh, 1979); A. G. Thomson: *The Paper Industry in Scotland* (Edinburgh, 1974); M. S. Moss and J. R. Hume: *The Making of Scotch Whisky* (Edinburgh, 1981). On landowners see L. Timperley: 'The Pattern of Landholding in Eighteenth Century Scotland' in M. L. Parry and T. R. Slater (eds.): *The Making of the Scottish Countryside* (London, 1980), pp. 147–154 and R. II. Campbell: 'The Scottish Improvers and the Course of Agrarian Change in the Eighteenth Century' in Cullen and Smout (eds.): *Comparative Aspects*, pp. 204–215. Merchants are examined in a series of studies by T. M. Devine viz.: *The Tobacco Lords* (Edinburgh, 1975); 'An Eighteenth Century Business Elite'; *Scottish Historical Review* LVII (1978), pp. 40–63; 'The Scottish Merchant Community, 1680–1740' in R. H. Campbell and A. S. Skinner (eds.): *The Origin and Nature of the Scottish Enlightenment* (Edinburgh, 1982), pp. 26–41; 'The Social Composition of the Business Class in the Larger Scottish Towns, 1680–1740' in T. M. Devine and D. Dickson (eds.): *Ireland and Scotland 1600–1850* (Edinburgh, 1983), pp. 163–176. See also T. Donnelly: 'The Economic Activities of the Aberdeen Merchant Guild, 1740–1790', *Scottish Economic and Social History* 1 (1981). For the legal classes see N. T. Phillipson, 'The Social Structure of the Faculty of Advocates in Scotland, 1661–1840' in Alan Harding (ed.): *Lawmaking and Lawmakers in British History* (Edinburgh, 1980). Banking has been analysed in S. G. Checkland: *Scottish Banking: a History, 1695–1973* (Glasgow, 1975) and C. W. Munn: *The Scottish Provincial Banking Companies 1747–1864* (Edinburgh, 1981). The colonial trades are assessed in J. M. Price: *France and the Chesapeake* (Ann Arbor, Michigan, 1973) and *Capital and Credit in British Overseas Trade* (Cambridge, Mass., 1980); Devine: *Tobacco Lords*;

'Colonial Commerce and the Scottish Economy, 1730–1815' in Cullen and Smout (eds.): *Comparative Aspects*, pp. 177–189 and 'The Colonial Trades and Industrial Development in Scotland 1700–1815', *Economic History Review*, 2nd series, XXIX (1976), pp. 1–13. Major advances in agrarian research are reported in I. D. Whyte: *Agriculture and Society in Seventeenth Century Scotland* (Edinburgh, 1979); R. A. Dodgshon: *Land and Society in Early Scotland* (Oxford, 1981) and 'Agricultural Change and its Social Consequences in the Southern Uplands of Scotland, 1600–1780' in Devine and Dickson: *Ireland and Scotland*, pp. 46–59.

9. H. R. Trevor-Roper: 'The Scottish Enlightenment' in *Studies on Voltaire and the Eighteenth Century*, vol. lviii (1967), p. 1636.

10. Whyte: *Agriculture and Society*, passim; Rosalind Mitchison: 'The Movement of Scottish Grain Prices in the Seventeenth and Eighteenth Centuries', *Economic History Review*, 2nd series, XVII (1965), pp. 278–91.

11. S. G. E. Lythe: *The Economy of Scotland in its European Setting, 1560–1625* (Edinburgh, 1960), pp. 15–23.

12. M. W. Flinn (ed.): *Scottish Population History from the Seventeenth Century to the 1930s* (Cambridge, 1977), pp. 164–186.

13. Whyte: *Agriculture and Society*, pp. 94–221; Dodgshon: *Land and Society*, pp. 205–270.

14. Smout: *Scottish Trade on the Eve of the Union*, pp. 194–236; P. W. J. Riley: *The Union of England and Scotland* (Manchester, 1978), pp. 200–201.

15. T. M. Devine: 'The Merchant Class of the larger Scottish Towns in the Seventeenth and early Eighteenth Centuries' in B. Dicks and G. Gordon (eds): *Scottish Urban History* (Aberdeen, 1983). pp. 92–111.

16. These developments are summarised in R. H. Campbell: 'Stair's Scotland: the Social and Economic Background', *Juridicial Review*, December 1981, pp. 110–127.

17. T. M. Devine: 'The English Connection and Irish-Scottish Development in the Eighteenth Century' in Devine and Dickson (eds.): *Ireland and Scotland*, pp. 12–31.

18. A. G. Frank: *Capitalism and Underdevelopment in Latin America* (New York, 1969).

19. Reported in Campbell: 'Union and Economic Growth', p. 61.

20. Gulvin: *Tweedmakers*, pp. 13–37; Durie: *Scottish Linen Industry*, pp. 8–21.

21. To appear soon in *Scottish Economic and Social History*.

22. Quoted in John S. Shaw: *The Management of Scottish Society, 1707–1764* (Edinburgh, 1983), p. 1.

23. Julia Buckroyd: *Church and State in Scotland, 1660–1681* (Edinburgh, 1980); P. W. J. Riley: *King William and the Scottish Politicians* (Edinburgh, 1979).

24. Quoted in G. Holmes: *British Politics in the Age of Anne* (London, 1967), p. 393, and in R. H. Campbell: 'The Scottish Improvers and the Course of Agrarian Change in the Eighteenth Century' in Cullen and Smout (eds.): *Comparative Aspects*, p. 206.

25. E. Cregeen (ed.): *Argyll Estate Instructions, 1771–1805* (Edinburgh, 1964), pp. ix-xxxix.

26. Shaw: *Management of Scottish Society*, p. 186.

27. Riley: *Union of England and Scotland*, pp. 1–22.

28. Louis M. Cullen: *Anglo-Irish Trade, 1660–1800* (Manchester, 1968), passim.

29. Shaw: *Management of Scottish Society*, p. 124.

30. Ibid., pp. 154–164.

31. T. C. Smout: 'Scotland and England: Is Dependency a Symptom or a Cause of Underdevelopment?', *Review*, III (1980), pp. 613–614.

32. From the *Wealth of Nations* quoted in R. H. Campbell and J. B. A. Dow: *Source Book of Scottish Economic and Social History* (Oxford, 1968), p. 20.

33. Eric Richards: *A History of the Highland Clearances: Agrarian Transformation and the Evictions, 1746–1880* (London, 1982), pp. 41–110.

34. Devine: *Tobacco Lords*, pp. 50–102; Richard F. Dell: 'The Operational Record of

the Clyde Tobacco Fleet, 1747–1775', *Scottish Economic and Social History*, 2 (1982), pp. 1–17.

35. Durie: *Scottish Linen Industry*, pp. 143–166.
36. Ibid.
37. T. M. Devine and D. Dickson: 'In Pursuit of Comparative Aspects of Irish and Scottish Development' in Devine and Dickson (eds.): *Ireland and Scotland*, p. 264.
38. R H. Campbell: *The Rise and Fall of Scottish Industry* (Edinburgh, 1980); pp. 30–36.
39. Cullen: *Anglo-Irish Trade*, p. 198.
40. Smout: *Scottish Trade*, pp. 47–56.
41. L M. Cullen and T. C. Smout: 'Economic Growth in Scotland and Ireland' in Cullen and Smout (eds.): *Comparative Aspects*, pp. 10–11.
42. David Dickson: 'An Economic History of the Cork Region in the Eighteenth Century', unpublished Ph.D. thesis, Trinity College, University of Dublin, 1977; J. Mannion: 'The Waterford Merchants and the Irish–Newfoundland Provisions Trade, 1770–1820' in L M. Cullen and P. Butel (eds.): *Negoce et Industrie en France et en Irelande aux XVIIIe et XIXe Siècles* (Bordeaux; 1980), pp. 27–43; Norman E. Gamble: 'The Business Community and Trade of Belfast, 1767–1800', unpublished Ph.D. thesis, Trinity College, University of Dublin, 1978; Devine: 'Business Class of the Larger Scottish Tovens' in Dicks and Gordon (eds.): *Scottish Urban History* pp. 92–111.
43. Cullen: *Anglo-Irish Trade*, p. 97; Devine: 'English Connection and IrishScottish Development' in Devine and Dickson (eds.): *Ireland and Scotland*, pp. 21–22.
44. These points are elaborated in my unpublished paper, 'Irish and Scottish Merchant Communities in the Seventeenth and Eighteenth Centuries', given at the inaugural conference of the Scottish Institute of Maritime Studies, University of St. Andrews, September 1983.
45. For example, P. Kriedte, H. Medick and J. Schlumbohn: *Industrialisation before Industrialisation* (Cambridge, 1981).
46. As reported in Devine and Dickson (eds.): *Ireland and Scotland*, p. 265.
47. Malcolm Gray: 'Migration in the Rural Lowlands of Scotland, 1750–1850' in Devine and Dickson (eds.): *Ireland and Scotland*, pp. 104–116.
48. L Timperley: 'Patterns of Landholding in Eighteenth Century Scotland' in Parry and Slater (eds.): *Making of the Scottish Countryside*, pp. 147–154.
49. For a more detailed examination of the peaceful transition to agrarian capitalism in the lowlands see T. M. Devine: 'Social Stability in the Eastern Lowlands of Scotland during the Agricultural Revolution, 1780–1840' in T. M. Devine (ed.): *Lairds and Improvement in the Scotland of the Enlightenment* (Dundee, 1979), pp. 59–70.
50. John Burrell's Arran Journal, 1766–1773, vol. 1, p. 20, 4 June 1766, Arran Castle, Arran. I am grateful to Lady Jane Fforde for permission to read and quote from this invaluable source.
51. T. M. Devine: 'Scottish Farm Service during the Scottish Agricultural Revolution' in T. M. Devine (ed.): *Farm Servants and Labour in Lowland Scotland. 1770–1914* (Edinburgh, 1984). pp. 1–8

4

THE ENGLISH CONNECTION AND IRISH AND SCOTTISH DEVELOPMENT IN THE EIGHTEENTH CENTURY

Both Scottish and Irish society were profoundly influenced by English political, economic and cultural connections in the eighteenth century. Indeed, Scottish historians have long argued that the relationship with England was the *sine qua non* of Scottish commercial and industrial success in the decades following the achievement of the Parliamentary Union of 1707. The principal staples and supports of economic advance, the trade in cattle, transatlantic commerce and the linen manufacture, seemed to rest securely on the privileges of free trade and protection afforded in the Union. As one writer has put it, 'When after the 1780s the Scottish economy was resting on a basis laid by achievements apparently its own, it was in reality resting on a foundation established through Union with England'.[1] The thesis is persuasive and becomes doubly so when the more subtle relationships with England are considered. English technology was of crucial importance to the growth of the Scottish lead, coal and cotton industries while 'English methods' became very rapidly an integral part of the process of agrarian 'improvement' in rural Scotland.[2] The British empire provided a new range of career opportunities for ambitious Scots in military and administrative service, merchanting and medicine, and much of the resulting income percolated through the Scottish economy in consequence of the adventurers' habit of returning to their homeland with the profits of their varied enterprises.[3] Furthermore, the Scottish élite became increasingly open to English cultural influences through the immense popularity of eighteenth-century London periodicals and the stimulus of closer political connections.[4] This provided a new dynamic of competitive emulation which helped to release energies for social and economic improvement among the indigenous governing class. Indeed, without the advantages conferred by full union and the English connection, Scotland seemed likely in 1700 to face a bleak future sunk in the economic doldrums as the terms of trade in continental Europe began to move ruthlessly and decisively against her traditional activities.[4]

There seems little doubt of the central importance of the Anglo-Scottish

Union in Scottish economic expansion before 1770, but it is more difficult to determine the exact relationship between the English connection and *structural change* in economic activity after c.1780. Historians traditionally assert that in the later period a mix of indigenous strengths and English economic pressures serves to explain the more fundamental and important transition from a society firmly rooted in a phase of proto–industrialisation to one in which the motors of growth were located in new manufacturing and urban development. Comparison with the Irish experience in this area of analysis is invaluable. Irish society was subject to a similar range of influences from England but, in the period after c.1780, and especially after 1815, reacted differently to them and, instead of structural change on the Scottish model, eventually endured the horror of widespread famine and the trauma of mass emigration. Comparison of the origins of this divergence helps to clarify the relative importance of indigenous and external factors in Scottish success. It is useful to begin with a discussion of the precise political relationship which each country had with England in the eighteenth century and to ask whether the particular form which this tie assumed in each case is perhaps itself sufficient to account for differentials in economic performance.

I

In essence the new English political connection with Scotland was forged in 1707 for strategic reasons in order to secure the northern flank against the feared threat of French and Jacobite attack.[6] Superficially at least, the end of the Scottish parliament in that year also implied the end of Scottish independence, since ultimate authority now derived from a London executive and Westminster legislature in which Scottish representation was numerically weak and politically subservient. Yet the reality of power relationships was somewhat different. Scottish 'independence' in the seventeenth century had been more apparent than real. Sir John Clerk, writing in 1730, may have put the point in extreme terms but his verdict contained a core of truth: 'As to our civil government [before 1707], it was an entire state of dependence on the councils of England. We had frequent sessions of Parliament, a constant Privy Council, a Treasury and Exchequer, but all these subservient to such administrators as the chief ministers in England thought fit to recommend to the Sovereign'.[7] Scotland had retained control over economic policy through Parliament and Privy Council in the era of the Union of the Crowns but none over foreign policy and precious little over the conduct of her commercial affairs abroad, as the notorious 'Darien Disaster' graphically illustrated. Moreover, after 1707, Scotland had free access to English domestic and colonial markets and at the same time enjoyed the protection of British tariffs which proved the keys to growth in her premier manufacture of linen. Yet this bonus was achieved with only marginal sacrifice in real political power. Essentially the

Union was successful because it was incomplete and enhanced rather than eroded the traditional authority of the Scottish governing class. In no sense was Scotland merged with England. The great institutions of law, education and the Scottish Kirk, the primary sources of nationality rather than a Parliament which had only lost its ancient impotence two decades before Union, were preserved intact. The existing privileges of landowners and royal burgh merchants were maintained. The changes in the treason law and the Patronage Act, passed after Union, served only to buttress the existing influence of the landowing élite, while the ensuing 'semi-independence' allowed this class to promote Scottish interests through the formation of such bodies as the Board of Trustees for Manufactures and Fisheries, the Society of Improvers and the Committee for the Annexed Forfeited Estates.[8] Thus, as the political relationship between England and Scotland became clearer by the middle decades of the eighteenth century, it was apparent that Scotland had obtained vital commercial privileges while retaining an indigenous élite with an enhanced apparatus of power and also the survival of a series of institutions which both defined her nationality and provided the social base for modernisation. In no sense, therefore, could Scotland be described as an English colony, a characterisation often applied to eighteenth-century Ireland.

Ironically, Ireland did acquire the separate Parliament which Scotland lacked in the eighteenth century. As in the Scottish case, London was in theory the ultimate source of power, but specifically Irish interests were not neglected because London generally avoided direct legislative interference. Moreover, the increasing political initiative taken by the Anglo-Irish meant that the Dublin Parliament began to devote greater attention to economic matters. The Irish economy eventually enjoyed enthusiastic parliamentary support for transportation development, bounties on corn exports and significantly, in the later eighteenth century, protection for the infant indigenous cotton manufacture.[9] For unlike Scotland, Ireland in the eighteenth century possessed its own import and export duties and customs service and was able to provide a separate tariff system which was not completely synchronised with or subordinate to that of England. On the other hand, while Irish linen, provisions (after the 1750s) and shipping were given favoured treatment in the English market, Irish merchants were legally barred from importing certain 'enumerated' goods from the colonies before 1780, and unilateral advantages were often conceded in the Irish tariff system to English products especially in the early eighteenth century.

Indeed, the mere existence of a separate Irish Parliament could not conceal the fact that the relationship between England and Ireland was a profoundly colonial one. The native governing class had been destroyed in the troubles of the seventeenth century and the confiscation of their lands resulted in the emergence of deep social, religious and political divisions between the native population and the new dominant Anglo-Irish élite over vast tracts of the countryside. Ireland's colonial and dependent status was also exemplified by the settlement of immigrants from protestant England and Scotland, recently estimated at about 27 per cent of the total population in the early eighteenth century, and by the notorious 'Penal Laws', repealed only in 1778.[10] These sought to exclude the native catholic majority from landownership and the professions, and contributed to the development of social fissures in the community which had no parallel in Scotland. The colonial status of Ireland can also be discerned in the acquisition of lands by English and Scottish gentlemen, several of whom already owned property in Britain and as 'absentees' have been regarded until recently as a parasitical class diverting rental to external consumption rather than energetic investment in Ireland.[11] A case can be argued, then, that in the realm of political economy the English connection was more favourable to Scottish development than to Irish because the Scots obtained commercial privileges without southern interference. Can such a thesis be sustained and, in particular, can the precise form assumed by the English connection in each case help to account for the divergence in economic development between the two countries in the later eighteenth and early nineteenth centuries?

II

Both Scotland and Ireland gained successively through their commercial association with England in a number of similar ways of which the most striking example of a mutual bonus was in linen manufacturing. In 1693 and 1696 special English tariffs were imposed on French goods which were virtually prohibitive as far as manufactured goods were concerned and which remained in force until the Eden Treaty of 1786. Linen imports from both Ireland and Scotland developed to replace these and later Dutch and German substitutes. Irish linen expansion was aided by the removal of duties in 1696 and Scottish by the Union of 1707. Further measures, including the abolition of the Irish export duty on linens, creation of linen boards in both countries and the provision of export bounties, meant that by 1774 most of the linen used in England and her colonies came from within the British Isles.[12] By the 1760s an estimated 60 to 70 per cent of linen manufactured within Scotland for public sale was sold within the English domestic and colonial markets, while in 1758 linen cloth and yarn made up 80 per cent of total Irish exports to Great Britain.[13] In fact, Irish growth was even more spectacular than that experienced in Scotland. Here was a development which was entirely dependent on English commercial policy. There was no market for an export industry of such magnitude outside the protected walls of the British Empire and, as recent research on the Scottish manufacture has shown, expansion occurred primarily through favourable tariffs and bounties, not through productivity gains which reduced costs.[14]

Yet, at the same time, behind the apparent similarity of experience the historian immediately encounters a major difference in the eventual evolution of the two industries. In Ireland, linen can be interpreted as a major force perpetuating the era of proto-industrialisation and, partially at least, a regional factor in the fragmentation of land units which was a basic cause of the Irish disaster of the mid-nineteenth century.[15] But in Scotland the industry has enjoyed a dramatically different historiography, being regarded as the source of enterprise, capital and labour for cotton, the 'leading sector', which ushered in the age of industrialisation and future prosperity.[16] Plainly only indigenous elements can explain this contrasting development.

English markets for Scottish and Irish livestock and provisions were instrumental in the growth of rural income in the two societies. If anything, however, the English connection in this respect favoured Ireland rather than Scotland. In the eighteenth century the Scottish trade in food products to England and her colonies was essentially in live cattle, fish and only to a lesser extent in grain. The famous black cattle trade to the south was not, *pace* Adam Smith, the key to agrarian change in Scotland. Indeed, the expansion of the trade in the eighteenth century came about partly because it did not require fundamental improvements either in the productive process or in existing transportation systems. The business was based on cattle-rearing not fattening, and the cattle travelled to market on the hoof along the drove roads. It can be argued that the cattle trade merely perpetuated the archaic societies of the Highlands and Galloway whence most beasts originated and which maintained a stubborn resistance to fundamental improvement into the nineteenth century.

The indigenous multiplier effects of the provision and grain trades from Ireland to Great Britain and her colonies were probably more extensive, and in this sense the late seventeenth-century Cattle Acts, which prohibited the export of Irish live cattle to England, were a paradoxical bonus in the long term. The provision trade, centred on Cork and Waterford, nearly tripled in volume between 1700 and 1765 and had important backward linkages in the growth of barrelling and packaging facilities and in the intricate expansion of inter-regional trade within Ireland.[17] Again, there is no parallel in Scotland of the sustained penetration of Irish grain into England (and Scotland) in the later eighteenth century, especially after 1806 when the English market was thrown open to Irish corn.[18] Despite the greater stimulus to Irish rural products from market expansion in England and Irish supply responsiveness, no systematic reorganisation of agriculture along Scottish lines occurred. A massive swing to tillage did take place but no 'agricultural revolution' was achieved.[19] Once again, therefore, one is presented with differences in development which can only primarily be explained by indigenous factors within the two societies.

The Scots, unlike the Irish, enjoyed direct access to the English colonies and, in consequence, built up highly lucrative re-export trades in tobacco and sugar. Ireland, excluded for most of the eighteenth century from the privilege of direct colonial commerce, had no re-exports to compare with this Scottish bonus. Undoubtedly, the Scottish tobacco trade, accounting for 40 per cent of imports and 50 per cent of overseas exports in 1762, cannot be neglected in any analysis of eighteenth-century Scottish growth. It was a key element in Scotland's favourable balance of trade, widened the manufacturing base of west central Scotland, provided a stimulus to banking development and encouraged investment in agriculture through merchant purchases of land.[20] It is unlikely, however, to be a central factor in explaining why Scotland drew rapidly ahead of Ireland in the later eighteenth century. For one thing, Scottish success in the trade was not solely dependent on the Union, which merely provided an opportunity for a growth rate which rested ultimately on the efficiency of Scottish trading practices and hence on indigenous sources of enterprise. Secondly, the impact of industrial investment by tobacco merchants began to weaken in relative terms after c.1780, precisely at the time when the Scottish economy began to pull ahead.[21] Third, the Irish provision trade to the colonies had substantial and beneficial income and employment effects on both regional rural and urban economies which partly compensated for the lack of a trade in re-exports. Fourth, the Irish were granted direct access to the USA and the British plantations in the 1780s but continued to depend on Great Britain for most of their tobacco and sugar, a trend which can possibly be interpreted in terms of enterprise limitations in Ireland as well as conditions of comparative advantage within the two merchant communities.[22]

There is probably more merit in the view that the 'colonial' apparatus of 'Penal Laws', alien settlement and land confiscation handicapped the Irish economy. There is a consensus that in the short term the 'new' Irish landlord class in the seventeenth century, with no emotional or patriarchal ties with the indigenous peasantry, could promote efficient practice and more rational use of land resources.[23] In the longer term, however, the existence of social, racial and religious gulfs between many landlords and their dependent tenantry may have impeded the easy transmission of 'improving' ideas and provided more encouragement for resistance to change on the part of the peasantry in a way which was less likely to happen in the culturally homogeneous society of lowland Scotland. Certainly there was no Scottish parallel to the widespread incidence of Irish agrarian discontent in the later eighteenth century which, while primarily fuelled by land hunger, often had sectarian ramifications and overtones.[24] The mere existence of such fissures in society may have discouraged the thinning of the rural population—often an integral feature of improvement in Scotland—because of the effect on social stability which such policies might have produced.

There is now, however, less force in the old argument that absentee English landlords drained Ireland of her wealth. The material demands of the absentee in both Scotland and Ireland often produced a need to extend the revenue-producing capacity of the estate and in that sense were a positive force for change. Equally residence in itself did not always or necessarily guarantee action.[25] In fact absenteeism was a characteristic and inevitable feature of *British* landed society in the eighteenth century because primogeniture ensured that eldest sons inherited scattered estates.[26] However, absenteeism was a political issue in Ireland because the estates from which landlords absented themselves often came to them through confiscation. As we shall see in more detail later, there do appear to have been significant differences in the policies of Irish and Scottish landlords, but it is more difficult to assert that these were mainly due to the racial origin of landed families.

Finally, both Irish and Scottish producers relied heavily on English technical invention in both industry and agriculture, a reflection of England's more advanced economic condition, geographical proximity and particular commercial relationships with the two other societies. Belfast and Glasgow, for example, had historic connections with Yorkshire and Lancashire in the fine yarn trade and these undoubtedly helped the rapid diffusion of knowledge of the new cotton technology in the later eighteenth century in these two towns.[27] Furthermore, the Scots borrowed substantially from England in other fields, varying from iron-making and lead-smelting to coal-mining and agricultural technique. But English investment and innovation in Scotland, relevant in the early days of cotton-spinning and iron-making, were quickly superseded by vigorous native initiatives which often improved rapidly on southern models.[28] The best-known instances were in cotton; Kelly of New Lanark was the first to apply power to Crompton's mule, and Snodgrass of Glasgow invented the scutching machine for cotton wool, both in the 1790s. Similar advances were made in steam-engine design, in steamship propulsion and in agricultural technology, where some of the most revolutionary designs, such as Small's plough and Meikle's threshing machine, were notable instances of Scottish ingenuity. There is no similar record of technical achievement in Ireland, and it is noteworthy how derivative was such innovation as there was there; interestingly too Scotland rather than England quickly became the source of techniques which were later adopted across the Irish Sea.[29] This is eloquent testimony either of the differing social values in the two countries or of the contrasting levels of economic development which in Scotland created a context where the need for labour-saving innovation became more pressing.

To sum up: it would seem apparent that the nature of the English connection with Scotland and Ireland is not in itself sufficient to explain the striking differences in economic performance between the two societies in the later eighteenth century and afterwards. While no precise measurement of the impact of English policy, market, technology and capital is possible a rough judgement suggests that the Scots did gain over the Irish because their social structure and cohesion was not disturbed by English conquest and confiscation. Against this, however, has to be set the fact that Irish producers of linen, beef and grain seem to have exploited English demand more successfully and consistently than their counterparts in Scotland. The key point, nonetheless, is the fact that the particular *response* to the English connection was critically dependent on indigenous social, geographical, economic and cultural traditions in each country. Put simply, Scottish society possessed more of the prerequisites for successful modernisation in the eighteenth century than Ireland.

III

In their provocative analysis of the comparative development of Scotland and Ireland, Cullen and Smout assert, principally on the basis of export figures, that, at the beginning of the eighteenth century, 'Ireland seemed to hold more promise of a bright economic future than Scotland'.[30] The sources on which their calculations depend are hazardous and incomplete and it is quite possible that the statement exaggerates the economic equality of the two societies before c.1750. A number of other indicators suggest that Scottish superiority was not suddenly established in the later eighteenth century but had been developing for some time before that. First, Irish peasant society presents an image of much greater levels of destitution than normally prevailed in lowland Scotland in the early eighteenth century. Holdings were abandoned in large numbers in years of crisis: Kerry and Sligo, two counties far apart and representative of poor, but by no means the poorest, areas in Ireland, show reductions in the hearth-money returns by as much as a third in the crisis of the 1740s.[31] This suggests a society which lacked sufficient surplus for savings and contrasts markedly with the resilience of rural society in Scotland where food shortage, not crisis, was experienced in 1756, 1776, 1782–3 and 1799 and where, in the lowlands at least, such habitual abandonment of buildings had long since disappeared.[32] For whatever reason the Scots seem already to have accumulated the reserves to maintain themselves in years of difficulty. Second, one gains the impression that town growth was more significant in Scotland by the later seventeenth century. As L. M. Cullen has recently suggested: 'there was a fundamental contrast between the largely unurbanised Irish society (of the later seventeenth century) and the small-scale but closely-knit urban life, the many 'royal boroughs yoken on end to end' of lowland Scotland . . . the poorness, smallness and isolation of Irish towns is eloquent testimony to the backwardness of Irish society'.[33] Third, and most importantly, the balance of population to resources probably favoured Scotland by the mid-eighteenth century. The precocious development of the linen manufacture and potato cultivation in Ireland can both be interpreted in these terms. Their pattern of expansion in Ireland resembles the proliferation of bi-employments in the north-west Scottish highlands rather than the superficially similar developments of the lowland zone. Linen production in Ireland, and especially in the poorer areas of that island, was primarily a means of increasing income in a society where population was already growing rapidly and standards falling. It thus tended to cause fragmentation of holdings in many parts as it became embedded within the farming structure.[34] In lowland Scotland, on the other hand, the richer areas such as the Lothians had hardly any textile tradition at all because a supplementary source of income of this type was less necessary. Where spinning and weaving elsewhere did become established they tended to concentrate in the cottages of farm servants or in villages, not in the homes of leaseholders.[35] In Scotland, therefore, linen production and farming income became insulated and there was little temptation for landlords to sub-divide units in the Irish fashion to maximise income from textile production.[36] Such a strategy was more typical of the Highland landed class who did encourage in that poorer society a smallholding system linked to kelping, fishing and illicit whisky-making. Significantly, too, the deprived north-west of Scotland was the Scottish home of the potato, not as an item in crop rotation but as a primary source of subsistence.[37]

If, on this evidence, Scotland was already a richer society by the mid-eighteenth century, developments thereafter merely increased her lead. Central to the process of differential advance post-1750 (and possibly before that date) was the contrasting rate of population growth. Over the period 1755 to 1821 Scottish population grew at a rate of 0.77 per cent per annum, while some recent calculations suggest an Irish rate of over 1.5 per cent per annum or more than twice as fast as that in Scotland.[38] Even this remarkable difference considerably underestimates the contrast in demographic pressure in the two societies because Scotland was also more successful in removing a proportion of its rural population from crop cultivation, where marginal productivity was close to zero, to industrial work in the towns and villages. The social consequences were plain: in Ireland population growth produced a pattern of farm fragmentation in densely settled areas and in more advanced farming districts an oversupply of labour and a decline in real wages.[39] In Scotland, the relatively slow rate of demographic expansion meant less pressure on land resources (except in the north-west highlands where population rose more rapidly and arable lands were scarcer) and rising real wages as farmers competed for labour with industrial producers.[40] In turn, with a buoyant home market, manufacturing growth was sustained in a fashion impossible in Ireland where rural incomes became depressed as the eighteenth century proceeded.[41]

It is easier to speculate on the effects than on the origins of this fundamentally important contrast in the demographic experience of the two societies. Sub-division of land was undoubtedly easier in Ireland than in lowland Scotland, and this may have contributed to earlier marriage through a greater facility in the setting up of separate holdings temporarily viable through potato cultivation and bi-employments.[42] Irish landlords have often been blamed through hindsight for allowing this potentially disastrous development. But landlords were less powerful than their critics allowed, and clandestine sub-division in defiance of estate authority was often practised. Partible inheritance apparently lay deep in the social institutions of the population, and its economic value exerted a powerful attraction for a population which was unlikely to find much in the way of long-term alternative employment off the land. In any case, Irish age at marriage seems to have been abnormally low by European standards, a pattern well established before the eighteenth century.[43]

Scottish social values and institutions were more conducive to economic growth in a wider sense. The apparent facility with which the economy recovered after 1770 from crises such as that of the American War of Independence and proceeded to exploit new avenues in West India trade, European commerce and East Indian connections reflected a society capable of rapid adjustment to new opportunities for profit and enterprise.[44] The Irish economy was encouraged by parliamentary assistance and landlord initiative but the population, even at élite levels, do not seem to have accepted growth as a social goal in the enthusiastic manner of the Scots. The great Scottish institutions of law, church and education partly inspired and at the same time reflected this approach. Legal thought evolved to accommodate the new demands of the emerging capitalist economy. Viscount Stair, in his *Institutions* of 1681, emphasised that man's obligations, not only to God but to the public interest, were 'anterior to and inductive' of property. By 1751, however, Lord Bankton was arguing, contrary to Stair, that property is anterior and that society really came into existence to protect property.[45] The same assumptions filtered through into the intellectual assumptions of the political economists who taught in the same universities and frequented the same clubs as the lawyers. The reader of the *Wealth of Nations* is left in no doubt that the main function of a country's legal system is to protect private property. At the more mundane level of burghal law and practice, equally important advances had occurred before the later eighteenth century. By the 1730s, the old legal constraints on entry to trade and apprenticeship seem to have been abandoned in practice in the larger towns, and competition rather than privilege became the governing influence on social status.[46]

In the age of the 'Moderates', the weight of the established church was thrown behind the cause of economic reform. The new rationalism of the Scottish Enlightenment quickly permeated some branches of the local parish ministry, not simply in the sense that Calvinism was able to accommodate the new realities of a commercial society but also, and more fundamentally, in the way in which many of the clergy enthusiastically commended material progress as a reflection of the will of God. In the *Old Statistical Account*, for instance, ministers were inclined to emphasise the contribution of religion, sobriety and industry to beneficient economic change. This was an important element in the legitimisation of growth. Of course, at a deeper level of analysis, no one can deny the relevance to Scottish economic success of the Calvinist inheritance and the social values it promoted. Historians dispute its precise influence, but there is a fair amount of agreement that it helped to strengthen the commercial virtues by encouraging social action and seriousness of purpose. As R. H. Campbell has argued: '. . . the social action was one in which the individual, as one of the elect, could find himself called to be a direct and active agent of God's Will. In that way the individual was a partner of the Almighty, a junior partner, but still a partner, and so was provided with a major incentive to the utter self-confidence and assurance in his actions which is necessary for a successful entrepreneur'.[47] There is less controversy over the importance of the elementary educational system, which was itself an integral feature of the Calvinist tradition. Schooling in the eighteenth century was not free nor was it compulsory, yet attendance in the lowlands was widespread. The system was one means by which the discipline of regular work was inculcated. The link achieved between parish and burghal schools and the universities was a route to social mobility for the *petite bourgeoisie* who made up the majority of students in higher education.[48] Trinity College, Dublin on the other hand had a mainly genteel intake and failed to develop vocational subjects when they were flourishing in the Scottish universities.

Little is known about the specific effect of basic educational skills upon growth, but it is likely that as a shift occurs to a more dynamic economic system, literacy acquires new value. The praise bestowed by contemporaries on Scottish farmers and labourers for their intelligent use of new methods and work patterns might suggest that literacy encourages processes of rationalism, raises expectations and stimulates the examination of alternatives. Comparison with Ireland reveals striking contrasts: in rural Ireland in 1841 only two-fifths of men over twenty-five years and less than a sixth of the women declared an ability to read and write.[49] Might this help to explain the technological conservatism and the aversion to risk of which Irish farmers were traditionally accused? Certainly current evidence suggests the survival of flail, spade and reaping hook in nineteenth-century Irish agriculture, but this might reflect the low labour cost structure of Irish farming (relative to Scottish) as much as anything else.[50]

Finally, some attention must be given to the three social groups, landlords, tenant farmers and merchant classes, in both Ireland and Scotland, who were primarily responsible for directing the course of economic change. The obvious contrast between an Irish Protestant landed class out of sympathy with a loyal Catholic peasantry and a Scottish landed élite with strong connections and much influence over its tenantry has already been mentioned. Equally significant were major differences in the composition of the landed classes. The large number of small estates in lowland Scotland permitted the relatively easy promotion of successful merchants, colonial adventurers, lawyers and military men to landed status. As non-landed fortunes rapidly accumulated in the period after 1750, so the speed and extent of this penetration increased.[51] Two-thirds of Roxburghshire changed hands and one-third of Renfrewshire between 1760 and 1815.[52] The widespread diffusion of urban wealth in the lowlands ensured that the pattern was not simply limited to the counties around Glasgow and Edinburgh though it was certainly more common in the central zone.[53] Such a social change brought new ideas, fresh horizons and more money to Scottish agriculture. No similar development occurred in Ireland. Irish adventurers, especially successful Catholics, tended not to return home to a landed estate in the Scottish fashion. Only in the Galway area and to some extent around Cork and Belfast did similar relationships form to those which were commonplace around every large Scottish town.[54] Connections were equally weak in the opposite direction. The Anglo-Irish tended to identify closely with land and to seek careers outside trade. Ironically, this helped to sustain business immigration from Britain to the Irish towns, of which the influx of Scots into Irish wholesale trade and manufacture was a particularly striking feature.[55] This partly reflected contrasting attitudes to commerce among the Scottish landed classes. The coincidence of small estates, traditions of primogeniture and the limited number of more desirable professional posts in the law and the church ensured that the younger sons of lairds saw trade as an entirely respectable and acceptable occupation. In turn, this two-way contact between land and trade meant that a deeply ingrained commercialism developed within the Scottish laird class.[56]

There were other differences. Scottish landlords were renowned for their enormous traditional and legal powers. They had an accepted right to control the organisation of the farm structure through the medium of the baron court, and legislation of the Scottish Parliament in the later seventeenth century had both strengthened these proprietorial privileges and given increased legal power to enclose and consolidate. The delicate ties of hierarchy and dependence within the social structure of their estates were maintained through their influence over education, poor relief and church appointments as well as by hereditary privilege. This helped to ensure the extraordinarily peaceful transition to capitalist agriculture which was such a striking feature of the Scottish agricultural revolution.[57] Their links with the world of the intellectuals through close association with the legal classes, residence in Edinburgh for the season and attendance at university helped to develop systematic ideas about the reorganisation of agriculture as both a morally enlightened and materially beneficial course of action.[58] Eric Hobsbawm has recently shown that the remarkable characteristic of the Scottish improvers and agronomists was the intellectual lucidity with which they viewed the task of rural transformation and their vehement but often uncritical condemnation of all practices associated with what they perceived as the old feudal régime of reciprocity and communalism.[59] The 5th Duke of Argyll spoke for his class when he asserted in 1800: '. . . farms should be divided so that every man may have his own separate farm to manage and improve in his own way, and the skilful and industrious may reap the benefit of their labours and knowledge and at the same time be examples to others.'[60] Scottish landowners were committed to reorganisation of traditional agriculture along the lines of consolidation into compact farms and utterly opposed to sub-division as an unmitigated moral evil and enemy of agrarian efficiency.

Irish landowners cannot easily be classified because, like the Scots, there were significant local variations in estate practice and landlord personality but, as in Scotland, some common characteristics emerge.[61] Irish landlords were often confronted with a hostile tenantry whom they were perhaps unwilling to alienate further by attempting radical surgery on their estates. It is relevant to note that they sometimes had to take into account the sectarian mix of their estate populations when formulating improvements. Eviction was less common in Ireland before 1815, but there was more rural violence.[62] The division of labour and function between landlord and tenant in Scotland was notably different from that in Ireland. In Scotland the landlord assumed financial responsibility for the maintenance and extension of roads, farm buildings and outhouses, leaving the tenant to concentrate on labour management, crop rotations and animal husbandry. In Ireland, much more of the burden for 'fixed capital' improvement tended to fall on the shoulders of the tenant.[63] Landlord ability to influence the direction of change was further limited by the very long leases, often for three lives, which proliferated on Irish farms and by the 'middleman' system of tenure which, while important in the effective pursuit of agrarian operations, especially in pastoral regions, was conducive to the practice of uncontrolled sub-division in a social context of rising population.[64]

All this tended to create an effective barrier to even the most enthusiastic of Irish improvers. Recent work on Ulster has shown how committed reformers were ultimately overwhelmed by the appetite for land of a rapidly increasing peasant population, traditions of partible inheritance, the weakness of alternatives to landholding and the temptations of easy income before 1815 from a smallholding economy based on linen, cattle and grain sales.[65] Indeed, it would be difficult to argue that the striking differences between Irish and Scottish agricultural systems by 1800 were solely or even mainly due to contrasts in landlord performance.[66] Ultimately, what mattered was the response of the tenants because increasing yields depended on their adjustments to land use, crop selection and livestock preferences. In Scotland, highland and lowland landowners were equally committed to raising the revenue-producing capacity of their estates, but the greater success of the latter was due primarily to the existence on their properties of a much larger pool of tenant farmers capable of adjustment and vigorous response to new ideas. Here perhaps lay a crucial difference from the social structure of rural Ireland, at least outside favoured regions in the province of Munster and some other parts. The Scottish capitalist farmer did not emerge fully formed in the last quarter of the eighteenth century from the plans of often dilettante improving landlords who were occasionally more interested in elaboration than efficiency. Consolidation of farm units had been underway on a considerable scale since the seventeenth century and this, by c. 1780, had produced in lowland Scotland groups of tenants well capable of responding to market trends and better methods after that date.[67] Indeed, the outlines of the conventional 'improved' farm were already present in several favoured areas—even outside the well-known example of East Lothian—by the middle decades of the eighteenth century. Interestingly, sub-tenancy on these farms, rapidly abandoned after 1780, was somewhat different from the smallholding structure in the central and western areas of Ireland. Often Scottish sub-tenants held the merest fragments of land and so had no option but to seek work on larger units for long periods in the year to gain a full subsistence. They had evolved to an intermediate rank which gave them a social position between that of peasant and agricultural labourer. Sub-division was thus partly prevented because sub-tenancies were effectively tied in with the specific labour needs of the larger farms and were altered when these changed after 1780.[68]

The Scottish tenant farming class were then provided with fresh incentives as the market for their products increased but it also did so for their Irish counterparts in the later eighteenth century. One key factor explaining different responses was that each group faced a quite different labour supply position. Labour was easy to come by in an Ireland experiencing high population growth and slow urban expansion. In lowland Scotland, however, population rose much more slowly while industrial and town growth proceeded apace. Irish farmers had less need to look for more productive methods as their labour costs fell in real terms; Scottish farmers on the other hand were confronted with sharp increases in wage levels as they competed with towns and industry. They reacted by organising labour more efficiently and produced by 1815 the classic Scottish structure of a small corps of dedicated, well-paid, full-time employees, the ploughmen, and a much larger number of poorly paid seasonal workers recruited mainly from Ireland, the Highlands and neighbouring towns and villages.[69] The contrast, therefore, which emerged between Ireland and the Scottish lowlands was reminiscent of that which developed between England north and south of the Trent line. In southern England, as in rural Ireland, there was a similar combination of rising population, decaying ancient manufacturing industry, slow migration and low labour efficiency, suggesting that it was the spatial concentration of new industry in Britain which was the decisive conditioning factor in agrarian development rather than the more dramatic and better documented intervention of landlord personalities.[70]

The roots of the Scottish achievement in urban and industrial growth, at least until the widespread use of steam-power after 1800, lay to a significant extent in the business resources and risk capital of the nation's commercial classes. It was not so much that Scotland had more investment capital than Ireland; rather it may be that there was more of it in the hands of the venturesome and the enterprising.[71] Again, the contrast between the two societies cannot be painted wholly in black and white terms. Irish merchants and producers, though constrained within the Navigation System to a greater extent than the Scots, were nevertheless able to take full advantage of national comparative advantage in provision supply and linen manufacture. However, the contrasts with the Scottish merchant community perhaps remain still more conspicuous than the parallels.[72] Irish traders tended mainly to do business on a commission basis, especially in English commerce, though less so in their European activities. The Scots normally traded on their own account but since the later seventeenth century had been effectively tapping London financial resources to help them do so. Mercantile activity in Ireland seemed more passive and dependent than in Scotland: the energetic fashion in which the Scots moved from emphasis on American trade before 1780 and then to Caribbean, European and Asian connections is striking in this respect though, it might be added, the Scots trading community by then had the 'irresistible bundles of products of the Industrial Revolution'[73] to offer their customers. By contrast with the Scots, the capitals of Irish merchants were low, and while banking in Scotland, outside the chartered institutions, was dominated by the merchant class, the system in Ireland was more likely to be supported by landowners.[74] Recent work has drawn attention to the array of small capitalists in domestic industry and inland trade in lowland Scotland whose numbers rose rapidly in the later eighteenth century.[75] It was from this social group that the enterprise and finance for the textile revolution primarily derived.

IV

It is entirely accurate to assert that a central reason for the Scottish achievement of industrialisation was the country's favourable natural endowment of coal and raw materials in close proximity to navigable water. Yet proven advantages in such resources cannot in themselves adequately explain why Scotland drew so rapidly ahead of Ireland in the period before 1815 if only because, in the eighteenth and early nineteenth centuries, such factor endowments played a much less crucial part in Scottish industrial expansion than they were to do after 1830. The argument of this paper has been that the origins of the different rates of growth lie deeper and go much further back in time than some have suggested. Both societies from the mid-seventeenth century were faced with the challenge and stimulus of English competition, markets, cultural influences and technological inge-nuity and reacted to them in dramatically contrasting ways. These responses were conditioned by the prevailing social structure, value systems, and business regimes of Ireland and Scotland and, perhaps most fundamentally of all, by the fact that by the early decades of the eighteenth century the two countries were already at somewhat different stages of development.

REFERENCES

1. R. H. Campbell, *Scotland since 1707* (Oxford, 1965), p. 42.
2. See, *inter alia*, B. F. Duckham, 'English influences on the Scottish Coal Industry, 1700–1815', in J. Butt and J. T. Ward, eds., *Scottish Themes* (Edinburgh, 1976), pp. 28–45; T. C. Smout, 'Lead-mining in Scotland, 1650–1859', in P. L. Payne, ed., *Studies in Scottish Business History* (London, 1967), pp. 103–35; J. E. Handley, *The Agricultural Revolution in Scotland* (Glasgow, 1963); H. Hamilton, *An Economic History of Scotland in the Eighteenth Century* (Oxford, 1963).
3. T. M. Devine, 'An Eighteenth Century Business Elite: Glasgow West India Merchants, 1750–1815', *Scott. Hist. Rev.*, LVII 1978, pp. 40–63; *idem*, 'The Scottish Merchant Community, 1680–1740', in R. H. Campbell and A. Skinner, eds., *The Origins of the Scottish Enlightenment* (Edinburgh, 1982); L. Timperley, 'The Pattern of landholding in Eighteenth Century Scotland', in M. L. Parry and T. R. Slater, eds., *The Making of the Scottish Countryside* (London, 1980), pp. 137–154.
4. John Clive, 'The Social Background to the Scottish Renaissance', in N. T. Phillipson and Rosalind Mitchison, eds., *Scotland in the Age of Improvement* (Edinburgh, 1970), pp. 225–244.
5. T. C. Smout, *Scottish Trade on the Eve of Union, 1660–1707* (Edinburgh, 1963).
6. P. W. J. Riley, *The Union of England and Scotland* (Manchester, 1980).
7. T. C. Smout, ed., 'Sir John Clerk's observations on the present circumstances of Scotland 1730', in *Miscellany of the Scottish History Society* X (Edinburgh, 1965), p. 184.
8. Alexander Murdoch, *The People Above: Politics and Administration in Mid-Eighteenth Century Scotland* (Edinburgh, 1980).
9. F. G. James, *Ireland in the Empire, 1688–1770* (Cambridge, Mass. 1973), pp. 190–127; L. M. Cullen, *Anglo-Irish Trade 1660–1800* (Manchester, 1968), pp. 1–28; E. M. Johnston, *Ireland in the Eighteenth Century* (Dublin, 1974), pp. 54–55.
10. L. M. Cullen, *The Emergence of Modern Ireland 1660–1900* (London, 1981), p. 87.
11. The basis of the revised view of the absentee landlords can be found in David Large, 'The Wealth of the Greater Irish Landowners, 1750–1815', *Irish Historical Studies*, XV (1966–7), pp. 22–41; A. P. W. Malcolmson, 'Absenteeism in Eighteenth Century Ireland,' *Irish Economic and Social History*, I (1974), pp. 15–30; W. A. Maguire, *The Downshire Estates in Ireland, 1801–1845* (Oxford, 1972).
12. R. Davis, 'English Foreign Trade 1700–1774', *Econ. Hist. Rev.* 2nd ser., XV (1963), pp. 286–7; N. B. Harte, 'Protection and the English Linen Trade', in N. B. Harte and K. Ponting, eds., *Textile History and Economic History* (Manchester, 1973), pp. 108–9.
13. A. J. Durie, 'The Markets for Scottish Linen, 1730–1775', *Scott. Hist. Rev.*, LII, (1973), pp. 30–49; Cullen, *Anglo-Irish Trade*, p. 51
14. A. J. Durie, *The Scottish Linen Industry in the Eighteenth Century* (Edinburgh, 1979), pp. 143–166.
15. W. H. Crawford, 'Landlord Tenant Relations in Ulster, 1609–1820', *Irish Economic and Social History* II (1975), pp. 12–16.
16. J. Butt, 'The Scottish Cotton Industry during the Industrial Revolution, 1780–1840' in L. M. Cullen and T. C. Smout, eds., *Comparative Aspects of Scottish and Irish Economic and Social History 1600–1900* (Edinburgh, 1977), pp. 116–128.
17. D. Dickson, 'Economic Development in Scotland and Ireland in the Eighteenth Century: Some thoughts on the Irish Case', Paper presented at the Economic History Society Conference, University College, Swansea, 1978; J. Mannion, 'The Waterford Merchants and the Irish-Newfoundland Provisions Trade, 1770–1820' in L. M. Cullen and P. Butel, eds., *Négoce et Industrie en France et en Irelande aux XVIIe et XIXe Siècles* (Bordeaux, 1980), pp. 27–43.

18. Raymond H. Crotty, *Irish Agricultural Production* (Cork, 1966), pp. 18–20; Laura E. Cochran, 'Scottish Trade with Ireland in the Eighteenth Century', Paper presented at the Economic History Society Conference, Loughborough University, 1981.

19. Sometimes reorganisation of farm structure on the Scottish pattern was attempted in areas of dense settlement but achieved little as population pressures increased. See D. McCourt, 'The Decline of Rundale, 1750–1850', in Peter Roebuck, ed., *Plantation to Partition* (Belfast, 1981), pp. 119–139.

20. The impact is discussed in detail in T. M. Devine, 'The Colonial Trades and Industrial Investment in Scotland 1700–1815', *Econ. Hist. Rev.*, 2nd ser. XXIX (1976), pp. 1–13, and *idem*, 'Colonial Commerce and the Scottish Economy 1730–1815', in Cullen and Smout, eds., *Comparative Aspects*, pp. 177–189.

21. *Ibid.*

22. Cullen, *Anglo–Irish Trade*, p. 19.

23. Donald Woodward, 'A comparative study of the Irish and Scottish livestock trades in the seventeenth century', in Cullen and Smout, eds., *Comparative Aspects*, p. 157.

24. T. Desmond Williams, ed., *Secret Societies in Ireland* (Dublin, 1973), pp. 13–25, 26–35; J. J. Lee, 'Patterns of Rural Unrest in Nineteenth Century Ireland', in L. M. Cullen and F. Furet, eds., *Ireland and France: 17th–20th Centuries* (Paris, 1981), pp. 223–237. For *The English Connection and Irish–Scottish Development in the Eighteenth Century* to the Scottish contrast, see T. M. Devine, 'Social Stability in the Eastern Lowlands of Scotland during the Agricultural Revolution, 1780–1840', in T. M. Devine, ed., *Lairds and Improvement in the Scotland of the Enlightenment* (Glasgow, 1979), pp. 59–70.

25. See references in note 11 and R. H. Campbell, 'The Scottish Improvers and the Course of Agrarian Change in the Eighteenth Century', in Cullen and Smout, eds., *Comparative Aspects*, pp. 204–215.

26. Peter Roebuck, 'Absentee Landownership', *Agricultural History Review* XXI (1973), pp. 11–14.

27. C. H. Lee, *A Cotton Enterprise 1795–1840: a History of McConnell and Kennedy* (Manchester, 1972), pp. 23–46; G. Kirkham, 'Economic Diversification in a Marginal Economy: a Case Study', in Roebuck, ed., *Plantation to Partition*, pp. 64–65.

28. T. C. Smout, 'Scotland and England: is Dependency a Symptom or a Cause of Underdevelopment?' *Review* III (1980), pp. 621–622.

29. J. S. Donnelly, *The Land and the People of Nineteenth Century Cork* (London, 1975), p. 11; E. R. R. Green, *The Lagan Valley 1800–50* (London, 1949), p. 98.

30. Cullen and Smout, eds., *Comparative Aspects*, p. 4.

31. Cullen, *Emergence of Modern Ireland*, pp. 30, 41–2, 90.

32. T. C. Smout, 'Famine and Famine-Relief in Scotland', in Cullen and Smout, eds., *Comparative Aspects*, pp. 21–30; I. D. Whyte, *Agriculture and Society in Seventeenth Century Scotland* (Edinburgh, 1979), pp. 7–28. Even in the north-western islands, the most primitive part of Scotland in the seventeenth century, little trace of this practice survives. See Frances J. Shaw, *The Northern and Western Islands of Scotland: their Economy and Society in the Seventeenth Century* (Edinburgh, 1980), *passim*.

33. Cullen, *Emergence of Modern Ireland*, p. 26.

34. Crawford, 'Landlord-Tenant Relations', p. 12; Eric L. Almquist, 'Mayo and Beyond: Land, Domestic Industry and Rural Transformation in the Irish West', *Irish Economic and Social History*, V (1978), p. 72.

35. Malcolm Gray, 'Scottish Emigration: the Social Impact of Agrarian Change in the Rural Lowlands, 1775–1875', *Perspectives in American History*, VII (1973), pp. 150–153.

36. T. C. Smout argues that it was the ease with which flax could be grown in Ireland which tied the proto-industrial family to the land, whereas in Scotland flax was

largely imported from the Baltic, the weaver bought his raw material and became a specialist in the village. This might have been an additional influence contributing to the wider demographic pressures which are seen here as the central factors in the contrast between the two societies. See T. C. Smout, 'Centre and periphery in history—Scotland', *Journal of Common Market Studies*, XVIII (1980), p. 266.

37. James Hunter, *The Making of the Crofting Community* (Edinburgh, 1976); T. M. Devine, 'The Rise and Fall of Illicit Whisky-Making in Northern Scotland, 1780–1840', *Scott. Hist. Rev.*, LIV (1975), pp. 155–177.

38. S. Daultrey, D. Dickson and C. O'Grada, 'Eighteenth Century Irish Population: New Perspectives from Old Sources', *Journal of Economic History*, XII, 3 (Sept. 1981).

39. For a discussion of a regional example of this process around the city of Cork, see D. Dickson, 'Property and Social Structure in eighteenth century South Munster', in Cullen and Furet, eds., *Ireland and France*, pp. 129–138.

40. For Scottish agrarian wages between 1740 and 1798, see Valerie Morgan, 'Agricultural Wage Rates in late Eighteenth Century Scotland', *Econ. Hist. Rev.*, 2nd ser., 24 (1971), pp. 181–201. For the period 1800 to 1840, see T. M. Devine, 'Social Stability and Agrarian Change in the Eastern Lowlands of Scotland, 1810–40', *Social History*, III (1978), pp. 331–346; *idem*, 'The Demand for Agricultural Labour in East Lothian after the Napoleonic Wars', *Trans. E. Lothian Antiquarian and Natural History Soc.*, Vol. 16, 1979, pp. 49–61; Ian Levitt and Christopher Smout, *The State of the Scottish Working Class in 1843* (Edinburgh, 1979), pp. 70–99.

41. Cullen, *Emergence of Modern Ireland*, p. 171.

42. There may well be contrasts in marriage ages. In Ireland they appear to have hovered around 22 years for males and 20 for females (Cullen, *Emergence of Modern Ireland*, p. 83). Material on the subject is fragmentary for eighteenth-century Scotland, but such data as do exist indicate substantially later ages at marriage: a mean 'rural' age for women in Central Ayrshire of 26; Laggan parish (Inverness) 29 to 32 for men and between 27 and 30 for women; Lochcrutton (Kirkcudbright) average age at marriage 33 for men and 24 for women. See Michael Flinn, ed., *Scottish Population History from the 17th century to the 1930s* (Cambridge, 1977), pp. 274–9.

43. L. M. Cullen, 'Population Trends in Seventeenth Century Ireland', *Economic and Social Review*, 61 (1974–5).

44. T. M. Devine, 'The American War of Independence and Scottish Economic History', in Owen Dudley Edwards and George Shepperson, eds., *Scotland, Europe and the American Revolution* (Edinburgh, 1976), pp. 61–65.

45. Peter Stein, 'The General Notions of Contract and Property in Eighteenth Century Scottish Thought', *Juridical Review* (1963), pp. 3–4, 11–12.

46. T. M. Devine, 'The Business Class of the Scottish Towns in the later Seventeenth and Early Eighteenth Centuries', in T. R. B. Dicks and G. Gordon, eds., *Studies in Scottish Urban History* (forthcoming).

47. R. H. Campbell, *The Rise and Fall of Scottish Industry, 1701–1939* (Edinburgh, 1980), p. 28. For other discussions of Calvinism and economic development, see Gordon Marshall, *Presbyteries and Profits* (Oxford, 1980); S. A. Burrell, 'Calvinism, Capitalism and the Middle Classes', *Journal of Modern History*, XXXII (1960); T. M. Devine and S. G. E. Lythe, 'The Economy of Scotland in the Reign of James VI: a Revision Article', *Scott. Hist. Rev.* 50 (1972), pp. 91–106.

48. W. H. Matthew, 'The Origins and Occupations of Glasgow Students', *Past and Present 33 (1966)*.

49. C. O Grada, 'On Some Aspects of Productivity Change in Irish Agriculture, 1845–1926'. Paper presented to the Seventh International Economic History Congress, Edinburgh University, 1978, p. 10.

50. *Ibid.*
51. Timperley, 'Pattern of Landholding', pp. 148–9.
52. Sir John Sinclair, *Analysis of the Statistical Account of Scotland* (1825), I, p. 175; Thomas Somerville, *My Own Life and Times* 1741–1814, (Edinburgh, 1861), pp. 359–60.
53. T. Donnelly, 'The Economic Activities of the Aberdeen Merchant Guild, 1750–1799', *Scottish Economic and Social History* I (1981), pp. 35–38; Timperley, 'Pattern of Landholding', pp. 148–9.
54. L. M. Cullen, 'Merchant Communities, the Navigation Acts and Irish and Scottish Responses', in Cullen and Smout, eds., *Comparative Aspects*, pp. 165–176.
55. Cullen, *Emergence of Modern Ireland*, pp. 16, 127–8, 189, 248.
56. Devine, 'Scottish Merchant Community'.
57. Devine, 'Social Stability during the Agricultural Revolution,' pp. 59–70.
58. N. T. Phillipson, 'The Social Structure of the Faculty of Advocates in Scotland, 1661–1840', in Alan Harding, ed., *Lawmaking and Lawmakers in British History* (London, 1980).
59. E. J. Hobsbawm, 'Capitalisme et Agriculture: Les Réformateurs Ecossais au XVIIIe Siécle', *Annales* (1979), pp. 580–601.
60. The 5th Duke of Argyll's Instructions to Mr. Duncan Campbell as Chamberlain of Tiree (1800), in Eric R. Cregeen, ed., *Argyll Estate Instructions* (Edinburgh 1964), p. 51.
61. This is well brought out in Maguire, *The Downshire Estates, passim.*
62. Lee, 'Patterns of Rural Unrest', in Cullen and Furet, eds., *Ireland and France*, pp. 223–237; McCourt: 'Decline of Rundale', in Roebuck, ed., *Plantation to Partition, p. 137.*
63. Maguire, *Downshire Estates*, pp. 70–71 and sources mentioned therein.
64. D. Dickson, 'Middlemen', in T. Bartlett and D. W. Hayton, eds., *Penal Era and Golden Age* (Belfast 1979), pp. 162–185.
65. McCourt, 'Decline of Rundale', in Roebuck, ed., *Plantation to Partition*, pp. 119–139. Again the comparison with similar landlord disappointments in the Scottish highlands is a compelling one.
66. Irish landlords founded villages, sponsored rural industry and supported tenurial change but they had much less room for manoeuvre than their Scottish counterparts. See, for example, Ingeborg Leister's study of Tipperaray, *Das Werden Der Agrarlandschaft in der Grafschaft Tipperary, Irland* (Marburg, 1963). Racial and religious links between landlord and peasantry were not necessarily conducive to successful development. Connaught, where a Catholic landholding rump survived, was probably the most conservative part of Ireland in the eighteenth century. See J. G. Simms, 'Connaught in the Eighteenth Century', *Irish Hist. Studies*, XI (1958–9), pp. 119–124.
67. I. Whyte, 'The Emergence of the New Estate Structure', in Parry and Slater, eds., *The Making of the Scottish Countryside*, pp. 117–136; R. A. Dodgshon, 'The Removal of Runrig in Roxburgh and Berwickshire', *Scottish Studies*, 16 (1972), pp. 121–7; J. di Folco, 'The Hopes of Craighall and Land Investment in the Seventeenth Century', in Devine, ed., *Lairds and Improvement*, pp. 1–10.
68. Devine, 'Social Stability during the Scottish Agricultural Revolution', pp. 59–60.
69. T. M. Devine, 'Agrarian Change in Ireland and Scotland in the Eighteenth Century', Paper presented at the Economic History Society Conference, University College, Swansea, 1978, pp. 8–10. Production rose markedly in both societies but in Western and Northern Ireland such increments often derived from small-scale intensive farming related to potato cultivation. Yields tended therefore to be increased through the *intensification of labour* rather than (as in lowland Scotland) through the greater efficiency of a given unit of labour input. By the

1840s the contemporary agricultural statistician, William Burness, concluded that the ratio of arable acres to each labourer in Scotland was about 20 whereas in Ireland it was almost 3. See W. Burness, 'Our Agricultural Labourers: English, Irish and Scotch', *Journal of Agriculture*, new ser. 1849–51, p. 450 and the important French exercise in early productivity comparisons, Leonce de Lavergne, *Essai sur l'Economie Rurale de l'Angleterre, de l'Ecosse et de l'Irlande* (Paris, 1854).

70. Eric L. Jones, 'The Constraints on Economic Growth in Southern England, 1650–1850', in *Third International Conference of Economic History: Munich*, 1965 (Paris, 1974), V, pp. 423–30.

71. One is struck, for example, by the more significant role played by landowners in banking and industrial development in Ireland compared to Scotland.

72. This paragraph is based mainly on Cullen, *Anglo-Irish Trade*; D. Dickson, 'The Cork Merchant Community in the Eighteenth Century: a Regional Perspective', in Cullen and Butel, eds., *Négoce et Industrie*, pp. 45–50; Devine, 'Scottish Merchant Community'; *idem, The Tobacco Lords* (Edinburgh, 1975), pp. 3–34.

73. Ralph Davis, 'English Foreign Trade, 1700–74', *Econ. Hist. Rev.*, 2nd ser. XV (1963), p. 298.

74. C. W. Munn, *The Scottish Provincial Banking Companies 1747–1864* (Edinburgh, 1981), pp. 152–163.

75. A. Dickson and W. Speirs, 'Changes in Class Structure in Paisley, 1750–1845', *Scott. Hist. Rev.* LIX (1980), pp. 54–72.

5

GLASGOW MERCHANTS AND THE
COLLAPSE OF THE TOBACCO TRADE
1775–1783

By the 1760s Glasgow had become the first tobacco port in the United Kingdom. Its rise from a late seventeenth-century position as an important centre of regional activity on the west coast of Scotland to a late eighteenth-century rôle as an entrepôt of international standing can fairly be considered spectacular.[1] Yet, if the expansion of the city's colonial commerce warrants this description, its collapse in 1775–6 merits it even more. Tobacco importation into Greenock and Port Glasgow, which had stood at just less than 46,000,000 lbs in 1775, slumped dramatically two years later to a gross total of 210,000 lb.[2] Further, with the British recognition of the independent 'United States' in 1783 the political structure which had underpinned Clyde-North American commercial relations was permanently altered. Once outside the regulation of the Navigation Acts, American interests could establish direct links between the tobacco plantations of Virginia, Maryland and North Carolina and the tobacco marts of continental Europe. The Clyde entrepôt status would then, in theory at least, be an irrelevance and indeed, although some Glasgow firms did manage to renew contact with former planter-customers after 1783, the city's tobacco trade after the American War of Independece never operated at more than twenty-five per cent of its pre-1776 level.[3]

This chapter is concerned with an examination of the short-term adjustments made by Glasgow merchants to what was a potentially disastrous situation. Apart from the obvious problem of ruptured commercial links there was the additional difficulty of the merchant community's financial stability because the operation of the tobacco trade had resulted in extension of credit to North American planters on an increasingly vast scale. 'The town of Glasgow', thought the city banker, John Brown, in 1766, 'reckoned itself to have been owed £1 million sterling'.[4] Certainly the historians, hagiographers and antiquarians whom Victorian Glasgow produced in such rich profusion insisted that there had indeed been widespread distress and extensive financial failure among the colonial merchant élite in the first few years of the American War. James Denholm, writing about thirty years after the collapse of the tobacco trade, considered that the year 1776 had dealt 'a dreadful stroke to Glasgow' and that 'it proved the ruin of great numbers who before reckoned themselves possessed of independent fortunes'.[5] Robert Reid was convinced that 'the dispute with our American colonies . . . had nearly annihilated the commerce of our city and ruined a great proportion of her enterprising merchants'.[6] This comment was reinforced by his contemporary George Stewart, a compiler of biographical data on leading eighteenth-century merchant families.[7] He thought 'heavy failures were of daily occurrence' among the tobacco aristocracy.[8]

Historians writing in the twentieth century have, however, approached these claims with increasing scepticism. In a pioneering article, published in 1930, Professor W. R. Scott, while admitting the reality of crisis, stressed that the speedy adjustment of the city's external commerce was the feature of 1775–83 which ought to be examined; so impressed was Scott with the positive reaction of the merchant group to its weakening position that he used the Glasgow case as an example of what he called 'economic resiliency'.[9]

Succeeding writers, following Professor Scott's cue, have since endeavoured to explain why tobacco merchants were able to weather the storm and why the series of bankruptcies which might well have been expected did not in fact occur. The work of the late Professor Hamilton,[10] Miss M. L. Robertson[11] and Professor R. H. Campbell[12] has been particularly noteworthy in this regard. Put in general terms, the synthesis which has evolved from the labours of these scholars is as follows:

(i) there were a number of failures resulting from the collapse, but these were not extensive and were mainly concentrated in the years 1778–80.

(ii) that financial ruin was not more widespread was due principally to the operation of three factors: (a) merchants were aware of the imminence of rebellion in the colonies and so took the necessary precautions; (b) in the early 1770s firms put into effect comprehensive plans to liquidate the debt owed them and were broadly successful in doing so; and (c) factors and storekeepers were urged to purchase as much tobacco as they could in the years before the war with the expectation that the heavy stocks would later be sold at inflated wartime prices.

Thus, by the enunciation of these theories, the paradox of a trading collapse with but little proportionate increase in the rate of bankruptcy would seem to be resolved in an elegant and satisfactory manner. This essay proposes a model which in some ways opposes that outlined above. It will be suggested that the extent to which Glasgow interests anticipated rebellion, as distinct from a further weakening in colonial relations, may have been exaggerated. As a result, exceptional buying of tobacco was confined to the summer of 1775 and so immediately predated by a matter of months the outbreak of revolution. Certainly in 1775-6 merchant houses appear to have had on hand uniquely large stocks of tobacco, but it will be argued that this was due as much to the vagaries of the weather and the behaviour of market prices for the crops of 1773-4 as to the shrewd stockpiling of the merchants themselves. It will further be stressed that the incidence and success of debt-collection would seem to have been over-emphasised; yet, at the same time, bankruptcies *were* few and some of those failures which did occur were not necessarily caused by the shock administered by the dramatic fall in tobacco imports after 1775. The probable reasons for Glasgow's good fortune will therefore be examined in the final section of the article.

I

There is little doubt that merchant opinion was well informed on the developing difficulties in the relationship between mother country and colonies before 1775. Such journals as the *Caledonian Mercury, Glasgow Journal, Glasgow Mercur* and *Scots Magazine* faithfully reported the successive crises, incorporating transcriptions of news and comment originally published in London newspapers. They also included items of specific Glasgow interest concerning the colonies, the source of which was often excerpts from private letters received in Scotland and written for the most part by Scots in America.[13] Storekeepers and factors of Glasgow firms were, of course, the major sources for detailed reports on the troubles: it was their duty to relate not only the movement of tobacco prices, the state of the weather and the prospects of the future crop but also to give full descriptions of prevailing political conditions especially in so far as they affected the city's commerce.[14]

The fact that companies were aware of developments in North America is certain; what, however, is perhaps more debatable is how they interpreted the information received, and, more important, how they reacted as the possibilities of permanent disruption of the tobacco trade became known. A review of the instructions sent out to factors by two leading Glasgow firms, William Cunninghame and Co. and Speirs, French and Co., reveals that merchants were much less pessimistic concerning the prospect of outright rebellion than is often suggested. Evidence extracted from the records of these two organisations should prove to be of particular value because, with the Glassford group of companies, they shipped the lion's share of tobacco in the three years previous to the American War. Thus of the 31,090 hogsheads landed at Clyde ports in 1774 the Speirs group, consisting of Speirs, French and Co. and Speirs, Bowman and Co., owned 5,629 hogsheads and the Cunninghame concerns (W. Cunninghame and Co., Cunninghame, Findlay and Co. and Cunninghame, Brown and Co.) 5,018 hogsheads. In effect, the interlocking units which made up these two combines imported in that year over one-third of the Glasgow total.[15] Evidence from the Cunninghame records might also be of special interest since William Cunninghame has long played the rôle in Glasgow hagiography of the extremely shrewd man of business, skilfully extricating himself from an impossible situation as commercial collapse loomed and, in the process, making vast windfall profits on imported tobacco as wartime prices rocketed.[16]

Cunninghame's letters in late 1774 to James Robinson, his chief factor in Virginia, show a determined reluctance to believe that the rebellious noises emitting from North America would ever come to anything. 'I imagine', he noted in September of that year, 'all your associations will come to nothing, the prudent Pennsylvanians will not be pushed into such violent plans . . . what madmen the Virginians are. How can they live or keep their negroes alive without coarse linens and cloths.[17] In the summer of 1774 his aim had been the extension rather than the contraction of his company's interests in North America. He planned to set up 'a lasting establishment' on the upper Potomac in Virginia in order to compete effectively with the stores of Messrs Buchanan.[18] As late as March 1775 he was still unwilling to accept the possibility of rebellion, maintaining that any attempt by the colonials to stop exportation must come to naught just as their 'non-importation agreements' had inevitably collapsed in the past.[19]

As a result of these assumptions, Cunninghame was left in a position of some indecision; there is little indication in his correspondence that a grand strategy was being marked out to exploit the developing political circumstances for maximum commercial advantage. In April 1775, a mere four months before the Virginian ports were closed, he confided to his chief factor that he was not alone in his anxieties:

> I really am at a loss how to act with regard to the purchase of cargoes and postpone doing anything until I heard from you, but from Findlay's letter now before me, informing me with certainty that all our ports are to be shut instantly I wish I had attempted purchasing. *The merchants here at present are undetermined what to do.*[20]

His mind was no more firmly set in May—'I am almost at a loss how to behave'[21]—and one gains the impression from his letters in the spring and early summer of 1775 that his anxiety was not so much the imminence of revolution as the fact that the bumper crop expected that year would glut European markets and so deflate prices.[22] Cunninghame was thus bent, at this point, not in concerning as much tobacco as funds would allow but in deferring purchase until the trend of prices became more explicit.

Finally, in May, he observed the beginnings of a rise in prices and how 'one or two gentlemen' were starting to buy at the higher level but he continued to order his storekeepers to refrain from heavy purchasing.[23] In that month he wrote to Robinson in some relief, stating how glad he was that his chief factor, with his long experience of the trade, agreed with him that 'it would be imprudent purchasing tobacco in these times'.[24]

The Cunninghame group was not unique in its rather optimistic appraisal of the political situation in the early summer of 1775. Indeed the resident factor in Virginia of James Brown and Co.reported to his parent house in April a rumour in that state which suggested that the United Kingdom parliament had 'put a stop to any proceedings against the Americans for a certain number of years'. This, he added had cooled many colonial tempers.[25] The intructions of Messrs Speirs, French and Co. to their storekeepers in Maryland illustrate that the firm did accept the possibility of a non-exportation agreement becoming a reality yet hardly envisaged a complete collapse in commerce. If the export of the year's crop should be temporarily halted, their factor was advised in June 1775 to keep his stores open and to dispose of the company's goods to those planters whose payment could be depended upon. Bonds were to be taken for existing debts, although no special effort was to be made to liquidate outstanding advances. Such a course of action, it was pointed out, 'will procure you the good will of your customers which may be of use when trade is open'.[26] The firm saw the emerging crisis as yet another in a series which had plagued their activities since the early 1760s and not as a watershed which would end in a permanent adjustment of the political structure on which the tobacco trade was based. Their final instructions demonstrate their optimism over future commercial links with Maryland: 'We desire you may contribute all in your power to dispose of the goods you have . . . as we would wish to have all our old goods disposed of before a new importation is allowed.[28]

John Herries, the Scottish agent for the farmers-general of the French customs who were the most important customers of the Glasgow firms, was a man closely in touch with the feelings and opinions of the colonial merchant group in the city.[28] His comments on the negotiations in early 1775 with the leading tobacco merchants add further weight to the argument that they did not anticipate rebellion long in advance. According to Herries, the merchants based their discussions with him on the assumption that 'disputes between the mother country and the colonies would soon be settled and that the prices of tobacco would ere long return to their former level'.[29]

Two points can be made in explanation of what, with the benefit of hindsight, can be dismissed as a basic misconception. In the first instance, Glasgow traders had been accustomed since the early 1760s to political instability in the colonies and to the non-importation agreements which were their normal accompaniment; they were also used to the collapse of such arrangements after short periods.[30] Cunninghame's faith in the inevitable logic of the forces of supply and demand is perhaps to be seen in this context. An additional factor, however, was the assumption that even if rebellion did break out, 'normal' relations would be speedily re-established by the British army: merchants, whether in private correspondence or in letters to the press, were at one in 1775–6 in looking forward to a speedy and inevitable victory over this 'petty little province, the creature of our own hands, the bubble of our breath'.[31]

It would appear that it is only from late May 1775 that one can speak of a concerted and feverish effort to buy up tobacco and load ships for home as the reality of incipient rebellion crystallised before company representatives in the colonies. By June, for instance, a virtual seller's market had been established in Virginia; factors eschewed the normal method of acquiring tobacco as payment for debts incurred at their stores and instead cash purchases were increasingly employed.[32] Transport costs rose as extra vessels were hired to ship out the annual crop before ports closed in September. At Alexandria in Virginia, for example, in August 1775 'there was no such thing as craft to be got' and one observer noted how the decks of Glasgow vessels, traditionally used to store staves and barrel hoops, were, in this particular summer, loaded with tobacco.[33]

While stressing the vigorous purchasing of the period May–August 1775, it would be unwise to conclude from this that atypically large importations of tobacco were reaching the Clyde throughout that year. An analysis of Scottish imports of the commodity for the years 1771–5 reveals that 1775 was by no means exceptional in the extent of imports:

Scottish imports of tobacco, 1771–5[34]

Year	Total (lb.)
1771	47,268,873
1772	45,259,675
1773	44,543,050
1774	41,348,295
1775	45,863,154

Yet, at the same time, there is substantial evidence to suggest that merchant firms had uniquely large stocks of tobacco in Clyde warehouses both in 1775 and 1776. Thus the collector of customs at Port Glasgow and Greenock complained in the autumn of 1775 that the tobacco cellars in these two ports were so overstretched that 'temporary sheds' and private stores had been filled but that 'there was still a good deal of tobacco which cannot be landed for want of the places to put it in'.[35] As late as August 1776 Messrs Dunwiddie, Crawford and Co. petitioned the Board of Customs that they were unable to discharge their 322 hogsheads of tobacco from the *Blandford*: 'On examining the cellars and enquiring at the person who has the management of them . . . we find we cannot yet get room.'[36]

One element in the overstocking of warehouses at this time was almost certainly the unusually short period allowed for firms to ship out the annual crops. Messrs Colin Dunlop and Sons, Bogle, Somervell and Co. and John Glassford and Co. noted how

our factors in these ports [i.e. Virginia and Maryland] were obliged to
hurry away our ships with tobacco and other goods, then on board,
otherwise there we had been precluded from bringing them to a
European market so hereby there has been a great and sudden
importation of tobacco from these two colonies.[37]

Again, merchants may have resolved to stockpile in the expectation of
steady increases in price as fear of wartime scarcities inflated demand.[38] In
August 1776 the Glassford group of companies had over 3,300 hogsheads
still in store in the Clyde; this was about two-thirds of their total importation
for 1775. Cunninghames held almost 5,000 hogsheads and in all, at this date,
there remained 14,404 in cellars in the two Clyde ports. Only a minimal
proportion of this total—1,521 hogsheads—had actually been landed in
1776.[39]

The effect of other elements partly outwith the control of the merchants
concerned has, however, been neglected. Importers gained also in 1775–6
through the incidence of bumper tobacco crops and the relatively sluggish
continental demand for the commodity in the period 1773–5; this meant
that *of necessity* they had extensive supplies on hand by the beginning of the
American War.

Market reports in the summer and autumn of 1774 indicated how the
French farmers-general were offering only 13/4d. per lb. and that crops that
season had been abundant. As a result 'every mercatt in Europe if full'[40]
Demand nearer home was no more vigorous. One house observed that
London had been 'empty for some time' but recalled that 'in a few months
on the arrival of their shipping it will be full enough of every kind'.[41] John
Glassford and Co. noted ruefully that there was 'nothing doing in tobacco
. . . mainly due to the French staying firm at 13/4 which we imagine they
will get exceedingly little'.[42] According to Sir William Forbes, Edinburgh
banker and friend of both the Scottish agent of the French buyers and of the
Glasgow merchants,[43] dullness in the market continued into 1775. His
comments are worth quoting in full:

Early in the year 1774 a new struggle took place between Mr. Herries
and the merchants of Glasgow who held at that time considerable
quantities of tobacco on hand about a small difference in price
between what he offered and they demanded. Things continued in
this situation till the beginning of 1775, when, instead of improving,
they grew worse, owing to the disputes which had by that time begun
to take place between Great Britain and the colonies of America, and
which threatened to put a stop to all commercial intercourse between
the two countries. The merchants of Glasgow instantly took alarm and
began to rise in their demands. Herries, who thought, as many others
did at that time, that the dispute between the mother country and the
colonies would be amicably adjusted, and that the prices of tobacco

would ere long return to their former level, advised the Farmers General to wait a little rather than yield to the increase demanded.[44]

II

As immediate a problem as the interruption of tobacco imports was the debt owed to Glasgow from the colonies. The size of the sums involved had expanded on a significant scale from the 1740s as a result of three factors.[45] In the first place, Scottish firms increasingly specialised in commerce with Virginia and in particular with the relatively new tobacco-growing areas in the piedmont region of that state. Here resided, in the valleys of the James and Potomac Rivers, the less wealthy planters, who in their exploitation of virgin land had quite exceptional needs for external credit. Linked with this was the operation of the 'store system', by the 1760s the normal mechanism of trade between North American tobacco planter and Glasgow merchant house. Customers were allowed to take goods in advance at company stores in return for the promise of a proportion of the future crop: such loans were rarely self-liquidating. Indeed, a representative for Alexander Cunninghame and Co. estimated that, for the 'store system' to function adequately, planters would require to have credit at individual stores for at least four years 'or in other words, supposing the value of a hogshead of tobacco to be only £6 sterling there must be at least £25 of stock such in Virginia for every hogshead imported if it was purchased for goods in the store way'. Thus, according to his estimate, the 2,200 hogsheads shipped by his house in 1772 needed about £55,000 'sunk' in the colony.[46] Finally, it became an integral part of the policy of many of the Glasgow organisations to make advances to planters in order to attract and secure custom; opportunities were also given to customers to draw bills on firms for mutually agreed sums.[47]

By the late 1760s all the indications are that the sum owed to Glasgow was truly enormous. In 1768 John Glassford, testifying before a select committee of the house of commons, alleged that the gross total was around £500,000 sterling.[48] Professor Thomas Reid, writing three years earlier, put the figure at 'above £400,000'.[49] By 1775, if one is to believe a petition submitted to the government from the city, the extent of ascertainable debt had more than doubled to 'one million and upwards'.[50] Yet, a mere six months after the submission of this petition, the *Caledonian Mercury* announced that 'more than half a million of the debts due from America to Glasgow have, by the activity and prudence of the storekeepers, been recovered and sent home in the course of a few months past' and that 'what is owing to this country is now very trivial'.[51]

It is plain that efforts were made to liquidate debt but it is much more difficult to ascertain how far such attempts were prompted by fear of future rebellion or were simply reactions to credit pressures within the tobacco trade. For instance, in the depression year of 1772, policies of retrenchment were planned by William Cunninghame and Co. and storekeepers were instructed 'to force payment of many of our overgrown large debts'.[52] Yet, as the financial crisis eased in 1773, so factors were once again permitted to extend credit judiciously to needy planters.[53] There was nothing exceptional about attempts at retrenchment in the years immediately preceding the war in relation to other periods: as one writer has put it,

> all surviving correspondence between Scottish or English merchants and their American employees is but a variation on the theme of the near-bankrupt employee beseeching his extravagant representative to be less easy with credit in the future.[54]

What is of importance, however, is how successful such endeavours were likely to be in the economic and political context of North America at this time.

The logic of the 'store system' meant that speedy reduction of debt was very difficult, especially as the trade itself was expanding and generating fresh grants of credit as old debts were liquidated. As a contemporary lawyer pointed out,

> every one who is acquainted with the trade, must know that this was unavoidable: for it is impossible at any one time, to get more out of the debts due by the planters than about a fourth part. They have credit at the several stores with which they deal for four years produce, and they never can deliver more than the produce of one year.[55]

A second major problem was the nature of the debts. John Glassford considered in 1768 that some were for large sums but that the vast majority were for relatively small amounts, most for under £30 sterling.[56] Those owed in the 1770s to William Cunninghame and Co., for instance, were almost all under £10, in thousands of separate accounts.[57] Recovery of such sums would demand an administrative operation of some complexity; amounts of £30 sterling were not necessarily trivial to the less wealthy planters of the interior of Virginia who were the Glasgow firms' best customers. The issue was further complicated by the fact that planters often had outstanding accounts with several different companies and thus their total debts could be quite considerable.[58] One merchant wrote to his brother despairingly in 1759, that 'they [the debts] commonly are endless— they are so small and numerous that it requires posterity to finish a concern'.[59]

Again, it may be doubted whether the agricultural economy of Virginia and Maryland in the colonial era, suffering as it was from a profound scarcity of specie,[60] was able to cope with the repayment of a sum of the order of £1 million sterling. After all it was the American planter's perennial need for working capital to acquire plantation equipment, purchase slaves and clear land for cultivation that had encouraged credit extension on such a vast scale. One store-keeper of Dunmore, Gilmour and Co. put the matter in a nutshell: 'I never knew money so hard to collect as at present, the Courts' business being stopped. Indeed, were they willing, I know not whether it would be in their power, there being so little money in circulation among us.'[61]

At the very best, successful collection would imply a major administrative operation necessarily involving the powers of law on the creditor's side. Yet such activity took place not in an atmosphere of relative goodwill but rather in one of explicit hostility to the Scots factors, traditionally one of the most hated elements in colonial society. Some argued that even the threat of legal action was enough to encourage a debtor to flee: 'the remote situation of the planters', thought one factor, 'will give them an opportunity to make away with their estates without our knowledge and, besides, it is the principle of many people of that neighbourhood not to pay debts'.[62] Alternatively, court actions might endure for months, a result which, according to John Hamilton, chief factor for John Brown and Co., arose from 'the tediousness of the law . . . and the generally litigeous disposition of the people who are well-acquainted with every chicanery that the law will admit of to keep off paying their debts'.[63] Even if a debt action was successful, judgment in a merchant's favour could mean simply the transfer of a debt from one individual to another rather than the collection in cash of the sum owed. Such was the limited property of many planters, and such was the shortage of cash, that sequestration of a debtor's assets was unlikely to bring about a speedy sale and release the sum due. Even the threat of imprisoning a debtor was considerably blunted by the widespread knowledge of the expense the creditor had to bear to keep him in jail and the hope of a quick release if the creditor's resources and/or his determination gave out.[64]

Such intrinsic problems were considerably exacerbated in the years 1774–6. Maryland and Virginia courts were shut from the summer of 1774. One court in Berkshire County, Maryland, did try to sit but a mob invaded the courtroom, seized the chief judge and kept him prisoner until he consented to adjourn the sitting *sine die*. One witness coyly observed that 'by such methods they meant to avoid the payment of their just debts'.[65] Direct intimidation might hinder debt collection as effectively as the shutting of courts. It was freely admitted that 'the Glasgow factors seem to be the great objects of their resentment, the case is plain to them they owe the money'.[66] Even in New York the judges and sheriffs were imprisoned by the mob in the spring of 1775.[67] Before the courts closed it was exceedingly difficult to overcome the prejudice of a section of the colonial magistracy as the United Kingdom government began to pass punitive legislation against North America.[68] Often patriotism and indebtedness became intermingled in a curious alchemy. Thus William Woodford, later commander of the rebel forces which burnt Norfolk, Virginia, and with it the property of several

Glasgow firms, related how he was indebted to two Scots' stores 'more than he was worth . . . but never had the least inclination to pay'; indeed, by 1777 he was exulting in the thought of 'discharging his debts to Britain with the broad brush, meaning the destroying of the books and papers of the merchants'.[69]

Undoubtedly, whatever the magnitude of the problems involved in debt collection, some companies did retrench successfully in 1775.[70] Yet, equally, the debts of others mounted appreciably in the few years before the outbreak of war. The sum owed to Speirs, Bowman and Co. quintupled between 1770 and 1776 from £6,299 7s. 4d. to £33,740 11s. od.,[71] and an analysis of other surviving mercantile records does suggest that the sums owed to Glasgow remained significant in 1776. As befitted its position as one of the largest tobacco-importing combines, the Cunninghame group had the largest ascertainable debts with a gross total of £111,300, excluding bad debts, owing to its three firms.[72] However, there was no exact correlation between a firm's importance, as measured by the extent of its importation, and the level of the sums owing. Baird, Hay and Co., which shipped 41 hogsheads in 1774 as opposed to the Cunninghame total of 5,018 hogsheads, or about 0.011 per cent of the volume of tobacco landed by the giant group, still had £16,100 owed to them, or about one-seventh of the Cunninghame debt.[73] Clearly, the many variables implicit in the abilities of factors to weigh up good credit risks, the credit-worthiness of the customers of respective companies and the changing sympathy of the courts over time must destroy and precise relationship between size of organisation and extent of debt.

The 'subject' of Colin Dunlop and Sons in Virginia and Maryland, exclusive of fixed property, calculated in October 1776, stood at £24,041 18s. 7d.[74] Around £20,000 was owed to John Glassford and Co., one of the four concerns which made up the Glassford syndicate.[75] Logan, Gilmour and Co., a much smaller unit, had debts of between £15,000 and £20,000 in Virginia in 1776.[76] The two major companies in which Alexander Speirs had a preponderant interest were owed over £46,000 in the same year.[77] Four leading Virginians were indebted to George Kippen and Co. for £10,000.[78]

Other firms made reference to their debts in more general terms. William Scott blamed 'the American troubles' for locking up 'a vast part' of the funds of Bogle, Scott and Co. 'as in the case with many others'.[79] James Somervell, partner in Bogle, Somervell and Co., foresaw that in 1776 'their funds being locked up in America, it would be a difficult matter for them to pay their debts'.[80]

III

It is plain that Glasgow's merchant élite had to contend with a stubbornly high level of debt owed to them from North America in 1776. Yet, paradoxically, the financial ruin which might have been expected to follow inevitably, both from this and from the collapse of the major sector of the city's external commerce, did not ensue. It seems probable that much of the confusion among nineteenth-century historians over the extent of bankruptcy was caused by their assumption that firms which became insolvent in the 1770s and 1780s obviously owed their plight to the disruption of the tobacco trade in 1775–6. For example, according to Robert Reid, William French 'was ruined by the American War'.[81] Yet French's assets were not sequestrated until 1787[82] and, between 1775–6 and the end of the war in 1783, he was buying up land in the Old Monkland parish of Lanarkshire.[83] Furthermore, he was an important partner in Speirs, French and Co. and Speirs, Bowman and Co., two firms which made immense profits from the sale of tobacco at inflated wartime prices.[84] Given his circumstances and the date of his bankruptcy, it would be fair to argue that his financial problems were not directly connected with the American War.

The firm of Wilson, Brown and Co. was adjudged by 'Senex' to 'have failed for £40,000 due to the collapse of the tobacco trade'.[85] It is difficult to find convincing evidence to justify this suggestion. On the contrary, the customs accounts demonstrate that the firm was still functioning in the last two years of war and, far from being 'importers of tobacco to a considerable extent', had been throughout the 1770s specialising more as manufacturers of roll tobacco, principally engaged in the export trade to Dublin, Belfast and Newry.[86] The company did not fail until 1786.[87] James Brown and Co. have also been described as ruined by the American War.[88] However, in evidence to the 'Loyalists Commission' in 1786, Browns asserted how, as soon as hostilities were terminated, they renewed links with Maryland. There is no mention of impending or past financial disaster which might well have aided them in their petition for compensation from the commission.[89]

The method adopted to enable an approximate estimate of the real extent of bankruptcy to be made was, in essence, a fairly straightforward though laborious one. A list of firms engaged in tobacco importation in 1774 was compiled from the customs accounts. Thereafter an examination was conducted through a variety of sources (customs accounts, the records of the firms, local and national registers of deeds, the local press and sample processes in the court of session records) to obtain proof of a company's survival into the later 1780s. If the company was found not to have continued, it was investigated, where source material allowed, to determine whether its demise had come about by bankruptcy, by mutual agreement among the partners or through the termination of a particular contract of co-partnership. Considerable success was achieved in this exercise. There were thirty-seven firms involved in tobacco importation in the selected year and it was possible to trace thirty-three of these and reach conclusions on their experience during the American War.[90]

On the basis of the data thus assembled, it is scarcely possible to describe the effects of the collapse on Glasgow as catastrophic. Indeed, so far-reaching was the rôle of the three giant groups of Speirs, Cunninghame and Glassford—they shipped over fifty per cent of the 1774 importation[91]—that their continued solvency would perhaps itself dispel any such suggestion. The seven units which did fail imported only 2,358 hogsheads of the 31,000 credited to the Clyde in 1774. Only one bankrupt concern was numbered among the eleven firms which each landed more than 500 hogsheads. Four of the insolvencies (those of Hugh Wylie and Co., Wylie, Mackenzie and Co., Baird, Hay and Co. and Jamieson, Johnston and Co.) were, however, concentrated among the ten companies which imported the least amount.[92]

By far the greatest and most famous series of bankruptcies was that of Buchanan, Hastie and Co. and of its sister concerns, Bogle, Jamieson and Co. and James Jamieson and Co.[93] This combine accounted for over two-thirds of the 2,358 hogsheads imported in 1774 by insolvent firms and it failed in December 1777 for £62,500.[94] One suspects, however, that even this disaster was due only partly to the locking-up of their debts and property in North America. James Gourlay, a pioneer historian of the tobacco trade, observed that the Buchanan group was one of the few which actually owned plantations in the colonies and so argued that the loss of these assets, as a result of the sequestration of British property in 1778, afforded a central reason for the failure.[95] Although it would be wrong to dismiss altogether the rôle of the existence of debt and property in America, certain other matters require evaluation.

The Glasgow bankers, Moore, Carrick and Co., a major creditor of the firm, pointed out that the total 'subject' of Buchanan, Hastie and Co. in the colonies in 1777, inclusive of debts and fixed assets, was a mere £13,000.[96] This compares very unfavourably with the figure of over £60,000 owed by the Buchanan concerns at their bankruptcy. Thus, even if total assets had been open to company control, it would appear that the ultimate fate of the undertaking would have been little affected. Again, it seems inaccurate to suggest that the loss of fixed property was an important factor in the firm's collapse when it is recalled that the company went bankrupt in December 1777 and that British property in Virginia was not sequestrated until March 1778.[97]

A more plausible line of enquiry might concentrate on the history of the three companies before the collapse of the tobacco trade. One could justifiably argue after examining this record that misfortune arose from defects in capital structure and in the business qualities of the partners. Throughout the early 1770s, the group was chronically short of working capital and had been borrowing heavily on land and on the security of the individual partners: sources as diverse as the trust funds of widows and orphans, the Faculty of Advocates, the marquis of Annandale and the purse of HMS *Panther* were all utilised.[98] The vast proportion of creditors were not trade creditors but persons who had deposited their money on loan. Clearly such a structure would be highly vulnerable in a period of depression such as emerged in late 1777.[99]

Yet the very fact that this syndicate had such a disastrous experience while the vast majority of firms continued to survive may imply that it lacked qualities which others possessed. Certainly the partners expanded their credit base to a perilous extent: as one contemporary pointed out, they were 'once reckoned capital people'.[100] John Brown, the Glasgow banker, writing in his private diary, perhaps put his finger on the root of the Buchanan troubles:

It seems one of the great causes of the failure was when others of the tobacco trade were getting home great quantities of tobacco which on account of the troubles were giving a very great price, the Company was delaying and arguing with their agents and factors abroad. Besides, their affairs seem to have been miserably managed at home. Instead of the partners minding the business they are making pleasures and advocations at their town and country houses. From a state of their affairs laid before their creditors, they appear to be owing £50,000, mostly bonded money.[101]

In the broad context of eighteenth-century Scottish commercial history, therefore, the failures of the American War period were not unique in extent nor in the degree to which they came about by the dramatic disruption of the tobacco trade. The direct effects hardly bear comparison with the failure of the Ayr Bank in 1772 for over £1 million,[102] nor with the depression in Scottish industry and trade in 1793 when several cotton firms collapsed and James Dunlop went bankrupt for £169,000,[103] nor yet with the spectacular failure of Alexander Houston and Co. in the early nineteenth century for over £1.2 million.[104] Again, although very profitable the colonial trades were also notoriously risky, dependent as they were on the vicissitudes of the weather and on an extended and vulnerable network of credit: thus failures were not uncommon. The years 1728 and 1772 easily rivalled the years 1777–8 in this regard, if they did not take precedence over them.[105] The final question must then be asked: given that the vast bulk of outstanding debt owed to Glasgow was at best only minimally reduced, how is the endurance of most tobacco firms to be explained?

IV

It ought first to be noted that by the early 1770s the Glasgow colonial merchant community had evolved to a level of organisation which was well adapted to coping with the stresses of a financial crisis. The merchant group itself was so small, power within it was so concentrated, and companies were so inter-linked by family and partnership that firms were unlikely to indulge in a *sauve qui peut* as pressure on credit slowly developed from the later months of 1777. Merchants were so involved in one another's affairs as insurers, as fellow partners, as creditors, as cautioners, as co–obligants and as members of the one social, economic and political élite, that salvation lay in mutual restraint and, indeed, in mutual aid. The train of financial disaster would begin when the delicate balance of the bill–of–exchange network became upset. Mutuality at least helped to restrain the dangers of such an eventuality.[106]

Between about 1770 and 1815 there were something of the order of 170 merchants involved in partnerships in both the tobacco and West India trades. In 1775–6, in the tobacco trade alone, fewer than eighty merchants were represented in the thirty–seven companies.[107] How tiny this group was in the context of the Glasgow merchant community as a whole may be seen by the fact that even in the four years 1776–80 no fewer than 236 men became Glasgow burgesses 'of the merchant rank'.[108] The extent of personal funds required to prosecute colonial commerce and to pay customs duties on imported tobacco and sugar helped to reserve the Caribbean and American trades to all but a wealthy few.[109] Professor Price, comparing the structure of units in 1728 with those of 1773, found that in the latter year two–fifths as many firms handled ten times as much business as in the former year.[110] Yet even this does not give a comprehensive picture of the concentration of control over importation. The thirty–seven companies were not individual units in competition with one another. Many were linked by common partnership: thus the Speirs group consisted of three firms, Cunninghames of three, McCalls of four, Donalds of two, and Glassfords of four.[111] The very size of these huge combines and the individual wealth of their partners afforded them credit status. Successive financial crises had thinned the ranks of the smaller fry and helped to establish the domination of the few.

The web of integration and cooperation was further extended by individuals who became members of various companies and by the popularity of family copartnerships.[112] In this regard it might be noted that the merchant dynasties of Murdoch, Dennistoun, Alston, Dreghorn, Donald, Dunlop, Campbell, Wylie, Robertson, Elliot, Hamilton, Marshall, French, Speirs, Buchanan, Bogle, Findlay and Cunninghame were all united by blood and marriage in one massive kinship group.[113]

The structure of companies presented further obstacles to fullscale financial disaster. In Scotland, unlike England the partnership was a legal entity which cut risk in several ways.[114] When partners subscribed to a particular contract their share became part of the common stock and, to quote a familiar line in several agreements, the share was to remain with the company 'ay and till the private and particular debts due, or that may be due, by one partner to another be paid off and ay and until the bonds and other securities wherein they are or may be engaged with and for each be also paid off . . .'.[115] Again, in a sample of fifteen contracts examined, an important clause in each stressed that on the bankruptcy of an individual partner his stock in the concern would not fall in the first instance to his creditors but rather to the solvent partners, to do with as other articles in the contract specified. This normally entailed the paying of a partner's outstanding debts to the company and the liquidation of his share of the firm's own obligations. Only then would his share be paid to external creditors, in phases over anything up to a two-year period. This type of regulation was an important braking mechanism on the multiplier effects of a credit crisis.

Risks were also spread by the traditional Scottish practice of holding individually small amounts of capital in various concerns;[116] in effect, by the formation of a sort of unit trust structure. Whereas the norm in London tobacco businesses was combination of two or three partners, groupings of six and often of nine individuals were not unusual in Glasgow companies. However, many of the Glasgow shareholders might have interests in three or four different units.[117] Diversification of risk also meant involvement in West India firms,[118] investment in land,[119] banking and in domestic industry. The major accruals of income came from colonial commerce, but many, especially the greater, merchants had important secondary investments which lent them flexibility when the disruption of the tobacco trade took place. Between *c.* 1770 and 1800 a minimum of seventy-seven Glasgow colonial merchants had financial interests in a series of industries, ranging from malleable ironworks, printworks and dyeworks to coal-mining, bottle-making and brewing.[120]

It was of importance, too, that fixed costs formed so minimal a proportion of the commercial regime of tobacco merchants. This allowed for rapid adjustment to changes in trade patterns. Fixed costs normally lay in stores and ships—only rarely did tobacco firms own plantations.[121] Of course, the sequestration of property did represent a loss in absolute terms—some 'stores' were considerable both in size and in architectural appeal: the Virginia and Maryland state governments took over several of them for use as official buildings. The property of John McDowall in Virginia was set aside for the auditor's office; that of Speirs, French and Co. for the use of the treasurer. Until the state capital was completed in 1789 the Virginia assembly met in a house which formerly belonged to W. Cunninghame and Co.; and 412 acres in Prince Edward County, owned by the Speirs group of companies, were given to Hampdon and Sydney College.[122] Yet in proportion to their debts and working capital such properties formed a relatively small proportion of the total assets of firms. For example, Dunmore, Gilmour and Co. had only £700 in colonial property but £15,000–£20,000 in other assets; the relevant figures for Colin Dunlop and Sons were £1,764 and £24,000. These ratios were by no means untypical.[123] Stocks of merchandise remaining in North America after rebellion were likely to be at risk; but in the two years before war broke out there had been a marked diminution in Scottish exports there, partly because of the enforcement of the non-importation and non-consumption clauses of the Continental Association after December 1774. Thus the value of exports fell from £260,033 in 1774 to £41,637 in 1775.[124]

After trade disruption, employees of firms in the colonies could be paid off and thus cease to be a burden[125] or could be directed to loyal areas such as New York, Charlestown and the West Indies to act as links in the much attenuated tobacco trade which developed through such channels after 1776. Thus Robert Burton, chief factor for Speirs, French and Co. in Maryland, was ordered to the Caribbean and directed to draw on his parent firm for bills up to the value of £10,000 and to establish a flow of tobacco via the neutral islands of St. Eustatius and St. Thomas.[126] Some factors remained in the colonies although officially expelled by an act of September 1776; there is solid evidence that Scottish merchants were resident in Richmond and Petersburg throughout the war, permitted to stay either as a result of taking an oath to Congress and declaring their neutrality to the satisfaction of the citizenry or because they satisfied a specific economic need in the community.[127]

Shipping formerly employed in the pre-1776 trade could be adequately utilised throughout the war. The interruption of American commerce did indeed mean that in the very short term there was a superfluity of merchantmen: thus one source noted in January 1776 that 'Glasgow vessels are mostly out of employ'.[128] However, from 1777 complaints of scarcity of shipping began to predominate. The foreign trade boom of 1776–7,[129] demands of the transport service in 1776 and 1778,[130] the extensive investment in privateering after 1778—between that date and 1783 there were about thirty-seven Glasgow vessels cruising as privateers—[131] the re-opening of the tobacco trade on a much diminished scale after 1777[132] and the capture of merchantmen by enemy action[133] were all elements in this. Yet above all was the fact that a state of war existed between the traditional source of Glasgow's ships, North America, and the United Kingdom. As a result, vessels formerly engaged in the tobacco trade were at a premium in the market between 1776 and 1783.

What has been offered thus far in explanation of the resiliency of the merchant group during the war are the constant elements in the structure and organisation of the Glasgow trades from the 1760s. Yet there were also elements unique to 1775–7 which favoured tobacco companies and enabled the majority of them to negotiate the depression years of 1778–9 successfully. It may first be said that the extent of outstanding debt in the colonies was not necessarily an insurmountable obstacle. Firms which operated the 'store system' were geared to large-scale extension of credit over long periods; the huge organisations which dominated the trade did not exist on such a shoe-string basis as to require comprehensive and speedy recovery of debt if they were to escape bankruptcy. On the contrary, since by the 'store system' merchants became owners of the tobacco, their primary concern was the price that a year's crop was likely to fetch in home (and above all in European) markets. Credit to planters was, as it were, a necessary cost in the mechanism of the trade and would only prove a drawback if it were not carefully rationed in relation to the capacity of a firm or if prices in a particular year were depressed. To put it in another way, income from tobacco sales was in effect the return for the sum invested in loans. Disaster, of course, might very well occur if most companies had a low liquidity preference and/or if accruals from markets in 1775–6 did not offer sufficient remuneration for outlays in the colonies.

On the first point it may be said that the balances of resources of most firms were probably sufficiently fluid. Generally, partners were allowed a return of only five per cent interest on their shares, the remainder being retained within the capital structure. Thus, in the case of George McCall and Co., 'None of the partners shall be allowed to withdraw any part of his stock except the dividend mentioned . . . until the whole money borrowed and other debts due by the company shall first be paid and cleared off.'[134] Moreover, partnership links between several of the tobacco firms and the Glasgow banks,[135] which were important purveyors of short-term credit for the trade,[136] helped to exert a stabilising influence and to avert the dangers of a liquidity crisis. Much of the tobacco purchasing in 1775 was done with cash and this obviously indicates availability of liquid resources.[137]

Perhaps most important of all, however, was the fact that merchants were not confronted with a crisis of confidence in the early stages of war, especially during the crucial period between the last bulk purchases of tobacco in the autumn of 1775 and the final bulk sales to European customers in the summer of 1777. The healthy functioning of the trade was dependent in the final analysis on the condition of the London money market, itself notoriously vulnerable to political shock. Glasgow firms drew bills on London agents payable on average within sixty days, and before this the latter would draw on their principals in Scotland for the agreed sum plus interest and commission.[138] Usually even a rumour of war was sufficient to shake the delicate structure built up on this foundation. Yet in 1776–7 there was an easing rather than a restriction of credit. The *Scots Magazine* was only one of the contemporary journals which noted a 'great plenty of money now in circle'.[139] The beginnings of tobacco speculation at wartime rates, the demands made on surplus shipping by the transport service and an upsurge in trade with England and Holland were all factors in this prosperous period. Yet most fundamental of all was the unwillingness to treat the war at this stage as a serious threat to Britain's security, in the same way that the conflict with France and Spain after 1778 undoubtedly was. There was an almost total underestimation of the ability of American colonists to resist for any extended period the counter-measures of British regular troops.[140] This was a natural mistake. There was no precedent for such a contest; the formidable logistics problem which was involved was only dimly realised,[141] and French intervention was hardly contemplated at the time. It is significant that not until the British defeat at Saratoga in October 1777 and French involvement in 1778 did Glasgow adopt the conventional postures of a city at war. Only then did significant investment in privateering begin and loyal addresses flow to the monarch; only then was the Glasgow Regiment raised and a general restraint on credit commenced.[142]

The period of relaxed credit from 1775 to late 1777 was of immense importance because it meant that importers were not compelled to release their large tobacco stocks on to the market to satisfy pressing creditors; rather it allowed them to retain supplies and await market developments.[143] Thus as late as August 1776 there remained 14,404 hogsheads in cellars in Greenock and Port Glasgow although only 1,521 actually arrived in that year.[144] Market developments in 1776–7 could not have been more attractive. As the *Caledonian Mercury* justly stated: 'The loss of American trade has been of great advantage to that place (Glasgow). Fortunes will be made by the advance of tobacco and other American goods of which a great store is still on hand.'[145] Merchants were able to make up for the relatively lean years of 1773–4. Speirs, French and Co. calculated that in the earlier period they made 'no profit equal to our debts on remittance'.[146] So great were the returns in 1776–7, however, that in those years Alexander Speirs was able to acquire estates in Renfrew and Stirlingshire totalling over £60,000 in value.[147] In the depression year of 1778, William Cunninghame could pay £24,000 cash down for the estate of Lainshaw in Ayrshire.[148] Even some small units, such as Baird, Hay and Co., participated in the bonanza: their profits rose from £388 in 1773 to over £2,600 in 1776.[149]

The most rapid advances took place from the summer of 1776 until the autumn of 1777. By then incoming cargoes from the colonies were few and far between, the rebels themselves had not yet established extensive connections with European customers, the previous year's stock of the tobacco purchasers had run out and commercial opinion was less ready to accept the inevitability of instant victory. Tobacco which had sold at Glasgow for little more than 3d. per 1b. in September 1775 was by September 1776 selling for 6d.[150] A month later the price had quadrupled to 2S.[151]; in August 1777 Glasgow merchants 'sold a great quantity of tobacco to the French at a very great price'; and a gross figure of £150,000 was quoted as the extent of a month's return on the sale.[152]

Even when prices began to falter on the Continent from late 1777 spectacular gains could still be realised in the domestic market. Indeed, some firms were re-shipping exported tobacco home from Dieppe, Rotterdam and Ostend, 'by which means they imagine they shall sell off their large stocks of an inferior sort of tobacco to London traders and that after the rate of 2/- per 1b.'[153] Of course, not all companies figured in the bonanza. Significantly, none of the smaller firms which failed between 1778 and 1780 seem to have been able to retain tobacco stocks until the remarkable price rise began in 1776.[154] Yet for most merchants the returns of 1776–7 were sufficient to compensate them, at least in the short term, for uncollected debts and dislocation of trade.

NOTES

1. For the expansion of the city's commerce during this period see T. C. Smout, 'The Development and Enterprise of Glasgow, 1550–1707', *Scot. Journ. Pol. Econ.*, vii (1960), 194–212; Jacob M. Price, 'The Rise of Glasgow in the Chesapeake Tobacco Trade, 1707', *William and Mary Quaterly*, 3rd ser., xi (April 1954), 179–99, reprinted in P. L. Payne (ed.), *Studies in Scottish Business History* (London, 1967), 299–318; [James Gourlay], *A Glasgow Miscellany: the Tobacco Period in Glasgow, 1707–1775* (privately printed, n.d); J. H. Soltow, 'Scottish Traders in Virginia, 1750–75', *Econ. Hist. Rev.*, 2nd ser., xii (1959), 83–98.

2. M. L. Robertson, 'Scottish Commerce and the American War of Independence', *Econ. Hist. Rev.*, 2nd ser., ix (1956), 123.

3. H. Hamilton, *An Economic History of Scotland in the Eighteenth Century* (Oxford, 1963), 416–17.

4. M[itchell] L[ibrary, Glasgow], Bogle MS, xci, John Brown's Recollections, i, 112–13.

5. James Denholm, *A History of Glasgow* (Glasgow, 1804), 407.

6. Robert Reid, *Old Glasgow and its Environs* (Glasgow, 1864), 175.

7. See, for example, his *Curiosities of Glasgow Citizenship as exhibited chiefly in the Business Career of its Old Commercial Aristocracy* (Glasgow, 1881).

8. George Stewart, *Progress of Glasgow* (Glasgow, 1883).

9. W. R. Scott, 'Economic Resiliency', *Econ. Hist. Rev.*, ii (1930), 291–9.

10. Hamilton, *Economic History*, 269–71; 'The Founding of the Glasgow Chamber of Commerce in 1783', *Scot. Journ. Pol. Econ.*, i (1954).

11. M. L. Robertson, 'Scottish Commerce', 123–31.

12. R. H. Campbell, *Scotland since 1707; the Rise of an Industrial Society* (Oxford, (1965), 45–46.

13. See, generally, D. I. Fagerstrom, 'The American Revolutionary Movement in Scottish Opinion, 1763 to 1783' (unpublished Ph.D. thesis, Edinburgh University, 1951).

14. E[dinburgh] U[niversity] L[ibrary], Mercantile Accounts, Virginia and Maryland, Microfilm 23, Letters of James Brown and Co., passim; S[cottish] R[ecord] O[ffice], GD 247/58/0, Cunninghame-Robinson Correspondence.

15. SRO, E 504/28/23–4; E 504/15/23–5. For the partnership structures of the two groups see P[ublic] R[ecord] O[ffice], AO 12/56/292; PRO, AO 12/9/53; G[lasgow] C[ity] A[rchives], TD 131/7/45.

16. Stewart, *Curiosities*, 194.

17. SRO, GD 247/141, W. Cunninghame to J. Robinson, 29 Sept. 1774.

18. Ibid., W. Cunninghame to W. Henderson, 18 July 1774.

19. SRO, GD 247/59/Q/I, W. Cunninghame to J. Robinson, 28 Mar. 1775.

20. Ibid., Cunninghame to Robinson, 25 Apr. 1775. My italics.

21. Ibid., Cunninghame to Robinson, 10 May 1775. It may be noted here that Cunninghame was not merely relying on factorial advice and information in forming his assessment of the situation. He himself was visiting Alexandria in Virginia in 1774–5.

22. Ibid., Cunninghame to Robinson, 28 Mar. 1775.

23. Ibid., Cunninghame to Robinson, 4 May 1775.

24. Ibid.

25. EUL, Mercantile Accounts, Virginia and Maryland, Alex. Hamilton to Messrs John Brown and Co., 25 Apr. 1775.

26. S[ignet] L[ibrary, Edinburgh], Court of Session Process 190/13, extract of a letter from Messrs Speirs, French and Co. to George Sherriff, 15 June 1775.

27. Ibid.
28. Sir William Forbes of Pitsligo, *Memoirs of a Banking House (London, 1860), 9, 27–28, 44–43*.
29. Ibid., 45–46.
30. Hamilton, *Economic History*, 268–9.
31. *Scots Magazine*, xxxvi, May 1774; for an analysis of this attitude see T. M. Devine, 'Glasgow Merchants in Colonial Trade, 1770–1815' (unpublished Ph.D. thesis, Strathclyde University, 1972), i, 179–80; and below, 72–3.
32. SRO, GD 247/59/Q/1, W. Cunninghame to James Robinson, 27 May and 4 Aug. 1775; SL, Court of Session Process, 190/13, G. Sherriff to Speirs, French and Co., 3 June 1775.
33. SRO, GD 247/59/Q/1, Cunninghame to Robinson, 17 and 26 Aug. 1775; James Crosby to Robinson, 20 July 1775.
34. PRO, Customs 14/2, quoted in Hamilton, *Economic History*, 416.
35. SRO, CE 60/1/8, Collector, Greenock and Port Glasgow, to H. M. Board of Customs, 12 Sept. 1775.
36. SRO, CE 60/1/9, Dunwiddie, Crawford and Co. to H. M. Collector of Customs, 13 Aug. 1776.
37. Ibid.
38. Stewart, *Curiosities*, 194; *Edinburgh Evening Courant*, 4 Sept. 1776; Robertson, 'Scottish Commerce', 126.
39. SRO, CE 60/1/9, Account of the quantities of tobacco in the hands of each importer, Port Glasgow and Greenock, 5 Aug. 1776; SRO, E 504/15/26–7; E 504/28/25–6.
40. SRO, GD 247/59/Q/1, W. Cunninghame to John Turner, 18 July 1774. The years 1771–5 have been described by Professor Price as 'glut years'; see Price, 'Rise of Glasgow', 301.
41. SRO, GD 247/141, W. Cunninghame to J. Robinson, 13 Aug. 1774.
42. SRO, GD 247/59/Q/1, W. Cunninghame to Thomas Gordon, 15 July 1774.
43. ML, Chamber of Commerce MS, Sir W. Forbes to Patrick Colquohoun, 26 Mar. 1782.
44. Forbes, *Memoirs*, 45–46.
45. For a detailed examination of the expansion of credit see Devine, 'Glasgow Merchants', i, 104–44; Soltow, 'Scottish Traders', 95–97.
46. SL, Court of Session Process, 162/3, Information for James Dougal . . ., 44.
47. GCA, Dunlop Papers, Additional observations for James Dougal . . ., 7; SRO, GD 247/58/0, James Robinson to Bennet Price, 7 Oct. 1767.
48. B[ritish] M[useum], Add. MS. 33030/31.
49. W. Hamilton (ed.), *The Works of Thomas Reid* (Edinburgh, 1846–63), i, 43.
50. *Caledonian Mercury*, 1 Feb. 1775.
51. Ibid., 19 Aug. 1775. This comment is quoted with approval by Miss Robertson and Professor Hamilton.
52. SRO, GD 247/59, W. Cunninghame to J. Robinson, 2 Apr. and 1 July 1772.
53. SRO, GD 247/158/0, J. Robinson to W. Cunninghame and Co., 26 Feb. 1773.
54. Price, 'Rise of Glasgow', 311.
55. GCA, Dunlop Papers, Additional observations for James Dougal . . ., 2.
56. BM, Add. MS, 33030/32.
57. PRO, AO 12/56/188.
58. SL, Court of Session Process, Information for Messrs Thomas, Peter and William Bogle, 15 Oct. 1769.
59. Quoted in A. J. Voke, 'Accounting Methods of Colonial Merchants in Virginia', *Journal of Accountancy*, xlii (1926), 5.
60. Soltow, 'Scottish Traders', 94–95.

61. PRO, AO 13/30/130, Letter of Ben Toter, 15 Apr. 1775.
62. EUL, Mercantile Accounts, Virginia and Maryland, Microfilm 23, Robert Ferguson to Thomas Mundell, 27 July 1787.
63. Ibid., John Hamilton to John Brown and Co., 28 May 774.
64. Soltow, 'Scottish Traders', 96.
65. N[ational] L[ibrary of] S[cotland], Charles Steuart Papers, MS 5028, James Parker to Charles Steuart, 14 Aug. 1774.
66. Ibid., Parker to Steuart, 29 Sept. 1774.
67. *Caledonian Mercury*, 31 May 1775.
68. NLS, MS 5028, James Parker to Charles Steuart, 17 May 1774.
69. *Edinburgh Evening Courant*, 10 Nov. 1777.
70. David Macpherson, *Annals of Commerce* (London, 1805), iii, 581.
71. GCA, Speirs Papers, TD 131/6/14, States of the Private Affairs of Alex. Speirs, Esq., Dec. 1770; TD 131/4, Ledger B, 1773–80, 61.
72. PRO, AO 12/56/288.
73. GCA, Journal of Baird, Hay and Co.; SRO, E 504/28/23–4; E 504/15/23–4.
74. GCA, Dunlop Papers, State of James Dunlop's subjects.
75. SRO, GD 247/151/3, State of the funds of Neil Jamieson.
76. Ibid., State of Robert Dunmore's subjects; SL, Court of Session Process 369/3, Petition of Robert Dunmore of Ballindalloch.
77. GCA, Speirs Papers, TD 131/13, Sederunt Book of Alexander Speirs' Trustees, 5; TD 131/5, Ledger C, 28.
78. P. J. Ford (ed.), *The Writings of Thomas Jefferson* (New York, 1892–9), iv, 348.
79. ML, Bogle MSS, Bundle 54, William Scott to George Bogle, 29 Nov. 1780.
80. SRO, Unextracted Process 1 Currie Dal B/5/8, Petition of Thomas Buchanan and Co. (1778). For similar comments see the testaments of George Kippen (SRO, CC 9/7/79), William French (SRO, CC 9/7/82/150) and John McCall (SRO, CC 9/7/79/650).
81. Reid, *Old Glasgow*, 173.
82. *Glasgow Mercury*, 25 July 1787.
83. SRO, General Register of Sasines 415/45; Particular Register of Sasines, Glasgow, 28/337.
84. PRO, AO 12/9/49–53; GCA, Speirs Papers, Ledger B.
85. Senex (J. M. Reid), *Glasgow Past and Present* (Glasgow, 1884), iii, 280.
86. GCA, B 10/5/8140, Agreement between Messrs Wilson and Brown.
87. SRO, GD 247/140, Information for Robert Dunmore and Co . . . 20 Dec. 1786, 10.
88. W. J. Addison (ed.), *The Matriculation Albums of the University of Glasgow, 1728–1858* (Glasgow, 1913), matric. no. 1420.
89. PRO, AO 12/9/59–61. See also SRO, E 504/15/33, where James Brown and Co. are shown as importing tobacco in 1781–2 from the Caribbean.
90. For the detailed evidence on this see Devine, 'Glasgow Merchants', ii, 557–61. James Pagan, *Sketch of the History of Glasgow* (Glasgow, 1847), 80, considered that there were 46 firms involved in the trade in 1774. The discrepancy may have occurred because Pagan occasionally lists as units individuals who were merely registering the cargoes in the customs accounts for their respective companies.
91. SRO, E 504/28/23–4; E 504/15/23–5.
92. Devine, 'Glasgow Merchants', ii, 557–61.
93. GCA, Probative Writs, B 10/12/4; Register of Deeds, B 10/5/8045.
94. SRO, Currie Dal Seq., B I/I, Buchanan, Hastie and Co. (1777).
95. Gourlay, *The Tobacco Period in Glasgow*, 65.
96. ML, Bogle MSS, xcl, John Brown's Recollections, i, Dec. 1777, 54.
97. *Edinburgh Evening Courant*, 13 June 1778.

98. For a sample of the sums lent see SRO, Register of Deeds, 223/411 Dal; 237/1/31 Dur; 223/1/198 Mack; 223/1/756 Mack.
99. SRO, Currie Dal Seq., B 1/1, Buchanan, Hastie and Co. (1777).
100. My italics. ML, Bogle MSS, xcl, John Brown's Recollections, i, 54.
101. Ibid., 54–55.
102. H. Hamilton, 'The Failure of the Ayr Bank, 1772', *Econ. Hist. Rev.*, 2nd ser., viii (1956), 405–17.
103. Hamilton, *Economic History*, 334; GCA, Dunlop Papers, State of the funds of James Dunlop, 23 Mar. 1793.
104. SRO, GD 237/143, Minutes of meeting of the sureties of Government for William McDowall . . ., 30 Nov. 1805, 7.
105. For 1728 see Robert Wodrow, *Analecta* (Maitland Club, 1842–3), iv, 10; for 1772 see Hamilton, *Economic History*, 319–25.
106. For evidence of 'mutuality' in the Liverpool merchant community see S. G. Checkland, 'Finance for the West Indies', *Econ. Hist. Rev.*, 2nd ser., x (1958), 461–9.
107. Devine, 'Glasgow Merchants', i, 1–16.
108. J. R. Anderson (ed.), *The Burgesses and Guild Brethren of Glasgow, 1751–1846* (Edinburgh, 1935).
109. Devine, 'Glasgow Merchants', i, 17–27.
110. Price, 'Rise of Glasgow', 308.
111. PRO, AO 12/9/53, GCA, Speirs Papers, TD 131/19/54; PRO AO 12/56/292; GCA, Probative Writs, B 10/12/4, B 10/12/9; *Glasgow Herald and Advertiser*, 7 Feb. 1812; PRO, AO 12/9/37, SRO, CE 60/1/10.
112. Devine, 'Glasgow Merchants', ii, 525–7.
113. Ibid., i, 34; ii, 519–20
114. R. H. Campbell, 'The Law and the Joint-Stock Company in Scotland', in Payne, *Studies in Scottish Business History*, 139–49.
115. GCA, Probative Writs, B 10/5/8123, Bond of co partnership between Messrs John McCall etc.
116. S. G. E. Lythe, *Economy of Scotland in its European Setting, 1550–1625* (Edinburgh, 1960), 126–7.
117. Devine, 'Glasgow Merchants', i, 118–23.
118. T. M. Devine, 'Problems of Glasgow West India Merchants during the American War of Independence', *Transport Hist.*, iv (1971), 266–304.
119. T. M. Devine, 'Glasgow Colonial Merchants and Land', in J. T. Ward and R. G. Wilson (ed.), *Land and Industry* (Newton Abbot, 1971).
120. Devine, 'Glasgow Merchants', ii, 316–409, 583–91.
121. Gourlay, *The Tobacco Period in Glasgow*, 65.
122. I. S. Harrell, *Loyalism in Virginia* (Durham, North Carolina, 1926), 95–100.
123. PRO, AO 12/124/187; AO 12/126/2207.
124. Robertson, 'Scottish Commerce', 124.
125. SRO, GD 247/59/Q/i, Walter Colquhoun to James Robinson, 7 June 1776; William Cunninghame to James Robinson, 13 Aug. 1776.
126. SL, Court of Session Process 190/13, Speirs, French and Co. to Robert Burton, 10 Mar. 1779.
127. Samuel Mordecai, *Richmond in Bygone Days* (privately printed, n.d.), ch. 2, passim.
128. *Caledonian Mercury*, 13 Jan. 1776.
129. Robertson, 'Scottish Commerce', 125–6.
130. *Edinburgh Evening Courant*, 22, 27 Jan. and 10, 24 Feb. 1776; SRO, CE 60/i/10, Collector, Greenock and Port Glasgow, to H. M. Board of Customs, 13 May 1778.
131. Calculated from *Glasgow Mercury*, 1777–83.

132. Devine, 'Problems of West India Merchants', 268.
133. Richard Champion, *Considerations on the Present Situation of Great Britain and the USA* (London, 1784), 14–15.
134. GCA, Probative Writs, B 10/12/9, Contract of Messrs. G. McCall and Co.
135. Price, 'Rise of Glasgow', 305.
136. The Glasgow Arms Bank, Ship Bank and Thistle Bank were all dominated by tobacco 'lords' at this time. Cf. [John Buchanan], *Banking in Glasgow during the Olden Time* (Glasgow, 1862), passim; GCA, B 10/5/8314 (Thistle Bank); GCA, Speirs Papers TD 131/4, Ledger B (Arms Bank). Moore, Carrick and Co. had two tobacco merchants in their first copartnership, GCA B 10/5/7904.
137. SRO, GD 247/59/Q/1, W. Cunninghame to J. Robinson, 4 Aug. 1775; SL, Court of Session Process, 190/13, G. Sherriff to Speirs, French and Co., 3 June 1775. The financial transactions of one Glasgow house in 1775–6 hardly suggests that it was under severe financial pressure. Neil Jamieson, chief factor of Glassford, Gordon and Co. in Virginia, was able to arrange a deal in early 1776 between Lord Dunmore, commander of the British forces in New York, and his parent firm in Glasgow. By this Dunmore was permitted to draw bills on Glassfords to the extent of £30,000 to pay for troop provisions. See PRO, AO 12/55/47.
138. Soltow, 'Scottish Traders', 95.
139. *Scots Magazine*, xxxviii, July 1776; *Caledonian Mercury*, 20 May 1775, 12 Sept. 1775.
140. Robertson, 'Scottish Commerce', 124–6.
141. Devine, 'Glasgow Merchants', i, 179–80.
142. For this, see David Syrett, *Shipping and the American War, 1775–1783* (London, 1970).
143. *Edinburgh Evening Courant*, 5 Sept. 1778; SRO, E 504/15/25–30; E 504/28/24–30; GCA, Town Council Minute Book, C 1/1/36/28–9, 37, 25 and 29 Dec. 1777; NLS, MS 8793, Letterbook E, Alexander Houston and Co. to David Macfarlane, 30 Nov. 1777.
144. SRO, CE 60/1/9, Account of quantities of tobacco held at Greenock and Port Glasgow reported by H.M. Board of Customs, 5 Aug. 1776.
145. 17 July 1776.
146. SL, Court of Session Process, Answers by Speirs, French and Co. . . ., 2.
147. GCA, Speirs Papers, TD 131/4, Ledger B; TD 131/5 Ledger C.
148. SRO, GD 247/140, Answers for William Cunninghame . . ., 5.
149. GCA, Journal of Baird, Hay and Co., 1772–7.
150. *Edinburgh Evening Courant*, 4 Sept. 1776.
151. Ibid., 20 Nov. 1776.
152. Ibid., 30 Aug. 1777.
153. MLS, MS 8759, A. Houston and Co. to John Turris, 9 Dec. 1777; SRO, E 504/28/28–9; *Caledonian Mercury*, 9 June 1777.
154. SRO, CE 60/1/9.

6

THE AMERICAN WAR OF INDEPENDENCE
AND SCOTTISH ECONOMIC HISTORY

There is a long-standing historiographical tradition that the American War of Independence was a turning-point in Scottish economic history. It is often asserted that the collapse of the lucrative tobacco trade was signalled by the outbreak of hostilities in 1775 and confirmed by the peace of 1783 when an independent United States was finally released from the constraints of the Navigation Laws. Since the old Virginia trade then seemed to have been eliminated, historians were concerned to explain what had become of the fortunes made from it, the capital employed in it and the enterprising merchants who had been responsible for its growth.[1] Until recently, for example, it was fashionable to explain the economic expansion of late eighteenth-century Scotland as the fruit of a transfer of capital from foreign commerce to domestic industry and, in particular, to the new cotton manufacture.[2] This view is certainly no longer favoured but the assumption persists that under-employed capital was available for new purposes after 1783: 'The collapse of the rich Glasgow tobacco trade after the War of American Independence is clearly associated with the movement of capital into cotton, coal and iron, though not usually in the form of crude transfers'.[3] Other writers have argued that an additional indication of diversification was the rise of the Caribbean trade when the American war came to an end, a development initiated by 'former' tobacco merchants striving to rebuild a new structure of colonial commerce on the ruins of the old.[4] On the face of it, Scotland's profitable associattion with the thirteen American colonies was to the end in 1775. Imports of tobacco, which stood at an enormous 45 million lb. in that year, rapidly shrivelled to 294,000 lb. in 1777 and only recovered marginally to 5 million lb. three years later.[5] But U.K. customs figures can give only a very partial indication of the condition and dimensions of tobacco commerce during the war. Imports of tobacco to Scottish ports after 1777 represented only that proportion of the commodity meant for home sale since no tobacco was re-exported to Europe from then until April 1783.[6] Yet, before the war, the &ottish tobacco business had been essentially based on re-export with over 98 per cent of imports being shipped, after paying duty at the Clyde, to France, Holland and the Gerrnan states. It is plain, therefore, that the supply of tobacco to U.K. domestic consumers not only persisted after 1775 but actually marginally increased in volume, possibly because Glasgow was now intervening in a sector previously controlled by London. There was an even more dramatic rise in the value of imports. Between 1770 and 1775 tobacco prices at the Clyde had averaged below 2d per lb. By Spring 1776 prices averaged between 8d and ls 6d and by December 1777 had climbed further to 2s per lb.[7] Average prices in 1781 were between 2s 5d and 2s 10d per lb.[8] What is equally clear is that merchant houses carefully controlled the level of importation into Scottish ports in order to retain these inflated price levels.[8a] This was a strategy made possible by the oligopolistic nature of the Glasgow trading structure and the high costs of wartime commerce which confirmed the dominance of the larger firms. The low imports of the period 1776 to 1783 were therefore as much a token of business sense as proof of an interruption in trade. Certainly in themselves they are not informative about the true nature of tobacco commerce during the war. This was based on a combination of the clandestine supply of consumer goods to the embattled thirteen colonies and the sale of tobacco direct to continental markets.

Scottish exports to the thirteen colonies did decline from an annual average of £298,922 (official sterling values) between 1770 and 1774 to £24,193 in 1775, £905 in 1776 and £35,553 in 1777.[9] But the bulk of the trade was channelled through other routes. The official value of Scottish exports to Canada rose from £4,742 in 1774 to £12,882 in 1775 and to £28,215 in 1777. Nova Scotia, of little account before the war, took goods to the value of £126,136 in 1777–78.[10] But Canada was not the preferred intermediate market for long. Of the ten ships freighting for North America at Clyde ports between January 1776 and April 1777, seven sailed for Nova Scotia and two for Quebec.[11] By the end of 1778, however, there had been a marked shift in the direction of trade towards ports in the thirteen colonies under British control. During the period January–April 1779, for instance, only two vessels sailed for Nova Scotia from the Clyde while seven freighted for such ports as New York, Philadelphia and Charlestown.[12] As a consequence Scottish exports direct to the thirteen colonies rose from £35,210 in 1778, at official values, to £62,626 in 1778, £171,317 in 1780 and £147,508 in 1781, although direct exports to Virginia and Maryland remained at zero between 1775 and 1782.[13]

Probably even more significant was the emergence of the West Indies as the focus of a clandestine commerce between North America and the United Kingdom in both tobacco and goods, a development which was associated with tobacco's new scarcity value in international trade. In an important sense, war came as a blessing, not as a disaster, for the tobacco merchant. The period 1772–75 had been one of glut crops and sluggish demand and only when direct trade was cut off did market prices move markedly in favour of the seller rather than the consumer.[14] Throughout most of the war, production in Virginia and Maryland averaged between one-half and one-third of the levels prevailing before 1775[15] while, on the European continent, demand for North American tobaccos proved only partially vulnerable to competition from indigenous substitutes.[16] At the same time, neither American nor European firms were able to organise a substantial transatlantic trade to satisfy this market. The blockade of the Royal Navy, the unfamiliarity of foreign sea captains with the Chesapeake and an intolerable rise in shipping costs combined to ensure its failure.[17] Ironically, however, war conditions accentuated not only the economic but also the strategic value of tobacco. Of all the major American export crops it lent itself more readily to development of trade with other powers, affording great possibilities of financing military operation and paying for much needed manufactured goods. The reality of the situation was, nevertheless, that only through utilising handled sales, could the American tobacco trade with Europe survive.

From the colonial side, the Caribbean was probably the most suitable area of exchange especially after France entered the war in 1778. The naval balance in the West Indies did not entirely favour the British; neutral Dutch (until 1780) and Danish islands there were obvious entrepots and the well-established provision trade with the thirteen colonies provided a ready-made channel for a rerouted tobacco commerce. Thus, the states of Virginia, Maryland and North Carolina began to maintain a regular correspondence with the mercantile firm of Harrison and Van Bibber in the West Indies. State authorities chartered ships, bought flour and tobacco, consigned the cargoes to their Caribbean representatives from whom they obtained in return military stores and consumer goods.[18] The principal centres of trade were the Dutch colony of St Eustatius and later, when Holland entered the war, the Danish islands of St Thomas and St Croix. When Admiral Rodney's forces took St Eustatius in 1781, John Adams saw the irony: 'There was found in that island a greater quantity of property belonging to the British themselves than to the French, Dutch or Americans. They have broken up a trade which was more advantageous to them than any of their enemies as it was a channel through which British manufactures were conveyed to North America'.[19]

Scottish merchants were able to enter this sector in a vigorous fashion. The early years of the American war and, in particular, the financial crisis of 1778, had not ruined their fortunes. Between 1775 and 1785 seven Glasgow tobacco firms did fail but their demise was not a catastrophic blow to Scottish enterprise. Only one bankrupt concern was numbered among the eleven large companies which shipped more than 500 hogsheads of tobacco in the years immediately before the war. Instead, four of the seven failures occurred among the ten firms which imported least.[20] Indeed, in the first two years of war the handful of great syndicates which controlled the Clyde tobacco business were able to achieve windfall gains which left them flush with capital and well able to adjust to the circuitous routes and high operating costs of Caribbean commerce at the time.

The direct purchase method of the Glasgow traders was very well suited to acquiring cargoes quickly in Virginia and Maryland during the crisis months of the summer of 1775. Evidence from the upper James River valley indicates that English merchants shipped approximately the same amount of tobacco in 1775 as in 1774.[21] Yet the larger Scottish firms managed to substantially increase their share. Cunninghame shipments rose from 1,654 hogsheads in 1774 to 1,771 in 1775; Speirs, Bowman and Co. cornered the lion's share, their exports rising from 4,853 hogsheads in 1774 to 5,451 the following year. As a result, Glasgow probably managed to secure more of the crucial 1775 crop than any other port in the United Kingdom.[22] In addition, the relatively sluggish demand of 1773–75 and the glut harvests of the same period meant that they had unsold stocks on hand anyway. The situation was even more favourable because the purchasing agents of the French monopoly in Scotland had cut back their orders before the war in an effort to push prices down.[23] Thus when the American ports were closed they were left in an exposed position with insufficient stocks and the possibility of an interrupted supply. Finally, the Glasgow houses benefited from the easy availability of credit in 1775–76. Unlike most wars, the early stages of the rebellion did not impair confidence in U.K. money markets.[24] So importers were not compelled to release their stocks because of pressure on credit. Instead those with sufficient nerve could await the anticipated rise in prices. Thus although only 1,521 hogsheads were landed at Clyde ports in 1776, there still remained 14,404 hogsheads, or about 25 per cent of the 1775 importation, in cellars there in August 1776.[25] In early 1777 one company estimated that there were 7,000 hogsheads at Port Glasgow and a further 8,000 at ports abroad 'belonging to this place and the whole quantity at market (in Europe) is reckoned to be about 30,000 hogsheads, so that half of the quantity at market belongs to this place'.[26] Inevitably, therefore, several of the great Glasgow houses did very well out of the ensuing bonanza as prices rose from around 3d per lb. in the autumn of 1775 to 10d by late 1776.[27] It was in this period that the financial resources became available to support investment in the Caribbean sector after 1778.

Not only did the larger merchant firms have the capital after 1775–77, they were also familiar with the West Indies. Some traders had always been more interested in sugar from that area than tobacco from West Virginia. Even companies normally more concerned with tobacco frequently made 'adventures' there when sugar prices merited it or when tobacco markets were sluggish. Furthermore, American traders had to retain correspondents to supply West Indian produce to their store outlets in Virginia and Maryland. But during the period 1775–77 contacts were sporadic because it was only when France entered the war that the commercial world finally adjusted to the possibility of an extended disruption in peacetime trade patterns.[29] By the end of 1777 the rerouting of Scottish exports via the Caribbean becomes apparent. Exports of plain linen to Virginia dropped from 700,000 yards in 1772 to zero in 1777, while exports to Jamaica rose rapidly from 250,000 yards in 1772 to 760,000 in 1777.[30] At the same time, Glasgow houses began to embark in the clandestine tobacco trade on a considerable scale. James Ritchie and Co., a medium sized concern, despatched an agent to the West Indies, gave him 'unlimited credit' and ordered him to engage in the purchase of tobacco. In 1779–80 he was spending £4,000 carrying out these directions.[31] Speirs, French and Co., one of the largest Scottish ventures, had, by 1781, secured a dominant position in this trade. By that date, their agent, Robert Burton, was reckoned one of the greatest merchants in the Caribbean. His annual outlay was an enormous £50,000 and he was dealing direct with European ports such as Hamburg, Ostend and Amsterdam in tobacco and employing neutral vessels as carriers. Manufactured goods came most often directly from London and the entire business was financed by Thomas Coutts and Sons, the Anglo-Scottish banking firm in the capital, with accounts later charged to Speirs, Murdoch and Co., bankers in Glasgow.[32]

Perhaps, in one sense, it might appear that the coming of peace in 1783 would pose a greater problem for Scottish tobacco merchants than the outbreak of war had done in 1775. Under the new relationship the independent United States were no longer compelled to send their export staples first to the United Kingdom, whatever their ultimate destination, or to acquire manufactures only from British traders. In other words, the legislative framework of the old tobacco entrepôt trade had been dismantled. In consequence, Scottish imports of tobacco in the following decade never reached more than a quarter of pre-war levels.

But when looked at in the round the overall commercial connection between Scotland and the United States after 1783 was much stronger. Scottish exports direct to the U.S.A. quickly regained the levels prevailing before 1775. Official sterling values of exports between 1784 and 1788 averaged £243,244 per annum compared with £222,497 from 1765 to 1769, and £298,922 between 1770 and 1774.[33] Moreover, while the number of vessels from the former thirteen colonies to Clyde ports fell from 136 to 84 between 1772 and 1790 (a drop of 38 per cent), the number to the U.S.A. only diminished from 103 to 95 (a drop of 11 per cent).[34] In addition, Glasgow merchants managed to maintain a substantial role in the American tobacco trade to Europe. The city's trading houses described four years after the war ended how the supply of American tobacco to the Continent employed 200–250 ships of all nations. But more than three-quarters of this number were British owned and, even more significantly, at least two-thirds of the tobacco cargoes carried in them were on British account.[35] Plainly, therefore, Scottish customs data can give only a partial indication of the survival of the Scottish tobacco trade after 1783.

Because, when peace came, the Scots factors returned in force to Virginia and Maryland. By the middle of 1784, on one estimate, there were 80 stores in Petersburg and as many in Richmond.[36] In Georgetown the Scots controlled 17 or 18 outlets.[37] As one contemporary remarked: 'the Glasgow goods continue still to be much liked . . . and Glasgow may yet have a great share of the trade'.[38] Both long-established and new organisations were involved in the revivial. The three most famous 'tobacco lords' of an earlier generation, Alexander Speirs, John Glassford and William Cunninghame had all disappeared from the scene. Cunninghame seems to have retired from a dominant role in his firm but remained a sleeping partner in Robert Dunmore and Co.[39] Both Speirs and Glassford had died before peace was signed. Yet their three great syndicates survived and continued to play a major role in the Chesapeake after the war. Robert Findlay, Cunninghame's kinsman and protégé, became associated with the Hopkirks and a branch of the Buchanan clan to form Findlay, Hopkirk and Co., while the Speirs and Glassford organisations continued under the leadership of men long experienced in the trade before 1775.[45] In 1785, these three groupings, together with Colin Dunlop and Sons and Corbett, Russell and Co. shipped more than 90 per cent of the Clyde's tobacco imports.[41] In the Chesapeake, therefore, Scottish business ability once again became a factor of consequence. In Petersburg in 1784, 'Messrs Donalds have been grasping all the trade' and, a year later, Patrick Henry complained to Thomas Jefferson that Scottish hegemony had not come to an end: 'We are much disappointed in our expectations of French and Dutch traders rivalling the British here. The latter engross the greatest share of our trade, and was it not the Irish bid up for our produce, the Scotch would soon be on their former footing'.[42]

The Glasgow merchants were very eager to re-establish themselves in order to recover the enormous pre-war debt (reckoned in 1778 at over £1,300,000) owed them by American planters.[43] Ironically, however, the only practical way of doing so was to provide further credit and consumer goods to their former clients in order to support a revival in tobacco cultivation. Indeed the Scottish firms were more necessary than ever to the economies of Virginia, Maryland and North Carolina after 1783. Put simply the British commercial role in North America had begun to function independently of the Navigation Laws by the later eighteenth century. Whatever changes had occurred in the political sphere a powerful alien merchant class remained vital to the efficient disposal of the produce of the agrarian economy in European markets. For investment capital planters still depended on UK sources and, moreover, the consumer habits of generations could not be broken by the accident of constitutional change. After 1783 it was only the British merchants who could supply the range of commodities in demand, at attractive cost and on long credit.[44] If anything, in fact, in the era of the Industrial Revolution, British goods were even more competitive than before. Therefore, seven years after independence was granted to the former colonies, their commercial dependency lingered on: '. . . there are not imported into all the United States from Europe five thousand pounds value of manufactures but what comes from Britain; the French and the Dutch are quite drove out of the trade by the superior quality and cheapness of British articles'.[45]

There was thus no need or desire for Scottish disinvestment from the American sector. Certainly, over the 1780s and 1790s the Scottish economy expanded rapidly and Scottish involvement in the West Indies trade was consolidated but neither of these two developments were associated with changes in the tobacco trade. Tobacco merchants invested in industry after 1783 but they had always done so and there is no evidence of an acceleration in the diversion of trade resources to the domestic economy. Between 1780 and 1795 colonial merchants took up shares in 21 new industrial partnerships but between 1796 and 1815 this figure declined to nine. Moreover, colonial merchants supplied at most about 17 per cent of the total capital in the Scottish cotton manufacture in 1795 but of the 25 merchants concerned, 17 were primarily involved in Caribbean rather than North American commerce.[46] The fact that needs to be stressed surely is the new strength and maturity of the Scottish economy which allowed both a renewal of the American link and substantial investment in indigenous industry.

Similarly, after 1783, the growth in the West Indies trade was related to industrial needs for cotton and increased consumer demand for sugar rather than to new strategies by tobacco firms. Although these concerns were associated with the Caribbean during the war this was primarily because they sought to continue the American connection. When peace came, the importation of West India commodities was controlled by companies long experienced in that trade (such as Alexander Houston and Co. and Somervell, Gordon and Co.) or by relatively new concerns with no previous interests in tobacco commerce. The link between the American and Caribbean sectors remained close but it was based on the diversified nature of the Glasgow business community which allowed wealthy merchants, long before 1775, to retain commitments in both areas.[47]

NOTES

1. M. L. Robertson, 'Scottish Commerce and the American War of Independence', *Economic History Review*, 2nd ser., IX (1950), 123–31; B. Crispin, 'Clyde Shipping and the American War', *Scottish Historical Review*, 41 (1962), 124–133.
2. For the older view see H. Hamilton, *The Industrial Revolution in Scotland* (Oxford, 1932), 121: L. G. Saunders, *Scottish Democracy: the Social and Intellectual Background* (Edinburgh, 1950), 98. For the modern reassessment, Robertson, *loc cit, 130*; R. H. Campbell, *Scotland Since 1707* (Oxford, 1965), 40; S. G. E. Lythe and J. Butt, *An Economic History of Scotland 1100–1939* (Glasgow, 1975), 147–8.
3. B. F. Duckham, *History of the Scottish Coal Industry* (Newton Abbot, 1970), 179–80.
4. Campbell, *op cit, 78*; Crispin, *loc cit*, 128–9; A. Slaven. *The Development of the West of Scotland* (London, 1975), 6; Lythe and Butt. *op cit*, 147–8.
5. Public Record Office (PRO), Customs 14.
6. Scottish Record Office (SRO). Collector's Quarterly Accounts. Port Glasgow and Greenock, E.504/28/22–36; E.504/504/15/22–38.
7. SRO, Oswald Papers, GD 213/53, John Anderson to Richard Oswald, 22 September 1776. 4 October 1776: *Edinburgh Evening Courant*, 20 November 1776: *Caledonian Mercury*, 9 June 1777.
8. Library of Congress, Washington (LC), Dunlop Family Papers, Box I. James

Ritchie and Co. to James Dunlop, 28 April 1780; Henry Ritchie to James Dunlop, 2 November 1781 (I am very grateful to Mr Stuart Butler for kindly lending me his transcripts of these papers): Strathclyde Regional Archives (SRA), Speirs Papers. TD131/9. Alexander Speirs to J. G. Martens, 11 October 1781.

8a. LC, Dunlop Family Papers, James Ritchie and Co. to James Dunlop, 29 January 1779.

9. Jacob M. Price, 'New Time Series for Scotland's and Britain's Trade with the Thirteen Colonies and States, 1740 to 1791', *William and Mary Quarterly*, 32, 2 (April 1975), 307–325.

10. PRO, Customs 14; SRO, RH 20/22, Customs Account Book, Newfoundland, 1771–85.

11. SRO, Customs Accounts, E,504/28/29–35; E.504/15/28–37.

12. Ibid.

13. Price, *loc cit*, 320–1.

14. SRO, GD 247/59/Q/1, William Cunninghame to John Turner, 18 July 1774; to J. Robinson, 13 August 1774; to Thomas Gordon, 15 July 1774; Sir William Forbes, *Memoirs of a Banking House* (London, 1860), 45–6.

15. R. W. Coakley, 'Virginia Commerce during the American Revolution', University of Virginia, PhD (1949), 380.

16. Jacob M. Price, *France and the Chesapeake* (Michigan, 1972).

17. Coakley, *op cit*, 166–7, 335.

18. L. C. Gray, *History of Agriculture in the Southern United States to 1860* (Washington, 1933), II, 578; David Macpherson, *Annals of Commerce, Manufactures, Fisheries and Navigation* (London, 1805), III, 719–20.

19. Quoted in C. B. Coulter, 'The Virginia Merchant' (University of Princeton PhD, 1944), 152. In fact official acquiescence had been given a year earlier when the U.K. Parliament legalised the trade in American tobacco from foreign islands in the West Indies and placed a special duty on it (20 Geo. III, c 39).

20. This is a brief summary of T. M. Devine's 'Glasgow Merchants and the Collapse of the Tobacco Trade, 1775–83', *Scott. Hist. Rev. LII* (1973), 50–74.

21. R. P. Thomson, 'The Tobacco Export of the Upper James River Naval District 1773–75', *William and Mary Quarterly*, 3rd ser., XVIII (1961).

22. T. M. Devine, *The Tobacco Lords* (Edinburgh, 1975), 108–9.

23. SRO, GD 247/59/Q/1, William Cunninghame to John Turner, 18 July 1774; to James Robinson, 13 August 1774; Price, *op cit*, 646.

24. Robertson, *loc cit*, 123.

25. SRO, CE 60/1/9, Account of quantities of tobacco in the hands of each importer, 5 August 1776.

26. SRO, Oswald Papers, GD 213/53, John Anderson to Richard Oswald, 18 February 1777.

27. Ibid, John Anderson to Richard Oswald, 1 February 1776; *Edinburgh Evening Courant*, 4 September 1776.

28. Ibid, John Anderson to Richard Oswald, 22 September 1776. For details of mercantile profit at this time see Devine, *op cit*, 110–111.

29. Devine, *op cit*, 106–7.

30. PRO, Customs 14.

31. LC, James Dunlop Family Papers, Hugh Wylie to James Dunlop, 22 December 1779; James Anderson to James Dunlop, 15 March 1780.

32. Strathclyde Regional Archives (SRA), Speirs Papers, TD 131/9, Letterbook of Alexander Speirs, *passim*.

33. Price, *loc cit*, 320–321.

34. SRO, Collector's Quarterly Accounts, E.504/28; E.504/15, Port Glasgow and Greenock.

35. PRO, B.T.6/20, Answers to the several questions respecting the commerce and shipping between Great Britain and the United States of America, 16 December 1789.

36. LC, James Dunlop Family Papers, James Dunlop sen. to James Dunlop, 20 July 1784.

37. Ibid, Thomas Montgomerie to James Dunlop, 10 August 1784.

38. Ibid, David Buchanan to James Dunlop, 5 April 1784.

39. SRO, GD 247/140 (Copy) Memorial and queries for the Trustees of the late Mr Cunninghame of Lainshaw.

40. SRO, RH 15/2237, Contract of Findlay Hopkirk and Co., S.R.A., TD 131/3, Sederunt Book of the Trustees of Alexander Speirs of Elderslie, 1782–85. *Glasgow Advertiser*, 22 January 1790; *Glasgow Mercury*, 19 January 1790.

41. SRO, E.504/28/38–40, Port Glasgow Customs Accounts, October 1784–April 1786.

42. LC, James Dunlop Family Papers, James Dunlop sen. to James Dunlop, 16 September 1784. Patrick Henry to Thomas Jefferson, 10 September 1785 in *Jefferson Papers*, VII, 509.

43. For the figure quoted as the pre-war debt see SRA, Speirs Papers, TD 131/10–12, Diary of Alexander Speirs, 2 March 1778. For company motivation see PRO, AO 12/9/35; LC, James Dunlop Family Papers, Box 6. Instructions from Messrs James Ritchie and Co., 31 March 1784; SRA, Speirs Papers TD 131/13, Sederunt Book of the Trustees of Alexander Speirs of Elderslie, 8–9.

44. Price, *op cit*, 728–31; Gray, *op cit*, II, 597; W. A. Low, 'Merchant and Planter Relations in Post-Revolutionary Virginia, 1783–1789', *Virginia Magazine of History and Biography*, 61 (1953), 208–17.

45. Extract of a letter from Philadelphia, 10 October 1789, in *Glasgow Advertiser*, 8 January 1790.

46. T. M. Devine, 'The Colonial Trades and Industrial Investment in Scotland, 1700–1815', *Econ. Hist. Rev.*, 2nd ser., XXIX (1976), 1–13.

47. Devine, *op cit*, 165–7.

7

THE MAKING OF INDUSTRIAL AND
URBAN SOCIETY: SCOTLAND 1780–1840

Scottish society before the later eighteenth century was far from static. The commercialisation of agriculture both in the Highlands and Lowlands was advancing as proprietors began increasingly to extract more revenue from their estates to support higher standards of living. Foreign trade, especially the Atlantic sector in general and Glasgow commerce in particular, experienced precocious growth from the 1740s. The significance of urban life became greater, not simply because of the expansion of the larger burghs of Glasgow, Edinburgh and Aberdeen but also as a result of the proliferation of smaller regional and local centres. But in a structural sense, Scotland was still relatively unchanged. Such economic expansion as did occur tended to develop along existing lines: for the most part it was relatively sluggish and the overwhelming predominance of agriculture and rural society remained. As late as 1750 probably no more than one Scot in eight was a townsman.

From the last quarter of the eighteenth century there was a significant change of gear. Economic growth not only became faster but was sustained on a broad front. One estimate suggests that the volume of grain brought to market doubled and animal products increased six-fold between 1740 and the 1820s. Exports rose nine-fold from 1785 to 1835 and the relative share of manufactures in this total consistently increased. Linen output climbed from over 12 million yards in the 1770s to over 30 million yards by the early 1820s. One clear sign that Scotland was a much wealthier society as a consequence of this huge increase in production and productive capacity was its ability to absorb increasing numbers of people and to feed and employ them. Webster put Scottish population at over 1,265,000 in the 1750s. By 1801 this had risen to over 1,600,000 and by 1831 to well over 2 million. Growth had occurred before but this was a rate never equalled in previous periods. More importantly, it was sustained expansion which was not impeded as it had been in the past by limitations on food supply or in employment opportunities.

It is, of course, important to stress that there was no complete break with the past. By 1830 most Scots still worked in a rural environment as their ancestors had done. The governing class of the old society, the greater landowners and their kin and associates in the legal profession, still dominated despite the active criticism of the reform movements of the 1790s and during the years after the end of the Napoleonic Wars. Furthermore, industrial expansion before 1830 was narrowly based on cotton, linen and woollen textiles and growth in coal-mining and iron production was much more sluggish. Sir John Sinclair confidently estimated that over ninety per cent of Scottish industrial workers in the early nineteenth century were occupied in the textile sector. The process of industrialisation was therefore far from complete in 1830. The great late-nineteenth-century staples of coal, iron, engineering and shipbuilding were all underdeveloped. Their phase of vigorous expansion lay in the future. Moreover, technical change, the substitution of machinery for human effort, was mainly confined to some of the textile, chemical and metal industries. In consequence, the factory, the classic symbol of the new age, had not yet become the characteristic working environment. Most Scots still laboured on the land, in the home, or in the workshop rather than in the new industrial complexes each employing several hundred people.

Yet, recognition of these continuities should not obscure the fundamental changes in Scottish life which took place during this period and which do suggest a major and decisive break with the past. It is true that as late as 1821 as many as two Scots in three still lived and worked on the farm, on the croft, in the country village or in the small town. However, their way of life was quite different from that of their forebears. Before the middle decades of the eighteenth century there were few entirely landless groups in the Scottish countryside. Rural tradesmen normally had a patch of land, much of the agricultural labour force was recruited from cottar families, small tenants practising subsistence husbandry proliferated in many areas, and even 'landless' farm servants were reared in peasant households before they were hired in their teenage years by larger farmers. On the very eve of the great movement towards agrarian reorganisation the vast majority of rural dwellers in Scotland depended to a greater or lesser extent on access to land. In that sense, there was a closer resemblance to the characteristic peasant societies of continental Europe than to many areas in England where the 'modern' social structure of landowners, farmers and landless labourers was already in place by the early eighteenth century.

That system was imposed on Lowland Scotland over a much shorter period of time. From the 1780s the pace of agrarian change quickened as small farms were reorganised and consolidated, fields enclosed and the subtenantry, the single most numerous social class in the old world, rapidly eliminated. The process occurred with little protest and perhaps for that reason its scale and speed has not been sufficiently recognised. Over two or three generations the traditional peasant society was removed and a new rural social order which survived into the twentieth century established in its place. This was radically different from that of the past in the sense that the vast majority of those who worked in Lowland agriculture no longer depended on subsistence plots to survive but rather on their capacity to sell their labour power to employing farmers in the market place.

At first glance, the pattern in the Highlands seems to be somewhat different. The connection between the people and the land which was severed in the Lowlands was maintained in many parts of the region and above all along the western mainland and throughout the inner and outer Hebrides. There the indigenous population continued to eke out a living on crofts, smallholdings and subtenancies through a combination of potato cultivation, cattle rearing, subsistence fishing and temporary migration. Ironically, however, social change in this region was probably more traumatic and cataclysmic than anywhere in the Lowlands. The old military society, already in decline in the early eighteenth century, was replaced by an entirely new order in which the land and the population of the region were subordinated to the revenue needs of the proprietors and the huge increase in external demand from the Lowlands and England for such Highland products as kelp, fish, cattle, wool, mutton, whisky, timber and slate. These forces of commercialisation produced two major phases of Clearance. In the first period the communal farming settlements or *bailetoun* were dissolved between c. 1730 and 1820 and replaced by a structure of individual smallholdings or crofts in which the people worked the land but also produced cash commodities for southern markets. After the end of the Napoleonic Wars, however, a collapse in kelp markets, stagnation in fishing and a slump in cattle prices ushered in the second phase of Clearance as proprietors laid down more territory for sheep farming. This led to an even more radical shift in the distribution of population, increases in eviction and an acceleration in the rate of migration and emigration. Unlike the pattern in the Lowland countryside economic change in the Highlands provoked embittered if sporadic protest and much social alienation. Yet both regions were subjected to the same fundamental pressures on social relationships and social structure: the new revenue demands of the landowners, the ideological forces of 'improvement' and above all, the influence of burgeoning markets for food, raw materials and labour.

The principal source of this market growth was the Scottish towns and cities. Recent research has established a truly remarkable rate of urban expansion from the later eighteenth century. In 1700, Scotland was tenth in a league table of 'urbanised societies' in Europe as measured by the proportion of population living in towns of 10,000 inhabitants or above. By the 1750s it had risen to seventh and by 1800 was already one of the five most urbanised countries in western Europe, alongside England, the Netherlands, Belgium and northern Italy. But Scotland had achieved this position over a much shorter period of time. Furthermore, the process of urbanisation continued to accelerate, so that by the 1850s more Scots lived in large towns than in any other European society with the single exception of England. This was indeed a fundamental social transformation even when it is recognised that the majority of the Scottish population still remained rural dwellers. The rapidly expanding urban areas were no longer simply adjuncts to an overwhelmingly rural society as they had been in the early eighteenth century. Rather they had become the dynamic centres of economic change. The lives of people in the countryside were altered by the needs of the teeming cities for foods and raw materials and the impact these needs and the sale of their products had on the social structure of countless communities in the Highlands and Lowlands.

A number of factors help to explain this extraordinary rate of town growth. It was assisted by the changes in Scottish agriculture already surveyed which through reorganisation of farms, more efficient use of labour and improved rotations contributed to an increase in food supply which allowed the urban masses to be fed. Again, as the movement of goods and raw materials expanded, towns had to develop as centres of exchange, providing the commercial, financial and legal services now required by the market economy. Thus Perth, Haddington, Ayr, Dumfries and Stirling owed much of their growth in this period to the requirements of their rural hinterlands for such facilities. Urban development was also influenced by foreign trade. In the eighteenth century, Scotland was in a superb geographical position to exploit the changing direction of international commerce from the Mediterranean to the Atlantic. This momentous alteration in transcontinental trade was a highly dynamic factor in port development along the whole western coast of Europe from Cork to Cadiz. Scotland was virtually at the crossroads of the new system and the Clyde ports grew rapidly to become great centres for the importation of tobacco, sugar and raw cotton. It was no coincidence that in the period after 1780 four of the five fastest-growing towns in Scotland were in the Clyde basin. Greenock may be taken as the archetypal port town, expanding from a population of 2,000 in 1700 to 17,500 in 1831.

Yet, in the long run, the most critical factor was the expansion of manufacturing industry. Of the thirteen largest towns in early nineteenth century Scotland, five at least trebled their population size between c. 1750 and 1821. In addition to Greenock these were Glasgow (from 31,700 to 147,000), Paisley (6,800 to 47,000), Kilmarnock (4,400 to 12,700) and Falkirk (3,900 to 11,500). Greenock apart all these towns depended directly or indirectly on manufacturing industry. It was clearly industrial concentration in towns which set the pace of Scottish urbanisation.

But the process was not inevitable in the short run. Indeed, by the 1830os, most industrial activity was still located in the village or the small town rather than the large city and this pattern helps to explain why most Scots still lived and worked in a rural setting at that date. The water-powered cotton factories, coal-mining and pig-iron manufacture were all in the country. In the long run, however, there were obvious advantages in industrial concentration in towns; firms saved the cost of providing accommodation and other facilities for their workers from their own resources; they were also guaranteed access to a huge pool of labour; transport costs between sources of supply, finishing trades and repair shops could be markedly reduced or virtually eliminated by the close proximity of complementary economic activities. In cotton-spinning, and eventually in other textile industries, steam power encouraged industrial settlements on the coalfields and removed the one major obstacle which had previously limited the expansion of manufacturing in the large towns. Glasgow provides the most dramatic case of the pattern of change. In 1795 the city had eleven cotton-spinning complexes but rural Renfrewshire had twelve. The basic need to have secure access to water power obviously diluted Glasgow's other attractions as a potential centre of textile production. However, the adoption of steam-based technology after 1800 allowed expansion on a massive scale in the city and its immediate environs. By 1839, out of 192 cotton mills in Scotland, 98 were in or near Glasgow.

Urban growth at such speed suggests a remarkably high rate of human mobility because the towns grew primarily through inward migration. In most areas of western Europe, most people lived and died in the parishes of their birth. But in Scotland, temporary and permanent migration was the norm rather than the exception. Only 47 per cent of the inhabitants of the ten principal Scottish towns in 1851 had been born in them. The majority of migrants were young adults who had travelled relatively short distances within the Lowlands. Increasingly, however, Highland movement, especially to the western towns, became significant though it was soon quickly dwarfed by Irish immigration. Population pressure, difficulties in the Ulster linen industry and ease of access to the Clyde ports afforded by the new steamships all contributed to this. By 1841 it has been estimated that almost a quarter of the people of the western Lowlands were of Irish extraction. The majority were Catholic but a substantial minority were Ulster Protestants. The scale of the movement, indigenous Scottish anti-Catholicism and the transfer of ancient rivalries from Ireland fuelled sectarian tensions in the developing urban society.

It was primarily because of the sheer speed of urban expansion and inward migration that the larger towns steadily became more lethal in this period. The contemporary structures of sanitation and waste disposal were often simply overwhelmed in a rising tide of humanity. Scottish conditions were worse than elsewhere in Britain. As Edwin Chadwick put it in 1842: 'There is evidence to prove that the mortality from fever is greater in Glasgow, Edinburgh and Dundee than in the most crowded towns in England.' By that decade, urban Scotland was approaching a social crisis of unprecedented proportions. Meaningful efforts at reform were constrained by contemporary ideologies which blamed poverty and squalor on weaknesses of character rather than on environmental pressures. The urban society had been born but not until the second half of the nineteenth century were its problems addressed in a serious way.

The rapid expansion of industry and the larger towns also inevitably imposed immense strain on the institutions of government. The Scottish political system was notoriously unrepresentative and dominated by the greater landed families and their associates. In 1831, one Englishman in thirty could vote, while at the same date only one Scot in six hundred was enfranchised. About three thousand 'county freeholders' voted for the thirty county members and the fifteen burgh members were elected by the oligarchic town councils. The system reflected the belief that only the small élite who possessed a great deal of property in land, those who had a major stake in the country, could be trusted to govern the country with prudence. However, as industrial and urban wealth increased, the existing political structure seemed to many to be both unjust, corrupt and anachronistic. From the later eighteenth century it was confronted by a series of challenges both from those members of the propertied classes who were outside the 'political nation' and, even more ominously, from the common people who achieved in this period a new awareness of their democratic rights.

There had been a movement for burgh reform in the 1780s and this was followed in 1792–3 by a short-lived but significant campaign for electoral reform stimulated by the French Revolution. The Societies of Friends of the People were eventually crushed by draconian government action and their leadership sentenced to transportation to Botany Bay. Not until after the Napoleonic Wars did the reform movement recover enough confidence to mount a fresh challenge. Huge public meetings, especially in the west of Scotland, the development of a radical press, the interaction between trade unions and reform groups and closer contact with English radicals culminated in the so-called 'Radical War' of 1820. Economic distress and the new political ideas of the time fused to produce a major political crisis. For several days, an estimated 50,000 in the industrial west stopped work and some groups openly carried weapons and took part in military drill. In the event, the threatened revolution did not take place and the few skirmishes which occurred were easily won by the army. Poor planning, the failure of English radicals to respond and the loyalty of the Scottish propertied classes and the military were all important factors in explaining the victory of government. But the events of 1820 were nevertheless significant in demonstrating a new if ephemeral collectivity of purpose among the working classes, the alienation of many from the existing system and the widespread popularity of democratic ideas.

All this represented a significant change from the middle decades of the eighteenth century. But the reform movements were not powerful enough to force any fundamental alteration in the political structure. Even the Reform Act of 1832 can be seen as a means of perpetuating old authority by partially extending the franchise within the propertied classes. It was not so much a resounding defeat for the existing regime as a further demonstration of its essential resilience and capacity for survival. Despite structural changes in both economy and society, Scotland in the 1830s was still dominated by the same social class who had held power in the old world. To some extent this was because many of the economic changes of the period strengthened the material foundations of landed political supremacy. Estate rentals rose in the wake of urban demand for foods, raw materials and fuel. Much industrial activity, especially in mining, metal-working and textile processing, took place in the country village or small town rather than the large city. Furthermore, there was no massive social or ideological gulf between urban and rural elites. They shared a common faith in property ownership as the best guarantee of political stability. They were both committed to the ideals of improvement and economic progress. Many landowners were in the vanguard of the process of material transformation not only as agriculturalists but also as the founders of industrial villages and as partners in banks, road and canal companies and a host of manufacturing ventures. The Scottish aristocracy may have been political conservatives but they were also economic revolutionaries who went with the grain of the developing capitalist order. The old political elite therefore demonstrated considerable flexibility in the field of economic legislation. It was the unreformed political system which presided over the removal from the statute book of such paternalistic laws as the controls on wages and prices. This not only helped to accelerate the complete dominance of market forces; it also illustrates the capacity of the traditional rulers of Scottish society to adapt to the new era and, by so doing, to perpetuate their power.

In the final analysis, however, old authority survived because no effective alliance of the unenfranchised developed to threaten it. Temporary accommodation between the middle classes and the labouring classes, as 1792–3 and 1816–19 revealed, was possible. But no enduring revolutionary combination was likely to emerge. Many middle class groups feared the threat to property implicit in democratic demands and were increasingly alarmed by the menace of popular unrest and the danger of anarchy. Ironically, the French Revolution at once stimulated bourgeois interest in reform and at the same time crystallised deep concerns about the profound social instability which might follow in the wake of radical political change. The Scottish middle classes therefore preferred to flirt with reform rather than commit themselves to it as a basic ideal. The working classes increasingly turned to it as a means of alleviating their social and economic difficulties. But they also were split along ethnic, occupational and ideological lines. A common front was difficult to achieve and virtually impossible to maintain for long. The old political order therefore emerged from the first phase of Scottish industrialisation remarkably unscathed. The power of the landed classes had been modified but was not yet supplanted.

8

SCOTTISH URBANISATION

The Process of Urbanisation

Town growth in the period covered by this volume forms a bridge between the old world of rural Scotland and the urbanised society of the later nineteenth century and modern times. In 1830 urban development had still some way to go before it began to ebb. But its acceleration from the middle decades of the eighteenth century had been dramatic and is perhaps only underestimated through knowledge of the continued expansion which was to occur later in the nineteenth century. While historians recognise the scale and speed of town growth between 1760 and 1830, they differ in their interpretation of its significance. One writer claims that as early as 1800, 'Scotland was well on the way to becoming an urban society'. Yet another can assert that as late as 1820, '. . . the farm and the village were still not replaced as the typical social environment in which a man spent his life'.[1]

In part the disagreement derives from different definitions of what constitutes a 'town'. Some authorities regard a population of 1,000 as the minimum size while others prefer a threshold of 5,000 or even 10,000. But the dispute is also caused by the absence, until recently, of a comparative perspective. The extent to which Scotland was an 'urbanised society' by 1830 depends not on absolute measures alone but on the proportion of the population living in large towns relative to patterns in other European societies. New work by Jan de Vries on European urbanisation since the sixteenth century enables the Scottish experience for the first time to be examined in an international context and its significance evaluated against standards of comparison drawn from the example of several continental societies.[2] The de Vries team collected data from sixteen European 'territories' over the period 1500 to 1850 in order to measure the proportion of total population in each area at fifty-year intervals who lived in towns with over 10,000 inhabitants. Complete precision in all aspects of such an ambitious project is obviously impossible. The reliability of the data varies significantly over time and between different countries. For instance, as far as Scotland is concerned, there is real difficulty in establishing the *size* of the national population before c. 1700, even before any attempt can be made to estimate the *proportion* living in an urbanised environment. Yet the figures can indicate the general direction of urbanisation over the long run and are useful for determining significant differences between countries. The data are also most solid for the period after 1750 which is the primary focus of the present discussion.

Table I makes fascinating reading for a Scottish social historian. The numerical data confirm the conventional view that in the seventeenth century and in the early part of the eighteenth, Scotland was a predominantly rural society. In a league of 'urbanised societies' (as measured by the percentage of total population inhabiting towns of 10,000 or over), Scotland was eleventh out of sixteen in both 1600 and 1650 and was still only tenth in 1700. The distribution of her population was more like that of Ireland, the Scandinavian countries, Spain, Austria and Poland than of such advanced economies as England and the Low Countries. On the other hand, it has to be remembered that the threshold of 10,000 significantly underestimates the absolute size of the real urban enclave in Scotland before 1750. In the seventeenth century, for instance, there was considerable town development, not only through the expansion of the major burghs of Glasgow and Edinburgh, but in the rise of the salt and coal centres around the Forth estuary. The dynamism of the early modern town has been further clarified by recent research.[3] Yet even recognition of the fact that there was more Scottish urban growth before 1750 than Table I implies does not entirely invalidate the proposition that the country was one of the least 'urbanised' in Western Europe in the seventeenth century.

Table 1 Percentage of Total Population in Western European Territories Living in Towns with over 10,000 Inhabitants, 1600–1850

	1600	1650	1700	1750	1800	1850
Scotland	3.0	305	5.3	9.2	17.3	32.0
Scandinavia	1.4	2.4	4.0	4.6	4.6	5.8
England and Wales	5.8	8.8	13.3	16.7	20.3	40.8
Ireland	0	0.9	3.4	5.0	7.0	10.2
Netherlands	24.3	31.7	33.6	30.5	28.8	29.5
Belgium	18.8	20.8	23.9	19.6	18.9	20.5
Germany	4.1	4.4	4.8	5.6	5.5	10.8
France	5.9	7.2	9.2	9.1	8.8	14.5
Switzerland	2.5	2.2	3.3	4.6	3.7	7.7
N.Italy	16.6	14.3	13.6	14.2	14.3	20.3
Central Italy	12.5	14.2	14.3	14.5	13.6	20.3
Southern Italy	14.9	13.5	12.2	13.8	15.3	20.3
Spain	11.4	9.5	9.0	8.6	11.1	17.3
Portugal	14.1	16.6	11.5	9.1	8.7	13.2
Austria-Bohemia	2.1	2.4	3.9	5.2	5.2	6.7
Poland	0.4	0.7	0.5	1.0	2.5	9.3

Source: After J. de Vries, *European Urbanisation, 1500–1800* (London, 1984 pp. 39–48).

From that period, however, the data reveal a dramatically different pattern and indicate an explosive increase in the numbers in Scotland living in large towns. By the 1750s, Scotland was seventh in the league table of 'urbanised societies', fourth in 1800 and second only to England and Wales by 1850. Less than ten per cent of Scots lived in towns with 10,000 inhabitants or above in 1750 but almost one third did so in 1850. In the long-run perspective of historical development a change of this magnitude represented a decisive break with the past. Plainly a new social order was in the process of formation. By 1800, according to Table I, Scotland was already one of the five most urbanised societies in western Europe, alongside England and Wales, the Netherlands, Belgium and northern Italy. But it had achieved this position only in the previous few decades. The Netherlands, Belgium and northern Italy were already highly urbanised two centuries before and town development there did not intensify in the period after 1750. Similarly, there is no evidence of any other territory on the continent (apart from Poland which started from a much lower base) experiencing such a rapid rate of urban expansion as Scotland between 1750 and 1850. The Scottish pattern was execeptional also in relation to England and Wales. Throughout the two and a half centuries after 1600, the tabulation suggests that a higher proportion of the population in the south lived in large towns than north of the Border. But, equally, it is clear that the gap between the two countries, which had been enormous in the early eighteenth century, narrowed very rapidly after that. Table 2 confirms that though England was still the more urbanised society, the Scottish rate of urban growth in the later eighteenth century was significantly higher. Until 1800 the English pattern seems to have been more one of a continuous and protracted process of steadily intensifying urban development. Town expansion in Scotland on this evidence was altogether more abrupt and swift and was therefore more likely to inflict much greater strain and pressure on urban social relationships, amenity and sanitation.

Table 2 Percentage Increase in Urban Population (as defined in Table 1) from Previous Date. Scotland, England and Wales

	1600	1650	1700	1750	1800
Scotland —	–	17	51	124	132
England and Wales –		94	45	42	83

The scale and speed of urban growth in this period is confirmed in Table 3 which employs a different and probably more meaningful measure of 'urbanism', namely the percentage of total population in towns with populations of *5,000* and over. The rates of town expansion achieved in Scotland between the censuses of 1801 and 1831 were the fastest of any period in the nineteenth century and raised the proportion of the population in towns of over 5,000 inhabitants from about one fifth to

116

nearly one third of the Scottish total. At the end of the period covered by this volume most Scots still lived in quasi-urban settlements, in country villages, and in farm steadings. But the growing urban areas had now become the strategic presence in the society and economy of Scotland. The towns were no longer adjuncts to an overwhelmingly rural social order hut had become the dynamic centres of economic change. The lives of the country population were themselves altered fundamentally by the needs of the teeming cities for food and raw materials and the impact which these requirements had on the social structure and stability of countless rural communities in the Highlands and Lowlands.

Table 3 Urbanised Proportion of Scottish Population, 1801–1901

	Percentage of Total Population in centres of 5,000 or over	Percentage Increase over previous decade
1801	21	29.4
1811	24	31.7
1821	27.5	31.7
1831	31.2	28.2
1841	32.7	16.2
1851	35.9	17.3
1861	39.4	16.2
1871	44.4	23.6
1881	48.9	12.8
1891	53.5	17.6
1901	57.6	19.7

Source: M. W. Flinn (ed.), *Scottish Population History from the 17th Century to the 1930s* (Cambridge, 1977), p.313.

The Bases of Urban Growth

Why Scotland should experience such a precocious rate of urban growth is a question which requires detailed consideration since its consequences for the long-run development of Scottish society were so profound. The essential foundation, though not the principal direct cause, was the revolution in agriculture which occurred in parallel with town and city expansion. Urbanisation could not have taken place without a substantial increase in food production to sustain the needs of those who did not cultivate their own food supplies. At the same time, agrarian productivity had to improve in order to release a growing proportion of the population for non-agricultural tasks in towns and cities. Later in the nineteenth century, industrialisation in Scotland allowed manufactured products to be exchanged for imported foods, and at that point the relevance of the indigenous system of food production became less critical. However, for much of the period of this analysis, the urban masses mainly relied on grain, milk, potatoes and meat supplied from Scottish farms. They were fed through a rise in both the production and productivity of agriculture achieved by a reorganisation in farm structure, a more effective deployment of labour and higher yields derived from improved fallowing, the sowing of root crops and the adoption of new rotation systems.[4] No authoritative measures exist of the precise rate of increase in food production but it must have been very substantial. One knowledgeable contemporary, for example, took the view that from the 1750s to the 1820s the output of corn and vegetables had doubled in Scotland while that of animal foods multiplied sixfold.[5] Grain prices rose significantly after c.1780 and especially during the Napoleonic Wars. Yet, though this did stimulate some social discontent in the form of meal riots, price inflation also tended to encourage innovation in better agricultural practices which in the long run continued to sustain urban expansion. It was vital that this response should take place. If it had not, town growth might have been hampered by growing social unrest and diversion of too much of the society's resources to current consumption and away from investment in residantial construction and the urban infrastructure.

Agrarian change was a necessary precondition for urbanisation but the process of agricultural reform also contributed directly to town growth at two other levels. First, the increasing orientation of agriculture towards the market further stimulated the function of urban areas as centres of exchange. There was a greater need than before for the commercial, legal and financial facilities which concentrated in towns. Perth, Ayr, Haddington, Dumfries, Stirling and several other towns owed much of their expansion in this period to the increasing requirements for their services from the commercialised agricultural systems of their hinterlands. Regional specialisation in agrarian production also enhanced the need for growing centres of exchange. Inverness, for example, expanded on the basis of its crucial role as the sheep and wool mart of the Highlands as that area became a great specialist centre of pastoral husbandry in the first half of the nineteenth century. Secondly, the prosperity of Scottish agriculture during the Napoleonic Wars boosted the incomes of tenant farmers and inflated the rent rolls of many landowners. The increase in the purchasing power of these classes had major implications for urban growth because it resulted in rising demand for the products of town consumer and luxury industries, and for more and better urban services in education, in leisure and in the provision of fashionable accommodation.[6]

Yet agrarian improvement was the necessary condition for Scottish urbanisation rather than its principal determinant. Towns which acted mainly as exchange and service centres for rural hinterlands expanded only relatively modestly, at a rate which was only slightly more than the national rate of natural increase.[7] Moreover, the rise in population which occurred in all western European societies from the later eighteenth century encouraged food producers throughout the continent to increase their output to cope with enhanced demand. The nature of the Scottish Agricultural Revolution may have been distinctive but agrarian improvement was too common in Europe at this time to provide the basic explanation for Scotland's exceptional pace of urban development.[8] It is more likely that Scottish town expansion was a direct consequence of Scotland's equally remarkable rate of general economic growth between 1760 and 1830. The Industrial Revolution before 1830 was mainly confined to mainland Britain and it is hardly a coincidence that in this same period urbanisation occurred more vigorously in England and Scotland than in any other European country. Scottish industrialisation and Scottish urban growth were both results of the same economic forces: '. . . non-agrarian occupations do not absolutely demand location in an urban environment but they certainly favour it, as offering prompt access to concentrations of producers, distributors and consumers'.[9]

This process had two interlinked aspects. The first was commercial in origin. In the eighteenth century, Scotland was in a superb geographical position to take advantage of the changing direction of international trade towards the Atlantic world. This momentous alteration in transcontinental commerce was a highly dynamic factor in port development along the whole western coast of Europe from Cork to Cadiz. Scotland was virtually at the crossroads of the new system and the Clyde ports grew rapidly to become the great tobacco emporia of the United Kingdom until diversifying later into the importation of sugar and cotton.[10] It was no coincidence that in the later eighteenth century four of the five fastest-growing towns in Scotland were in the Clyde basin.[11] Commercial success was bound to foster urban expansion.

The carriage and merchandising of goods in bulk were all highly labour-intensive in this period and demanded large concentrations of labour. Considerable investment was also needed to build up the complex infrastructure of trade: warehouses, ports, industries, merchants' mansions, banks, exchanges, inns and coffee houses. Greenock may be taken as the archetypal part town of the western Lowlands: it mushroomed in size from a population of 2000 in 1700 to 17,500 in 1801 and 27,500 by 1831. By that date Greenock had become one of the six largest towns in Scotland. Irish trade, coastal commerce and continuing economic connections with Europe also stimulated port development along both the east and west coasts.

But, in the long run, the expansion of manufacturing industry was even more critical for urbanisation than the stimulus derived from international and interregional commerce. Of the thirteen largest towns in early nineteenth-century Scotland, five at least trebled their population size between c.1750 and 1821. In addition to Greenock these were Glasgow (from 31,700 to 147,000), Paisley (6,800 to 47,000), Kilmarnock (4,400 to 12,700) and Falkirk (3,900 to 11,500). Greenock apart, the inhabitants of all these towns mainly depended either directly or indirectly on manufacturing industry. It was the larger industrial towns and the constellation of smaller urban areas with which they were associated which set the pace of Scottish urbanisation. It is important to emphasise, of course, that industry did not necessarily or inevitably generate large-scale urban expansion in the short run. As late as the 1830s, for instance, around two-thirds of Scotland's handloom weavers of cotton, linen and woollen cloth lived in country villages or small towns.[12] The water-powered cotton-spinning factories of the last quarter of the eighteenth century were more often to be found in rural settlements such as Catrine. New Lanark or Deanston than in the cities. Throughout the period under consideration both coal-mining and pig-iron manufacture were also located in small towns and country villages. The continued presence of industry in a variety of forms in the countryside helps to explain why a majority of the Scottish people still lived outside large urban areas by 1830.

Yet, in the long run there were obvious advantages in industrial concentration in towns.[13] Manufacturers were able to gain from 'external economies': firms saved the costs of providing accommodation and other facilities for their workers from their own resources; they were guaranteed access to a huge pool of labour and transport costs between sources of supply, finishing trades and repair shops could be markedly reduced or virtually eliminated by the close proximity of complementary economic activities. These advantages built up a dynamic for urban expansion even before 1800. Thereafter the new technology of steam propulsion and conspicuous progress in transport developments through the construction of canals and roads steadily intensified the forces making for urban concentration. In cotton-spinning, and eventually in other textile industries, steam power encouraged industrial settlements on the coalfields and removed the one major obstacle which had previously constricted the expansion of manufacturing in the larger towns. Glasgow provides the most dramatic case of the pattern of change.[14] In 1795 the city had eleven cotton-spinning complexes, but rural Renfrewshire had twelve. The fundamental need to have secure access to water power obviously diluted Glasgow's other attractions as a centre of textile industrial production. However, steam-based technology was rapidly adopted after 1800 and concentration accelerated on an enormous scale in the city and its immediate environs. By 1839 there were 192 cotton mills in Scotland employing 31,000 workers. All but seventeen were located in Renfrew and Lanark and ninety-eight were in or near Glasgow. In Paisley, or its vicinity, there was a further great network of forty factories employing almost 5000 workers. A similar process of intensifying convergence evolved over a longer time-scale in the Border wool towns of Hawick and Galashiels and the linen centres of the eastern Lowlands: '. . . there emerged a strong urban concentration—Dundee specialised in heavy flax and tow fabrics, Arbroath was the seat of the canvas trade, Forfar and Brechin produced heavy linens such as osnaburghs and northern Fife specialised in finer linens and bleached goods'.[15] Before 1830 textile manufacturing was the principal motor of this process of agglomeration. Up till then, for example, it was the cotton centres of Glasgow and its suburbs and Renfrewshire which grew most rapidly in the western Lowlands. Only thereafter, and especially from the 1840s, did intensive urban development spread from them to the coal and iron towns of Coatbridge, Airdrie and Wishaw in north Lanarkshire.

The Urban Structure

Despite fast urban growth there remained considerable continuity between the old world and the new. The four major cities of the early nineteenth century, Edinburgh, Glasgow, Aberdeen and Dundee, were also the biggest Scottish burghs of the seventeenth century, although of course they had experienced substantial changes in size, occupational structure and economic specialisation over that period. Again, the thirteen largest Scottish towns of the early eighteenth century were the same, with only one or two exceptions, as those of 1830. The biggest urban areas, therefore, were all ancient places and the traditional county and regional capitals also continued to play a role whether as centres of administration, local government or as markets for prosperous agricultural hinterlands. But by 1830, the Scottish urban system had also developed some characteristic features typical of the new era.

First, urbanisation was mainly concentrated in the narrow belt of land in the western and eastern Lowlands. Between 1801 and 1841 never less than 83 per cent of the entire Scottish urban population (defined as those inhabiting towns of 5000 or more) lived in this region. Within the area there was heavy concentration in Glasgow and Edinburgh where, as early as 1800, 60 per cent of Scottish urban dwellers resided. This remarkable pattern had implications for the demographic structure of Scottish society because population concentration on such a scale could not have taken place without considerable redistribution of people over a relatively short period of time. Thus, whereas the percentage of total Scottish population in the central Lowlands rose from 37 per cent to 47 per cent of the whole between c.1750 and 1821, it fell from 51 per cent to 41 per cent in northern Scotland and remained roughly static at 11 per cent in the southern region of the country over the same period. The modern population profile of Scotland was beginning to take shape. Within the urbanising zone the fastest growth among the largest towns was in the west, with four towns in that area at least trebling in population. Paisley expanded more than six times, Greenock more than five, and Glasgow grew four-fold.

Second, there was wide diversity within the urban structure. Any attempt at neat categorisation of Scottish towns is bound to be arbitrary, but it is important that the effort should be made because differences in size, economic composition and employment opportunities had fundamentally varying effects on the health, living standards, education, religious practice and the class relationships of urban dwellers which are considered in detail in later chapters of this volume. It is necessary at least to emphasise that there was such a diversity of urban experience that generalisations about the impact of urban expansion on Scottish society at this time must be made with great care. In very broad terms, most Scottish towns fitted into three categories: first, the four major cities; second, industrial towns; third, local capitals in historic sites which performed marketing and service functions for their immediate neighbourhoods. In addition, there was a miscellany of other urban settlements including the fishing ports of the Fife and Moray coast, the old coal and salt burghs of the Forth estuary and the new inland spas of Bridge of Allan, Peebles and Strathpeffer. Of these groups, the industrial staple towns and some of the cities were most likely to suffer the adverse consequences of expansion which are often associated with urbanisation at this time. Such places as Paisley, Falkirk, Kilmarnock and Hawick grew swiftly, and their mainly working-class inhabitants were usually heavily concentrated in one or two industries which were often geared to overseas markets and hence were vulnerable to the changes in demand for international commodities. The ordinary people of these towns endured great suffering in the serious commercial depressions of 1816–17, 1825 and 1836–7. In relative terms, at least, those who dwelt in the regional centres were better placed. Their typically moderate rate of population growth ensured that the existing organisation of sewage and waste disposal was not so easily overwhelmed as elsewhere, though it must be stressed that sanitary problems were a familiar feature of all Scottish towns, whatever their size, this time.[16] In addition, their occupational structure was more diverse than that of the staple towns and, because the economy of such centres primarily depended on their service function to surrounding rural areas, they were less vulnerable to the social crises provoked by cyclical unemployment. Again, however, distinctions should not be drawn too neatly because some towns of this type, such as Perth, for instance, had a considerable industrial presence and could not be entirely insulated from the ebb and flow of external demand for manufactured goods. The differences between centres like this and the staple towns were sometimes of degree rather than kind.[17]

The main contrasts in the occupational structure of Scotland's four cities are best studied from Tables 4(a) and 4(b).[18] One similarity, however, is worth emphasising initially. The dominance of textile employment, except in the case of Edinburgh, is very obvious from the tabulation, and underscores the point made earlier in this chapter about the essential importance of cotton, linen and, to a lesser extent, woollen manufacture in Scotland's first phase of urbanisation. The relative stability and balance of Edinburgh's economic base is also apparent. The majority of the employed population worked in small-scale consumer industries many of which depended on demand from a middle and upper-class clientele. Domestic service was far and away the largest employer of female labour. This occupational pattern reflected Edinburgh's metropolitan status, the significant numbers of salaried professionals in the city who represented a large pool of demand for services and luxury consumer goods and the major functions of the capital in the areas of law, banking and education. Poverty and destitution were endemic in certain parts of the city, notably in the Old Town and elsewhere, but the ordinary people of the capital were less likely to experience the full horrors of cyclical unemployment on the same scale as their counterparts in Dundee and Glasgow.

Aberdeen, though smaller, was closest to Edinburgh in occupational structure. It performed the same key legal, educational and financial services for the north-east region as Edinburgh did for the whole of Scotland. The proportion of professionals in the employed population was second only to Edinburgh and there was also a significantly high number of domestic servants. On the other hand, there was extensive textile employment and, alone among the major cities, Aberdeen had a significant proportion of males occupied in fishing. By and large, the city possessed a relatively balanced occupational structure and by the standards of other large towns experienced a moderate rate of growth before 1830. Not surprisingly, therefore, it was spared some of the worst of the social problems which afflicted Glasgow and Dundee.

Table 4(a): Occupational Structure in the Scottish Cities, 1841

Percentage of Workforce in:	Glasgow	Edinburgh	Dundee	Aberdeen
Printing & Publishing	1.12	3.88	0.56	0.91
Engineering, Toolmaking and Metals	7.17	6.07	5.59	6.32
Shipbuilding	0.35	0.17	1.14	1.24
Coachbuilding	0.40	0.92	0.21	0.34
Building	5.84	5.73	6.05	5.99
Furniture & Woodmaking	1.06	2.73	0.77	0.87
Chemicals	1.22	0.24	0.19	0.37
Food, Drink & Tobacco	5.24	8.31	5.27	4.66
Textiles & Clothing	37.56	13.04	50.54	34.68
Other Manufacturing	2.90	3.02	1.29	3.18
General Labouring	8.40	3.69	3.84	6.87

Source: Census of 1841 (*Parliamentary Papers*, 1844, XXVII) and R. Rodger, 'Employment, Wages and Poverty in the Scottish Cities, 1841–1914', Appendix 1, in George Gordon (ed.), *Perspectives of the Scottish City* (Aberdeen, 1985).

Note that occupational classification in the 1841 census is questionable and imprecise. The precise figures presented here are unlikely to be wholly accurate; they provide an impression of overall structures rather than an exact measurement of them.

Glasgow and Dundee were alike in their heavy dependence on textile employment, the speed of their growth in the nineteenth century (though Dundee grew most rapidly from the 1830s and 1840s) and the relative weakness of the professional element in their occupational structures. It was these two cities which suffered very severe problems of health, sanitation and poverty. In the short term, and especially before 1840, Glasgow's difficulties attracted most attention. In the long run, however, Dundee appeared even more vulnerable. Over half of its employed population were engaged in textiles alone and increasingly these were low-paid females occupied in the heavy linen and jute industries. Already by 1841, the urban economy of Dundee had become dangerously lop-sided.

Table 4(b): Occupational Structures in the Scottish Cities, 1841 By Sector (Percentage of Total Workforce).

	Professional		Domestic		Commercial		Industrial		Agriculture & Fishing	
	M	F	M	F	M	F	M	F	M	F
Glasgow (and suburbs)	4.53	0.57	2.03	31.60	15.09	2.87	73.92	64.59	4.43	0.37
Edinburgh (and suburbs)	13.34	1.93	6.53	70.36	14.10	2.71	63.26	23.61	2.77	1.39
Dundee	4.98	0.88	1.95	27.30	13.70	2.79	76.57	68.65	2.80	0.38
Aberdeen	6.46	2.24	4.05	40.37	14.57	2.44	68.71	53.98	6.21	0.97

Source: As for Table 4(a).

Migration and Urbanisation

Not all towns in this period grew by migration. But those which experienced a rate of increase substantially greater than the national rate of natural population growth had to do so. Unfortunately, it is not possible to say much in precise terms about migration to towns in Scotland before the publication of the 1851 census which first printed the birthplaces of the population. Reliance on data extracted from this source in this analysis exaggerates the scale of Irish immigration, which was less for the period before 1830 than for that after the Great Famine. Otherwise the patterns recorded in 1851 are unlikely to drastically misrepresent trends in earlier decades.

Several points are worthy of comment. Migration was obviously very extensive. Of the ten principal Scottish towns in 1851, only 47 per cent of their inhabitants had been born in them. The majority of the migrants were young adults, more concentrated in the marriageable and child-bearing age groups than were the native inhabitants. High migration because of its age composition was therefore likely to fuel natural increase in the urban areas. Of those born in Dundee in 1851, only 37 per cent were aged 20 and over, whereas 70 per cent of the migrants to the city were in that age group. The overwhelming majority of migrants had only travelled short distances. Most new Aberdonians, for instance, were from the north-east counties; the largest number of Greenock's Highland immigrants came from localities in the vicinity of the town in the neighbouring southern Highlands. During the 1820s, burial records show that one-third of those buried in Dundee who were not natives of the city had been born in the city's county of Angus, and most of the rest came from the surrounding east coast areas.[19] The big towns, as Table 5 indicates, all had population catchment areas which were usually in their immediate regions.

Long-distance migration (again as revealed in Table 5) was surprisingly slight. In the main, only the largest centres, such as Glasgow and Edinburgh, had apparently the capacity to attract many people over long distances. Despite Scottish myth, which sometimes portrays the Highlands as being emptied to furnish labour for the large towns, permanent migration to the south from the north-west in this period was relatively limited and most of those who left tended to make for such western towns as Glasgow, Paisley and Greenock. As late as 1851, however, only around 5 per cent of Glasgow's population were born in the Highlands, and the majority of these came from the southern districts adjacent to the Lowlands rather than from the crofting region of the far west. The inhabitants of that area clearly preferred transatlantic emigration to permanent movement to the cities. Temporary migration to the Lowlands was, however, much more extensive and important.[20]

Table 5: Birthplaces of the Residents of Glasgow, Paisley and Edinburgh (Percentages), 1851.

	Far North	High- lands	North- East	W. Low- lands	E. Low- lands	Borders	Ireland	Rest of G. B. & overseas	Same City
Glasgow	0.3	5.2	0.8	16.9	9.7	1.8	8.2	3.1	44.1
Paisley	–	2.9	0.2	17.9	3.4	0.6	12.7	1.4	60.9
Edinburgh	2.0	2.4	2.2	4.8	20.8	5.5	6.5	5.9	50.3

Source: 1851 Census, *Parliamentary Papers*, 1852–3, LXXXVIII, Pt. II; Flinn (ed.), *Scottish Population History*, p. 462.

Highland movement was dwarfed by Irish migration which accelerated from Ulster and eastern Connaught in the 1810s and 1820s due to the difficulties there of the native linen manufacture and the quicker and cheaper access to the Clyde ports afforded by the new steamships. The Irish immigrants of this period were both Catholic and Protestant and it was the transfer of traditional sectarian animosities to Scotland as much as native Scottish prejudice which provoked religious and social bitterness in the wake of this movement. In 1851, after the even greater immigration of the Great Famine, 7 per cent of the total Scottish population were Irish-born, more than twice that of England. But this bald figure underestimates the Irish influence on Scottish urban expansion. J. E. Handley rightly stresses that those of Irish extraction should be included in the count as well as the Irish-born.[21] Handley's revised estimates would suggest that in 1841 almost a quarter of the people of the western Lowlands were of Irish extraction. Moreover, Irish immigration tended to concentrate on specific urban areas, and global figures conceal the impact of the distribution. Thus 44,000 of Glasgow's population in 1841, or 16 per cent of the total of 274,000, were Irish-born. But if Handley is correct, it would mean that around one in three of the city's inhabitants were of Irish descent at that date.

No single factor was decisive in explaining the increasing scale of rural-urban migration within Scotland. There was undoubtedly a distinctive urban pull: 'urbanisation meant more jobs, a wider diversity of social contacts and infinitely greater colour and excitement in the lives of the masses'.[22] Higher wages than were usual in the rural economy and a greater range of employment opportunities helped to hasten migration to towns *in the later eighteenth century* to such an extent that Scottish farmers in the zones where urban growth concentrated were forced to raise wages to retain labour. Even after the Napoleonic Wars, when urban demand for labour slackened, and clear signs emerged of a labour surplus in some of the cities, the towns still retained their allure. The poor health record of the large towns did not deter migrants, and indeed there is evidence that urban crises of mortality were sometimes followed by 'replenishment migration'. The fact that the overwhelming majority of newcomers to the towns came from adjacent districts was itself confirmation of the importance of the 'pull' factor.[23]

The close proximity between the source of migrants and the host towns facilitated migration. The urban areas were near and familiar. Migration did not mean that all contact with the native rural community was lost. There was much seasonal and temporary migration, and a connection could be retained with kinfolk who normally lived short distances away. Many of the migrants to the cities already had some experience of town life. One of the biggest migrant streams was that which linked different *urban* areas: not all or even the majority of new arrivals were the rural innocents of legend. It should not be forgotten either that extensive migration was not unique to the era of urbanisation. Mobility over short distances was common in pre-industrial Scotland long before the late eighteenth century. Again, the apparent obstacles to rural-urban migration were often more apparent than real. A crude contrast is occasionally drawn between the radical change in life-style enforced upon peasant cultivators who moved to factory employment in the cities. But this stereotype did not necessarily apply to the majority of migrants. Most townspeople before 1830 worked outside the factory, in workshops, homes and in the open air. There were, therefore, often important continuities between rural and urban employments, especially when it is remembered that before 1760 the spinning and weaving of textiles was so extensive in Lowland Scotland that most country families must have had some members with experience of such industrial labour. The migrant could also ease the process of urban assimilation by lodging with kinfolk or with family friends from the same locality. Movement from country to town was in this way facilitated both by the previous experience of the migrants themselves and the strategies they adopted to adjust to a new life.

The most controversial aspect of migration at this time is the question of how far people were 'forced' off the land into towns as the process of agrarian reorganisation gathered pace from the later eighteenth century.[24] The numbers with either a legal or customary right to land in Lowland Scotland did decline rapidly after c.1780 as main tenancies were consolidated and subtenancies eliminated when rationalisation quickened. On the other hand, in the short run at least, the creation of the modern agrarian structure (through the construction of farmhouses, roads, fencing and dykes and the adoption of the new rotation crops of sown grasses and turnips), seemed to require more rather than less labour than the old system. The new ploughs were certainly labour-saving and labour productivity increased as work organisation was improved, but most farm tasks remained unmechanised and there was an overall increase in demand for labour as production of foods and raw materials intensified. In addition, textile and other manufactures expanded in the country villages and small towns. There was therefore often less need for dispossessed cottars with craft skills to move to the big cities to make a living. Rather, surviving wage data for the later eighteenth century, when agrarian reorganisation accelerated, suggest that rural employers were forced to offer increasing wages in order to compete with their urban counterparts. In that period, therefore, it would seem that many migrants from the country, far from being forced off the land, were being lured to the towns by the positive attractions of higher wages and a greater range of employment opportunities.

Yet, there were indeed fundamental links between rural–urban migration in Scotland and the social changes initiated by the Agricultural Revolution, even if they were more subtle than is sometimes suggested. The creation of a landless labour force did not necessarily cause people to leave their rural environment but it did facilitate it. Peasant farmers are notoriously reluctant to give up their holdings. As Pierre Goubert has written, 'No peasant willingly surrenders land, be it only half a furrow'. Landless wage labourers are, however, much more mobile. They survive through selling their labour power in the market and they cannot fall back on scraping a living from a smallholding, no matter how meagre. Again, outside the south-east Lowlands, Fife and some other districts, most regular farm workers in Lowland Scotland were unmarried male and female servants, hired on six-monthly contracts. At marriage, many were forced to move to alternative employments. They were a highly mobile group and one option among several for them was movement to the towns. All the local studies demonstrate a great haemorrhage from farm service at 23 to 25, the average age at marriage in Scotland at this time.

In the final analysis, however, the main momentum was probably generated by the acceleration in Scottish population growth, which occurred from the early nineteenth century, and the social effect that this had in country areas, as well as agrarian reorganisation in itself. As was shown in Chapter 1, Scottish demographic expansion in the later eighteenth century was unusually moderate by the standards prevailing in Ireland, England and several continental societies. Between 1755 and 1801, the annual rate of increase was only about 0.6 per cent. From 1801 to 1811, however, this doubled to 1.2 per cent and increased again to 1.6 per cent per annum from 1811 to 1821. Such a rate of growth might well have swamped rural labour markets and the problem would have been aggravated by the great demobilisation of soldiers and sailors after the Napoleonic Wars. Though farmers had a need for more hands, the demand for labour was not increasing at anything like the pace of population growth, especially as agricultural income and hence employment opportunities contracted with the slump in grain prices after the Napoleonic Wars. One might realistically have anticipated, therefore, a huge expansion in structural unemployment in rural districts. This did happen in the western Highlands but not in the Lowlands. This was partly a result of the expulsive force of the Scottish structure of engagement for farm service. Both single and married servants in Scotland lived on the farm. Their accommodation was provided as part of their contract of employment. For many, to be unemployed, to fail to gain a 'fee' at the biennial feeing markets, meant not simply to be without work but also to be without a home. In the later eighteenth century, it became a major principle of Scottish improving policy that only the population essential for proper cultivation should be retained permanently on the land. Accommodation in and around the farm was strictly limited thereafter to the specific labour needs of the farmer. Cottages surplus to these requirements were pulled down and the building of new accommodation strictly controlled. This inevitably became a mechanism for channelling excess labour off the land, especially when it is remembered that the able-bodied unemployed had no legal right to be relieved under the Scottish Poor Law, even if occasional assistance was sometimes provided in several areas. The combination of this system, a natural and accelerating rise in population and only slowly growing or stagnant employment opportunities in agriculture after 1812–1813, helped to ensure an increasing movement of people from country to town. In the 1810s and 1820s Scotland had a growing problem of structural unemployment. But it did not concentrate in the Lowland agricultural sector and was mainly confined to the large towns, the western Highlands and the communities of industrial workers (and especially handloom weavers) in the countryside. Some of its effects will be considered in the final section of this chapter.

The Urban Problem

The speed of Scottish urban expansion did not have a significant impact on mortality rates until the second and third decades of the nineteenth century.

The larger towns were mainly free of epidemic fevers from 1790 to 1815 but these diseases (mainly typhus) reappeared at recurrent intervals between 1817–20, 1826–7 and 1836–7. Scotland also experienced its first major cholera attack, which claimed 10,000 victims, in 1831–2. Interpretation of mortality statistics for any period in the first half of the nineteenth century is hazardous. But the careful enumerations carried out by some local doctors leave little doubt that the urban environment was steadily becoming more lethal. In Edinburgh, where conditions were by no means the worst of the larger towns, the death-rate which had fallen to 25 per 1000 in 1818–19, climbed to 26.2 in the following decade and reached 29 between 1830 and 1839.[25] So marked was the general rise in urban mortality rates that students of Scottish demographic history can demonstrate that they explain why *national* death rates also began to move upwards after a sustained decline in earlier decades.[26] There could be no more telling or ominous illustration of the new significance of the large towns in Scottish life. By the 1830s and 1840s some were approaching a social crisis of unprecedented proportions. Meaningful efforts at reform rather than temporary palliatives were not even contemplated until the 1840s. Not before the second half of the nineteenth century were some of the worst aspects of the urban problem effectively tackled.[27]

Urban growth brought major health problems throughout Britain, but both available statistical evidence and contemporary comment suggest that conditions were worse in Scotland than England. As Edwin Chadwick concluded in his *Sanitary Report* of 1842: 'There is evidence to prove that the mortality from fever is greater in Glasgow, Edinburgh and Dundee than in the most crowded towns in England'.[28] The influences which promoted environmental decline in cities in the first half of the nineteenth century have been chronicled in detail by a number of historians and there is no need to explore them at great length here.[29] They included, *inter alia*, the absence of effective sanitation; the Scottish tradition of accommodating people in high-built tenements, courts and wynds; little or no street cleansing in poor neighbourhoods; inadequate supplies of uncontaminated water; the inertia of unreformed municipal authorities; medical ignorance of the causes and nature of the major killer diseases; and ideologies which blamed poverty and squalor on weakness of character rather than environmental constraints. These and other factors control until the 1850s. But most were common to both England and Scotland and cannot in themselves explain the peculiarly bad conditions in several of the Scottish cities. To do that, distinctive Scottish influences must be considered.

Some are already obvious from previous discussion. Scottish urbanisation proceeded at a faster pace than probably anywhere else in Western Europe between 1760 and 1830 and the rate of growth simply overwhelmed the primitive contemporary structures of sanitation and amenity in a huge rising tide of humanity. Much of Glasgow's notoriety as the unhealthiest city in Britain at this time stemmed from the simple fact that it was growing more swiftly than any other British city of its size, adding a staggering 5,000 every year to its population in the 1820s. It must also be remembered that the larger Scottish towns, especially those in the western Lowlands and Dundee, played host to migrants from Ireland and parts of the Highlands, two of the poorest societies in the British Isles. The Irish, in particular, often arrived in a semi-destitute condition, concentrated in the poorest quarters of towns, were more vulnerable to the diseases of the city and inevitably aggravated pressure on accommodation and amenity.

But the familiar plight of the Irish was but a part of a more general and deeper social problem in early nineteenth-century Scotland. The rapid industrialisation of the society was partially due to the fact that Scottish labour costs were lower than England's.[30] This, in turn, was a reflection of the relative poverty of the country, a poverty which persisted throughout this period.[31] Many thousands in the booming towns of Scotland eked out an existence close to the margins of destitution, a condition aggravated by the fact that the able-bodied unemployed had no legal right to relief within the terms of the Scottish Poor Law.[32] One calculation, for instance, suggests that in 1834 about half of Scotland's handloom weavers, a very large occupational group, fell below the primary poverty line as defined by late nineteenth-century social analysts.[33] In addition, all the large towns had significant numbers of casual labourers who worked in the varied urban tasks of fetching, carrying and construction. James Cleland estimated that almost one quarter of Glasgow's labour force in 1831 were casual workers.[34] They endured a regime of very poor wages, broken time and employment which fluctuated throughout the year. Groups such as these had little economic power to create market demand for decent housing.[35] Instead they were accommodated cheaply in the old centres of the cities, notably the Old Town in Edinburgh and the High Street-Gallowgate area of Glasgow, through existing buildings being subdivided and their backcourts filled in with additional dwellings. Housing conditions in such areas were appalling simply because many had no alternative but to accept them.

The connection between poverty and urban mortality was vividly demonstrated during the three great industrial recessions of 1816–18, 1825 and 1836. It was these rather than poor sanitation as such which precipitated the first upswing in urban death-rates in Scottish cities in the nineteenth century. Significantly, fever was much rarer in the early years of the century despite the fact that then too sanitary provision was very inadequate. Typhus only became a major killer in the crisis years of profound economic difficulty following the Napoleonic Wars. All three depressions were followed by savage epidemics in 1816–18, 1827–8 and 1837–9 which drove up mortality rates in all the larger towns. Poverty and destitution were obviously as lethal as inadequate sewage and poor housing. This was not the result of urbanism *per se* but the inevitable consequence of a general imbalance between population and employment opportunities in

Scotland in the two decades before 1830. It was an imbalance which only began to be reduced in the second phase of industrialisation when iron, coal and engineering expanded from the middle decades of the nineteenth century. Industrial expansion and its offspring, urbanisation, significantly increased the volume and range of jobs down to 1830 but not at the rate required to provide regular and decent employment for the constantly rising numbers of people entering the labour market. Economic change and industrial growth saved. Scotland from the demographic horrors experienced in Ireland in the 1840s but were not yet vigorous or extensive enough to prevent social suffering on a large scale in the growing towns.

NOTES

1. Anthony Slaven, *The Development of the West of Scotland. 1750–1960* (London. 1975), p. 145; T. C. Smout, *A History of the Scottish People, 1560–1830* (London, 1969), p. 260.
2. Jan de Vries, *European Urbanisation, 1500–1800* (London, 1987).
3. Michael Lynch (ed.), *The Early Modern Town in Scotland* (London, 1987).
4. T. M. Devine and R. Mitchison (eds.), *People and Society in Scotland 1760–1830* (Edinburgh, 1988), ch. 3
5. George Robertson, *Rural Recollections* (Irvine, 1829), p. 352.
6. L. J. Saunders, *Scottish Democracy 1815–40: the Social and Intellectual Background* (Edinburgh, 1950), pp. 79–96.
7. M. W. Flinn (ed.), *Scottish Population History from the Seventeenth Century to the 1930s* (Cambridge, 1977), p. 313.
8. On this point see T. M. Devine, 'Social Responses to Agrarian Modernisation: the Lowland and Highland Clearances in Scotland, 1500–1850', in R. A. Houston and I. D. Whyte (eds.), *Scottish Society, 1600–1800* (Cambridge, 1988).
9. P. J. Corfield, *The Impact of English Towns 1700–1800* (Oxford, 1982), p. 94.
10. T. M. Devine, *The Tobacco Lords: A Study of the Tobacco Merchants of Glasgow and their Trading Activities, 1740–90* (Edinburgh, 1975); L. E. Cochran, *Scottish Trade with Ireland in the Eighteenth Century* (Edinburgh, 1985).
11. Glasgow, Greenock, Paisley and Kilmarnock.
12. N. Murray, *The Scottish Handloom Weavers 1790–1850: A Social History* (Edinburgh, 1978), pp. 1–9.
13. J. Docherty, 'Urbanisation, Capital Accumulation and Class Struggle in Scotland, 1750–1914', in G. Whittington and I. D. Whyte (eds.). *An Historical Geography of Scotland* (London, 1983), pp. 244–5.
14. A. Gibb, *Glasgow: the Making of a City* (London, 1983), pp. 91–3.
15. Ian H. Adams, *The Making of Urban Scotland* (London, 1978), pp. 90–3; C. Gulvin, *The Tweedmakers* (Newton Abbot, 1973).
16. See, for example, S. Wood, *The Shaping of 19th Century Aberdeenshire* (Stevenage, 1985), ch. 2.
17. The whole issue of the smaller towns is well covered in Saunders, *Scottish Democracy*, pp. 145–160.
18. This paragraph is mainly based on R. Rodger, 'Employment. Wages and Poverty in the Scottish Cities. 1841–1914', in G. Gordon (ed.), *Perspectives of the Scottish City* (Aberdeen, 1985), pp. 25–63.
19. Flinn (ed.), *Scottish Population History*, p. 467.
20. T. M. Devine, 'Highland Migration to Lowland Scotland, 1760–1860', *Scottish Historical Review*. 63 (1983) pp. 137–49; T. M. Devine, *The Great Highland Famine:*

Hunger, Emigration and the Scottish Highlands in the Nineteenth Century (Edinburgh, 1988), chs. 6, 8, 9–11: C. W. J. Withers, *Highland Communities in Dundee and Perth, 1787–1891* (Dundee, 1986).

21. James Handley, *The Irish in Scotland, 1798–1845* (Cork, 1943). Amorerecent analysis of Irish immigration to Britain (including Scotland) in this period is contained in R. Swift and S. Gilley (eds.). *The Irish in Victorian Britain* (London, 1985).

22. A. S. Wohl. *Endangered Lives: Public Health in Victorian Britain* (London, 1983), p. 80.

23. This paragraph and the remainder of this section are based on: T. M. Devine (ed.). *Farm Servants and Labour in Lowland Scotland, 1770–1914* (Edinburgh, 1984); T. M. Devine, 'Social Stability and Agrarian Change in the Eastern Lowlands of Scotland, 1910–40', *Social History*, 3, no. 3 (October, 1978), pp. 331–46; M. Gray, 'Scottish Emigration: the Social Impact of Agrarian Change in the Rural Lowlands, 1775–1875', *Perspectives in American History*, VII (1973); M. Gray, 'Migration in the Rural Lowlands of Scotland, 1750–1850', in T. M. Devine and D. Dickson (eds.), *Ireland and Scotland, 1600–1850* (Edinburgh, 1983); Brenda Collins, 'Irish Emigration to Dundee and Paisley during the first half of the Nineteenth Century', in J. M. Goldstrom and L. A. Clarkson (eds.), *Irish Population, Economy and Society* (Oxford, 1981).

24. T. M. Devine, *The Transformation of Rural Scotland* (Edinburgh, 1994), *passim*.

25. James Stark, *Inquiry into some points of the Sanitary State of Edinburgh* (Edinburgh, 1847).

26. Flinn (ed.), *Scottish Population History*, p. 19.

27. E. Gauldie, *Cruel Habitations* (London, 1974).

28. M. W. Flinn (ed.), E. Chadwick, *Report on the Sanitary Condition of the Labouring Population of Great Britain, 1842* (Edinburgh, 1965).

29. The interested reader should consult the following, *inter alia*: J. H. F. Brotherston, *Observations on the Early Public Health Movement in Scotland* (London, 1952); S. D. Chapman (ed.), *The History of Working Class Housing* (Newton Abbot, 1977); R. J. Morris, *Cholera, 1832* (London, 1976); Gauldie, *Cruel Habitations*; Wohl, *Endangered Lives*.

30. R. H. Campbell, *The Rise and Fall of Scottish Industry, 1707–1939* (Edinburgh, 1980).

31. Devine and Mitchison (eds.), *People and Society in Scotland*, ch. 10.

32. *Ibid.*, ch.12.

33. Murray, *Scottish Handloom Weavers*, pp. 84–114.

34. James Cleland, *Enumeration of the Inhabitants of the City of Glasgow* (Glasgow, 1832), p. 231.

35. J. H. Treble, *Urban Poverty in Britain* (London, 1979), pp. 55–80.

9

THE HIGHLAND CLEARANCES

The Highland Clearances were the process by which between c. 1760 and c. 1860 the inhabitants of entire districts in the Scottish Highlands and Islands were displaced and evicted from their lands. It is one of the classic themes of Scottish history but also of much more general historiographical significance. The subject offers an unrivalled opportunity for an examination of the social consequences of agrarian modernisation. The Clearances bring into particularly sharp focus the titanic conflict between the forces of peasant traditionalism and agrarian rationalism. All the great themes are there: the powers of the landed classes; the constraints of economic and demographic pressure; dispossession; peasant resistance; cultural alienation; migration and emigration.

BEFORE THE CLEARANCES

Any assessment of the social impact of the Clearances vitally depends on some reckoning of conditions in the Highlands before the evictions began. Nineteenth-century critics argued that the majority of the population lived a secure and relatively comfortable existence which was later irreparably damaged by dispossession. Modern research has painted a quite different picture. Before 1750 the evidence suggests that the northern region, even by the standards of the rest of Scotland, was very poor; that its economy was precariously balanced between meagre sufficiency and intermittent shortage; that destitution was widespread and the people endured a constant struggle in a land of uncertain climate, limited arable resources and poor natural endowment. The Clearances did not in themselves cause Highland poverty; that was an inevitable fact of life, long before the later eighteenth century [Richards (1), Gray (2)].

VARIETIES OF CLEARANCE

The great evictions are commonly viewed in particularly stark and simple terms. It is still widely held that the Clearances refer to the process of wholesale expulsion of entire communities through the use of especially brutal methods, in order to clear land for the formation of large sheep ranches. While such a description does have validity when applied to many evictions at certain periods, it is essentially all over-simplification of a much more complex social development. Easy generalisation is impossible because each 'clearance' had individual characteristics dictated by landlord attitudes, and the varied influence of demographic and economic pressures.

Some removals occurred through a discreet and gradual thinning of the ranks of the small tenantry, in the manner reminiscent of many other parts of Britain in the age of agricultural improvement that has been discussed in the preceding chapters. There were striking differences in the scale, speed and modes of dispossession. Eviction was only one of a series of sanctions employed: others included confiscation of the cattle stock of those in arrears; controls over subdivision of land; refusal of famine relief. Some proprietors went to considerable lengths to accommodate displaced populations; others evicted without compunction or concern for the social costs of their actions. In the later eighteenth century it was common to plan for a redistribution of the population; after *c.* 1820 the strategy more often became one of an undisguised determination to expel. These different approaches were responses to the varied economic and social incentives and pressures of the period 1760–1860. They ensured that the phrase 'the Highland Clearances' is 'an omnibus term to include any kind of displacement by Highland landlords; it does not discriminate between small and large evictions, voluntary and forced removals, or between outright expulsion of tenants and re-settlement' [Richards (1)].

The fact that the Clearances were far from homogeneous either in origin or effect renders meaningful analysis very difficult. Some attempt, however, can be made to categorise them roughly in a more coherent manner in order to move towards a definition of particular phases and types of eviction. In very broad terms, therefore, five classes of clearance may be identified.

(i) *The southern and eastern Highlands*

Between *c.* 1780 and *c.* 1830, along the arable fringes of the Highlands in eastern Inverness, southern Argyllshire, Easter Ross and parts of Sutherland, the existing structure was dissolved and replaced by a pattern of larger farms, held by one man, employing wage labourers. Alongside the new order emerged a 'croft' or smallholding system which became a source of seasonal labour for the large units and also an efficient means of bringing marginal land into steady cultivation. Eviction of small tenants and sub-tenants was a central part of the process but these 'clearances' had less harmful results than elsewhere because the new agriculture was founded on a combination of mixed husbandry and pastoral specialisation. Thus the dispossessed were often absorbed within the labour-intensive regime of arable cropping or in the developing crofting structure [Gray (2)].

(ii) Cattle farming

For the most part the rearing of black cattle for sale in southern markets was accommodated within the traditional economic and social structure of the Highlands. This was in contrast to commercial sheep-farming which almost from its inception fell under the control of capitalist farmers from the Lowland and Border counties. Nevertheless, in some districts, extensive cattle ranches were established in response to external market pressures and many small tenants in consequence turned out of their holdings. This pattern was widely noted in a significant number of parishes in Dunbartonshire, Argyll and Perth as early as the 1750s [Richards (1)].

(iii) The creation of the Croft System

Throughout the western mainland north of the Ardnamurchan peninsula and the inner and outer Hebrides, the existing system of joint tenancies and communal agriculture was terminated beween *c.* 1760 and *c.* 1840. This region afforded only limited possibilities for arable or mixed farming and therefore lacked the potential for the moderate land consolidation and the formation of medium-sized farms characteristic of the southern and eastern Highlands and the Scottish Lowlands. Here the landlord strategy was devoted to the formation of individual smallholdings or 'crofts' which were allocated in 'townships' or crofting settlements [Hunter (3)]. It is important to stress that this change did not destroy the peasant class though it did dramatically affect status, size of holding and local distribution of population. Essentially it perpetuated the connection with land and, within the croft system, sub-division of units among kinfolk became commonplace. Yet, while the formation of the new structure did not possess the drama associated with the more notorious evictions for sheep-farming, it did result in substantial disruption, displacement and relocation of population. Over less than two generations it transformed the entire social map and pattern of settlement of the western Highlands and Islands. One expression of the social resentment which the process produced was the great wave of transatlantic emigrations which were triggered by it after *c.* 1760 and which predated the arrival of the large sheep farms by several decades [Bumstead (4)].

(iv) Sheep-farming

Commercial sheep-farming penetrated the southern and eastern counties of the region in the last quarter of the eighteenth century. After 1800 the pace of development quickened significantly. Inverness had a sheep stock of 50,000 at that date; by 1880 it had reached 700,000. The speed of expansion in Sutherland was even more rapid. That county had only about 15,000 sheep in 1811 but 130,000 nine years later. Almost inevitably pastoral husbandry practised on this huge scale would result in far-reaching population displacement. Commercial pastoralism was conducted most efficiently in large units: the conventional wisdom had it that the most economical ratio was single shepherd to 600 sheep. Again, the big farmers who controlled the business required the low-lying areas of arable on which the peasant communities clustered. At the very core of their operations was the vital need for suitable land for wintering in the harsh climate of the northern mountains. On this depended both the quality and the quantity of stock which they could maintain. The consequence was a sweeping increase in clearance: 'Where dispossessed families had been numbered in tens before, now there were hundreds. Kintail, Glenelg, Glendessary, and Loch Arkaig . . . names of bitter memory plot the movements of the sheep farming frontier' [Gray (2)].

Although these removals often resulted in emigration they did not necessarily cause wholesale depopulation, until at least the second decade of the nineteenth century. Frequently the dispossessed were relocated on coastal or marginal areas while the interior glens were laid down for sheep. The best known example of this pattern was the great clearances in Sutherland where between *c.* 1810 and *c.* 1825 an estimated 8,000 to 9,000 people were moved to the coastal fringe and settled in fishing and quasi-industrial communities. This was probably the most remarkable programme of social engineering ever undertaken in nineteenth-century Britain. In the short run, at least, it limited out-migration but, in the longer term, population levels on the estate began to fall rapidly.

(v) Emigration and clearance

Between *c.* 1840 and *c.* 1860 a new series of evictions began in the western Highlands and Islands. They differed from most previous clearances since they were intended to achieve depopulation. Attempts at resettlement were abandoned and increasingly those displaced were encouraged to emigrate. 'Compulsory emigration', to use the contemporary phrase, became wide-spread. Landlords offered the bleak choice to their small tenantry of eviction or dispossession together with assisted passage to North America or Australia. During the potato famines of the period 1846-56 an estimated 16,000 received assistance to emigrate in this way from either proprietors or charitable societies.

PRECONDITIONS FOR CLEARANCE

A useful approach here might be to consider initially those general, conditioning factors which made widespread population displacement possible. This can then be followed by an analysis of those influences which triggered the specific types of clearance outlined earlier.

The Jacobite defeat in 1746 and the imposition of effective rule by the state officially brought to an end the old clan-based martial society of the Highlands. Land could now more easily be regarded as a unit of resource than the basis of military power. This created the essential precondition for rationalisation of traditional agriculture. Landlords more than ever before came to value their estates principally as economic assets. It is important, however, not to exaggerate the significance of the aftermath of the '45 rebellion. Rather than a great watershed it can more reasonably be seen in the light of recent research as the final phase in the steady encroachment of state power in the Highlands, a process which can be traced back at least to the reign of James VI and I in the early seventeenth century. It is now clear also that southern civilisation and economic pressure were already influencing the *mentalité* of Highland proprietors, the markets for Highland products, such as cattle, fish and timber, and even tenurial structures in some districts long before 1745 [Hunter (3)]. Finally, there was no automatic link between pacification and clearance. Major structural change did not begin in the Highlands for about two decades or more after Culloden, indicative of the fact that the massive expansion in the markets for northern commodities in the last quarter of the eighteenth century was much more decisive in initiating innovation than political change.

Landlord authority was a vital precondition of the Clearances. If, as is often asserted, Scottish landowners were among the most powerful in Europe, the Highland élite was the most absolute of all. They had enormous capacity to displace population and radically alter settlement structure. The peasantry possessed land but did not own it; there were therefore few of the obstacles which restrained seigneurial power in many European societies. The vast majority of the small tenantry had no leases and held land on an annual basis. Below this rent-paying group, and forming as much as one third to one half of the population of some estates in the nineteenth century, was an undermass of semi-landless subtenants who paid no rent directly to the proprietor. Most inhabitants on a typical Highland property were therefore liable to eviction at the landlord's will. There were none of the complicated legal procedures associated with the enclosure of lands in England. Landowners merely had to obtain a Summons or Writ of Removal from the local Sheriff Court.

These tenurial weaknesses reflected the absence of bargaining power on the part of the small tenantry. With the expansion of capital-intensive commercial pastoralism, they rapidly ceased to have much economic value. The balance of power swung even more emphatically towards the proprietor in the subsistence crises of 1816–17, 1837–38 and, most importantly, the great potato famine of 1846–56. Many came to depend at these times on the largesse of landlords for life itself. With few legal, tenurial or economic restraints on the autocracy of social élite, the relationship between proprietor and the small tenantry could easily become an exploitative one. Only sustained and stubborn resistance in the fashion of the Irish peasantry might have inhibited the full implementation of landlord strategies but, although modern research shows that the Clearances were far from peaceful, effective and enduring protest before 1860 was relatively rare [Richards (1)]. The problem was, however, that even in times of severe destitution the crofters and cottars only grudgingly surrendered their land; contemporary observers also pointed out that the poorest class in the Highlands was also the least mobile. As the great French historian, Pierre Goubert, has said: 'No peasant willingly gives up land, be it only half a furrow'. Out of the inevitable conflict between landlord omnipotence and these unyielding peasant values came the agony of the Clearances.

Within this general context it is possible to identify three specific influences which contributed directly to population displacement at different times between 1760 and 1860.

(i) The landlord role

Pressure on the landlord class to exploit their estates more effectively intensified in the later eighteenth century due to the impact of 'improving' ideology, the growing hostility to communal practices and structures, the new faith in individualism and the increasing costs of maintaining social position in an age of rising inflation and competitive display. The Highland aristocracy had fewer choices and alternatives than their peers elsewhere in Britain due to the poverty of the resource base in the north, the virtual absence of coal reserves, the weakness of the urban sector and the very great suitability of the area for large-scale commercial pastoralism.

(ii) The expansion of markets

Growing landlord needs for more income coincided with a huge expansion in demand from the urban and industrialising areas of Britain for all Highland produce. The markets for cattle, sheep, whisky, fish, timber, slate and kelp were all buoyant. Increases in production of some of these commodities, notably cattle, could often be accommodated within the existing social and settlement structure. But sheep and kelp were less easily absorbed. Kelp manufacture was the highly labour-intensive production of alkali from seaweed which was used in the soap and glass industries. By 1815 it was reckoned to employ between 25,000 to 30,000 in the western Highlands and Islands. Landlords broke up the existing joint tenancies to create subsistence plots for both the kelp labour force and for fishermen [Hunter (3)]. Large-scale sheep-farming caused even greater displacement. The local population was mainly excluded; the new breeds were Cheviots and Lintons from the south and sheep-ranching quickly became a business of great efficiency absorbing large amounts of capital in which traditional society was very deficient. As the sheep frontier expanded, communities were uprooted and resettled in less favoured areas.

(iii) Economic and demographic strain

From the 1820s serious economic recession undermined many of the peasant bi-employments of the period before 1815. Fishing stagnated, cattle prices fell and above all kelp manufacture collapsed with the rise of the modern chemical industry and the removal of excise duty on salt. At the same time the population of the western Highlands and Islands continued to increase at a rate per annum which accelerated from 0.72 (1801–10) to 1.46 (1811–20) before falling to 0.51 (1821–30). The signs of escalating demographic strain were clearly revealed in the subsistence crises of 1816–17, 1837–38 and 1846–56. This was the background to a new wave of clearances through which landlords sought to remove the 'redundant' population because they feared the huge burden of relief costs in maintaining the people and increasingly saw no viable economic alternative to large-scale sheep husbandry. In a sence, this recognition simply reflected the imperatives of developing regional specialisation within the British economy and the tendency of many areas to move towards exploitation of comparative advantage.

THE SOCIAL RESPONSE

The Highland Clearances were associated with protest, trauma and bitterness when they occurred and bequeathed to posterity a popular tradition of lost rights and wrongful dispossession. Much recent work has focused on the reasons why agrarian reorganisation in the Highlands caused a deeper sense of alienation than anywhere else in Britain.

One likely explanation is that many of the evictions in the Highlands had more serious social costs than consolidation of land in other areas. The drive towards the expansion of commercial pastoralism created particularly large farms which were both capital- and land-intensive but had little need for many hands. The new agrarian sector excluded the local population while at the same time it monopolised much of the scarce arable lands and absorbed the pastures of the old peasant cattle economy. While the mixed husbandry of the southern and eastern Highlands, and in the Scottish Lowlands, released employment opportunities, sheep-farming, in particular, almost invariably led to the contraction of peasant resources and income.

The problem of absorbing the cleared populations was rendered even more acute by the fact that no permanent alternative to agriculture emerged in the region. Despite the efforts of several proprietors, southern business interests and even government, the infant industrial growths of the later eighteenth century withered in the recession after the Napoleonic Wars under the impact of intense competition from Lowland manufacturing centres. No dynamic urban or industrial sector developed, as in central Scotland, to absorb the dispossessed. Their sufferings were rendered even more traumatic by the fact that evictions tended increasingly to concentrate in years of subsistence crisis. At these times, hunger, disease and loss of land combined to cause terrible social destitution throughout the western mainland and islands [Hunter (3)].

There was also something distinctive about the nature of many clearances in the Highlands. They occurred within a predominantly peasant society in which, until the 1840s and beyond, land remained the primary source of food, fuel, drink, clothing and shelter. There was a widespread belief in the 'right to land', a claim which had no legal foundation but which may have rested on the ancient clan tradition of dispensing land in return for service. Ironically the old martial ethos survived in a new form long after the Jacobite defeat at Culloden, because of the landlord custom of raising regiments from the men of their estates for the British army, through the simple expedient of promising land in return for service. Not surprisingly after 1800, the assumption persisted on several properties that the right to the secure possession of land had been acquired in return for service not in the distant past but in the very recent present. Partly because of this the land issue stirred deeper passions in Gaeldom than anywhere else in Britain.

Yet, it was precisely in this society that eviction took place very rapidly on an especially enormous scale. This was partly because the new sheep and cattle ranches demanded huge areas of land and partly because removal could be accomplished relatively easily with minimal legal fuss. But it was also related to the phasing of agrarian change, especially along the west coast and the islands. Two coherent processes can be identified. The first, roughly covering the period *c.* 1760 to 1820, involved the concentration of a larger population than before along the coasts. The second, from about the 1820s to the 1850s, moved to the opposite extreme, to the consolidation of land and the dispersal of many communities. Draconian methods were widely employed in this phase to expel dense communities of smallholders. It was from this period and these districts that much of the sense of bitterness associated with the Clearances derives. These evictions also stirred emotions outside the Highlands because they were still taking place as late as the 1850s and were widely publicised. Thus this evoked the sympathies of an age with a more sensitive social conscience, a growing hostility to the excesses of landlord authority and a developing 'romantic' interest in Highland society. It was partly this growth in public sympathy which enabled Gladstone's government in 1886 to pass the Crofters' Holding Act, which considerably checked the powers of landlordism and provided for the crofting population the right to secure possession of land for which they had so long craved.

CONCLUSIONS

This topic is still at a relatively immature stage of historical investigation. There is a major need for both detailed empirical research and conceptual development in the methodology of analysis. A series of professional local studies of the type common in France would be most useful. No economic history of sheep-farming exists. Detailed studies of individual estates and of key phases in the processes of eviction would be very welcome. A systematic evaluation of the linkages between eviction, migration and emigration is a major requirement. However, it is already reasonably clear that the Clearances varied significantly over time and place, had complex origins and were not simply the result of the imposition of overweening landlord authority on a dependent peasantry. It is also firmly established that population displacement in the Highlands was mainly a consequence rather than a cause of the poverty and social distress of the region. At worst, the Clearances aggravated conditions of destitution which existed before they took place and which were then exacerbated by the combined influence of limited natural endowment, regional specialisation, rising population and weak economic diversification.

REFERENCES AND FURTHER READING

(1) E. Richards, *A History of the Highland Clearances: Agrarian Transformation and the Evictions, 1746–1886* (London, 1982).

(2) M. Gray, *The Highland Economy, 1750–1850* (Edinburgh, 1957).

(3) J. Hunter, *The Making of the Crofting Community* (Edinburgh, 1976).

(4) J. M. Bumstead, *The Peoples Clearance: Highland Emigration to British North America 1770–1815* (Edinburgh, 1982).

(5) E. Richards, *The Leviathan of Wealth* (London, 1973).

(6) P. Gaskell, *Morvern Transformed* (Cambridge, 1968).

(7) A. J. Youngson, *After the Forty Five* (Edinburgh, 1973).

(8) T. M. Devine, *The Great Highland Famine: Hunger, Emigration and the Scottish Highlands in the Nineteenth Century* (Edinburgh, 1988).

(9) A. I. Macinnes, 'Scottish Gaeldom: the First Phase of Clearance', in T. M. Devine and R. Mitchison (eds), *People and Society in Scotland, 1760–1830* (Edinburgh, 1988).

10

TEMPORARY MIGRATION AND THE SCOTTISH HIGHLANDS IN THE NINETEENTH CENTURY

By the late eighteenth century temporary migration from the Scottish highlands to the lowlands was already very significant. The fairs of Doune, Gartmore, and Drymen, on the fringes of the highlands, had become marts for the hiring of harvest labour and, 'were regularly frequented by multitudes of young men and women from the north'.[1] One contemporary, after extensive travel in the region, came to the conclusion that at least half the 'young women' in the southern highlands went south for the harvest, while more recent historical investigation has suggested that few families in Argyllshire could have broken even without the earnings of their young seasonal workers.[2] Yet, although agricultural employment almost certainly absorbed the largest number of temporary migrants at this time, it was by no means the only outlet of importance. Already, by about 1800, highlanders also worked for the season in the herring fisheries of the north-east and Clyde estuary, in the building industries of the lowland towns and cities, in industrial occupations like textile bleaching, and in domestic service.[3]

These migrations were essentially a reflexion of the differences in economic and demographic development between the highland and lowland zones. The north was a region of pastoral husbandry, slowly growing by-employments, such as kelping and illicit whisky-making, and steadily rising population. Increasingly, much of this natural demographic increase was shed either by permanent outmigration or more temporary movements to the lowlands where seasonal employments were available as a consequence of more vigorous agrarian and industrial change.[4]

Historians have long recognized the important function of temporary migration in highland society but, because of paucity of data for the eighteenth century, it has been possible to present only a very vague outline of the probable nature and impact of the phenomenon at that time.[5] In the nineteenth century, however, source materials are richer and more varied and, while not permitting precise quantification of migration trends, do enable a more detailed historical survey to be carried out. Ironically, however, it is precisely in this later period and particularly after about 1840, that present knowledge of highland temporary migration is most limited, partly because it has often been assumed that many of the opportunities formerly available to highlanders in the lowlands were absorbed by Irish immigrants in the few decades after the end of the Napoleonic Wars.[6] It is this phase which is the primary concern of this essay. First, it sets out to describe the broad determinants of temporary migration in agriculture, urban/industrial employment, and the fisheries. It will be argued that highland workers continued to play an important role in lowland agriculture until the final few decades of the nineteenth century. Increasingly, however, alternatives to agrarian employment became even more significant as a result of the growth of the lowland industrial economy, technical changes in the agricultural sector, which, by the 1870s restricted outlets for highland field workers, and an even greater dependence of the crofting population on temporary migration. In the second part of the discussion the effects of these population movements on the family economy of the highland population will be considered.

I

Because of the difficulties in the indigenous highland economy one might anticipate an even greater reliance on seasonal migration after *c*. 1815 than before. A number of studies have familiarised us with the process of economic decline.[7] The three decades after the Napoleonic Wars saw a collapse in the kelp industry, which had underpinned the economy of the Western Isles, a serious malaise in indigenous fishing, the gradual diminution of illicit whisky-making, the virtual disappearance of military employments, and, perhaps most disastrously of all, a sharp fall in the level of cattle prices. Cattle stocks had always represented the highland peasant's capital resource and traditionally the main base from which annual rentals, his single most important cash expense, were paid. Sagging prices were therefore inevitably reflected in a rapid accumulation of rent arrears on several estates. More seriously, they also resulted in a gradual depletion of stocks as beasts were sold off in a context of falling income, undiminished monetary need, and intermittent increase in the demand for imported food.[8]

Despite the weakening of the traditional economic structure the population of the highlands continued its seemingly inexorable rise. Depopulation was more typical of the later nineteenth and twentieth centuries than of earlier decades. Over the north-west highlands and islands, numbers rose by about 53 per cent between 1801 and 1841 and this occurred in an area where land resources, already limited, were further constricted by the spread of capitalist sheepfarming and the undisciplined subdivision of family lots. Temporary migration had always been attractive to many highlanders because it fitted so well into the cycle of activities and work-peaks characteristic of a pastoral economy. When the vulnerability of the mass of highlanders was exposed in the potato 'famine' of the later 1840s, however, their need to search for alternative employment, outside the highlands, either by permanent or temporary movement, was likely to become more pressing.

This suggestion of an increased reliance on seasonal income is, however, difficult to reconcile with established historical thinking on general migration patterns in nineteenth-century Scotland. A number of scholars have maintained that in the period after about 1820 seasonal employment opportunities for highlanders actually decreased, as their main traditional task, harvesting in the lowlands, was taken over by the Irish[9]. The latter, so the argument goes, were prepared to work harder, accept lower wages and, with the extension of steam navigation between Ulster and the Clyde in the first half of the century, could reach the hiring fairs more quickly and cheaply than their northern rivals. The fact that Irish seasonal migration did increase is beyond dispute. Numbers arose from an annual average of 6,000—8,000 disembarking at Glasgow in 1820 to 25,000 in the early 1840s[10]. However, it is less clear how far this 'forced' a general withdrawal of highlanders from the agricultural labour market in the lowlands.

One reason for initial doubt is that the orthodox view is mainly based on evidence submitted to the Select Committee on the State of the Irish Poor in Great Britain (1836)[11], and the Select Committee on Emigration, Scotland (1841)[12]. Self-evidently, these two sources may tell us much about the 1830s, when the general labour market in agriculture was relatively depressed, but nothing about the phase from the 1840s when it was more vigorous and, just as importantly, when the flow of seasonal migrants from Ireland to Scotland diminished very considerably[13]. Furthermore, the evidence presented to the committees must be treated with caution for three additional reasons. Firstly, most witnesses tended to treat temporary agricultural employment solely in terms of the grain harvest and were less inclined to draw conclusions concerning other aspects of farm work[14]. In the first half of the nineteenth century, however, the spread of green crops transformed and extended the farmer's labour needs by creating more seasonal work peaks in the year[15]. Secondly, much evidence, to the 1836 committee in particular, was inevitably framed in polemical terms, with the thinly veiled aim of curtailing Irish immigration to the United Kingdom. As a result, some witnesses may have been prone to exaggerate the adverse impact of the Irish on the labour market and, at the same time, willing to ignore or play down the contradictory evidence of a continuing highland presence in some parts of the lowlands despite the Irish penetration. Thirdly, most witnesses, in both 1836 and 1841, were inclined to limit their comments to the situation in the narrow central zone, stretching from Ayrshire in the west to the Lothians in the east and it is, indeed, apparent from other sources that here the Irish harvester did begin to play a dominant role.

The partial displacement of highland labour in this region was related to a subtle but nonetheless vital revolution in hand-tool technology: the adoption of the scythe-hook in preference to the toothed-sickle. The hook became popular because it could do a quarter to a third more work than the more traditional implement. But it was a man's tool, used with a slicing motion over a breadth measured by the arm. The toothed-sickle, the implement which it displaced in the central lowlands, was, however, favoured by women. It only cut small bunches at a time and was employed to remove stalks low down where they were firmer. Women were said to be physiologically better suited to bending than men.[16] Since Irish migration to the harvests was almost entirely male (in 1841, 49,911 of the total of 57,651 landing in Britain as a whole were men)[17] and highland movement mainly female, the victory of the Irish in some areas at least was perhaps inevitable.

Yet that victory could not have been complete because evidence from the highland zone itself does indicate a continued seasonal migration for harvest work in the 1830s, 1840s, and 1850s, despite the Irish presence. So, from the Hay Mackenzie estates in Wester Ross in 1844, 'many went for the harvest, some as far as the Lothians.'[18]. In 1841, 'the great part of the population of Badenoch and of the midland part of the county of Inverness' migrated south for the harvest.[19] It was suggested by Sir John McNeill, in 1851, after his inquiry into conditions in the western islands, that the people of Skye depended on such work for between one-half and two-thirds of their 'means of living'.[20] From one parish in that island (Strath) 300 set off annually for harvest work.[21] It was said of Tiree and Coll in 1842 that 'a great part of the young unmarried population especially of females, are in the habit of resorting to the low country in quest of harvest employment. Hundreds of these set off . . .'[22] Reports from Mull, Iona, and Barra in the 1840s and 1850s confirmed that harvesting in the south remained a major summer employment.[23]

A number of factors help to explain the survival of work opportunities for highlanders in lowland agriculture despite the Irish influx. In the first place, farmers in the central zone, from Ayrshire to the Lothians, seem only slowly to have abandoned the highlands as their main source of harvest labour. The Irish doubtless had an advantage in terms of labour productivity but employers had to balance this against the fact of a tried, traditional, and secure supply of workers for what was still the most critical task in the farming year. Thus, in the 1820s, contemporary press reports indicate a continuing annual migration of female reapers from the north. At this stage, the major impact of the Irish seems to have been to force down harvest wages rates rather than to monopolise employment.[24] Secondly, although the Irish scythe-hook did displace the highland toothedsickle throughout the central belt, it also increased the need for more female stackers and bandsters in the harvesting process. In some areas, this aspect of farm work continued to be carried out by women from the highlands.[25] Thirdly, by the middle decades of the nineteenth century, a regional division of labour had emerged between Irish and highlanders. While the former were strong in the western lowlands and to a lesser extent in the south-east, they apparently did not move in any force along that important arable zone stretching from the Tay, in the south, to Caithness, nor were they numerically strong around the southern fringes of the highland zone itself.[26] Much of this region seems to have remained a virtual monopoly of highland seasonal migrants until the mechanization of the harvest reached its climax in the 1890s with the widespread adoption of the mechanical reaper-binder.[27] Only in Aberdeen, Banff, and some parishes in Kincardine did they have only a marginal role. Farmers in those counties had developed their own indigenous labour supply for the busy season by establishing a structure of croft holdings alongside the larger farms.[28] Finally, during the 1830s and 1840s, there had been a further development of the 'bothy' system of accommodating farm labour in the counties of Perth, Fife, and Angus. In order to save on housing costs, some farmers in these areas began to pull down family cottages and instead boarded their ploughmen in sparsely furnished dormitories.[29] This, however, created a problem of securing extra hands during the harvest. In some districts this was solved by recruiting harvest workers from local weaving communities. Elsewhere, however, there developed a new dependence on the highland zone as a fruitful source of cheap female labour.[30]

The harvest was not, however, the only seasonal task in lowland agriculture which attracted migrants from the north. The tendency in the new husbandry had been to fill in the empty gaps in the summer months where previously there had been little to do around the farm. As the acreage of green crops rose so the farmer's busy time, formerly exclusive to the grain harvest of late August-September, began to extend from early spring until late autumn. In areas of turnip cultivation there was therefore a considerable increase in the demand for female workers for the associated tasks of hoeing, weeding, and singling.[31] One farmer, James Wilson of Foodie in Fife, reckoned that in 1844 he employed six ploughmen throughout the year and ten women as day-labourers from the beginning of April to harvest.[32] In 1836, Robert Hope of Fenton Barns in East Lothian estimated that he required 18 women and boys for weeding and hoeing turnips for 24 weeks in the year.[33]

But by the 1860s, the evidence suggests that farmers in many districts in lowland Scotland had great difficulty in recruiting the required number of females from local sources. The gradual triumph of factory industry in an urban context eventually restricted the earnings of country spinners and weavers and endangered the stability of many small industrial communities in the countryside which had previously supplied field-workers during the spring and summer months.[34] Again, women in some areas showed an increasing distaste for agricultural employment. As the Royal Commission on Labour reported authoritatively in 1893:

the chief cause of the abstention of women from farm work would seem to be the growing dislike to the work itself, coupled with a keen desire to enjoy the animation and variety of town life. With the general improvement of the domestic household of the married farm servant, the greater sense of refinement and the very general advance in education, young women feel ill-disposed to follow in the steps of their predecessors and engage in the rather rough though generally healthy requirements of Scottish farms. They prefer domestic service and town life to farm labour and a tidy respectable country girl can secure a nice place at a good wage by merely getting a character from the minister and farmer's wife, and replying to a few of the numerous advertisements in the *Daily Scotsman*.[35]

Yet in the period after *c.* 1850 there was an even greater need for female seasonal workers in the Scottish lowlands. Investment in more elaborate and carse lands of Perthshire, to extend turnip cultivation for the first time on a large scale. To do so they had to import female labour from the highlands and Western Isles; 'where a farmer can give constant employment to women by having cottar houses he can secure native female labour. Where he cannot give constant work he must fall back on the employment of Highland girls who will occupy a bothy for three quarters of the year and go home in the winter months or trust to occasional supplies of Irish women.'[36] In Lanarkshire in the 1880s, 'the principal permanent farm servants are usually natives of the county, but the extra hands are highlanders or Irish, both of whom are extremely numerous in the county.'[37] Also in Peeblesshire, in the 1860s, there was a 'fast increasing demand for high-landers and Irish', while even in the Lothians, despite the traditional dependence on the daughters of married farm servants, employers were forced to recruit highland girls.[38]

II

In 1851, after his tour of the western islands on behalf of the Scottish Board of Supervision, Sir John McNeill observed that a number of changes had taken place in the pattern of seasonal migration. He noted, in particular, that in the eighteenth and early nineteenth centuries, it had been the youth of both sexes who mainly sought outside employment. By the middle decades of the nineteenth century, however, he contended that the older males also felt the need to trek south and east. Furthermore, in his view, seasonal work had previously primarily attracted cottars and others at the bottom of the social scale who had only minimal access to land. By the 1850s, he argued, it had apparently become equally common among the majority of crofting females.[39] McNeill probably erred in detail by failing to consider military employment as a form of 'temporary migration' for adult males in the earlier period and by paying insufficient attention to participation by the same group in public work projects both within and outside the highlands. It is difficult, however, to object to his main thesis that by mid-century more highlanders than ever before had come to depend on seasonal incomes. As will now be seen, much other evidence seems to support his conclusion.

The new pattern was both a reflexion of the needs of the crofting population after the potato famines of the 1840s and the long-term consequence of the elimination of employments in the highland zone from the end of the Napoleonic Wars. It was also due to structural change and expansion in the lowland economy. On the one hand, this created an additional and varied range of casual employments.[40] On the other, economic change developed a new syncopation in seasonal troughs so encouraging migrants to dovetail one employment with another, and permitting extension in the period of residence away from home. Indeed, in evidence to the Napier Commission in 1883, crofter witnesses suggested that the overall trend was developing away from seasonal movement towards semi-permanent migration.[41] So, in the 1840s, men from the parish of Avoch in Ross spent the summer months building roads in Aberdeenshire and part of the winter digging drainage ditches on the county's farms. Those from the Ardnamurchan peninsula divided their time between field-work and general labouring in the dye works of Glasgow.[42] Highlanders recruited as labourers in the Glasgow gas-works during the winter months in the 1890s spent the summer months at the herring fisheries.[43]

Three outlets—domestic service, the construction industry, and the fisheries—require fuller comment because of their particular significance. The mid-Victorian boom and the growth of middle-class affluence, which was one immediate consequence, helped to boost demand for domestic servants. Not all, or even the majority, of this group were necessarily *temporary* migrants, but some undoubtedly were. Occupational mobility of female servants was very considerable as girls sought a better 'place' in the hierarchy of service. So, in Renfrewshire, in the 1790s, 'girls were in the habit of changing their residence every term' and, in the early nineteenth century, highland women employed as domestic servants in lowland towns tended often to return home for the winter.[44] This was one area of employment where, some contemporaries argued, Irish competition in the labour market was not as strong as in other sectors. Thus the Rev. Norman McLeod, the minister of a Gaelic church in Glasgow and a man of considerable personal experience of highland immigration, observed in 1841:

It may be a prejudice on the part of the Scotch but they generally prefer the Highland females in their families . . . I think the High-landers find it more easy to get respectable employment than the Irish; the Highlanders have many friends in Glasgow to whom they apply; there are very few days in which we do not receive letters of recommendation on behalf of poor highlanders coming to Glas-gow; they come with letters of recommendation to countrymen and clansmen who are in comfortable circumstances and those who come from one island do it for those from that island who have to get employment the Macdonalds for the Macdonalds and the Macleods for the Macleods.[45]

Modern research on highland migration to Greenock has supported Macleod's opinion. Between 1851 and 1891 about 25 per cent of all women engaged in private households were of highland origin, a figure markedly higher than that for any other migrant group.[46] Furthermore, in the main migrant district of Paisley in 1851, 57 per cent of the female highland work-force was employed in domestic service whereas only 19 per cent of the Irish, who made up a much higher component of the town's total population, were so occupied.[47]

The Scottish railway construction booms of the 1840s and the 1850s not only provided work for the Irish navvy but also for the highlander. Indeed, some sought and obtained railway employment as far away as France,[48] but more acquired it in the Scottish lowlands. More than half of the 2,124 men employed in railway construction in the Lothians in the 1840s were from the highlands. On the Hawick branch of the North British Railway, the respective numbers of employees were 1,310 Scots (mainly highlanders) and 731 Irish; while on the Caledonian there were 300 highland and 219 Irish navvies in the early 1840s. In the west of Scotland, too, highlanders worked on the line from Glasgow to Greenock in the 1830s and the line from Glasgow to Wemyss Bay in the 1860s.[49] The railway boom was dramatic but ephemeral. Probably of much greater significance, but much more difficult to document, was the role of highlanders as builders' labourers in Scottish towns and cities.[50]

Despite the importance of all these outlets, however, employment in the fisheries was probably the single most powerful influence on temporary migration from the outer Hebrides and the far north-west mainland in the second half of the nineteenth century. The seas around Ireland, the Isle of Man, the Clyde estuary, and the north-east coast (including Caithness) all attracted highland labour, but it was the two latter areas which exerted an especial magnetism for the crofting population.[51] Official figures for the 1870s and 1880s indicate that 5,000 men and women came in a great annual exodus from the two Hebridean islands of Lewis and Harris alone to the fishing ports of the east coast from Fife in the south to Caithness in the north. This represented almost 20 per cent of the total population of these two islands.[57] Some 10,000 crewmen, packers, and gutters from the highland zone as a whole descended on the town of Wick in the 1880s and almost as many, it was alleged, spent the season at Fraserburgh and Peterhead.[53]

Most communities in the north-west and outer isles were undoubtedly sending more seasonal workers to the fisheries by the later nineteenth century than ever before. In Lewis, about mid-century, at least one person from each family went to the north-east for the season.[54] Subsequently numbers increased until, three decades later, nearly 5,000 were involved or about one in five of the island's population.[55] There had been a particularly significant expansion in the size of the female labour force and as the Fishery Officer for Stornoway remarked in 1887: 'since 1854 the annual migration from the Lews to the east-coast fishing has been steadily increasing till latterly, and for a number of years back, every man and woman who was without regular employment went.[56] Other parts of this region, while perhaps not as dependent as Lewis on earnings acquired in the north-east, also supplied much labour for the fisheries. About 500 came from Harris in the 1880s.[57] All the young men of Barra served on the east-coast boats in the same period and, as early as the 1850s, it could be said of Mull that 'the number of people who go from hence to the Caithness and east-coast fishing may probably be equal to the number of families.'[58] Over the period 1850–80, seasonal fishing earnings were the main source of income on Skye and, in addition, on the north-west mainland, there was evidence that employment on the east coast was a vital factor in the material well-being of the population.[59]

Opportunities in the herring fishery blended well with the customary labour rhythms of these maritime areas. The phase of peak activity in the north-east from July to August fell midway between the earlier herring season of the Minch and the later white fishery in north-western waters. As a consequence, the crofter-fishermen attempted to derive returns from all three sources. Indeed, it was possible also for women gutters to seek harvest employment when the fishing season came to an end on the east coast.[60] Furthermore, despite marginal advances in technology, herring fishing fundamentally remained a labour-intensive industry in the second half of the nineteenth century. Thus, increases in catch and expansion in demand necessitated some augmentation of the labour force. This process only happened gradually. Between 1835 and 1854 there was a limited rise in the annual average cure of herring from 428,343 barrels to 495,879. The pace hardly quickened to 1864 (averaging 515,368 by that year). Thereafter, however, the industry entered a phase of very considerable expansion which endured for the subsequent twenty years. The average annual cure between 1865 and 1874 was 602,375 barrels and from 1875 to 1884 it rose to a figure approaching one million.[61] As a result, the number of herring boats on the east coast grew by about 51 per cent between 1855 and 1886.[62]

This vigorous development was accompanied by concentration of the industry in particular centres along the coasts of Aberdeen and Caithness. These foci could not themselves supply all the extra hands required during the busy season. The boats were operated through a system of owner-fishermen all of whom belonged to the same town or village. In July-August these four-five man consortia were each strengthened by the addition of one or two highlanders.[63] According to Fishery Board figures, the number of fishermen and boys (including seasonal migrants) rose as a consequence by about 60 per cent from 1854 to 1884.[64] Increasing catches necessarily also stimulated demand for processors since it was reckoned that, on average, three experienced women gutters and packers were needed throughout the season to cope with the catch of a single vessel.[65]

III

The vast scale of these various forms of temporary migration, involving as they did probably at least one member from the majority of families in the highland region, must have influenced northern society in a number of different ways. Most obviously, by providing a certain degree of income flexibility, temporary migration may have slowed down the rate of depopulation which would inevitably have been much more significant, at an earlier date, if highlanders had had to rely on a diminishing range of indigenous employments. The literature of the highland 'clearances' has tended to stress the drama of regional depopulation.[66] However, such polemic has obscured the reality of the relatively slow pace of the permanent exodus, which only accelerated in the final decades of the nineteenth century and the fact that population at the end of the century was still much larger than in 1800.[67] Clearances of population for sheep and movement of evicted communities to areas of inferior and marginal land might not automatically mean permanent movement from the region if temporary employment outlets were available and capable of providing a subsistence income in most years.

Moreover, the very fact that a significant proportion of the society had eaten away from home between May and September, when temporary migration was at its peak, was itself of major importance. This was the time of maximum pressure on food resources, the period when the old grain and potato harvests were running out and the new had yet to be gathered. Food, drink, and accommodation were normally available as part of the wage contract in farm work and in consequence it was sometimes possible for temporary migrants to save meal to take home to the family.[68] Travelling expenses to and from seasonal employment were not over-burdensome. Migrants from Lewis to the east-coast fisheries either joined the boats at the earlier Minch fishery or trekked across country to Wick, Peterhead, and Fraserburgh.[69] In the 1870s, at least, lowland farmers often paid part of the travelling expenses of their temporary workers, a custom which illustrated the serious problems of labour shortage which existed at that time in some sectors of agriculture.[70]

The period spent away depended not only on the availability of work in the lowlands and the level of earnings there but also on conditions at home. For example, in 1881, young migrant workers from Tiree prolonged their stay in the south because of the failure of the potato crop on their native island. Because of this, they did not want to come home and burden their parents.[71] At an earlier and more widespread crisis, the potato famines of

151

1847-8, temporary employment outlets provided an important alternative when the highland economy was threatened with collapse. The famine Relief Commission grasped their importance and allocated travelling expenses in some areas to those willing to seek work outside the stricken region.[72] As Sir John McNeil commented in the aftermath of the disaster. As a result of the famine, from the Pentland Firth to the Tweed from the Lews to the Isle of Man, the men of Skye sought the employment they could not find at home.[73] Indeed, the famine seems to have been a watershed in the evolution of temporary migration. Because of the shock it administered, more people than ever before were eager to seek work outside the highland zone rather than depend on the slender and uncertain returns from monoculture.

The new dependence on temporary migration automatically resulted in an increased flow of cash earnings to northern society. Temporary migrants had a very high propensity to save because on their efforts depended the survival of close relatives over the winter months.[74] In consequence, the erosion of the subsistence system was hastened as new resources of cash income and cheaper world grain prices in the 1870s and 1880s encouraged the purchase of meal from outside.[75] About mid-century, hardly any lowland products had infiltrated the peasant society of the north-west. Of Lewis it could be said in 1844 the produce of a foreign soil, as tea, coffee and sugar, and the common convenience of lowland art are to them altogether alien.[76] Thirty years later, however, meal, tea, tobacco, and even clothing had become commonplace purchases in the north.[77] Involvement in the exchange economy meant that many crofter families, became almost as acquainted with cash relationships as the working classes of the industrial cities to the south with whom they are usually contrasted. The highland equivalent of the urban pawnbroker and small shopkeeper was the meal dealer some areas, too, small banks flourished to provide the basis of this credit mechanism and in Skye, for instance, by the 1880s it was said the crofters are as *au fait* at discounting and receiving bills as men in the centres of business.[79]

Whether this augmented cash income altered material standards for the better in a marked way cannot at the moment be determined in precise terms. Certainly seasonal earnings did rise substantially in some sectors over the period in 1850-80. Wages formulae deck hands during the six-week east–coast fishing averaged £12 by the later 1870s in a moderately average season. This was about three times the levels prevailing thirty years earlier.[80] In the south-east, at current prices, increases of at least one-third occurred in general agricultural wages over the period 1838-52. By the late 1860s there had been a similar rise of a quarter and despite an inevitable annual fluctuation in the level of harvest earnings, the current value of wages was at least twice as great as it had been forty years previously.[81] Furthermore, this expansion in seasonal earnings, until the late 1870s at least was not cancelled out by rises in most crofter fixed costs or by a parallel malaise in other highland economic activities. On the contrary, the level of rentals on most estates after about 1850 remained stable;[82] grain, the other major cost apart from rent, dropped in price especially from the early 1870s as a result of low world prices and communications developments in steam and rail. Recovery in cattle prices and fresh stimulus to the native white fishery in the 1850s and 1860s also promoted economic stability while the acceleration both of emigration and permanent migration from mid-century partially relieved congestion and indirectly contributed to regional income through remittances sent home by relatives.[83]

On the other hand, these gains, tangible as they were, hardly implied permanent or fundamental amelioration. The very heavy incidence of temporary migration was itself proof of the slender basis of the region's recovery. Economic necessity, the need to scrape a subsistence living, compelled these mass movement.[84] Moreover, migrant workers were essentially vulnerable. Their prime advantage to the host economy was that they were removable. They and not the native population bore the greater brunt of unemployment and this disadvantage was compounded by the fact that temporary workers were concentrated in areas of the economy where demand for labour was most fluctuating.[85]

Entire communities in the Western Isles had by the 1880s become overwhelmingly dependent on an income source which was itself based on the market prices for herring in places as far apart as Scandinavia and Russia. The potential danger became a reality in the years 1883–9 when vast herring catches glutted markets and prices collapsed.[86] As a result boat-owners and curers changed their traditional bargain with the hired men to one in which the whole catch was sold by daily auction and each member of the crew shared in the proceeds. This was to expose the seasonal worker to the full impact of a chronically depressed market, a disaster which was exacerbated by a dramatic rise in unemployment among hired hands.[87] Furthermore; from about 1884–5, the difficulties of the crofting population were increased by the onset of an industrial depression in lowland Scotland which markedly reduced the opportunities for urban casual employment precisely at the time when highlanders were seeking alternatives to fishing.[88] As a result extreme privation once again visited the western highlands and islands and the feelings of discontent which this provoked were made manifest in the crofting agitation of that decade. The 'Crofters' War', in its early stages, antedated the economic depression and had complex political and cultural origins.[89] Nevertheless, the extent to which the momentum of protest was sustained by the fall in earnings from temporary migration in the period 1884–9 has, perhaps, not received the attention which it merits.

The very fact that these migrations were not permanent implied a determination to preserve a valued life-style and reject the supposed attractions of residence in the south. Ironically, however, closer contacts with lowland society helped to erode cultural and linguistic difference and therefore may have helped to facilitate permanent movement in the longer term. It has been argued that education in the English language in the late nineteenth century was a powerful influence in encouraging permanent movement.[90] Yet, in the view of many contemporaries, knowledge of English speech in Gaeldom was more associated with periods of employment in the south and less with formal schooling in the north.[91] Temporary migration also helped to acquaint the inhabitants of a peasant society with the complexities and attractions of a money economy. The new availability of consumer goods in the highlands in the last quarter of the nineteenth century was a direct consequence of the incomes released by temporary migration and this may have diluted the values and attractions of crofting society for some. Such an effect was perhaps especially likely because of the habit of spending even longer periods away from home in the later period.[92] Certainly, data on highland migration to the town of Greenock indicate a substantially higher level of permanent movement from parishes with traditions of seasonal migration than from those without. On the other hand, such arguments can be pressed too far. Income from temporary employment was as much a support of the old society as a potent contribution to the new. It did stimulate the trend towards a cash-based economy in the highlands but it did not, as the political programmes issued during the 'Crofters' War' showed, remove the old hunger for land. On the contrary, temporary migration was a consequence of the desire to retain a foothold on the land and, as such, provided a vivid-demonstration of the strength and resilience of an old-established peasant society.

NOTES

1. A. Whyte and D. Macfarlane, *General View of the Agriculture of the county of Dumbarton* (Glasgow, 1811), pp. 248–9. I am grateful to Malcolm Gray of the University of Aberdeen for his valuable comments on an earlier draft of this article. The map was drawn by the Cartography section of the Department of Geography, University of Strathclyde. I am grateful to the cartographers and to Prof. Keith Smith for their help.
2. J. Knox, *A Tour through the Highlands in 1786* (1787), p. 60; E. Cregeen, 'The Changing Role of the House of Argyll in the Scottish Highlands', in N. T. Phillipson and R. Mitchison, eds. *Scotland in the Age of Improvement* (Edinburgh, 1970), p. 9.
3. D. F. Macdonald, *Scotland's Shifting Population* (Glasgow, 1937), pp. 129–37.
4. E. J. T. Collins, 'Migrant Labour in British Agriculture in the Nineteenth Century', *Economic History Review*, 2nd ser. xxix (1976), 30–59; M. W. Flinn, 'Malthus, Emigration, and Potatoes in the Scottish North-West, 1770–1870', in L. M. Cullen and T. C. Smout, eds. *Comparative Aspects of Scottish and Irish Economic and Social History, 1600–1900* (Edinburgh, 1977), pp. 47–64.
5. Malcolm Gray, *The Highland Economy, 1750–1850* (Edinburgh, 1961), p. 53; Cregeen, loc. cit. p. 9; Collins, loc. cit. 36–59; A. Redford, *Labour Migration in Great Britain, 1800–1838* (Manchester, new edn. 1964), pp. 132–49; Macdonald, op. cit. p. 129; James Hunter, *The Making of the Crofting Community* (Edinburgh, 1976), p. 50.
6. Hunter, op. cit. p. 50; Redford, op. cit. pp. 132–49; James Handley, *The Irish in*

Scotland, 1798–1845 (Cork, 1945), p. 34; Macdonald, op. cit. pp. 132–3; Collins, loc. cit. 47–8.

7. See, *inter alia*, Gray, op. cit. Hunter, op. cit. Flinn, loc. cit. P. Gaskell, *Morvern Transformed* (Cambridge, 1968); A. Youngson, *After the' 45* (Edinburgh, 1973); T. M. Devine, 'The Rise and Fall of Illicit Whisky-Making in Northern Scotland, 1780–1840', *Scottish Historical Review*, LIV (1975), 155–77.

8. Gray, op. cit. p. 182.

9. See references quoted in p. 345, n. 2.

10. Handley, op. cit. p. 38.

11. P.P. 1836, XXXIV, app. G.

12. *First and Second Reports from the Select Committee on Emigration, Scotland* (P.P. 1841, VI) (hereafter *Reports on Emigration*).

13. Between 1841 and 1881, the number of Irish seasonal workers resident in Ireland but labouring during the summer months in Scotland declined from about 25,000 to about 4,000. See Collins, loc. cit. 51.

14. See, for example, *Reports on Emigration*, evidence of J. Bowie. p. 4, Rev. N. Macleod, p. 70, A. Scott, p. 146.

15. P. Brodie, 'On Green Crops', *Prize Essays and Transactions of the Highland Society of Scotland* (hereafter *Trans. H.S.*), **1** (1799), 110—11.

16. A. Taylor, 'On the Comparative Merits of Different Modes of Reaping Grain', *Trans. H. S. n.s. (1843–5)*, 263–8; A. Fenton, *Scottish Country Life* (Edinburgh, 1976), p. 54; *First Report from the Select Committee appointed to inquire into the state of Agriculture and into the Causes and the extent of the Distress which still presses on some important Branches thereof* (P.P. 1836, VIII) (hereafter *S. C. on Agricultural Distress*), evidence of Robert Hope, QQ. 9046–55, George Robertson, Q. 12254.

17. C. Larcom, 'Observations on the consesus of the Population of Ireland in 1841,' *Journal of the Statistical Society of London*, VI, (1843), 323–51.

18. *Appendix to the Report from H. M. Commissions for Inquiring into the Adminsitration and Practical Operation of the Poor Laws in Scotland* (P.P. 1844, XXII) (hereafter *Report on the Poor Laws*), p. 61, Seasonal migration can only be described in this impressionistic fashion because there is little reliable statistical information on numbers engaged in agricultural (and especially harvest) work. Apart from the year 1841, the occupational census was not taken in summer when seasonal migration was at its peak but in the relatively quiet months of March or April. In addition, the distinction between 'temporary' and 'permanent' movement from a native parish cannot be rendered precisely in the census returns.

19. *Reports on Emigration*, p. 70.

20. *Report to the board of Supervision by John McNeill on the western Highlands and Islands* (P.P. 1851, XXVI) (hereafter *McNeill Report*), app. 4, p. 1067.

21. Ibid.

22. *New Statistical Account of Scotland* (hereafter *N.S.A.*) VII, 214.

23. Ibid. VII, 356, 402, 562, XIV, 172; *McNeill Report*, app. A, reports on Iona and Mull. Evidence from other parts of the western mainland and islands confirm the pattern. Parish of Knockbain, Ross, 1844; 'many go to the harvest to the low countries and fishing at Caithness.'—*Report on the Poor Laws*, 1844, app. 1, pt. II, parish of Knockbain. Parish of Lochcarron, Ross, 1844; 'Population employed in harvesting and fishing in the north-east.'—Ibid. parish of Lochcarron. Parish of Urquhart, Inverness, 'women go in crowds for harvest work; about 200 are absent annually'.—Ibid. parish of Urquhart. Similar statements came from the parish of Applecross, Inverness (*McNeill Report*, app. A, parish of Applecross); Tongue, Sutherland (*N.S.A.* XV, 178); island of Gigha (*N.S.A.* VIII, 32); South Knapdale, Argyllshire (*N.S.A.* VII, 263).

24. Anon. 'On Reaping with the Scythe', *Quarterly Journal of Agriculture*, IV (1832–4),

355,; 'Agricultural view of Edinburghshire', *Farmer's Register and Monthly Magazine*, II (1828), 527, I, (1827), 429; *Farmer's Magazine*, XXI (1820), 490.

25. *Farmer's Register and Monthly Magazine*, II (1828) 527.

26. Anon. loc cit; *Royal Commission on Labour, the Agricultural Labourer, Scotland*, II, pt. II (P.P. 1893–4, XXXVI) (hereafter *R.C. on Labour*), pp. 13, 40, 109, 152.

27. J. Macdonald, 'On the Agriculture of the County of Caithness', *Trans. H.S.* 4th ser. VII (1875), 253; *Reports on Emigration*, 1841, p. 118; *Fourth Report on the Employment of Children, Young Persons and Women in Agriculture*, app. I (P.P. 1870, XIII) (hereafter *Fourth Report on Women in Agriculture*), pp. 110, 123, 126; *Royal Commission on the Depressed condition of the Agricultural Interest, Assistant Commissioner's Reports* (P.P. 1881, XVI) (hereafter *R.C. on Agricultural Depression*), QQ. 35980, 36530, 39968.

28. M. Gray, 'North East Agriculture and the Labour Force, 1790–1875', in A. A. Maclaren, ed. *Social Class in Scotland: Past and Present* (Edinburgh, 1976), pp. 86–104.

29. *Report on the Poor Laws*, evidence of P. Jack, session clerk of Flisk, Fife, pp. 94, 271, 282.

30. Ibid.

31. Brodie, loc. cit; R. S. Skirving, 'On the Agriculture of East Lothian with Special Reference to the Progress made in Husbandry during the last Twenty-five Years', *Trans. H.S.* 4th ser. V (1873), 19–20.

32. *Report on the Poor Laws*, p. 282.

33. *S.C. on Agricultural Distress*, p. 21, Q.9693.

34. The process has been described in detail by M. Gray, 'Scottish Emigration: the Social Impact of Agrarian Change in the Rural Lowlands, 1775–1875', *Perspective in American History*, VIII (1973), 95–174. See also *Fourth Report on Women in Agriculture*, p. 40, and J. W. Paterson, 'Rural Depopulation in Scotland: Being an Analysis of its Causes and Consequences', *Trans. H.S.* 5th ser. IX (1897), 64.

35. *R.C. on Labour*, pp. 13, 98.

36. *Fourth Report on Women in Agriculture*, pp. 51–2.

37. J. Tait, 'The Agriculture of Lanarkshire', *Trans. H.S.* 4th ser. XVII (1885), 77.

38. *Fourth Report on Women in Agriculture*, pp. 51, 55. It would be a mistake to assume, however, that the demand for agricultural workers from the highlands was exclusively for females. Throughout the middle decades of the nineteenth century the elaboration of drainage schemes, a result of the invention of the cylindrical clay pipe, and the allocation of government funds at low interest rates, provided employment throughout the lowlands for male highlanders as day-labourers. The vast majority of permanent employees on Scottish farms were specialist ploughmen and occasional labour for additional tasks had to be recruited from other sources including the highlands. See J. Macdonald, 'The Agriculture of Fife', *Trans. H.S.* VIII (1876), 11–12; J. Dickson 'The Agriculture of Perthshire', *Trans. H.S.* II (1868–9), 167–8.

39. *McNeill Report*, p. xxxvi.

40. See G. Stedman-Jones, *Outcast London: A Study in the Relationship between Classes in Victorian Society* (Oxford, 1971), pp. 33–158, for a consideration of the structure of the casual labour market in one urban context.

41. *Report of the Commissioners of Inquiry into the Condition of the Crofters and Cottars in the Highlands and Islands of Scotland* (P. P. 1884, XXXII–XXVI) (hereafter *Napier Commission*), QQ. 258–65, 1006–16, 26998, 29153–65, 33681.

42. *Report on the Poor Laws*, p. 68.

43. *Royal Commission on the Poor Laws and Relief of Distress, Appendix XIXA, Report by the Rev. J. C. Pringle on the Effects of Employment or Assistance given to the 'Unemployed' since 1886 as a Means of relieving Distress outside the Poor Laws in Scotland* (Cd. 5073 of 1910), p. 61. I owe this reference to my colleague Dr. J. H. Treble.

44. R. D. Lobban, 'The Migration of Highlanders into lowland Scotland, *c.* 1750–1890, with particular reference to Greenock' (unpublished Ph.D. thesis, University of Edinburgh, 1970), p. 122; J. Macdonald, *The Agriculture of the Hebrides* (1811), p. 150.
45. *Reports on Emigration*, pp. 115–18.
46. Lobban, thesis, p. 136.
47. Scottish Record Office, Edinburgh, Census Enumerator's Books for Abbey Parish, Paisley. vols. 469, 471, 474.
48. *McNeill Report*, p. xxxvii.
49. *Report from the Select Committee on Railway Labourers* (P. P. 1846, XIII) (hereafter *S. C. on Railway Labourers*), pp. 15–30; Lobban, thesis, p. 35.
50. See, for example, *Report on the Poor Laws*, evidence of Donald Macpherson, superintendent of police in Arbroath, p. 51.
51. *Annual Reports by the Commissioners of the Fishery Board, Scotland, 1879–89*, passim.
52. *Report on the Condition of the Cottar Population of the Lews* (P. P. 1888, LXXX) (hereafter *Report on the Lews*), p. 33.
53. *R. C. on Agricultural Depression*, Q. 30192; *N.S.A.* xv, 145.
54. *McNeill Report*, p. xix.
55. *Report on the Lews*, Statement of the Fishery Officer for Stornoway, p. 33.
56. Ibid.
57. Ibid.
58. *Napier Commission*, Q. 10460.
59. Ibid. Q. 29153, app. A, pp. 45, 64.
60. *R. C. on Labour*, p. 129.
61. *Fourth Report of the Fishery Board for Scotland* (P. P. 1886, xv), p. xi.
62. M. Gray, 'Organisation and Growth in the East Coast Herring Fishing, 1800–85', in P. L. Payne ed. *Studies in Scottish Business History* (1967), p. 188.
63. *Report on the Lews*, pp. 4–5.
64. *Annual Reports of the Fishery Board for Scotland, 1852–84*, passim.
65. R. J. Duthie, *The Art of Fishcuring* (Aberdeen, 1911), pp. 6–32.
66. See, for example, John Prebble, *The Highland Clearances* (1963).
67. As the following table indicates:

Year	Total highland population	Percentage change in previous decade
1801	312,817	—
1811	318,266	+5.1
1821	362,184	+13.8
1831	381,876	+7.4
1841	396,045	+1.8
1851	395,540	−0.1
1861	380,440	−3.8
1871	371,840	−2.5
1881	369,453	−0.5
1891	360,367	−2.5
1901	352,371	−2.1

The demographic pattern of the island of Lewis, in the outer Hebrides, perhaps provides the clearest evidence of the function of seasonal migration in this respect. Population stood at around 8,300 in *c.* 1795, rose to 17,037 in 1841, 19,694 by 1851, and 25,487 by 1881. As the Select Committee on the Condition of the Cottar Population of the Lews concluded in 1887: 'this rate of increase in prosperous agricultural districts would be remarkable but occurring where, with a population of only 8,311 as in 1790–97, concurrent testimony represents the produce of the land as insufficient to maintain the inhabitants, it clearly indicates the extent to which they are indebted for the means of subsistence to sources other than those which their holdings afford.'—*Report on the Lews*, p. 7.

68. *Napier Commission*, QQ. 33812, 2787, 3377.
69. *R.C. on Agricultural Depression*, QQ. 30128–30.
70. *Fourth Report on Women in Agriculture*, pp. 61, 108; *Napier Commission*, QQ. 1739–41.
71. *Napier Commission*, QQ. 33812–13.
72. *Report on the Poor Laws*, evidence of Rev. Alexander Adams, United Presbyterian Congregation, Portree, Skye, p. 986.
73. *McNeil Report*, p. xii.
74. S.C. on Railway Labourers, pp. 16, 30; *Report on the Poor Lawns*, p. 986; *Reports on Emigration*, 1841, p. 4; *Fourth Report on Women in Agriculture*, p. 51; *Napier Commission*, app. A, p. 2.
75. *Report on the Lews*, p. 4; *R.C. on Agricultural Depression*, Q. 30107; *Napier Commission*, app. A, pp. 46–7, QQ. 28180, 29153–65, 41120.
76. N.S.A. XIV, 147. *R.C. on Agricultural Depression*, Q. 30107. See also references in n. 7.
78. *Report on the Lews*, p. 5.
79. *Napier Commission*, app. A, p. 46.
80. *Report on the Lews*, p. 4; *N.S.A.* XV, 101, 181.
81. *Fourth Report on Women in Agriculture*, pp. 61; 129; A. L. Bowley, 'The Statistics of Wages in the United Kingdom during the last Hundred Years, Part I, Agricultural Wages', *Journal of the Royal Statistical Society*, LXII (1899), 141–8; G. Houston, 'Farm Wages in Central Scotland from 1814 to 1870', ibid. ser. A, CXVIII (1955), 224–8.
82. *R.C. on Agriculture Depression*, pp. 555, 560; Hunter, op. cit. p. 244.
83. Hunter, op. cit. pp. 107–30; Flinn, loc. cit. pp. 47–64.
84. *Napier Commission*, Q. 1016; 'Young lads stayed as long as they wished in the south; many young women went to the Lothians. It is sheer necessity that compels them to go.'
85. Collins, loc. cit. 54. In harvest employment this difficulty was exacerbated by the fact that dependants of permanent farm workers were first taken on and only afterwards were stranger hired. See *Farmer's Magazine*, XXI (1820), 490.
86. *Annual Report of the Fishery Board for Scotland, 1879–87*, passim.
87. Ibid.
88. *Third Report of Select Committee on Distress from want of employment* (P. P. 1895, IX), p. 515. I am indebted for this reference to Dr. J. H. Treble.
89. H. J. Hanham, 'The Problem of Highland Discontent, 1880–5', *Transactions of the Royal Historical Society*, 5th ser. XIX (1969), 21–67; Hunter, op. cit. pp. 31–183.
90. A. Geddes, *The Isle of Lewis and Harris* (Edinburgh, 1955), p. 226.
91. *N.S.A.* VII, 263, 562; XIV, 122, 172; *Fourth Report on Women in Agriculture*, p. 103.
92. In the 1870s and 1880s census data for certain of the Hebridean islands begin to show an increasing number of wives and children with birth places beyond the highland region. This was one spin-off from temporary migration which may have facilitated permanent residence in the south in the longer term. See Margaret C. Storrie, 'The Census of Scotland as a Source in the Historical Geography of Islay', *Scottish Geographical Magazine*, LXXVIII (1962), 165. It is difficult, however, to generalize in this complex and under-researched area. The establishment of such marital connexions was very rare among highland female field workers in the eastern lowlands but much more common among their sisters in domestic service.—*Fourth Report on Women in Agriculture*, app. B, p. 100.

11

HIGHLAND LANDOWNERS AND THE
HIGHLAND POTATO FAMINE

I

The last great subsistence crisis on the British mainland in modern times
occurred in the 1840s and 1850s in northern Scotland. During that period,
when the United Kingdom was consolidating its position as the most
advanced economy in the world, the inhabitants of the western Highlands
and islands were reduced to serious destitution and even threatened with
starvation when blight destroyed the potato, their main source of food.
Widespread failure of the crop first occurred in 1846 but endured to a
greater or lesser extent for almost a decade thereafter in most parts of the
crofting region. Not until 1856 did reports finally begin to appear of a
general recovery throughout the area. The epic tragedy of the Great Famine
in Ireland has caused this regional disaster to be partially overlooked by
British historians.[1] The Highland potato famine certainly did not cause the
appalling crisis in mortality suffered by the unfortunate population across the
Irish Sea, but it was nonetheless an episode of major significance in the
history of the Scottish Highlands with fundamental effects on the living
standards, emigration patterns and social structure of the region. The
concern of this essay, however, is not with the impact of the famine on
the Highland people as a whole, but with its effects on the élite of the
society, the landowners who were more likely to be hit in their pockets
rather than their stomachs by the most devastating Scottish subsistence crisis
since the notorious Lean Years of the 1690s.

It is important to begin by stressing that the crisis was both much wider
and deeper than a simple crop failure. Poor harvests had been a fact of life in
the western Highlands from time immemorial. The loss of oats and bere in
years of bad weather always inflicted widespread suffering and usually
provoked a wave of emigration. Such was the predictable pattern in
1771–2, 1782–3, 1795–6, 1806–7, 1816–17, 1825 and 1836–7, as well
as in a series of other less serious episodes. But the grain crop normally only
failed in part and rarely for more than two consecutive seasons. In 1846 and
1847 the potatoes were almost entirely diseased in most areas of the western

159

Highlands and islands, with the exception of parts of Sutherland, and the blight continued to inflict widespread damage for almost a decade after that. The extent of dependency on the crop by the 1840s in this region must also be borne in mind. Many of the subtenant or cottar class, a group which accounted for as much as half of all the inhabitants on some Hebridean estates, eked out an existence almost exclusively on the basis of potato cultivation and some fishing, while even the small tenant or crofter class relied to a considerable extent upon potatoes as a vital element of diet in combination with varying amounts of meal, milk and fish.[2]

But the period of the potato famine was not simply one of biological disaster. Three economic factors intensified the magnitude of the calamity and the impact it was likely to have on the lives of the population and the financial position of the landlord class. First, the potato failure was the climax to the gathering crisis which had beset the crofting economy since the end of the Napoleonic Wars. From the early 1820s through to the 1840s, its fragile supports crumbled as the north-west region was mercilessly exposed both to the postwar recession and the irresistible impact of savage competitive pressures from the urban manufacturing centres of the Lowlands to the south. Kelp production, reckoned to employ between 25,000 and 30,000 people in the Hebrides at its peak, disintegrated to minor proportions; illicit whisky-making for the wider market had all but ceased; military employment, a huge source of regional income during the Napoleonic Wars, dwindled rapidly during the peace which followed; commercial fishing, the great hope for a prosperous economy in the eighteenth century, stagnated in some districts and vanished entirely from others. The famine was then the culmination of three decades of creeping despair, the end not the beginning of an epoch of extended economic agony which not only intensified the burdens on the poor but increasingly exposed the traditional élite of the society as a debilitated and beleaguered class.

Second, during the famine itself, the failure of the potatoes was accompanied by a collapse in the prices of black cattle from 1847. Between that year and 1853 average prices fell by between one-third and one-half. The principal influence here was a change in external market circumstances but demand was also affected by the poor condition of Highland stock being presented at the trysts during the famine years.[3] With their main subsistence crop destroyed in some districts and badly diseased in others, the peasantry was even more likely to depend on income from cattle sales to pay rent and buy meal. But, virtually from the end of the first year of the blight, returns from this vital source contracted.[4] Third, difficulties also soon began to emerge in the labour market for temporary Highland migrants. In 1846 and 1847 there had been a happy coincidence between the needs of the crofting population for jobs in the south and the requirements of the Lowland economy for casual labour. The potato blight struck the western Highlands in the year of the greatest Scottish railway construction boom of the nineteenth century. The demand for navvies together with the effect of railway building on the Lowland economy as a whole stimulated a huge increase in temporary migration which produced a stream of income that did much to compensate for the failure of the potato crop. However, this windfall was short-lived as the boom years were followed by the serious industrial recession of 1848 and 1849 and the labour market for temporary migrants stagnated from then until about 1853.[5]

The potato famine can, therefore, indeed be seen as a disaster of exceptional magnitude. Because of its duration and through the interaction of crop failure and economic crisis it inflicted a quite unprecedented scale of misery. Contemporary observers were stunned into semi-apocalyptic utterances. The Free Church newspaper, the *Witness*, proclaimed that it was a calamity '. . . unknown in the memory of this generation and of many generations gone by, even in any modern periods of our country's history'. A national day of Fasting and Atonement was proclaimed, '. . . the hand of God has indeed touched us'.[6] Another commentator drew a close parallel between the trauma suffered by the Highlands in the aftermath of Culloden in 1746 and the even greater calamity which the potato blight would assuredly bring upon the people. For the landlords, the first effect of the disaster was seen in the rapid contraction of rental income from the small tenant class as they desperately switched their meagre resources from payment of rent to the purchase of meal during the bleak months of the autumn, winter and spring of 1846 and early 1847. In the first year of the blight, 25 per cent of all tenants on the Mackenzie of Gairloch estate in Wester Ross (by no means one of the poorest properties in the region) were in arrears; by 1848, the proportion had swollen to 63 per cent.[8] Rental income on Lord Macdonald's Skye estates collapsed by almost two-thirds between 1845 and 1850.[9] On the property of Sir James Riddell in Ardnamurchan, arrears surged from £269 in 1847 to £3,219 five years later and in the three western parishes of Sutherland arrears as a proportion of total small tenant rental climbed from 21 per cent in 1842 to an average of 89 per cent in 1849.[10] These data tend to confirm the accuracy of Sir John McNeill's observation in 1851 that the combined effect of the potato blight and the decline in cattle prices made it virtually impossible for those with rentals of £5 or below, who comprised the majority of the small tenants, both to feed their families and maintain payment of rent at the same time.[11]

But landlords had also to contend with the prospect of a potentially disastrous increase in costs as well as the collapse in small tenant rents. By the early decades of the nineteenth century, many traditional landed families were heavily burdened with hereditary debts which had inexorably grown larger during the recession after the Napoleonic Wars.[12] In some cases, the lion's share of annual income from rents was absorbed in the servicing of interest charges on these accumulated debts. In 1845, for instance, no less than 71 per cent of the gross income of Lord Macdonald's estates in Skye and North Uist was employed in the funding of such payments.[13] The critical factor here was interest rates. In 1848 and 1849 rates moved up during the recession precisely at the same time as the scale of the increase in rent arrears began to become evident. It was reckoned that any rise of half of one per cent in interest rates would further reduce Lord Macdonald's 'free' annual income of £7,000 by a further £560.[14] More seriously it might cause the whole unsteady financial edifice to crumble as creditors became uneasy and sought to secure their assets by having embarrassed estates placed under trusteeship or even by proceeding to drive proprietors into complete bankruptcy.

Such an outcome seemed even more likely when the broad outlines of the government's response to the emergency became apparent. It was clear as early as autumn 1846 that the state was determined that Highland landowners should bear the main responsibility for famine relief. At most, government was only willing to play the role of an enabling agency which would facilitate the measures to be taken by the proprietors. It was not prepared to replace or supersede them. As Charles (later Sir Charles) Trevelyan, Assistant Secretary at the Treasury, and the most influential figure in the management of the government's relief operation, put it: '. . . it is by no means intended to afford relief in such a way as would relieve the landowners and other persons of property from the obligations they are under to support the destitute poor . . . any assistance contemplated would be rather in the form of giving a proper organisation and direction to the efforts of the proprietors'.[15] This was no idle or paper threat. During the course of the first two years of the famine, those landowners unwilling to fulfill their obligations as defined by the state were warned that they would be charged the full cost of grain should government be finally forced to intervene and send supplies to save the inhabitants of their estates. Particularly recalcitrant proprietors were threatened with public condemnation in Parliament and even with sequestration of their assets to defray the cost of government relief measures on their properties should these be deemed necessary. At the same time, both the Lord Advocate of Scotland and the Chairman of the Board of Supervision of the Scottish Poor Law urged local poor law committees to use their powers of discretion under the 1845 Act to provide 'occasional' relief to the destitute able-bodied population of the Western Highlands.[16] Either by insisting on direct landlord intervention to feed the people or by pressing for an extension of the responsibilities of the poor law authorities, and hence an increase in poor rates, government in 1846 seemed determined to ensure that Highland proprietors would bear the prime responsibility for Highland relief.

The prospects for the landed class now seemed miserable indeed. They were apparently caught in an irresistible and powerful vice between sharply contracting income and the probability of enormous increases in expenditure. In 1846 and early 1847 many petitions from landowners were dispatched to the Lord Advocate's office in Edinburgh and the Treasury in London pleading for assistance as a wave of virtual panic swept across the western Highlands.[17] Given the nature of the crisis, a great transfer of estates precipitated by the insolvency of many proprietors, on a scale akin to that which occurred in the western Lowlands after the dramatic failure of the Ayr Bank in the 1770s, might well have been anticipated.[18] Whether or not this was indeed the eventual outcome will be assessed in the next section of this essay.

II

A search was carried out for the period 1846 to 1860 in the contemporary press,[19] estate papers[20] and petitions and sederunt books of sequestration in the Court of Session[21] in order to determine the extent of financial crisis among Highland proprietors during the potato famine and in the years following it. The exercise was not designed to assess in a comprehensive fashion the range of economic problems caused by the famine but rather to reveal the extent to which these led to 'crisis'. This was a condition which was measured (a) by the number of estates put on the market because of the financial difficulties of the owner, (b) sales of particular sections of estates brought about by the extreme financial circumstances of the owner, and (c) the number of properties which were placed under the formal administration of trustees because of an owner's increasing indebtedness. Entail arrangements sometimes might limit estate sales even when owners were in grave difficulty. However, the greater Highland landowners, whose estates were most often entailed also held property which was unentailed, and the sales of many smaller properties, as the buoyancy of the regional land market between 1810 and 1840 confirms, were not always constricted by such legal arrangements.[22]

The investigation revealed only five cases where acute financial pressure caused estates either to be sold in whole or in part or to come under the administration of trustees in the western Highland and Islands between 1846 and 1856. W. F. Campbell of Islay and Sir James Riddell of Ardnamurchan were the only two proprietors to become insolvent and only Campbell suffered sequestration of his assets.[23] The estate of Knoydart, the last remaining property of the Macdonnels of Glengarry, was brought to market by the family's trustees in 1855.[24] North Uist, part of the patrimony of Lord Macdonald, whose principal lands were in Skye, was sold in 1856. These estates and those of Norman Macleod of Macleod, also in Skye, had earlier been placed under temporary trusteeship. Parts of these properties were put on the market during the famine period.[25]

Several points about this pattern are worth noting. First, acute financial difficulty was obviously very much the exception rather than the rule among west Highland landowners in this period. There were at least 86 separate estates in the region most seriously affected by the potato blight but in only a very small minority of cases did owners either suffer bankruptcy or concede control of their properties to the authority of trustees.[26] Second, even in the five examples described, the crisis precipitated by the famine was often the immediate cause rather than the fundamental explanation of insolvency. Lord Macdonald, for instance, already had an accumulated debt burden of over £140,000 on the eve of the potato failure and an annual rental income of £7,971.[27] He was clearly teetering on the edge of disaster long before the onset of the subsistence crisis of the 1840s completed his discomfiture. The same could also be said of Walter Campbell of Islay and Norman Macleod of Macleod.[28] There basic problems did not derive from the famine *per se*, but rather from the inability of several hereditary landed families to maintain the rising standards of living associated with their rank in society on the limited rent rolls of Highland estates during the era of economic recession after the Napoleonic Wars.

Third, when examined over the long-run, there seems little especially significant about the scale of land transfers in the western Highlands between 1846 and 1856. In the previous decade, 1836 to 1846 for example, at least eleven large Highland estates were sold by hereditary proprietors to newcomers.[29] The famine, on the evidence presented here, provoked some land sales but not apparently on a sufficient enough scale to radically alter the long-term structure and development of the Highland land market. It is possible, indeed, that in the short-run, the problems experienced by the region's landed class during the famine, may have temporarily reduced external demand for Highland estates.[30] What emerges, however, is an interesting paradox: the resilience and survival of the regional social élite during the greatest single economic and social disaster in the modern history of the Highlands.

III

Many Highland landowners escaped relatively unscathed simply because their properties were located outside the distressed region itself. The most devastating impact of the famine was felt only in the western maritime districts, north of Morvern and Ardnamurchan, and in most of the Inner and Outer Hebrides.[31] The population most affected was about 120,000 or around 40 per cent of the total population of the four Highland counties of Argyll, Inverness, Ross and Sutherland. Relief operations, which took place all over the Highlands in 1846 and early 1847, terminated in the southern, eastern and most parts of the central districts by the end of that year and thereafter were confined to the crofting parishes of the far west. An examination of the rentals of several estates in the eastern and central Highlands reveals little indication of a significant or enduring increase in rent arrears. Indeed, it would be difficult even to discover the existence of a *major* crisis in that region from these data alone.[32] The limited effects of the famine in this area are not difficult to understand.[33] The potato, though important, was not the crucial element in diet that it was in the west. Neither was there the same chronic imbalance of resources and population. A combination of heavy migration to the adjacent Lowlands and the labour-intensive requirements of mixed husbandry, which was important in some parts of the region, helped to preserve a rough equilibrium in most years between demand and supply of labour.[34] In other parishes, the rental income of landlords depended mainly on the operations of big sheep-farmers possessing tenancies of several hundred acres or more rather than impoverished crofters and cottars scraping a living from miniscule areas of land.

In the maritime and insular districts of the western Highlands, however, the landed class was exposed to the worst social consequences of the famine. The evidence suggests that in the short-term, at least, the majority do appear to have tried to assist the people of their estates through the distribution of meal at cost price and the provision of public works. Government relief officers carefully monitored the response of individual landowners during the winter, spring and early summer of 1846–47 and their reports confirm that most proprietors appeared willing, albeit sometimes grudgingly, to assume their responsibilities.[35] The responses of 77 per cent of landowners in the distressed districts are known. Twenty-nine per cent of this group were singled out for praise by government officers for their efforts while only 14 per cent were censured for their negligence. However, government threats to enforce sanctions rapidly reduced the number who were unwilling to provide assistance to a small handful. Charles Trevelyan was warm in his praise: '. . . the Treasury have been quite delighted with the whole conduct of the Highland proprietors . . . it was a source of positive pleasure to turn from the Irish to the Scotch case. In the former, everything with regard to the proprietors is sickening and disgusting'.[36] He asserted later that '. . . in Ireland the general disposition of these classes is to do nothing while in Scotland they are disposed to do what is in their power . . . if Skye were in the west of Ireland, the people would be left to starve in helpless idleness'.[37] Such intervention, however, could only be achieved at very considerable and increasing cost. On the Duke of Argyll's Tiree estate, for example, one of the islands which suffered the most extreme levels of destitution, expenditure on 'relief by employment' rose from £8 in 1845 to £1,850 in 1847 and on 'gratuitous relief' from £11 in 1845 to £2,174 in 1847. In the year before the famine, outlay on these forms of relief amounted to less than 4 per cent of total estate expenditure; by 1847, the proportion had climbed to over 74 per cent. The balance of income accruing to the proprietor in 1845 was £2,226. By 1847, on the other hand, the Tiree estate was operating at an annual deficit of £3,173.[38]

Yet, most west Highland landowners did not have to shoulder these burdens for long. From the early months of 1847 the main responsibility for famine relief began to be assumed by the Free Church of Scotland and the Edinburgh and Glasgow Destitution Committees which united in February, 1847 to form the Central Board for the Relief of Highland Destitution.[39] By the end of that year the Board had raised a sum of over a quarter of a million pounds from philanthropic sources at home and abroad. From 1847 to the end of 1850, when its operations came to an end, the bulk of this huge fund was distributed to the needy throughout the stricken region in the form of meal payments for labour. At peak periods of stress, such as the spring of 1849, almost four-fifths of the people of Barra, two-thirds of the population of Skye, one-half of the inhabitants of Wester Ross and one-third of the people of Mull, were in receipt of the Central Board's meagre pittances. But Lowland charity came to the rescue not only of hungry Highlanders; it also supported the position of the Highland landed class as a whole. Several proprietors continued to be active in relief measures after 1847 but the majority left most of the provision for the maintenance of the people to the Central Board and its Edinburgh and Glasgow committees. Above all, it was the charities which saved the landed class from what one contemporary described as 'the bankruptcy of public burdens'. The numbers of 'occasional poor', far from rising sharply and so leading to a huge increase in poor law rates, actually *fell* in the four Highland counties after 1847 to 1851 in the middle of the greatest social crisis in the region in the nineteenth century (see Table 1). There could be no more convincing confirmation of the crucial significance of the Central Board in the provision of minimal welfare services in these years.

Table 1 Occasional poor, highland counties, 1846–53

County	1846	1847	1848	1849	1850	1851	1852	1853
Inverness	296	1498	746	715	573	2099	2579	637
Argyll	553	932	838	719	716	843	946	602
Ross and C.	169	390	416	383	406	417	1503	464
Sutherland	34	26	39	52	70	120	81	71

Sources: *Parliamentary Papers, Annual Reports of the Board of Supervision for Relief of the Poor in Scotland*, XXVII (1847–8); XXV (1849); XXVI (1850); XXIII (1852); L (1852–3); XXIX (1854); XLV (1854–5).

Nor was the state entirely indifferent to the threat to the solvency of west Highland property posed by the famine. The government was indeed committed to the orthodoxies of political economy: that an economy thrived best when left to the free play of market forces and that any unnecessary interference with them was bound to do more harm than good. It was also determined to avoid the deep and costly involvement in famine relief which had absorbed its energies in Ireland. On the other hand, there was too much at stake for the tenets of political economy to be followed entirely to the letter. As the senior government official most closely asociated with the problem put it: 'The people *cannot under any circumstances*, be allowed to starve.[40] There was also recognition of the fact that the policy of relying mainly on individual landlords to provide relief would be inevitably counter-productive if the crisis persisted for very long.[41] Insolvencies would spread and the risk to the people on bankrupt estates would accordingly increase. State aid for the landed class was therefore approved, not in the form of a direct grant, which would have offended the political and economic conventions of the time, but by encouraging proprietors to apply for loans through the existing Drainage Act (9 and 10 Vic. cap. C1 (1846)) which had been passed by Sir Robert Peel's government to assuage opposition from the landed interest after the Repeal of the Corn Laws.[42] Loans were made available at an interest rate of 6.5 per cent per annum and repayment could occur over 22 years. The treasury, which administered the distribution of loans, was instructed to 'strain it (the Drainage Act) to the uttermost' in order to ensure that not only drainage works but fencing, roads and other developments 'subordinate to and connected with a system of drainage' might be approved.[43] In effect, the legislation became a mechanism for channelling state loans to a distressed region of the country which government could not assist directly because of its ideological predilections.

Not surprisingly, therefore, the eventual value of Highland applications for assistance through the Drainage Act was out of all proportion to the value of Highland property relative to that elsewhere in Britain. By the end of March 1847, the landowners in one of the poorest regions in Britain had applied for loans to the value of £488,000 under the Act, a figure which amounted to almost 20 per cent of all applications made in Britain as a whole.[44] As the factor of Lord Macdonald's estate put it: 'It [the Drainage Act] is not, however, altogether adapted to our circumstances but we have like drowning men catching at a straw, been obliged to lay hold of it'.[45] Perhaps more than any other single factor, the huge stream of income which flowed into the western Highlands through the funds released by the Act must have done most to alleviate the misfortunes of the region. The initial application was for a sum more than twice the value of the resources of the Central Board and additional loans were made available from 1850.[46] Many of the loans were used to reduce rent arrears through the wages paid to destitute crofters engaged in draining and trenching work under the Act. The actual payment was usually paid mainly in meal once per week. The residue of the 'wage' went to defray rent arrears and any balance was distributed in cash. In addition, crofts deemed to have been 'improved' by works carried out under the Act were charged the annual government interest rate of 6.5 per cent.[47] Landowners, therefore, sometimes passed on the 'cost' of the loan to their tenants. Some crofters were still paying these charges in the 1880s.[48] In this way, therefore, the Drainage Act not only alleviated the destitution of the people but made a powerful contribution to the economic stability of landed property in the distressed districts. The ground officer of one of the biggest estates in Skye noted how rents began to be 'generally well paid' again from 1849–50 and this he attributed mainly to the impact of the loans made available under the Act.[49]

The role of the charities and the influence of government legislation were, therefore, principal factors in allowing a destitute population to be supported without necessarily accelerating the ruin of large numbers of landed families. But these elements mainly explain how the *cost* of maintaining the people through the crisis was met. They do not adequately answer the question why the dramatic contraction in estate *income* from the small tenants did not produce serious financial problems for the landed class in general. The evidence suggests that it did not do so because a large number, and probably the majority of proprietors, by the late 1840s no longer depended on crofting rents as their major source of income. This was due both to the changing social composition of the west Highland landed class and to the new structure of the regional economy which had emerged in the three decades before the famine.

By 1846 the pattern of landownership in the western Highlands had undergone radical change. The hereditary landed families, apart from the two great ducal dynasties of Argyll and Sutherland, only clung on in North Uist, most of Skye, Islay and a few areas on the mainland such as Gairloch, Knoydart and Ardnamurchan. From the early nineteenth century, in a series of great land sales which reached a climax during the potato famine, the old Highland élite was replaced in many districts by a new class who had made their money in trade, industry and the urban professions of banking and law.[50] Typical of the new breed were such men as Octavius Smith, the wealthy London distiller, who in 1845 bought Achranich Estate in Morvern, a parish where between 1813 to 1838 every single property changed hands: James Matheson of the giant East India firm of Jardine, Matheson and Co., the new owner of Lewis, referred to in Disraeli's *Sybil* as '. . . richer than Croesus, one Macdrug, fresh from Canton, with a million in opium in each pocket'; Col. John Gordon, proprietor of Barra, South Uist and Benbecula, dubbed the 'richest commoner in Scotland' in the obituary written after his death; Francis Clark, a successful lawyer from Stirling, who had acquired the island of Ulva in 1835; James Baillie, a Bristol merchant and banker, who became the proprietor of Glenelg in 1837; Alexander Matheson, another very wealthy East India merchant, whose Ross-shire estates were more extensive by the 1860s than those of such grandees as the Dukes of Argyll and Atholl. In all, an analysis of the ownership of estates in the distressed region indicates that at least 74 per cent changed hands, several more than once, between 1800–40. This was a dramatic and exceptional rate of regional land transfer which was in sharp contrast to the pattern elsewhere in the first half to the nineteenth century.[51]

The reasons why this should be so are explored in detail elsewhere and need not be examined fully here.[52] They included the fact that much land was now available in the region as the pressures gripping the old Highland elite eventually overwhelmed many families in the post-war economic recession; the advances in steam navigation which rendered access less difficult from the rest of Britain; the new attractions of a Highland estate stimulated by the success of Scott's novels, the romantic appeal of scenic grandeur, Queen Victoria's well-published interest in the Highlands and the superb opportunities the region provided for the fashionable sports of hunting, fishing and shooting; the remoteness and solitude of the region which offered successful businessmen the possibilities of escaping occasionally from the space of life in the cities; the chance also for absentee proprietors to make speculative gains by buying up the possessions of insolvent families, laying the land down to sheep and then later selling at a greatly increased price. For present purposes, however, more important than the reasons for this changing pattern of landownership was its effects on the stability of the landed class during the famine. Quite simply the new men were not dependent on the petty payments of the impoverished crofters of their northern estates. Their income primarily derived from the profits of their manufacturing concerns, trading firms and professional activities. Many were tycoons of massive wealth for whom the provision of famine relief was easily submerged within their other investments in nco-Gothic castles, mansions, steam yachts, hunting lodges and bizarre schemes of agricultural improvement. Sir James Matheson, for example, spent almost £200,000 in famine relief and emigration assistance in Lewis and still had enough change to buy up several more properties in Wester Ross in the early 1850s.[53] Historians have underestimated the scale of this silent revolution in Highland landownership before 1846 and hence have tended to overestimate the vulnerability of the landed class as a whole during the famine after that date.

Table 2 Rental Structure of Hebridean and West Highland Estates

Parish/Estate	Per cent Share of Total Rental paid by Tenants with holdings rented at over £20 per annum. Selected West Highland and Hebridean Districts
Kilfinichen (Mull)	68
Kilmuir (Skye)	54
Snizort (Skye)	71
Portree (Skye)	43
Strath (Skye)	54
Sleat (Skye)	59
North Morar	73
Knoydart	90
Glenelg	87
Glensheil	97
Loschalsh	70
Kintail	77
Lochcarron	58
Applecross	52
Torridon	70
Average	74

Source: Parliamentary Papers, Report to Board of Supervision by Sir John McNeil, Appendix A. passim.

The changing economic structure of Highland estates was also conducive to the resilience of many proprietors. In all districts of the western Highlands for which we have detailed records the majority of tenants rented land at less than £20 per annum.[54] The numerical dominance of the crofting class is therefore not in doubt. What is more open to question is the *proportion* of rental paid by this group, because on that depended the real impact of the famine on landlord income. The available evidence suggests that tenants renting land above £20 per annum were more able to weather the storm and much better equipped to maintain their rent payments than those below them on the economic scale. For instance, on the Gairloch estate in Wester Ross, arrears among the bigger tenants rose marginally from £89 in 1845 to £214 in 1848 out of a total annual rental of £3,000 paid by this group. But this still represented only 12 per cent of total arrears which had accumulated on the estate by that year. Overwhelmingly, it was the smaller men who failed to maintain their rent payments.[55] The flow of rental income therefore crucially depended on the tenant composition of west Highland properties. An estate where the greater value of rents was paid by bigger tenants was self-evidently likely to be less vulnerable during the famine years than one where the bulk of revenue depended on the payments of destitute crofters.

Crofting rentals remained more important in several areas, such as the Ardnamurchan estate, Barra, South Uist, the Coigach section of the Cromartic estate and the Duke of Argyll's lands in Tiree and Mull.[56] But Table 2 demonstrates that in many other districts bigger tenants were now dominant, not numerically, but rather in the value of their contributions to total rental. A typical pattern was that in North Uist. There less than 6 per cent of all tenants paid £20 per annum or more, but they accounted for 76 per cent of the entire rental.[57]

There seems little doubt that the presence of these larger tenants mainly reflected the extensive development of sheep-farming in the western Highlands in the decades before the famine. A dual structure clearly existed on some estates. Large pastoral farms coexisted beside congested communities of crofters and cottars who possessed their own small fragments of land. By *c.* 1846 commercial pastoralism had penetrated virtually all the western Highlands and islands with the exception of Tiree, Barra, Islay and parts of Skye.[58] In the early 1840s, the *New Statistical Account* suggests that at least 85 per cent in Inverness and 35 per cent in Argyll, had experienced large-scale sheep farm development which resulted in the emergence of bigger tenancies and much land comsolidation.[59] It followed also that many estates primarily depended on the prices of wool and mutton for rental income rather than the cattle sales of a multitude of poor crofters. Significantly, as Figure I reveals, sheep prices began an almost uninterrupted climb from the mid 1840s from the doldrums of the period after the Napoleonic Wars, a trend which lasted until the later 1860s. The era of the famine was one of considerable difficulty for cattle farmers but it was also the early stages of a phase of buoyant prosperity for sheep farmers. For many Highland estate owners this expanding market was a crucial

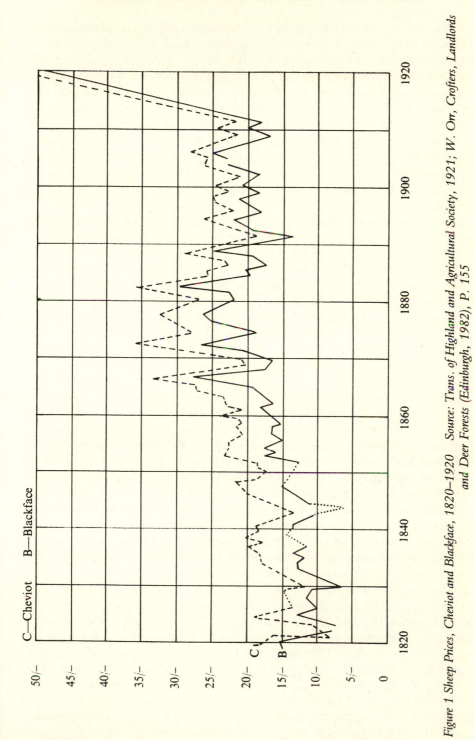

Figure 1 Sheep Prices, Cheviot and Blackface, 1820–1920   Source: Trans. of Highland and Agricultural Society, 1921; W. Orr, Crofters, Landlords and Deer Forests (Edinburgh, 1982), P. 155

advantage. It not only insulated them from the worst economic consequences of the potato failure but also stimulated further expansion of large-
scale pastoral husbandry during the crisis itself.[60] As the blight persisted,
several landowners began to turn the misfortunes of the small tenants and
cottars of their properties to their own advantage by enforcing policies
designed to increase income by altering the social and economic structure of
their estates. In order to understand their strategy and its effect it is necessary
in the first instance to outline the problems which had confronted them
during the three decades before the crisis of 1846.

IV

The basic issue in Highland history in the first half of the nineteenth century
was the imbalance between rising population and the contraction in
indigenous employment opportunities which was initially generated by
the post-war economic recession and then accelerated by the remorseless
advance of commercial pastoralism. The Select Committee on Emigration
(Scotland) of 1841 estimated that in the western Highlands and islands there
was a surplus of population of 44,600 people or almost 38 per cent of the
total inhabitants. The imbalance would have been even more acute if it had
not been for the increasing pace of out-migration.[62] But the exodus was still
not on a sufficient scale in all areas to effectively counterbalance natural
increase and the impact of the dramatic decline in the labour-intensive
sectors of the economy after 1820. Despite the increasing volume of
emigration, only in Sutherland and a few other districts was there *mass*
desertion from the land during the postwar crisis. In 1841 around 85,000
more people were living in the crofting region than the total recorded in
Webster's census of the 1750s. This represented an increase of about 74 per
cent over that period.[63] In addition, there were wide regional disparities in
the scale of haemorrhage. Depopulation was mainly confined to the county
of Sutherland itself and to a few parishes on the western mainland. Numbers
continued to rise in many of the islands of the Inner and Outer Hebrides
despite the collapse of profitable kelp manufacture and the stagnation in
fishing. Of those parishes which reached their maximum level of population
before the 1841 census, only 37 per cent were in the islands.

It is vital to this analysis, therefore, to recognise that before 1846, despite
dispossession, clearance, economic recession and harvest failure, the grip of
the people on the land had not been broken. This was still a peasant society
and its members possessed the tenacious attachment to land which is
characteristic of all such societies. As Pierre Goubert has remarked: 'No
peasant will voluntarily give up his land, be it only half a furrow'.[64] It was to
this set of social values that the parish minister of Duirnish in Skye referred
when he explained how the people '. . . feel a blind, and therefore, a very
powerful attachment to the rocks and glens amid which they were brought
up—an almost invincible aversion to abandon them'.[65] Even grinding

poverty, usually tolerated because it was familiar, could not easily or quickly dissolve these attitudes. Heavy emigration was normally confined to periods of great distress such as recurrent harvest failure. But even at such times there was often great reluctance to move. An enquiry into attitudes towards emigration in 1837–8, in the aftermath of the most serious nineteenth century subsistence crisis before the potato famine itself, revealed a very great diversity of response. In 16 of the 45 parishes which provided information, more than one-third of the inhabitants were disposed to accept offers of emigration assistance, in 21 less than a third and in 8 parishes few or none were keen.[66]

Not surprisingly, these attitudes were anathema to the landowners.[67] The continuing rise in the Hebridean population deepened destitution and forced up rent arrears. The people became increasingly vulnerable to the effects of harvest failure in 1816–17, 1825 and 1836–7. At each crisis several proprietors were forced to intervene to prevent starvation on their estates by distributing meal at cost price and adding the outlay to rents which were unlikely ever to be repaid in full. Some also provided employment in road-building and estate improvement for the destitute. Strategies of clearance and assisted emigration were more commonly employed as the social crisis in the western Highlands became more acute. Though these did have an effect in some areas of the region, they did little to solve the underlying problem. On several estates draconian measures actually exacerbated social destitution as dispossessed crofters were pushed further down the social scale into the impoverished mass of cottars and semi-landless people. Clearance in itself was just as likely to intensify congestion as cause depopulation since some of those who lost their lands crowded into slum villages or crofting townships in neighbouring districts rather than leave the region altogether for a new life elsewhere. If contemporary opinion is correct, it was often the poorest, those who could not easily raise the cost of passage and resettlement across the Atlantic, who were forced to remain.[68]

In the event only a disaster on the scale of the potato famine could reduce the intractable demographic problems which had harassed the administration of Highland estates since the early decades of the nineteenth century. The famine not only precipitated a huge increase in migration from the region in general but caused the greatest haemorrhage to occur in the Hebrides, which had sustained the fastest rate of actual population growth before 1846. Six of the nine crofting parishes estimated to have lost 20 per cent or more of their inhabitants between 1841 and 1851 were located in the islands.[69] In the following decade, ten of the twelve parishes which lost 20 per cent or more were also in the Hebrides. Over the two decades of the famine, Uig, in Lewis, lost an estimated half of its total population; Jura, almost a third (1841–51); the Small Isles, almost a half (1851–61); Barra, about one-third (1841–51). An examination of the census enumerator books for two representative insular parishes, Kilfinichen in Mull and Barvas in Lewis, shows a loss respectively of 45.5 per cent and 24.4 per cent of all *households* between 1841 and 1851 and a further substantial haemorrhage in the following decade.[70] The overwhelming majority of the 17,000 emigrants assisted either by individual landlords or the Highland and Island Emigration Society during the famine were also from the Inner and Outer Hebrides, 76 per cent of those assisted by landlords and 78 per cent supported by the Society were natives of the islands.[71]

Only a crisis of the severity and duration of the potato famine could have enforced such a radical increase in emigration. The long series of bad years, punctuated only by a few periods of ephermeral improvement, temporarily relaxed the peasant grip on the land. Communities where there had previously been little enthusiasm for emigration were seized with a desperate urge to get away. The Duke of Argyll's Chamberlain in the Ross of Mull and Tiree reported in 1849 that the cottars were '. . . ready to go in hundreds to Canada if provided with the means'.[72] During the course of the famine his correspondence indicates that many more wished to emigrate than the estate was prepared to assist.[73] Similarly in Skye, the termination of the operations of the Central Board in 1850 and the financial problems experienced by Lord Macdonald and Macleod of Macleod, the two greatest landowners on the islands, induced a mood of desperation in 1851–2 which resulted in a widespread anxiety to emigrate.[74] Only in Lewis did the old hostility to emigration apparently persist and that may have been due to the relief schemes of Sir James Matheson and the resilience of fishing around the coasts. As a result, the island's inhabitants may have suffered less than those elsewhere.[75]

The fundamental influence of the stress of hunger and destitution on the pattern of movement is confirmed by the cycle of emigration. The return of slightly better times, even if they did not last for long, could quickly dissipate the urge to leave. Thus, although 50 families from Edderachillis in Sutherland petitioned for emigration assistance in January 1847, only ten were still willing to go by March. Spring weather and improved prospects at the fishing had led to a change of heart.[76] There was an even more remarkable example of a similar type of response in the Macleod estates in Skye in 1855. Over 1,000 of its destitute inhabitants had sought to emigrate with the help of the Highland and Island Emigration Society. In the event, however, only 237 individuals finally presented themselves for inspection and registration by the Society's officials.[77] The vast majority had changed their minds because of the arrival of a steamer at Dunvegan with a cargo of meal and potatoes sent out for distribution by the Free Church and other sympathisers in the Lowlands.

The Society also found that the demand for emigration assistance fluctuated markedly with sudden changes in economic circumstances. Fifty-three per cent of the 4,910 emigrants it assisted to emigrate to Australia between 1852 and 1857 left in the first year of its operation which was a time of terrible destitution. However, only 13 per cent (628 individuals) emigrated in 1853 because conditions then were much better.[78]

The Secretary of the Society explained: '. . . the disinclination to emigrate is because their condition at home is so far better by the increased demand for labour, the high price of cattle and sheep, the abundance and good quality of their crops, especially of potatoes—and the success of the Herring Fishery on the West Coast.'[79]

But the volume, pace and timing of the exodus was not linked only to prevailing economic circumstances. Those who suffered most from the crops failures and the associated economic crisis were the very same families and individuals who could not normally afford the costs of passage and resettlement from their own resources. In the final analysis, the poor had to rely on landlord assistance, the efforts of such charitable organisations as the Highland Emigration Society and the Central Relief Board and kinsmen already settled abroad, to embark on emigration. The landed class was therefore able to develop a significant influence on the timing, the sequence and, above all, the social composition of the movement. In addition, though the Highland Emigration Society was an independent public charity, landowners were intimately involved in its operations as the Society's officials relied partly on proprietors and their agents in the selection of suitable candidates for assistance.[80] Their association with the Society was consolidated further after the passage of the Emigration Advances Act (14 and 15, Vic. c.91) in 1851 which made available public funds at interest rates of 6.25 per cent per annum to proprietors wishing to assist emigration from their estates. Those landowners who took advantage of these loans mainly sent out the emigrants they supported under the auspices of the Society to Australia. It covered two-thirds of the total cost from its own charitable resources, leaving only the remaining one-third to be contributed by individual proprietors.[81]

Landowners exploited these opportunities with considerable energy. From 1849, in particular, they intensified the pressures which were already fostering emigration by enforcing a series of sanctions designed to accelerate the flight of the very poor. As the Duke of Argyll proclaimed in 1851: 'I wish to send out those whom we would be obliged to feed if they stayed at home—to get rid of that class is *the object*' (underlined in original letter).[82] The measures taken towards this objective included the confiscation of the cattle stocks of those in considerable arrears of rent, a more resolute and thorough-going programme of clearance (especially in the linkage of eviction with schemes of assisted emigration on a much greater scale than ever before), a veto on tenants cutting peat during the summer who were scheduled for emigration assistance and denial or reduction of famine relief except in dire circumstances.[83] The development of coercion is made most apparent in the steep increase in summonses of removal obtained at west Highalnd sheriff courts in this period. Between 1846 and 1852, a total of 1,052 summonses were issued at Tobermory with over 84 per cent given from 1849 to 1852.[84] The Matheson estate in Lewis obtained no less than 1,180 summonses of removal in the three years after 1849.[85]

At the same time, much discrimination was employed in the selection of those to be given emigration assistance. The policy was framed not in a spirit of paternalistic benevolence but mainly out of a desire to exploit the circumstances of crisis to best economic advantage. In general, the retention of those communities who depended mainly on fishing was favoured while determined efforts were made to enforce the expulsion of those who traditionally relied more on kelp-burning and also, though to a lesser extent, on cattle farming. On several properties, indeed, such as Lewis and the Macdonald estate in Skye, a very close correlation developed between eviction, assisted emigration and removal or thinning of kelping townships. The policy, therefore, was designed above all else to eliminate or reduce the very core of the 'redundant' population. On the other hand, there was also a reluctance to provide emigration assistance for tenants paying rentals above £10 per annum and those with only small arrears of rent. Instead, it was the cottars and the poorer tenants who were more likely to receive aid. Most landowners and their agents sought to increase social differentiation among the population of their estates, to rigorously control subdivision after the famine emigrations had taken place, to drive out the weaker elements and consolidate the position of the stronger and, at the same time, to release even more land for the pursuit of large-scale pastoral husbandry. As a result several Hebridean estates were, in economic terms, in leaner and fitter condition after 1856 than they had been before.[86] The potato famine was certainly painful for some landed families and a disaster for a few others but the majority of proprietors were less at risk. They might regard it in a more sanguine light as a great crisis which eventually provided the opportunity at great social cost to reduce the social and demographic problems which had confronted their predecessors for over a generation.

NOTES

1. Aspects of the Highland famine are examined in James Hunter, *The Making of the Crofting Community* (Edinburgh 1976), ch. 5 and M. W. Flinn (ed), *Scottish Population History from the Seventeenth Century to the 1930s* (Cambridge 1977). The only attempt at a comprehensive analysis is T. M. Devine, *The Great Highland Famine: Hunger, Emigration and the Scottish Highlands in the Nineteenth Century* (Edinburgh 1988). The research for this paper was conducted as part of a larger project supported by ESRC (Grant no. B00232099). I am grateful for the Council's generous support and the energetic help of my research assistant, Mr W. Orr, in the collection of data.
2. Devine, *Highland Famine*, ch. 2.
3. These generalisations are based on market reports in the *Inverness Courier* and *John O'Groats Journal*, 1845–1854.
4. Prices were buoyant throughout most of 1846 and only declined sharply the following year. See, *Inverness Courier*, 21 October 1846; *Edinburgh Evening Courant*, 3 October 1846.
5. See Devine *Great Highland Famine*, ch. 6 for this paragraph.
6. *Witness*, 21, 25 November 1846.
7. Anon, *Extracts from Letters to the Rev. Dr Macleod regarding the Famine and Destitution in the Highlands of Scotland* (Glasgow 1847), p. 71.

8. Conon House, Mackenzie of Gairloch MSS, 'Gairloch Rentals, 1846–49'.
9. Scottish Record Office (SRO), Lord Macdonald Papers, GD221/43, 46, 62, 70, 82, 'Macdonald Rentals, 1796–1858'.
10. SRO, Riddell Papers, AF49/6, 'Report of T. G. Dickson for Trustees, 1852'; National Library of Scotland, Sutherland Estate Papers, Dep. 313/2283 2302, 'Small Tenant Rentals, Eastern and Western Districts'.
11. *Parliamentary Papers, Report to the Board of Supervision by Sir John McNeill on the Western Highlands*, XXVI (1851), IV.
12. M. Gray, *The Highland Economy, 1750–1850* (Edinburgh 1957), pp. 181–92.
13. SRO, Lord Macdonald Papers, GD221/62, 'General View of the Affairs of the Rt. Hon. Lord Macdonald, 3 February 1846'.
14. *Parliamentary Papers, Correspondence relating to the measures adopted for the Relief of Distress in Ireland and Scotland*, LIII (1847), Mr Trevelyan to Sir E. Coffin, 11 September 1846.
15. Ibid, Trevelyan-Coffin Correspondence, September–December, 1846.
16. SRO, Lord Advocate's Papers, AD58/86, 'Lord Advocate to Mr Tytler, 5 January 1847'.
17. SRO, HD7/26, Miscellaneous correspondence from Highland landowners, 1846–7.
18. This disaster resulted in the transfer of landed property estimated at a value of £750,000. Several of the bank's partners were substantial landowners. See H. Hamilton, 'The Failure of the Ayr Bank, 1772'. *Econ. Hist. Rev.*, VIII, 2nd series, 1955–6, pp. 405–18.
19. These included the files of the *Inverness Advertiser, Inverness Courier, Witness, John O'Groats Journal, Scotsman* and *Glasgow Herald* for the relevant years. Highland properties were regularly advertised in these papers.
20. SRO, Breadalbane Muniments, GD 112; Campbell of Barcaldine MSS., GD 170; Campbell of Jura Papers, GD 64; Clanranald Papers, GD 201; Cromartie Estate Papers, GD 305; Loch Muniments, GD 208; Lord Macdonald Papers, GD 221; Maclaine of Lochbuie Papers, GD 174; Riddell Papers, AF49; Seafield Muniments, GD 248. Inverarary Castle. Argyll Estate Papers. Achnacarry Castle, Cameron of Lochiel Papers. Conon House, Mackenzie of Gairloch MSS. Dunvegan Castle, Macleod of Macleod Muniments. Islay House, Islay Estate Papers.
21. SRO, CS 277, Sederunt Books in Sequestration; CS 279, Petitions in Sequestration, 1839–56.
22. J. Barron, *The Northern Highlands in the Nineteenth Century* (Inverness, 1907), vol. 1, *passim*.
23. SRO, CS 277, Sederunt Books in Sequestration, W. F. Campbell of Islay; SRO, Campbell of Jura Papers, GD 64/1/347/1, 'Report to the Creditors of W. F. Campbell of Islay'; SRO, Riddell Papers, AF49/6, 'Report of T. G. Dickson for Trustees, 1852'; *North British Advertiser*, 15 July 1854.
24. Anon., *The State of the Highlands in 1854* (Inverness 1855), pp. 21–44.
25. SRO, HD 20/31, 'Report of Committee on the Case of Macleod of Macleod, 5 March 1847'; SRO, GD 221/160/4, 'State of Debts due by Lord Macdonald, November 1849'.
26. The figure is based upon SRO, HD 6/1, 'Map of the Distressed Districts by D. W. Martin'.
27. SRO, Lord Macdonald Papers, GD 221/62, 'General View of the Affairs of Lord Macdonald, 3 February 1846'.
28. Dunvegan Castle, Macleod of Macleod Muniments, Box 51, 'C. E. Gibbons to Macleod, 27 December 1833'; I. F. Grant, *The Macleods: the History of a Clan, 1200–1956* (London 1959), pp. 584–5; J. Mitchell, *Reminiscences of My Life in the Highlands* (1833, reprinted Newton Abbott, 1971), pp. 299–300; SRO, Treasury

Correspondence relating to Highland Destitution, HD 6/2, 'Deputy-Commissary Dobree to Sir Edward Coffin, 21 April 1847'.

29. The estates and their purchasers with date of acquisition in brackets were: Kintail, Sir A Matheson (1840, 1844); Aros, Mull, D. Nairne (1842); Ulva; F. W. Clark (1835–6); Raasay, G. Rainy (1846); Glenelg, James Baillie (1837); Lewis, James Matheson (1844); Barra, S. Uist, Benbecula, Col J. Gordon (1838–45); Torridon, Col McBarnet (1838); Arisaig, Lord Cranstoun (?). The figure of eleven is unlikely to be definitive and should be taken as a minimum number based on land sales reported in the *Inverness Courier*, 1836–46 inclusive. For a more detailed examination of land sales see T. M. Devine, 'The Emergence of the New Élite in the Western Highlands and Islands, 1790–1860', in T. M. Devine (ed), *Scottish Society in the Era of Improvement and Enlightenment* (forthcoming, Edinburgh 1989). The references to estate sales during the famine period do not apply to all transactions but are confined to those where other evidence indicates that sales were rendered necessary either through the insolvency of the landowner or through the actions of trustees.

30. For instance, in December 1846, the Marquis of Lorne, heir to the Duke of Argyll, admitted that the 'potato panic' had reduced demand for Highland property (SRO, Loch Muniments, GD 268/45, 'Marquis of Lorne to James Loch, 12 December 1846'). However, this malaise was probably only temporary. In early 1848 Lord Cranstoun sold Arisaig to Mr Mackay of Bighouse without reducing the upset price. The estate of Lynedale in the distressed island of Skye was acquired by Alexander Macdonald of Thornbank, Falkirk at a cost of £9,000 in 1849. This represented an advance of about ten per cent on its 1837 price (*Scotsman*, 29 January 1848, 11 August 1849).

31. See Devine, *Great Highland Famine*, ch. 2, for the basis of the generalisations which follow in this paragraph.

32. National Library of Scotland, Sutherland Estate Papers, Dep. 313/2216–22; Conon House, Mackenzie of Gairloch MSS, 'Account of Charge and Discharge, Conon and Kernsaray estates, 1845–1849'; SRO, Cromartie Papers, GD 305/2/84–121, Strathpeffer and New Tarbet rentals, 1834–1855, SRO, Seafield Muniments, GD 248/408, Urquhart Rental, 1816–1856.

33. There is a useful summary of the main reasons for the varying regional impact of the potato famine in *Reports of the Edinburgh Section of the Central Board for the Relief of Destitution in the Highlands, 1847–50*, (Edinburgh, 1847–50), Second Report by the Committee of Management to the Edinburgh Section for 1850–11.

34. T. M. Devine, 'Highland Migration to Lowland Scotland, 1760–1860'. *Scottish Historical Review*, LXII (2) (1983), pp. 137–49.

35. SRO, Treasury Correspondence relating to Highland Destitution, February–September, 1847, HD 6/2; SRO, Lord Advocate's Papers, AD 58/81, 'Reports on conditions of various estates in the Highlands and Islands, 1846–7'.

36. SRO, Breadalbane Papers, GD 12/14/19, 'Alexander Campbell to Earl of Breadalbane, 23 April 1847'; Trevelyan's opinion was communicated in private correspondence to Campbell who then informed Breadalbane.

37. SRO, Destitution papers, HD 7/46, 'Sir Charles Trevelyan to William Skene, 2 March 1848'.

38. Inveraray Castle, Argyll Estate Papers, Bundle 1522, 'Abstract of Accounts etc. of Tiree, 1843–49'.

39. See Devine, *Great Highland Famine*, ch. 5 for detailed references for this paragraph.

40. *Parliamentary Papers, Correspondence relating to the relief of Distress* Mr Tevelyan to Mr Horne, 20 September 1846. The phrase is italicised in the original source.

41. Ibid, Mr Ellice to Chancellor of the Exchequer, 31 August 1846.

42. J. B. Denton, 'Land Drainage etc. by Loans', *Journal of the Royal Agricultural Society of England*, 4 (11), 1868.

43. *Parliamentary Papers, Correspondence relating to the relief of Distress*, Chancellor of Exchequer to Lord Advocate, 13 October 1846; Sir E. Coffin to Mr Trevelyan, 22 October 1846.
44. *Parliamentary Papers, Return of Applications under the Drainage Act*, XXXIV (1847); SRO, Papers relating to the Drainage of Land Act (1847) including returns, HD 7/33. £2 millions were allocated under the original legislation and a further £2 millions were made available by the Treasury from 1850.
45. *Parliamentary Papers, Correspondence relating to the relief of Distress*, Mr McKinnon to Capt Pole, December 1846.
46. See n. 44 above.
47. *Parliamentary Papers, report to Board of Supervision by Sir John McNeill*, Appendix A, Evidence of Angus McDonald, 60: evidence of C. Macleod, 81: *Witness*, 28 July 1849; *Inverness Courier*, 6 February 1851; Conon House, Mackenzie of Gairloch MSS, Black Deed Box, Bundle 53, 'Report by Mr Inglis on Management, 1854–57'; SRO, Lord Macdonald Papers, GD 221/46, 'Charge/Discharge, 1850–51'.
48. *Parliamentary Papers, Report and Evidence of the Commissions of Enquiry into the Condition of the Crofters and Cottars in the Highlands and Islands of Scotland*, 1884, XXXII–XXXVI, 302, Q.5564.
49. *Parliamentary Papers, report to Board of Supervision by Sir John McNeill*, Appendix A, 60.
50. What follows is based on Devine, 'The Emergence of the New Elite', *passim*.
51. Lawrence Stone and Jeanne C. Fautier Stone, *An Open Elite? England 1540–1880* (Oxford 1984), pp. 407–21.
52. Devine, 'The Emergence of the New Elite', *passim*.
53. *Parliamentary Papers, report to Board of Supervision by Sir John McNeill*, Appendix A. Evidence of J. M. Mackenzie, 93; MS. Diary of J. M. Mackenzie, Chamberlain of the Lews, 1851. (In private hands. Copy made available courtesy of Ms M. Buchanan.)
54. Gray, *Highland Economy*, ch. 5.
55. Conon House, Mackenzie of Gairloch MSS, 'Account of Charge and Discharge of the Intromission of Dr J. Mackenzie as Factor for the Mackenzie estates, 1846–8'. For a similar pattern on the Sutherland estate see National Library of Scotland, Sutherland Estate Papers, Dep. 313/2207–15, 'Sutherland Rentals'.
56. Inveraray Castle, Argyll Estate Papers, Bundle 1522, 'Abstract of Accounts, Tiree, 1843–50', 'Abstract of Accounts Mull property, 1843–50'; SRO, Cromartie Estate Papers, GD 305/2/84–121, 'Estate rentals'; SRO, Riddell Papers, A.F. 49/6, 'Report of T. G. Dickson for Trustees, 1852'; MS. Diary of J. M. Mackenzie, 1851.
57. SRO, Lord Macdonald Papers, GD 221/43, 'Report by D. Shaw, Factor for North Uist, 1839'; GD 221/70. 'North Uist Rentals, 1853–4'.
58. *Reports of Central Board of Management of the Fund Raiser for the Relief of the Destitute Inhabitants of the Highlands* (Edinburgh 1847–50), First Report of Central Relief Board (1847), 2; *Report on Mull, Tiree . . . etc. by a Deputation of the Glasgow Section of the Highland Relief Board* (Glasgow 1849), 8, 10; *Parliamentary Papers, Report to Board of Supervision by Sir John McNeill*, Appendix A, Evidence of Thomas Fraser, 35.
59. These estimates are based on a scrutiny of the parish accounts for the four Highland counties in the *New Statistical Account of Scotland* (Edinburgh 1835–45).
60. Devine, *Great Highland Famine*, ch. 12.
61. *Parliamentary Papers, Report from Select Committee on Condition of Highlands and Islands*, 21.
62. Flinn (ed), *Scottish Population History*, pp. 327–34, 338–9.
63. The region referred to in these figures is the West Highland survey area as defined by F. Fraser Darling in *West Highland Survey* (Oxford 1955), pp. 15–17.

64. P. Goubert, *The Ancien Regime: French Society 1600–1750*, (London 1973), p. 44.
65. *New Statistical Account*, XIV, p. 344.
66. A Fullarton and C. R. Baird, *Remarks on the Evils at Present affecting the Highlands and Islands of Scotland* (Glasgow 1838), p. 128.
67. The generalisations in this paragraph are based on a survey of the following material: Public Record Office, London, T1/4201, Correspondence and reports of Robert Grahame to Fox Maule, 6 March 6 May 1837; *Parliamentary Papers, Report from Select Committee on Condition of Highlands and Islands, passim*; SRO, Lord Macdonald Papers, GD 221/122/1,4,11,19; Fullarton and Baird, *Remarks on the . . . Highlands and Islands*; Inveraray Castle, Argyll Estate Papers, Bundle 1529, SRO; Brown MSS, TD80/100/4; National Library of Scotland, Sutherland Estate Papers, Dep. 313/2283–2302; SRO, Riddell Papers, AF49/4, Sunart and Ardnamurchan rentals; SRO, Cromartic Papers, GD 305/2/84–121, Estate Rentals, 1834–1855; Dunvegan Castle, Macleod of Macleod Muniments, 3/107/5, Macleod Rentals, 1800–58.
68. See, for example, SRO, HD 21/35, 'Petition of the Inhabitants of Glenelg (1848)'.
69. For the basis of these estimates see Devine, *Great Highland Famine*, ch. 8.
70. General Register Office, Edinburgh, Census Enumerators Books, Kilfinichen (Mull) and Barvas (Lewis), 1841, 1851, 1861.
71. For the Society's figures see SRO, HD 4/5, 'List of Emigrants of the Highland and Island Emigration Society'; for those of individual landlords see Devine, *Great Highland Famine*, Appendix 10.
72. Inveraray Castle, Argyll Estate Papers, Bundle 1535, 'J Campbell to Duke of Argyll, 27 February 1849'.
73. Ibid, Bundle 1805, J Campbell to Duke of Argyll, 17 May 1851.
74. *Report of the Highland Emigration Society* (Edinburgh 1853), 10. Another witness confirmed that 'the people are anxious and willing to get away'. See Dunvegan Castle, Macleod of Macleod Muniments, 659/7/3, 'J D Ferguson to Madam Macleod. 25 June 1852'.
75. MS. Diary of J M Mackenzie, Chamberlain of the Lews, 1851.
76. National Library of Scotland, Sutherland Estate Papers, Dep. 313/1512, 'E McIver to R Horsburgh, 27 March'.
77. SRO, HD 4/4, 'J Chant to H Rollo, 30 April 1855'. See also, Mitchell Library, Glasgow. Letterbook of Sir J McNeill, MS. 21506, 'McNeill to Sir Charles Trevelyan, 23 June and 21 August 1852.
78. SRO, HD 4/5, 'List of Emigrants of the Highland and Island Emigration Society'.
79. SRO. Letterbooks of the Highland and Island Emigration Society, HD 4/2, 'Sir Charles Trevelyan to Capt W Denison. 4 July 1853'.
80. For the Society see D S Macmillan, 'Sir Charles Trevelyan and the Highland and Island Emigration Society, 1849–59', *Royal Australian Society Journal*, XLIX, (1963) and R A C S Balfour, 'Emigration from the Highlands and Western Isles of Scotland to Australia during the Nineteenth Century'. Unpublished MLitt thesis. Edinburgh University, 1973.
81. *Parliamentary Papers, Seventh Report of Board of Supervision of Scottish Poor Law.* 1. (1852–3), XII: Eighth Report XXIX (1854), IX.
82. Inveraray Castle. Aryll Estate Papers. Bundle 1558, 'Duke of Argyll to ?, 5 May 1851'.
83. Unless otherwise indicated all generalisations until the end of the essay are based on a survey of: MS. Diary of J M Mackenzie, Chamberlain of the Lews, 1851; Inveraray Castle. Bundles 1522–4, 1804, Campbell–Duke of Argyll correspondence, 1848–55; SRO, Riddell Papers, AF 49/6, 'Report of T G Dickson for Trustees (1852); SRO. Campbell of Jura Papers, GD 64/1/347. 'Report to the Creditors of the late W Campbell of Islay'; Mitchell Library, Glasgow. MS. 21506

Letterbook on Highland Emigration of Sir John McNeill; SRO. Lord Advocate's Papers, AD 58/83. Threatened Eviction of the tenants of Strathaird, Skye'; SRO. Lord Macdonald Papers, GD 221/122/4, 11, 19', GD 221/123/1; SRO, Lord Advocate's Papers. AD 58/85. 'Evictions of Tenants from the District of Sollas'.

84. SRO, Sheriff Court Processes (Tobermory), SC 59/2/4–14.
85. SRO, Sheriff Court Processes (Stornoway), SC 33/17/26–33.
86. Devine, *Great Highland Famine*, ch 12.

12

UNREST AND STABILITY IN RURAL IRELAND AND SCOTLAND, 1760–1840

I

The Agricultural Revolution in Scotland produced profound social effects. In the Lowlands enlarged farms were created as the small farmer class was reduced and the sub-tenant or cottager group eliminated. In the Highlands the consequences of 'improvement' were even more dramatic and notorious. The scale of eviction of peasant communities increased in unprecedented fashion as landlords sought to rationalise estates and respond to the rise in prices for pastoral products. Social dislocation produced popular resistance in varying degrees. The most remarkable response came in the Lowlands. There the old order passed away with little dissent. Apart from the Levellers' Revolt in Galloway in the 1720s, two generations before the main phase of change, and one or two minor incidents thereafter, the consolidation of land proceeded peacefully.[1] There was no folk memory of dispossession and historians even assert that the success of the new farming system was partly due to the positive contribution made to the working of the new agriculture by the Lowland farming and labouring classes.[2] The tranquillity of the Lowland countryside is especially striking when comparing with the rise of popular protest in urban Scotland, ranging from the Associations of Friends of the People and the United Scotsmen in the 1790s to the major trade union and radical disturbances in the years after the Napoleonic Wars.[3] Protest as such was not uncommon in Lowland society between 1780 and 1840; it was specifically agrarian discontent which was notable by its absence.

The record was significantly different in the Highlands. There eviction or the threat of it did produce disturbances. But even in the north the scale of unrest needs to be kept in perspective. While we can no longer regard the Highlands as a 'pacific fringe', overt protest was still the exception rather than the rule.[4] More common were various forms of passive resistance. A significant number of incidents occurred in certain restricted areas such as Easter Ross and the Sutherland estate, but for vast stretches of the Highlands the record is quite. The authorities were forced to react vigorously in such years as 1814–16 and 1819–21, but even when resistance did take place it rarely lasted for longer than a few weeks, always collapsed when challenged by military power and, with only a few exceptions, had little enduring impact on landlord strategy. Indeed, even those landlords who feared to provoke peasant reaction were often less concerned with the threat to the success of their policies of 'improvement' than with the public odium their actions might incur outside the Highlands. Until the 1880s, then, Highland discontent, though indicative of the social misery caused by the clearances, was intermittent, ephemeral and limited in its effects.

Peasant unrest in Ireland offers both points of comparison and contrast with stability in the Scottish Lowlands and sporadic disturbance in the Highlands. As in Scotland, there were few indications of serious agrarian discontent until the second half of the eighteenth century. The Houghers of Connacht in 1711–12 were just as exceptional as the Levellers of Galloway in the 1720s.[5] In Ireland, too, there were pronounced regional variations in the scale of disorder. Though few areas were entirely immune, disturbances tended to concentrate in the west midlands, the south and the south-east of the country.[6] It is possible also to detect certain similarities in the aims of both Irish and Scottish peasant movements. The Whiteboys, Oakboys, and Houghers of rural Ireland, like Highland crofters, sought redress for such grievances as inflated rents, eviction and the conversion of arable land to pasture.[7] The concept of the right to a patch of land for the maintenance of family life was shared by Irish countrymen as well as Highland peasants. Both had traditionalist assumptions, were defensive of existing customary rights and had limited ends. They sought not to change the *status quo* but to preserve it, not to attack or abolish landlordism as such but to force individual landlords, whether they were landowners or employing farmers, to conform to a code which confirmed the customary relationships threatened by new pressures of market expansion and estate rationalisation.

Yet Irish unrest also differed from that of Scotland in certain key respects. Scotland was decidedly more tranquil. While it is vital to remember that only certain areas were prone to agrarian rebellion and that most of the country was quiet at any one time, every decade in Ireland between 1760 and 1840 was punctuated by at least one major outbreak of peasant unrest. Some Irish movements survived for years and in parts of such chronically disturbed areas as Tipperary, Leitrim, Kilkenny and Limerick had a continued existence throughout the first half of the nineteenth century.[8] In the main, Highland protests were desperate reactions to the threat of eviction and were by their nature poorly organised and ill-prepared. But several of the Irish movements had an almost military form of organisation, whose participants wore special dress and were bound together by oaths of secrecy and loyalty. The perceptive contemporary observer, G. C. Lewis, saw them as 'protective unions, coolly, steadily, determinedly and unscrupulously working at their objects but sleeping in apparent apathy so long as their regulations are not violated'.[9] The Irish organisations were indeed forces to be reckoned with; they used intimidation, threats, terrorism and murder against those who transgressed the peasant code and, therefore, had a considerable impact on landlord decisions.[10] Economic historians suggest that the movement towards pastoralism in the central counties of Ireland after 1815 would have occurred more rapidly but for the fear of provoking agrarian outrage and, more generally, that the inward flow of investment capital to Ireland could have been checked by the violent reputation of some districts.[11] On the other hand, not least of the peculiar advantages of the Scottish Lowlands in the development of a more efficient system of farming was

In essence, then, Irish peasant movements were better organised, had a longer life and were much more effective in pursuing their aims and objectives than those in Scotland. But unrest in rural Ireland was not limited to 'organised' resistance or even to disputes over the use and occupation of land. There was nothing in Scotland to compare with the vicious rivalries *within* the ranks of the rural poor of some districts which often reached the stage of open, armed conflict between factions, gangs and families.[12] Irish peasant discontent, then, was not simply based on the existence of class tensions between landlords, farmers, cottiers and labourers but also in some areas on the thriving jealousies and insecurities of the rural masses. The remainder of this essay will seek to clarify the social and economic context within which this instability developed and offer an explanation why collective protest was more common in Ireland than Scotland.

II

The capacity of Scottish society south of the Highland line to adjust to profound social change without visible internal conflict was in part at least a reflection of the tightness of social control within the affected communities. Social order in the Scottish Lowlands was supported by a series of influences. The landed class was an hereditary elite whose families had held the same estates over many generations. Before c. 1760 the land market was relatively sluggish and the rapid penetration of newcomers only occurred in the later eighteenth century in some areas close to the larger towns.[13] But the old-established governing classes were also enthusiastic innovators and were able to exploit their inherited authority to gain social acceptance for agrarian change.[14] The influence which flowed from their long tenure of hegemony legitimised reform of estate structure and practice. Their social authority was both symbolised and confirmed by the very late survival of feudal institutions in Scotland. The private courts of the lairds were only formally abandoned in the 1740s, but such practices as thirlage and the provision of labour services survived for much longer even in areas in the vanguard of agrarian progress.[15] Furthermore, Scottish landowners and large farmers were broadly unified in a political, ideological, religious and intellectual sense by the late eighteenth century. There were none of the inter-gentry feuds which characterised some European countries and might have paralysed or severly weakened the structures of civil order and authority.[16] Scottish politics had become a matter of patronage and debate rather than passionate struggle, thanks to the effects of the religious settlement of 1690, the Union of 1707, the final defeat of Jacobitism and the closing of ranks in the face of the twin threats of popular radicalism and French aggression in the 1790s.[17]

The social prerogative of Scottish landowners was also confirmed and reinforced by their relationship with the two national institutions of church and education. They had close links with both, partly through their responsibility as heritors and also through their rights as patrons. It would, of course, be too crude to portray parish ministers and schoolmasters as conscious agents of landed hegemony. The series of eighteenth- and early nineteenth-century disputes over patronage suggests a greater degree of ecclesiastical independence than some critics, who hold to this view, have allowed.[18] But, equally, both the Kirk and the schools were likely to be significant bastions of social order, professing as they did the value of social harmony and hierarchy. In Ireland, for instance, the vexed issue of the payment of tithes not only incited specific episodes of agrarian discontent but, in a more general sense, stimulated the development of deep tensions between the ecclesiastical and civil orders in society as all landholders, no matter how small, had to share in the tithe burden.[19] In Scotland, however, there was no payment of tithes in kind; they could be valued and, when valued, did not afterwards increase and so this obligation tended to fall in relation to rising land values.[20] An important potential source of stress between secular and religious interests was therefore removed. Indeed, the parish accounts in the *Statistical Account* suggest that the majority of local ministers accepted and supported the ideal of material progress. 'Improvement' was viewed as legitimate in moral terms and most ministers seem to have shared the broad intellectual assumptions of the landed classes in the Age of Enlightenment.

Both the Church of Scotland and the system of parish schools were weakest in the Highlands where social disruption came most violently and rapidly. But there a martial society had survived into the eighteenth century and Highland landlords had a peculiar and personal authority far stronger even than their counterparts in the Lowlands.[21] Vertical loyalties persisted in many areas and these made it difficult to articulate effective strategies of opposition to the plans of improving grandees who had only recently shed the role and function of clan chiefs. Indeed, even after 1760, when the pace of economic change accelerated, several Highland landlords perpetuated the old tribal and military role by seeking to encourage the recruitment of their tenantry to family regiments during the American and Napoleonic Wars.[22] This helped temporarily to disguise the speedy and dramatic shift in the nature of social and economic relationships on some estates, although in the long run it intensified bitterness when evictions finally came about. It is also significant that one of the recurring themes of the waulking songs of the Western Isles was praise of the aristocracy and preoccupation with the exploits of the elite.[23] As late as the 1880s the Napier Commission, during the Crofters' War, could still report authoritatively that 'there is still on the side of the poor much reverence for the owner of the soil'.[24] Such evidence suggests the inability of the Highland peasantry to sever their links with the tribal past; to recognise themselves fully as a social group with powerful interests separate and distinct from those of their landlords. At the same time it is eloquent testimony to the sheer desperation and anxiety of some communities during the Highland clearances that considerable resistance, no matter how fragile and short-lived, did occur.

In Ireland agrarian discontent was more widespread and enduring at least partly because the structures of social control were less effective than in Scotland. It is easy perhaps to discount the popular myth of an historic struggle between Catholic peasant on the one hand and an alien class of heartless and mostly absentee landlords on the other. First, Irish agrarian discontent was not a major recurrent feature of the seventeenth and early eighteenth centuries but only began to reach epidemic proportions *in some areas after* c. 1780.[25] Second, 'none of the perpetrators of outrage are recorded as having appealed to the despoiled rights of a great Gaelic past'.[26] Third, tensions were often as acute between big farmers and labourers of the same denomination as between Protestant landlords and the Catholic rural poor.[27] Fourth, there is no evidence that nationalist or religious affiliation was a significant factor in the selection of victims by the agrarian secret societies.[28]

On the other hand, to deny any link between Irish political and religious and Irish agrarian disturbances would clearly be naive. It has been suggested that religious loyalty among Catholics, when the Irish state apparatus was dominated by Protestants, may have provided a major source of integration, 'a bond of union' as G. C. Lewis had it, which might have facilitated mobilisation of peasant communities.[29] In Scotland, especially in the Lowlands, Protestantism lent a homogeneity to rural society, an ideology shared by both governors and the governed. In Ireland, on the other hand, the civil administration was carried on by Protestants and the penal system presumed that all Irish Catholics were potentially disaffected to the state. Furthermore, the spirit of defiance of the law manifested in the emergence of such political and sectarian movement United Irishmen and the rebellion of 1798 may not actually have caused specifically agrarian disturbances but did contribute to a massive and general weakening of social and political authority within which disorder could flourish. Indeed, recent research suggests that the 1790s were a key decade in the history of governmental authority in Ireland. It is argued that harmony rather than conflict characterised social relations before the 1790s but that this fragile consensus between governors and governed ended abruptly in that decade.[30] The Catholic Relief Acts of 1792 and 1793 fatally destabilised Irish society, leaving Protestants feeling bitter and betrayed while Catholics were initially elated but then disillusioned. These deep tensions came to the surface when the authorities over-reacted to the Militia Riots of 1793. There was always this danger in Ireland as all disturbances, whatever their origin, could be perceived by government as having the final potential for full-blooded Catholic insurrection. Indeed, it could be speculated in a more general sense that the 1790s constituted a sharp break in the character of Irish protest: the appalling experiences of that decade might have had a permanently brutalising effect on Irish society, accustoming all social groups to new levels of violence.[31] The point, nevertheless, needs to be kept in perspective, as areas prone to serious unrest in 1798 were not necessarily those which saw the rise of peasant agrarian movements in the early nineteenth century.

Scotland too had its anti-Militia riots in 1797 but they were rapidly checked by a combination of judicious military action and the speedy conviction of accused persons.[32] These riots occurred after almost a decade of radical reforming activity, but the war with France and the excesses of the French revolutionaries effectively suppressed the cause of political opposition for a generation. The Scottish governing classes emerged from the 1790s with their powers and influence unimpaired and the confidence to maintain their dominant position renewed political challenge after 1815. There was much greater scope for alienation in Ireland because there the unity of the elites was fissured by religious and political tensions, 'dormant in normal times, but susceptible to manipulation in times of crisis'.[33] As a result, the Irish state, with its draconian legal apparatus, large army and growing police force, had more power to coerce but much less ability to control than its Scottish counterpart.[34]

III

The fundamental causes of unrest and stability lay not in the methods of control available to local and national authorities but in the deep contrasts in the nature of social and economic development in Scotland and Ireland. Irish historians stress that while major outbreaks of discontent had a number of specific, short-term causes, such as protest over tithes, high rents, evictions and encroachment of pastoral farming on arable land, they also reflect the influence of deeper strains and pressures within Irish society. A number of factors can be identified in the literature.[35] First, acute demographic pressure increased as Irish population expanded from less than 2.5 million in 1753 to 6.8 million in 1821. This rate of growth was not only exceptional by European and especially Scottish standards but was paralleled by other developments which combined to ensure the appearance of a vast surplus of labour in the Irish countryside after the Napoleonic Wars. Irish town and industrial growth decelerated over the period 1815 to 1840 after an earlier phase of precocious expansion. In consequence, the great majority of the new generation had to depend on land and land-related employment for survival. There is considerable agreement in the literature that widespread land hunger was a root cause of peasant unrest.[36] Moreover, emigration, a potential safety-valve, was mainly restricted before the Famine to certain areas, such as Ulster and areas adjacent, and to particular groups, such as better-off peasants and redundant workers in declining industries.[37] Second, the Irish rural economy after c. 1760 became subject to an intense level of commercialisation with the enormous growth of English demand for grains, beef and pastoral products. Farmers and landlords became more exacting; the easier-going relationships of earlier days were replaced by more vigorous methods reflected in rent increases and encroachments of dairy and beef cattle on commonage. The resulting social pressures contributed to the first main wave of agrarian unrest associated with Whiteboys, Oakboys, Rightboys and Houghers of the last quarter of the eighteenth century.[38] Third, after 1815 there was an incentive to shift from tillage to pasture in response to price movements in Ireland's major external markets. Again, this provoked bitter resistance in parts of the central and south-east regions from cottiers and labourers who saw their source of subsistence threatened.[39] Fourth, the social structure of several areas outside the eastern zone was decidedly fluid.[40] For small farmers and cottiers both upward and downward mobility was possible and this tended to deepen anxieties in a society which lacked a Poor Law until 1837 and where insecurities were aggravated by the twin evils of unemployment and seasonal underemployment after the Napoleonic Wars.

This short précis of some of the underlying causes of peasant discontent suggests both parallels and contrasts with patterns in Scotland. In the Highlands the social and economic pressures were similar and, if anything, the scale of eviction was significantly greater than anything experienced in Ireland. Ironically, however, resistance was subdued, at least when compared to the chronic discontent of parts of the Irish countryside. Partly this may be explained by the social influences already described earlier in this essay. One detects, for instance, a longer tradition of protest on the fringes of the Highlands, in Easter Ross and some of the eastern parishes of Sutherland where clanship might have been weaker than in the central Highlands and the western isles.[41] Again, clearances affected different communities in widely contrasting ways and so provoked different responses. In some cases tenants were evicted without compunction or alternative accommodation; in others efforts were made to establish evicted communities on the coast and to encourage employment in fishing, kelping or textile manufacture. It is possible also that migration was either easier or more attractive for the Highlander than for many small farmers and cottiers in Ireland.[42] There was much 'group' emigration to the United States and Canada from all parts of the region, assisted no doubt by the traditional links of Highland communities with the transatlantic military settlements and the tacksmen-led parties of the later eighteenth century.[43] In Skye in the early nineteenth century, for instance, crofters on some estates used the threat of emigration to compel landlords to rescind or alter plans for improvement.[44] Throughout the period, too, there was a heavy haemorrhage of population from the southern and eastern Highlands to the industrialising and urbanising centres of the central Lowlands.[45]

But one can also argue that the partial quiescence of Highland society, even in the wake of profound social dislocation, was analogous to the social experience of the extreme west of Ireland. It, the poorest region in Ireland, was also one of the quietest.[46] Eric Wolf's well-known observation—that the poorest communities rarely protest because peasants require a certain degree of tactical power or leverage to give them sufficient independence to engage in collective action—may be as apposite to certain parts of the Highlands as to the poverty-stricken west of Ireland.[47] Furthermore, both in the north of Scotland and in the west of Ireland, it was still possible for the peasant family to maintain a foothold on the land, practise sub-division among kinfolk and employ young adults in temporary migration because much of the land itself was so poor that landlords were not always concerned to control access to it in rigorous fashion. Even clearances in the Highlands did not break the hold of the crofting class on the land; often eviction simply meant movement to the coast or resettlement on even poorer plots where families could still eke out a living before the 1840s by a combination of potato cultivation and seasonal migration.[48] Significantly peasant unrest in Ireland was most intense and violent in those midland and south-eastern counties where the population was not quite as deprived as in the far west, and where the deeper penetration of commercial pressures and the higher value of land made farmers and landowners more determined to resist sub-division of peasant holdings.[49] Here conflicts of interest between social groups existed in acute form.

IV

In the Scottish Lowlands consolidation of tenancies and the elimination of sub-tenancies failed to produce widespread resistance because the mode and context of economic change were conducive to peaceful adjustment. The process of tenant reduction was evolutionary and was already occurring on a considerable scale in the seventeenth and early eighteenth centuries in the Borders and eastern counties.[50] Recent work suggests that the ranks of full tenants in some areas were thinned as part of the normal process for reletting of farms.[51] There seems to have been little of the systematic eviction of entire communities so common in the Highlands. Sub-tenancy was crushed more dramatically but loss of land was not as serious a threat to survival as in some parts of Ireland. Demand for all forms of agricultural labour was buoyant in Lowland Scotland between 1770 and 1815 when sub-tenancy was destroyed, because of the expansion of labour-intensive rotation systems and the elaboration of the infrastructure of the new rural economy.[52]

Average agricultural money wages in the central Lowlands more than doubled between the 1750s and the 1790s as farmers competed with industrial and urban employers for assured supplies of labour.[53]

It is also vital to keep the disappearance of sub-tenancy in perspective. It was not necessarily a wholly radical upheaval for the rural population. There were important continuities between the old and new worlds, recognition of which can help to explain why no folk tradition of dispossession gathered round the 'Lowland clearances'. There were indeed differences between the sub-tenant system in which land was given for labour, and the new age where landless employees were engaged in return for payments in money and kind. Sub-tenants and cottagers seemed to possess a greater degree of 'independence' and security because of their access to land, whereas the 'landless' servant was more dependent on the employer class and hence more vulnerable to unemployment. But sub-tenants held the merest fragments of land and had little option but to work on adjacent larger farms to gain a full subsistence. Grinding poverty before 1750 was the lot of many sub-tenant families and there is considerable contemporary comment about the miserable conditions in which they often lived because of the chronic seasonal underemployment which characterised Lowland agriculture before the adoption of the new rotations.[54]

On the other hand, the married farm servants of the new order were hired by the year, were paid entirely in kind and allowed ground for planting potatoes and the keep of a cow. Single servants did not hold land in the manner of sub-tenants but were paid in cash, employed on six-monthly contracts and received food and accommodation as an integral part of the total wage reward. Employment, though more difficult to come by after 1815, was widely available for most grades of farm labour during the Napoleonic Wars and real wages rose during the phase of greatest disruption.[55] There was an obvious contrast with the experience of the Irish rural population. As one historian of Ireland has put it: 'In a period of rising prices, the value of payments in kind such as Scottish labourers received tended to rise, whereas the Irish labourer was caught in the scissors-like effect of nominal money wages which were depressed by competition for employment and rising rents for land as inflated produce prices pushed upwards farmers' valuations of land let to labourers'.[56]

By the early nineteenth century, then, a number of significant differences emerged between Lowland Scotland and those districts in central and southern Ireland most prone to agrarian disturbance. First, though both countries had experienced urban and industrial expansion after c. 1760, town development and manufacturing growth were already more pronounced throughout the Lowlands than in any area of Ireland, with the possible exception of Ulster. Both societies were still mainly ruralised but the alternatives to agricultural employment were already more fully developed in Scotland.[57] Second, the Lowlands had become a highly stratified society with landlords, farmers and labourers clearly demarcated and little possibility of movement between these social groups except where a smallholding structure survived, as in the north-east, or in areas such as the western dairying counties where family farms of limited size predominated.[58] There was therefore less risk of the proliferation of the social anxieties which characterised the more fluid social system common in whole areas of rural Ireland.[59] Third, the majority of the agricultural population in the Lowlands had become landless employees by 1815. This break with the land facilitated the very heavy rates of local migration which characterised nineteenth-century Scotland and served to reduce demographic pressure in country areas.[60] Much of Ireland, however, was still a peasant society where access to land remained vital. As numbers rose, many districts began to suffer the linked evils of chronic subdivision of land and relative population immobility which produced intense social strains within which rural disorder could thrive.

Furthermore, the transition from a sub-tenancy structure to one where landless employees were engaged in return for payment was sustained in Scotland by the maintenance of the farm servant system. This functioned to preserve social order at a number of levels.[61] The yearly and six-monthly contracts gave security of employment over extended periods. Payment in kind insulated farm servants from the market price for food and married ploughmen gained in periods of high prices because they were accustomed to selling a proportion of their 'in kind' earnings back to farmers, to day labourers wholly paid in cash, or in local markets.[62] The young male and female servants were boarded in the steading and were constantly under the eye of the master, a custom which helped to maintain the hierarchical relationship of the old days. But the farm servant system also allowed for a delicate balance of relationships between farmers and workers rather than the complete subservience of one group to the other. The hiring fair or feeing markets were an 'institutional alternative to strikes . . . wages had to be re-negotiated each year'.[63] When the labour market was tight, as it was in most years during the Napoleonic Wars, farmers had to maintain 'a good name' in order to ensure a supply of efficient servants who could (and often did) move at the end of the term if wages or conditions were not to their taste.[64] In Ireland, however, living-in servants were much less common and cottagers of considerably greater significance.[65] The latter often paid by their labour for the land they occupied, a system prone to gross exploitation when the numbers eager for land rose swiftly from the second half of eighteenth century.[66] Once again there existed potential for acute conflict between masters and men.

These contrasts became even sharper after the Napoleonic Wars. Rural Scotland like rural Ireland was affected by the downward trend in grain prices during the years of economic deflation. There was unemployment among farm workers in 1817–18, 1821 and 1827 but it is important to stress that there is no evidence of the emergence of a vast labour surplus of the type which was the main underlying cause of violent protest in Ireland.[67]

Rural unemployment in Lowland Scotland was cyclical rather than structural and had begun to diminish by the early 1830s.[68] Social stability was maintained even in the decades after 1815 because a rough balance was achieved in most years between the number of workers on the land and the range of employments open to them. This equilibrium in turn depended on a variety of factors. Scottish population growth accelerated from a rate of 0.6 per cent per annum in the later eighteenth century to 1.2 per cent between 1801 and 1811 and rose again to 1.6 per cent from 1811 to 1821. But this increased rate of expansion was still significantly lower than that of Ireland. Scottish population grew from 1,265,000 in the 1750s to just over 2 million in 1821; Ireland's from 2.5 million in the 1750s to 6.8 million in 1821. While Irish town and industrial development stagnated between 1815 and 1840, the Scottish industrial economy, despite cyclical fluctuations and slow expansion between 1815 and 1830, grew apace thereafter. By the early 1830s Scotland was entering the second phase of industrialisation as investment quickened in coal, iron and engineering production. Scotland, therefore, had the burgeoning alternative employment opportunities outside agriculture which Ireland lacked. By the 1840s no Lowland Scottish county had a majority of householders engaged in farming.[69] To this key advantage Scotland could add a highly mobile work force. Migration increased significantly over late eighteenth-century levels and was facilitated not simply because of rural proximity to urban employment but because of pressures making for movement within the fabric of the agricultural communities.[70]

Finally, the adaptation of the agrarian economy after 1815 did not threaten to reduce employment opportunities to the same extent as did the tendency towards pastoralism in Ireland. Scottish agriculture was less export-orientated than Ireland's and so was less exposed to the violent oscillations in demand in external markets. To this advantage was added the fact that the Scottish system of mixed farming allowed for adjustment to the new price structure. There was a more intensive cultivation of those crops, such as potatoes and barley, least affected by price falls.[71] The north-east Lowlands became a cattle-fattening rather than simply cattle-rearing area and the south-east, where grain farming had always been central, moved towards a more closely integrated regime of arable production and stock-fattening.[72] Flexibility of response rather than radical alteration was the favoured policy and there was therefore little significant shedding of labour in most years.[73]

Urban Scotland, like several rural districts in Ireland, experienced considerable unrest after the Napoleonic Wars. But the Lowland country-side was quiet. A social and economic structure had evolved which promoted stability rather than conflict and ensured the further development of advanced and internationally renowned systems of husbandry. In Ireland, on the other hand, the social pressures already emerging in the later eighteenth century became even more acute after 1815 and provoked the successive agrarian rebellions which in some districts at least aggravated the nation's economic weaknesses.

NOTES

1. T. M. Devine, 'Social Stability in the Eastern Lowlands of Scotland during the Agricultural Revolution', in T. M. Devine, ed., *Lairds and Improvement in the Scotland of the Enlightenment* (Dundee, 1979), pp. 59–70. I wish to acknowledge with thanks the assistance of Dr. Sean Connolly, University of Ulster, who read this paper in draft form and provided me with several useful comments. I also benefited from discussions with L. M. Cullen and David Dickson. The preparation of the material was aided by a generous grant from the Carnegie Trust for the Universities of Scotland.
2. Rosalind Mitchison, 'The Highland Clearances', *Sc. Ec. & Soc. Hist.*, I (1981), 4–20.
3. K. J. Logue, *Popular Disturbances in Scotland, 1780–1815* (Edinburgh, 1979); M. I. Thomis and P. Holt, *Threats of Revolution in Britain, 1789–1848* (London, 1977), pp. 5–28, 62–84.
4. E. Richards, 'Patterns of Highland Discontent, 1790–1860', in J. Stevenson and R. Quinault, eds., *Popular Protest and Public Order* (London, 1974), pp. 75–114; *idem, A History of the Highland Clearances*, I (London, 1982), pp. 249–283; R. Walker, 'The Insurrection of 1792 in Easter Ross and the Adjacent Parishes of Sutherland' (unpublished B. A. dissertation, Department of History, University of Strathclyde, 1983); J. Hunter, *The Making of the Crofting Community* (Edinburgh, 1976), pp. 89–106.
5. S. Connolly, 'The Houghers: Agrarian Protest in Early Eighteenth-Century Connacht', Paper read at the Irish Conference of Historians, 1983. I am grateful to Dr. Connolly for providing me with a copy of his paper.
6. J. Lee, 'Patterns of Rural Unrest in Nineteenth-Century Ireland: a Preliminary Survey', in L. M. Cullen and F. Furet, eds., *Ireland and France, 17th to 20th Centuries* (Paris, 1980), pp. 221–237; S. Clark and J. S. Donnelly Jr., eds., *Irish Peasants, Violence and Political Unrest, 1780–1914* (Manchester, 1983), p. 25; J. Hurst, 'Disturbed Tipperary, 1831–60', *Eire Ireland*, IX, 3 (1974).
7. Connolly, 'The Houghers'; Lee, 'Patterns of Rural Unrest', pp. 228–9; K. B. Nowlan, 'Agrarian Unrest in Ireland, 1800–45', *University Review*, II, 6 (1959); M. R. Beames, 'Peasant Movements: Ireland, 1785–95', *Journal of Peasant Studies*, II, 4 (1975), pp. 502–6; *idem, Peasants and Power: The Whiteboy Movements and Their Control in Pre-Famine Ireland*, (London, 1983); G. E. Christianson, 'Secret Societies and Agrarian Violence in Ireland, 1790–1840', *Agricultural History*, XLVI, 4 (1972); J. S. Donnelly Jr., 'The Whiteboy Movement, 1761–5', *I.H.S.*, XXI, 81 (1978), pp. 20–54; *idem*, 'The Rightboy Movement, 1785–8', *Studia Hibernica*, 17 and 18 (1977–8), pp. 120–202; 'Hearts of Oak, Hearts of Steel', *Studia Hibernica*, xxi (1981), pp. 7–73; 'Irish Agrarian Rebellion: the Whiteboys of 1769–76', *Proceedings of the Royal Irish Academy*, LXXXIII, C, 12, pp. 293–331; T. D. Williams, ed., *Secret Societies in Ireland* (Dublin, 1973), pp. 13–35; J. W. O'Neill, 'A Look at Captain Rock: Agrarian Rebellion in Ireland, 1815–45', *Eire Ireland*, XVII, 3 (1982).
8. Clark and Donnelly, eds., *Irish Peasants, Violence and Political Unrest*, pp. 25–35.
9. G. C. Lewis, *On Local Disturbances in Ireland and on the Irish Church Question* (London, 1836), p. 124.
10. *Ibid., passim* and works listed in n. 7 above.
11. L. M. Cullen, *An Economic History of Ireland since 1660* (London, 1972), p. 114; J. Mokyr, *Why Ireland Starved: A Quantitative and Analytical History of the Irish Economy* (London, 1983).

12. Lewis, *Local Disturbances*, pp. 280–294; D. Fitzpatrick, 'Class, Family and Rural Unrest in Nineteenth-Century Ireland', P. J. Drudy, ed., *Ireland: Land, Politics and People* (Cambridge, 1982), pp. 37–76.

13. L. Timperley, 'The Pattern of Landholding in Eighteenth-Century Scotland', in M. L. Parry and T. R. Slater, eds., *The Making of the Scottish Countryside* (London, 1980), pp. 137–176.

14. T. M. Devine, 'The Union of 1707 and Scottish Developments', *Sc. Ec. & Soc. Hist.*, 5 (1985), pp. 23–40.

15. I. Whyte, *Agriculture and Society in Seventeenth-Century Scotland* (Edinburgh, 1979), pp. 35–6, 45–6; Timperley, 'Pattern of Landholding', p. 138; E. Gauldie, *The Scottish Country Miller, 1700–1900* (Edinburgh, 1981), pp. 43–63; L. M. Cullen, 'Incomes, Social Classes and Economic Growth in Ireland and Scotland, 1600–1900', in Devine & Dickson, p. 257.

16. A. Murdoch, *The People Above: Politics and Administration in Mid-Eighteenth-Century Scotland* (Edinburgh, 1980), pp. 1–22.

17. W. Ferguson, *Scotland: 1689 to the Present* (Edinburgh, 1968).

18. See, for example, T. Dickson, ed., *Scottish Capitalism (London, 1980), p. 117.*

19. Donnelly, 'Rightboy Movement', pp. 120–202; P. O'Donoghue, 'Causes of the Opposition to Tithes, 1830–38', *Studia Hibernica*, 5 (1965), pp. 7–28; *idem*, 'Opposition to Payment of Tithes in 1830–1', *Studia Hibernica*, 6 (1966), pp. 69–98; M. J. Bric, 'Priests, Parsons and Politics: The Rightboy Protest in County Cork, 1785–88', *Past and Present*, 100 (1983), pp. 100–122.

20. A. A. Cormack, *Tithes and Agriculture: A Historical Survey* (Oxford, 1930).

21. E. Burt, *Letters from a Gentleman in the North of Scotland* (London, 1754), pp. 261–2.

22. Richards, *Highland Clearances*, pp. 147–154; J. Prebble, *Mutiny* (London, 1975); B. Lenman, *The Jacobite Clans of the Great Glen* (London, 1984), pp. 177–220.

23. T. J. Byres, 'Scottish Peasants and their Song', *Journal of Peasant Studies*, 3 (2) (1976), p. 240.

24. *Report of the Commissioners of Inquiry into the Condition of the Crofters and Cotters in the Highlands and Islands of Scotland* (Napier Commission), (P. P. 1884, XXXII, 36); see also S. Maclean, 'The Poetry of the Clearances', *Trans. of the Gaelic Society of Inverness*, XXXVIII (1939), p. 319.

25. M. Wall, 'The Whiteboys', ed., *Secret Societies*, pp. 13–25; Connolly, 'The Houghers'.

26. Lee, 'Patterns of Unrest', p. 228.

27. J. Lee, 'The Ribbonmen', in Williams, ed., *Secret Societies*, pp. 26–35; Cullen, *Economic History*, p. 114; G. O. Tuathaigh, *Ireland before the Famine, 1798–1848* (Dublin, 1972), p. 138.

28. Lewis, *Local Disturbances*, pp. 124–139; M. R. Beames, 'Rural Conflict in Pre-Famine Ireland: Peasant Assassinations in Tipperary, 1837–47', *Past and Present*, 81 (1978), pp. 75–91; Hurst, 'Disturbed Tipperary'.

29. Lewis, *Local Disturbances*, p. 155.

30. T. Bartlett, 'An End to Moral Economy: the Irish Militia Disturbances of 1793', *Past and Present*, 99 (1983), pp. 41–64.

31. I am most grateful to Dr. Sean Connolly for suggesting this point to me.

32. Logue, *Popular Disturbances in Scotland*, pp. 75–115.

33. M. Elliott, 'The Origins and Transformation of Early Irish Republicanism', *International Review of Social History*, XXIII (1978), p. 406; *idem, Partners in Revolution; the United Irishmen and France* (New Haven, 1982); J. S. Donnelly, Jr., 'Pastorini and Captain Rock', in Clark and Donnelly, eds., *Irish Peasants, Violence and Unrest*, pp. 102–141.

34. Galen Broeker, *Rural Disorder and Police Reform in Ireland, 1812–1836* (London, 1970), p. 235.

35. These are conveniently summarised in Clark and Donnelly, eds., *Irish Peasants, Violence and Unrest*, pp. 26–35.

36. Mokyr, *Why Ireland Starved*, p. 128; Fitzpatrick, 'Class, Family and Rural Unrest', pp. 43–4.

37. S. H. Cousens, 'The Regional Variation in Emigration from Ireland between 1821 and 1841', *Institute of British Geographers, Transactions and Papers*, 37 (1965), pp. 15–30; C. O Grada, 'Across the Briny Ocean: Some thoughts on Irish Emigration to America, 1800–1850', in Devine & Dickson, pp. 118–130.

38. Donnelly, 'The Whiteboy Movement', pp. 65–104; *idem*, 'Hearts of Oak', pp. 7–73; W. A. Maguire, 'Lord Donegall and the Hearts of Steel', *Irish Historical Studies*, XXI (1979), pp. 374–75.

39. Mokyr, *Why Ireland Starved*, pp. 130–1.

40. Cullen, 'Incomes, Social Classes and Economic Growth', p. 258; Beames, 'Rural Conflict', p. 58.

41. A. Charlesworth, ed., *An Atlas of Rural Protest in Britain, 1548–1900* (London, 1983), p. 25.

42. T. M. Devine, 'Highland Migration to Lowland Scotland, 1760–1860', Scott. Hist. Rev., LXII (1983), pp. 137–149.

43. J. M. Bumsted, *The People's Clearance, 1770–1815: Highland Emigration to British North America* (Edinburgh, 1982), pp. 55–107; I. Levitt and C. Smout, *The State of the Scottish Working Class in 1843* (Edinburgh, 1979), pp. 236–258.

44. R. A. Berry, The Role of Hebridean Landlords in early Nineteenth-Century Emigration (unpublished B. A. dissertation, Department of History, University of Strathclyde, 1979).

45. Devine, 'Highland Migration', pp. 137–149.

46. Lee, 'Ribbonmen', pp. 28–29; Lewis, *Local Disturbances*, p. 90.

47. E. Wolf, *Peasant Wars of the Twentieth Century* (New York, 1969), pp. 290–293.

48. Devine, 'Highland Migration', p. 142; *idem*, 'Temporary Migration and the Scottish Highlands in the Nineteenth Century', *Ec. H. R.*, XXXII (1979), pp. 344–59.

49. Cullen, *Economic History*, p. 113; O Tuathaigh, *Ireland before the Famine*, p. 138; Lee; 'Patterns of Unrest', p. 225.

50. Whyte, *Agriculture and Society*, pp. 137–172; R. A. Dodgshon, *Land and Society in Early Scotland* (Oxford, 1981), pp. 205–76.

51. R. A. Dodgshon, 'The Removal of Runrig in Roxburghshire and Berwickshire, 1680–1766', *Scottish Studies*, XVI (1972), pp. 121–7.

52. Devine, 'Social Stability', pp. 60–2.

53. V. Morgan, 'Agricultural Wage Rates in late Eighteenth-Century Scotland', *Ec. H. R.*, XXIV (1971), pp. 181–201.

54. P. Graham, *Agricultural Survey of Clackmannanshire* (Edinburgh, 1814), p. 332; O. S. A., VIII, p. 610; I. Carter, *Farm Life in Northeast Scotland, 1840–1914* (Edinburgh, 1979), pp. 16–17.

55. M. E. Goldie, The Standard of Living of Scottish Farm Labourers in Selected Areas at the time of the first Two Statistical Accounts, 1790–1845 (unpublished M. Phil. thesis, University of Edinburgh, 1970).

56. Cullen, 'Incomes, Social Classes and Economic Growth', p. 257.

57. L. M. Cullen and T. C. Smout, 'Economic Growth in Scotland and Ireland', in Cullen & Smout, p. 5.

58. T. M. Devine, ed., *Farm Servants and Labour in Lowland Scotland, 1770–1914* (Edinburgh, 1984), pp. 107–8.

59. T. M. Devine and D. Dickson, 'In Pursuit of Comparative Aspects of Irish and Scottish Development', in Devine & Dickson, p. 263; Fitzpatrick, 'Class, Family and Rural Unrest', pp. 54–68.

60. M. Gray, 'Migration in the Rural Lowlands of Scotland, 1750–1850', in Devine & Dickson, pp. 104–117.
61. T. M. Devine, 'Scottish Farm Service in the Agricultural Revolution', in Devine, ed., *Farm Servants and Labour*, pp. 1–8.
62. R. Somerville, *General View of the Agriculture of East Lothian* (London, 1805), p. 210.
63. J. P. D. Dunbabin, *Rural Discontent in Nineteenth-Century Britain* (London, 1974), p. 132.
64. Carter, *Farm Life in Northeast Scotland*, pp. 113–118; *idem*, 'The Peasantry of Northeast Scotland', *Journal of Peasant Studies*, 3 (1976), pp. 178–9.
65. O Tuathaigh, *Ireland before the Famine*, p. 133.
66. Lewis, *Local Disturbances*, pp. 311–13; M. Beames, 'Cottiers and Conacre in Pre-Famine Ireland', *Journal of Peasant Studies*, 2 (1975), pp. 352–3; Lee, 'Patterns of Rural Unrest', pp. 228–0; J. S. Donnelly, *The Land and People of Nineteenth-Century Cork* (London, 1975), pp. 16–19. Of course, once again, the force of these pressure varied according to the general economic and social context of particular districts. 254 outrages were committed in Tipperary in 1844 compared to only 32 in the much more populous county of Cork. Donnelly argues that the central difference between the two areas may have been the much greater difficulty faced by labourers and cottiers in obtaining adequate potato ground and conacre at reasonable rents in the grazing country of Tipperary. See Donnelly, *Land and People*, p. 54.
67. *Farmer's Magazine*, 'Quarterly Intelligence Reports', 1811–25; *Farmer's Register and Monthly Magazine*, 1827–8; *Report from Select Committee on the Present State of Agriculture*, (P.P. 1833, V), pp. 30, 56, 132; G. Houston, 'Farm Wages in Central Scotland from 1814 to 1870', *Journal of the Royal Statistical Society*, Ser. A (1955), pp. 118, 224–7; T. M. Devine, 'Social Stability and Agrarian Change in the Eastern Lowlands of Scotland, 1810–1840', *Social History*, 3 (1978), pp. 338–346.
68. I. Levitt and C. Smout, 'Farm Workers' Incomes in 1843', in Devine, ed., *Farm Servants and Labour*, pp. 167–8.
69. Devine & Dickson, 'In Pursuit of Comparative Aspects of Irish and Scottish Development', p. 269.
70. Gray, 'Migration in the Rural Lowlands', pp. 108–110; Devine, 'Farm Service in the Agricultural Revolution', p. 6.
71. *N.S.A.* (Edinburgh, 1845), IV, pp. 205, 304, 956; J. Dickson, 'The Agriculture of Perthshire', *Trans. of the Highland and Agricultural Society*, II (1868–9), pp. 167–8; *First Report from Select Committee on Agricultural Distress* (P.P. 1836, VIII), QQ. 11170, 10352, 10651–60, 11840.
72. *N.S.A.*, XI, pp. 140, 202, 684; G. Channon, 'The Aberdeenshire Beef Trade and London: A study in Steamship and Railway Competition, 1850–1869', *Transport History*, 2 (1969), pp. 1–23.
73. *Report from Select Committee on Agricultural Distress*, 1836, Q. 13640; *Farmer's Magazine*, XVIII (1817), p. 101; IXX (1818), p. 106; *Farmer's Register and Monthly Magazine*, II (1828), pp. 229, 231; Houston, 'Farm Wages', pp. 324–7; T. M. Devine, 'The Demand for Agricultural Labour in East Lothian after the Napoleonic Wars', *Trans. East Lothian Antiquarian and Field Naturalist Society*, 16 (1979), pp. 49–61.

13

SOCIAL STABILITY AND AGRARIAN CHANGE IN THE EASTERN LOWLANDS OF SCOTLAND, 1810–1840

At the end of the Napoleonic Wars, the boom which had sustained British agriculture in a phase of remarkable expansion came to an end. After *c.* 1812 there was a downward trend in grain prices, a marked reduction in the wage levels of farm labourers and a visible increase in the number out of work on the land. Unemployment, initially stimulated by the temporary decline in the fortunes of the farming class, was then exacerbated by postwar demobilization and a persistent natural increase in rural population.[1] In some parts of the country these adverse influences led to desperate and violent protest by the labouring classes as their material conditions deteriorated to miserable levels. The most serious and dramatic outbreaks occurred in the southern and eastern counties of England. There were risings by farm labourers in East Anglia in 1816, again in the same region in 1822, all over the south and east of England in the famous 'Captain Swing' riots of 1830 and again, though more scattered, in 1834–5 and 1843–4. Furthermore, these spectacular episodes were paralleled by the more common incidence of casual violence, of stacks being fired, of animals maimed and fences destroyed. Indeed, the evidence leaves little doubt that rural society in certain parts of southern England suffered from a deep and pervasive discontent which, at critical times, erupted into organized acts of protest.[2]

Outbreaks of a similar nature took place in the Scottish Highlands in rural Ireland and in Wales but they had few parallels in the north of England and lowland Scotland.[3] Contemporaries were particularly impressed by the stability of the Scottish countryside after the Napoleonic Wars. The tranquillity of the rural lowlands in their view contrasted remarkably with the troubles of other areas of Britain and with the social tensions manifested at the time in the towns and cities of industrial Scotland. As one East Lothian farmer commented in 1812:

> during this season of scarcity and distress, when part of the labouring classes in other districts of the Kingdom, almost driven to desperation

197

and madness by the want of employment and the high price of provisions have committed the greatest outrages against individuals and property, the lower orders in this district have sustained the pressures and hardships of the times with a degree of patience and regularity of conduct which entitle them to the highest confidence and respect from their superiors in rank and fortune.[4]

Again, during the difficult winter of 1817–18, the Justices of the Peace in the south-eastern lowlands, after the most careful enquiry, found no indication of an increase in social tension in their districts and so saw no need to appoint a single special constable.[5] Kincardine magistrates reported in 1820, the year of the so-called 'Radical War' in Scotland, that

> there was scarcely a murmur to be heard, and our 'little community' is too much of an agricultural cast for the spirit of *radicalism* to take root in it.[6]

Finally, in the year 1830, William Cobbett came north to find out why the Scots were quiet while the English burnt the ricks.[7]

Cobbett raised an intriguing question which has thus far attracted little attention from Scottish historians.[8] Indeed, the complex problem of social stability in nineteenth-century Britain is only now beginning to stimulate serious scholarly discussion.[9] Perhaps in the Scottish context, however, such relative neglect is understandable. On one level it is easy enough to explain the tranquility of the countryside. Rural society was not hard to govern. The successful maintenance of order depended not on the powers to coerce, which were relatively weak and primitive anyway, but rather on the delicate social ties of hierarchy and dependence which linked the various social groupings of the local community. In rural areas the concept of hierarchy was buttressed, both deliberately and subconsciously, in a variety of ways, ranging from preaching to education, from charity to paternalism.[10] These enormously important influences cannot be underestimated and any comprehensive explanation of social stability in the rural lowlands must take account of all of them. Smout, for example, has recently argued that, in Scotland, 'rural Calvinism worked against radicalism'.[11] The idea, stimulating as it is, does, however, require more detailed investigation before its relative importance in the context of a broader explanation can be evaluated.

In this paper I shall attempt to make a brief contribution to that final explanation considering the influence of the material factor on social stability. The evidence, both from England and from the Scottish Highlands, does suggest that acute material deprivation and insecurity could undermine even the most powerful traditional constraints on social disturbance. Nowhere, for instance, was the influence of paternalistic power and ancient authority more apparent than in the Highlands. But there some 'clearances' did from time to time provoke violent reaction on several estates.[12] Equally in England, the established networks of social control did not function effectively in some areas of severe deprivation and chronic unemployment. The material factor, therefore, while probably not the sole influence on tranquility is, neartheless, likely to be an important variable in any final analysis. Had the conditions of Scottish agricultural labourers been such as to provoke desperate action, it is doubtful if even the condemnation of the Calvinist Church would have had any appreciable effect restraining them.

William Cobbett's approach to the problem was to compare the social and economic structure of the Scottish lowlands with those regions in England which experienced discontent and to isolate those factors in Scotland which, in his view, favoured stability. Cobbett was probably wrong in the particulars of his explanation—he put too much emphasis, for instance, on the impact of the Scottish Poor Law which only affected a tiny minority of Scots—but probably correct in his general method. It is his comparative approach which will be adopted here.

One point of obvious contrast between the two regions lay in their differing systems of recruiting labour. By the end of the Napoleonic Wars, farm workers in the southern and eastern counties of England were paid and hired in a variety of ways depending on local custom and agrarian specialisation. In general, however, there had been a decided movement away from the traditional system of long-hires and from the habit of boarding labourers within farms and paying them in kind. Instead, the majority, by the early nineteenth century, were on a daily or weekly basis, and hence most workers in these regions had become a species of casual labour and in consequence vulnerable to both short- and long-term unemployment. Furthermore, these labourers were in the main recruited from local villages rather than boarded within the farmsteading and increasingly they were paid in cash wages with only vestigial remains of traditional allowances in kind. In sum, then, a very significant number of farm workers in the south of England were accustomed to sharp fluctuations in money wage-levels and to the direct impact of price changes on their material condition. Since they lived in villages with their peers rather than in the farmsteading with their masters they were also perhaps less amenable to the social control of the farming class.[13]

In the eastern lowlands of Scotland the structure of labour payment and recruitment was quite different. Until the end of our period, payments in kind, though they varied in detail, still formed a very substantial component of the total wage reward for most workers. In the south-eastern lowlands and parts of the east-central district, most permanent farm workers were married ploughmen. To a very significant degree, and certainly as far as the necessities of life were concerned, this class was insulated from the vicissitudes of the market when in employment. Their allowance invariably included stipulated measures of oats, barley, pease, the keep of a cow and ground for planting potatoes. The rental of the cottage was paid for by the labour of the wife or daughter during harvest. Fuel was carted from town at the farmer's expense and, by law, farmers were also obliged to provide for the servant employed on an annual basis for six successive weeks when unable to work through illness.[14] Similarly, unmarried farm servants, who were most prominent in the north-east lowlands of Scotland but also common elsewhere, obtained board and lodging within the steading in addition to a cash wage.

There is no doubt much truth in the assertion that payments in kind were 'a polite euphemism for truck in agriculture' and that they probably persisted because of a stubborn refusal by farmers to increase money wages.[15] Nevertheless, the system did give Scottish farm servants an enviable security in relation to their counterparts in south and east England. They were guaranteed the necessities of life when in employment according to familiar and acknowledged standards, while, at the same time, allowances in kind were less easily reduced in times of agrarian difficulty. The system also helps to explain why there was hardly any tradition of food-rioting in the Scottish countryside after 1750 whereas such disturbances were common in the towns and in several areas south of the Border where farm workers were affected by high bread prices because of their need to purchase food in the market.[16]

The length of contract of service also distinguished the systems of recruitment in south-east England and lowland Scotland. In Scotland, over the period considered in this discussion, there seems to have been no reduction in the length of the hiring period. Between 1810 and 1840 most Scottish farm workers continued to be hired for a year or six months. This divergence between the two systems was broadly related to the state of the late eighteenth-century labour market and also to differences in agrarian structure. By the 1790s, in southern England, there were probably already too many labourers for farmers' needs. At the same time, that region was a specialist centre of wheat production and, as the acreage under this crop grew as a result of the wartime increase in prices, so fluctuation in the seasonal demand for labour increased. Two influences were possibly responsible for this. On the one hand, more workers than ever before were required at harvest; on the other, the adoption of the threshing machine from the early nineteenth century began to absorb a traditionally important winter task for male workers. Because of the marked differences in the amount of labour required at different seasons, farmers in the south and east had a clear incentive to eliminate the principle of the long-hire and, instead, take on men as and when required.[17]

In northern England and in lowland Scotland, however, the system of long-hires was perpetuated because it fitted in so well with farmers' needs in these regions. Scottish farmers in the late eighteenth century had to compete to a much greater extent with industrial employers. Industrial and agrarian change proceeded simultaneously and, more importantly, in close geographical proximity in the Scottish lowlands. Indeed, since most spinning and weaving of textiles took place in the countryside in the 1790s industrial and agricultural work were rarely wholly separate activities. Ironically, however, it was precisely at this time that the new improved agriculture demanded a more specialist and dedicated labour force. Yet, equally, because of the elimination of sub-tenants and cottagers and the counter-attraction of the towns, the farming class may have found it more difficult to retain the necessary pool of extra workers.[18] These varied pressures, therefore, not only forced a marked increase in money wage-rates on the farm but also, perhaps, contributed to a consolidation of the Scottish long-hire system in order to secure labour supplies.[19]

Shortage of workers, however, could not have been the fundamental influence because, after 1815, when labour became more plentiful, there was still no incentive to convert the workforce into casual labourers. An additional influence was the Scottish climate which dictated a regime of mixed agriculture. Increasing production within this system automatically required an expansion in the acreage under turnips and artificial grasses. In turn, this encouraged an extension in the working year because of the manifold tasks of weeding, dunging, singling and, most importantly, of intensive and regular ploughing associated with this crop sequence.[20] In essence, then, the social effects of agrarian change in a mixed-farming region were almost the reverse of those in a specialist cereal zone. Since work was spread more evenly throughout the year, farmers had a vested interest in recruiting labourers over lengthy periods.

This was vital anyway because of the crucial position of the horseman in the agricultural workforce in Scotland. As Gray has pointed out, the key to the farmer's policy of hiring was the need to use his work horses economically.[21] The horse was an expensive item for which the cost remained the same however infrequently it was used. It became essential, therefore, in order to secure the best returns, to spread work for the horse throughout the year, and to ensure that it functioned as efficiently as possible when at work. Thus each ploughman assumed responsibility for a pair of horses and his entire routine from the early morning to evening was concerned with preparation, working and final grooming of his animals. Inevitably, therefore, the ploughman had to be a permanent servant. He lived in the farmsteading near his horses and was engaged for an extended period.

The long-hire system helps to explain why the adoption of the threshing machine was not followed by the massive increase in winter unemployment among male workers which was one important cause of discontent in the south of England. Wage data indicated that the hiring of male farm servants in the eastern lowlands of Scotland only fluctuated on a seasonal basis in a minor way. This was even the case in the south eastern counties of Scotland where the balance of production lay more towards grain farming. In three of the nine years, 1814–23, money wages for single male servants in East Lothian and Berwick were the same at both Whitsun and Martinmas; in one year, winter wages were actually higher than those offered in summer; in the remaining five years, winter wages fell below summer levels but the reduction was never more than 15 per cent.[22]

Furthermore, while giving security to the worker when in employment, long-hires also helped to reinforce the farmer's powers of labour discipline. The hired servant was utterly dependent on his master during the period of the contract.[23] The individual bargaining between farmer and servant at the feeing markets was, in the view of some contemporaries, inimical to the development of group organization while the custom of boarding unmarried servants in the steading and feeding them in the kitchen implied the continuation of a paternalistic function which seems to have been abandoned in many parts of southern England.

Among the permanent staff only the bothymen were apparently less amenable to social control. They were accommodated in a farm outhouse or bothy where they slept and also prepared their own food. Outsiders repeatedly denounced the 'bothy system' for its tendency to brutalize and demoralize. Moreover, bothy dwellers had the reputation of being more detached from their employers than other workers and, in consequence, more restless and easily discontented. For instance, while Chartism in the 1840s seems to have had little appeal for most Scottish farm workers it did attract adherents from the bothy districts.[24] Again in the same areas, there were clear attempts at collective action by ploughmen in the early nineteenth century. In 1805, an organization of farm servants in the Carse of Gowrie was suppressed under the Combination Acts. In 1834, the same area was agitated again. A meeting at Inchture was attended by around 600 ploughmen and addressed by Dundee trade unionists. A committee was elected to extend the movement throughout Perthshire and to press its demands for an 8–10 hour day and payment of overtime.[25]

But the bothy system was not typical of most farming regions in lowland Scotland. It was virtually unknown in the south east and, in the north east, bothies were uncommon outside the old red sandstone areas of southern Kincardine and parts of the coastal plain of Moray and Nairn.[26] In the Carse of Gowrie bothies were more popular because there and in the lower parts of Strathearn there was a good deal of stiff, clay land requiring a very large amount of horses and ploughmen for cultivation. Furthermore, there was less need for female labour in this district which could have been supplied from the cottages of married servants. Until the formation of drainage schemes in the mid-nineteenth century, the carse lands were not very well adapted for root crops which caused most demand for female and child labour.[27] There was an obvious incentive, therefore, to erect only basic accommodation for single male workers.[28]

The other section of the agricultural workforce in Scotland we should consider was the day-labourers, recruited as extra hands at the busy season or to carry out the draining and ditching work associated with the new farming régime. Superficially, this group bore a resemblance to the labourers of southern England; both were hired on a short-term basis[29] and both were paid mainly in cash. Yet their intrinsic differences were more important than their apparent similarities. Day-labourers in Scotland formed but a minor proportion of the total workforce. In the 1790s, 20 per cent of agricultural workers in Dalmeny parish, Fife, were day-labourers; 10 per cent in Gask, Perthshire; 7 per cent in Oldhamstocks, Berwick; 14 per cent in Auchentoul, Fife; 5 per cent in Birmie, Elgin; 11 per cent in Edzell, Forfar.[30] Second, a substantial proportion of this minority were the wives and children of married male servants. In the south east, for example, the cash wages of dependants formed a useful addition to the income of households predominantly paid in kind.[31] Third, Scottish farmers did not maintain the large pool of underemployed day-labourers which was needed in southern England to meet the exceptional requirements of harvest time. They had no need to do so. The Highlands and Ireland provided a large and growing reservoir of seasonal workers and the remainder were recruited from the families of permanent servants and from adjacent industrial towns and villages.[32]

It is clear, the, that the vast majority of Scottish farm workers were largely insulated from the vicissitudes of the market when in employment and this fact may help to explain the stability of the rural lowlands after 1815. However, this assertion rests on the fundamental premise that most workers on the land continued to find jobs in these years. It is this assumption which must now be scrutinized. Measurement of unemployment at any time before the late nineteenth century is notoriously difficult since there is no possibility of quantifying numbers out-of-work in precise terms because of the absence of suitable data. Nevertheless, such source materials as are available permit the historian to construct a rough guide to the problem and to draw some tentative conclusions about its nature and duration in this period. Wage data available both in the contemporary press and in parliamentary papers help to provide a general profile of the labour market.[33] Again, between 1811 and 1825, when it ceased publication, the *Farmer's Magazine* published very detailed quarterly reports on each agricultural zone in Scotland. These not only provide full comment on prices and products but also describe conditions of employment among various grades of farm workers. This information is essentially impressionistic but it was collected by experienced observers and, when used in conjunction with wage data can cast light on regional employment trends. The gap between 1825 and the 1830s can be partially filled by material contained in the 1833 and 1836 Select Committees into Agriculture, from the parish reports of the *New Statistical Account of Scotland* and from the *Farmer's Register and Monthly Magazine*, which appeared in 1827–8 and provided the same useful service on wages and employment as its predecessor, the *Farmer's Journal*.

Three main conclusions can be derived from this evidence.[34] First, the fall in produce prices, which first became apparent from 1812, was not reflected in an immediate reduction in money wages until 1816. Second, after 1816 there was considerable unemployment among farm workers in 1817–18, 1821 and 1827 but no evidence of the problem of structural unemployment which was characteristic of rural areas in the south of England. Third, the severity of unemployment in these exceptional years varied both regionally and between different groups of farm employees. In the crisis years unemployment in the south east was always most significant among unmarried servants hired on six monthly contracts. Redundancy was much less common in this region among married servants who formed a majority of the permanent staff on most of the farms.[35] But the south east was likely to be most vulnerable when wheat prices collapsed from the wartime peaks. Most other areas were in a more fortunate position. In the central district, which included the counties of Fife, Perth and Stirling, there was a more flexible response. So, even in 1816–17, there were few complaints that agricultural workers had difficulty in finding jobs. The contrast was even more striking between the pattern in the south east and the north-eastern counties of Banff, Kincardine and Aberdeen. Here the more balanced agrarian structure and the development of land reclamation projects after 1815 ensured a greater vigour in the labour market than elsewhere. In 1816–17, for example, the north east began to shed farm workers later than the south east and to take on additional hands at an earlier stage when the temporary crisis had begun to pass. Again, 1821 was a bad year in the south east but hardly at all in Aberdeen and Banff. Throughout the period, indeed, half-yearly money wages for single male ploughmen in these latter counties were consistently 15 to 20 per cent higher than those offered in the Lothians and Berwickshire.

The evidence seems to suggest then that no permanent surplus of labour emerged in the eastern lowlands of Scotland in the decades after 1815.[36] Social stability was consolidated there partly because a rough balance was achieved between the number of workers on the land and the range of employments open to them. The probable reasons for this equilibrium will be explored in the final section of this paper.

There is no doubt that part of the explanation is to be found in the continuing presence of textile and other industry in the eastern lowlands. It is clear that from the early nineteenth century there was a swift decline in linen spinning and stocking knitting in the Scottish countryside but that this was partly compensated for by a sustained expansion in linen weaving in the east-central district until the end of the period considered here. Weaving increasingly became a specialized activity, carried on mainly in rural villages rather than farm cottages and thus provided a real alternative to agricultural work since wage levels, although they declined after 1815, proved more resilient than in the cotton-weaving districts of the west.[37] But a more fundamental influence than textile work was the particular response of

Scottish agriculture to the postwar depression in grain prices.

Scottish farming was better placed than the specialist wheat-producing regions of southern England. The range of crops grown, the vital significance of animal rearing and fattening, and the relative unimportance of wheat cultivation, except in the south east, lent the agrarian system a versatility which regions of monoculture manifestly lacked. The grains commonly grown in the north, oats and barley, were notably less affected by the slump in prices than wheat. Between 1805 and 1812 the average annual price for wheat in the south-east zone, according to the Haddington fiars, was 85/- per quarter. Between 1813 and 1820 the annual average fell by 47 per cent to 45/- per quarter. On the other hand, the decline in barley and oat prices was much less severe. Barley fell by about 9 per cent between 1813 and 1820 in relation to the average of 1805–12; oats by 14 per cent.[38]

Scottish farmers had another basic advantage. Some of the money costs of agriculture were probably less onerous north of the Border. There was no payment of tithes in kind: they could be valued and, when valued, did not afterwards increase. Poor Law assessments were still only a marginal and indirect burden on Scottish tenant farmers; landlords paid half the amount directly, the remainder was passed on to their tenants. But as late as 1839 only 236 out of 900 parishes had assessments and the majority of these were to be found either in the south east or in the growing towns and cities of the central belt.[39] A more important expense, however, was labour costs and here the continuation of payment in kind as an integral part of the total wage was again of considerable significance. When grain prices were depressed and pressures on cash resources increasing it made economic sense to perpetuate such payments and minimise money outlay.

Yet, despite these advantages, Scottish farmers did not escape unscathed in the aftermath of the Napoleonic Wars. High rentals, set when prices were at inflationary levels, were soon found excessively burdensome and bankruptcies did occur among tenant farmers in 1818 and 1820–1.[40] But the period from 1821 to the end of the 1830s was much less gloomy. During this phase landlords had apparently no difficulty in leasing farms.[41] Furthermore, a series of expert witnesses to the 1833 and 1836 government inquiries into British agriculture were firmly convinced of the positive prospects for Scottish farming. Indeed, so optimistic were they that they declined to ask for any of the forms of state help which seemed to be so urgently required in some parts of England at the time.[42]

The Scottish recovery initially proceeded on the secure basis of rent adjustment. From about 1820 rents began to be linked to the annual fiars prices for wheat, the commodity which had shown the greatest decline in price since 1812.[43] Abatement in rentals added to this advantage. By 1820 there had been reductions of up to 40 per cent in the rental of some Berwickshire estates and in the central district rents had fallen by about a quarter by 1833 from the levels prevailing in 1815.[44]

Declining costs enabled the development of a more positive strategy of adjustment from the early 1820s. This took the form in the first instance of a more intensive cultivation of those crops, such as potatoes and barley, least affected by price falls. For the first time, from 1821–2 a major export trade developed in potatoes from the counties of Perth, Stirling, Angus and Kinross. Second, the real agricultural potential of the north east as a cattle-fattening area was realised from the later 1820s as a result of the establishment of a steamship connection with London. Previously beasts destined for the southern market had had to be sold lean and under-priced in Aberdeenshire and Banffshire. Third, areas such as the Lothians and Berwick, where grain-farming had always been of most significance, began to move towards a more closely integrated structure of arable production and stock-fattening.[45]

All those developments, to a greater or lesser extent, involved an increased intensity of work on a given area of land. Employment opportunities expanded in the north east because more acres were absorbed into cultivation by the draining of stiff, clay land and the extension of turnip husbandry. The impact of this development is clearly evident in wage-rates. Money wages for single male servants in Aberdeenshire had reached a wartime peak of 8 guineas per half year in 1810. By 1816 this figure had been sharply reduced to just over £4. Thereafter, however, the recovery became obvious. Rates rose to £6 in 1820, steadied around that figure until 1824, reached £7 by 1825 and remained at about that level until the early 1830s.[46]

In the south east agrarian adjustment resulted in heavy investment in drainage schemes and generous additions of rape and bone dust to boost turnip yields. These advances had a visible impact on the job prospects of single female servants and day-labourers. Female money wages in East Lothian and Berwick showed an impressive stability in spring and summer from about 1819. Indeed, between 1819 and 1825, Whitsun wage rates for women were actually higher than those for men on three occasions.[47] This, of course, was as much a reflection of the demand for female domestic servants in nearby Edinburgh as an indication of the more vigorous labour market in agriculture. The same qualification could not, however, be applied to male day-labourers. Between 1815 and 1817 unemployment was severe among this group as investment plans were abruptly curtailed. But in the following decade day-labourers apparently only encountered problems of similar dimensions in 1827.[45]

Agrarian change was a central influence on employment but it was perhaps equalled in its significance by the trend in migration. Comparison with the southern counties of England is again useful. In simple terms the social problems of that zone were fundamentally related to an imbalance between an expanding rural population and scarcity of employment. This was caused by the failure of the surplus population to migrate. Hobsbawm and Rudé have clearly demonstrated how, in the first half of the nineteenth century, a diminishing proportion of the natural increase migrated precisely at the time when grain-farming was itself in great difficulties after the Napoleonic Wars. There was thus increasing pressure on the Poor Law at a time when farmers and landlords were less able or less willing to raise their rate subsidies. Indeed, their attempt to reduce their rate pavments and cut the Poor Law dole was a major factor in the discontent which led to the 'Captain Swing' riots all over the south and east of England in 1830.[49]

The demographic experience of the eastern lowlands of Scotland was, however, quite different. In the later eighteenth century, migration from rural counties, although it had already begun, was proceeding at a relatively slow rate. The safety valve of migration and emigration was of much greater consequence in the nineteenth century. Indeed between 1801 and 1851 many parishes in the eastern lowlands showed a net decline in numbers as the movement from country to town began to accelerate.[50] In essence, the eastern counties of Scotland seem to have been able to shed their surplus numbers more effectively than the southern region of England.

The method of accommodating labour in some regions also influenced the movement of younger workers.[55] In districts where there were few others than employing farmers and unmarried servants, ploughmen had to come from a distance at their first engagement, and when they married, might have to move out again because of the lack of family cottages. So in Perthshire, the dependence on unmarried labour was sufficiently great to cause a drain from agricultural labour. In the mid-nineteenth century between a quarter and a third of the men in Perthshire who had been servants or agricultural labourers were likely to leave for some other occupation by the time they were thirty.

The labour structure in Perthshire was, however, almost unique. Of more general significance throughout the lowlands in promoting migration was the Scottish system of hiring farm servants. The long-hire did offer security of employment for a time but when it lapsed the majority of workers, and single adult males in particular, customarily discharged themselves and travelled to the hiring fair to seek a new master, better conditions and more experience.[56] The single farm servant was therefore habitually mobile even if his movements were mainly confined to a particular neighbourhood. Furthermore, the feeing market was a uniquely effective medium for relating the number of places to the number of potential servants required by farmers for periods of between six months and one year. Individuals not engaged at Whitsun or Martinmas were faced with the prospect of seeking work elsewhere, accepting the inevitability of unemployment until the next fair or trusting to the chance of being hired as day-labourers and accepting the fall in status that that implied. They could not, unlike the rural unemployed in England, depend on the Poor Law because in Scotland the rights of the able-bodied to relief were not officially recognized. Movement from their parish of origin, therefore, did not imply a loss of 'settlement' rights as it did in England and where it acted as a most effective deterrent to migration in that region. In the second and third decades of the nineteenth century the difficulties encountered in obtaining employment in East Lothian and Berwick were reflected in the emigration of married and single farm servants to North America and Australia. Between 1815 and 1832, for example, most Scottish applicants seeking to settle in the Australian colonies came from the south-eastern counties and, over the same period, observers frequently commented on the movement of farm servants from the same area to the United States and Canada.[57]

This paper has not tried to present a comprehensive answer to the question posed by William Cobbett in 1830. The definitive explanation of Scottish rural stability in the early nineteenth century must take account of cultural, religious and political influences which have been treated only marginally here. What has been examined, however, are the factors within the agrarian structure of lowland Scotland which may have limited the development of discontent. These elements helped to ensure that the labour market in agriculture only became congested for brief periods after 1815 and that rural society was therefore capable of adjusting to the postwar situation in ways which reduced the tensions evident elsewhere in Britain at this time.

Appendix A. Median half-yearly money wages for single male and female agricultural servants, 1812–1828 (£ sterling)

Year		East Lothian/Berwick		Aberdeen/Banff	
		Male	Female	Male	Female
1812	Whit.	6	—	8–8	—
1814	Mart.	6	—	—	—
1813		—	—	—	—
1814	Whit.	6–15	5–15	8	2–10
1814	Mart.	6–15	—	—	—
1815	Whit.	6–10	2	8–10	—
1815	Mart.	5	2	—	—
1816	Whit.	—	—	6–10	—
1816	Mart.	4	2	4–10	—
1817	Whit.	4	3–10	—	—
1817	Mart.	3–10	1–10	4	—
1818	Mart.	3–10	1–10	4	—
1819	Whit.	4	4	5–10	—
1819	Mart.	4–10	1–15	—	—
1820	Whit.	4–10	5–15	6–10	—
1820	Mart.	—	—	7	—
1821	Whit.	4–10	5–10	—	—
1821	Mart.	4–10	1–15	—	—
1822	Whit.	4–10	4–10	5–10	—
1822	Mart.	4–10	1–10	5	—
1823	Whit.	4–10	4	6	4
1823	Mart.	3–10	1–10	5–10	2
1824	Whit.	5–0	4–10	—	—

1824		Mart.	5–0	—	6–10	2–5
1825		Whit.	6–0	5–5	7	4
1825		Mart.	5–5	—	7	—
1826		—	—	—		
1827	Mart.	4	—	6	2–10	
1828	Whit.	5–10	—	7	3–5	

Farmer's Magazine, 1812–25; *Farmer's Register and Monthly Magazine*, 1827–8.

Appendix B. *Annual cash wage-rates of Perthshire ploughmen, 1814–1870 (£ sterling)*

Year	Cash wage-rates
1814	12 to 16
1815	–
1816	–
1817	10 to 11
1818	10 to 11
1819	10 to 11
1820	–
1821	10 to 11
1822	10 to 11
1823	–
1824	–
1825	13 to 14
1826	10 to 12
1827	11 to 13
1828	10 to 12
1829	11 to 12
1830	11 to 12
1831	11 to 12
1832	10 to 11
1833	–
1834	10 to 11
1835	–
1836	12 to 15
1837	–
1838	–
1839	12
1840	12 to 15

Source: *Perthshire Courier*, 1814–40; G. Houston, 'Farm wages in central Scotland from 1814 to 1870', *Journal of the Royal Statistical Society*, Series A (General), 118 (1955), 224–7.

NOTES

1. E. J. Hobsbawm and George Rudé, *Captain Swing* (London, 1973 edition), 18–70; E. L. Jones, 'The agricultural labour market in England 1793–1872', *Economic History Review*, 2nd serv. XVII (1965–6), 329 ff.; N. Gash, 'Rural unemployment, 1815–34', *Economic History Review*, VI (1935–6), 90–3; G. Houston, 'Farm wages in central Scotland from 1814 to 1870', *Journal of the Royal Statistical Society*, Series A (General), 118 (1950), 224–7.

2. Hobsbawn and Rudé, *op. cit., passim*; A. J. Peacock, *Bread or Blood* (London, 1965); Bernard Raney, *The Class Struggle in Nineteenth-century Oxfordshire: the Social and Communal Background to the Otmoor Disturbances of 1830 to 1835* (Oxford, 1970).
3. E. Richards, 'Patterns of Highland discontent, 1790–1860' in R. Quinault and J. Stevenson (eds.), *Popular Protest and Public Order* (1974), 75–114; Galen Broeker, *Rural Disorder and Police Reform in Ireland, 1812–36* (1970); David Williams, *The Rebecca Riots* (Cardiff, 1965).
4. *Farmer's Magazine*, XIII (1812), 413–14.
5. *Ibid.*, XVII (1817), 101.
6. *Ibid.*, XXI (1820), iii. For other references to stability in the rural lowlands in the period 1815–36 see B.P.P., *Report from the Select Committee appointed to inquire into the Present State of Agriculture and Persons employed in Agriculture in the United Kingdom*, 1833, v (henceforth called *Report on Agriculture*, 1833), QQ. 2745–6, 2755; B.P.P., *First Report from the Select Committee appointed to inquire into the State of Agriculture and into the causes and extent of Distress which still presses on some branches thereof*, 1836, VIII (henceforth called *S.C. on Agricultural Distress*, 1836), QQ. 10189, 10367, 12223, 14064.
7. G.D.H. and M. Cole (eds.), W. Cobbett, *Rural Rides . . . together with Tours of Scotland . . . and Letters from Ireland* (1930), 111, 783–5.
8. An exception is T. C. Smout who discusses the problem in *A History of the Scottish People* (1969), 324–31.
9. J.P.D. Dunbabin, *Rural Discontent in Nineteenth Century Britain* (1971), *passim*.
10. *Ibid.*, 13–14.
11. Smout, op. cit., 331.
12. Richards, 'Patterns of Highland discontent', 75–114.
13. Hobsbawm and Rudé, *op. cit.*, 3–70; Peacock, *op. cit.*, 12–38; Gash, 'Rural unemployment', 90–3.
14. *S.C. on Agricultural Distress*, 1836, evidence of George Robertson, 218, Q. 13640; Anon., 'On the hiring markets in the counties of Northumberland. Berwick and Roxburgh', *The Quarterly Journal of Agriculture*, v (1834–5), 379–85; Sir John Sinclair, *General Report on the Agricultural State and Political Circumstances of Scotland* (Edinburgh, 1814), III, 227–42.
15. The phrase is Professor O. R. McGregor's in his introduction to Lord Ernle, *English Farming, Past and Present* (1901 edn), CXVIII.
16. S. G. E. Lythe, 'Tayside Meal Mobs', *Scottish Historical Review*, XLVI (1967); J. Stevenson, 'Food riots in England, 1792–1818', in Stevenson and Quinault (eds.), *Popular Protest and Public Order*; Walter J. Shelton, *English Hunger and Industrial Disorders* (1973); R. B. Rose, 'Eighteenth-century price riots and public policy in England', *International Review of Social History*, VI (1961).
17. Gash, 'Rural unemployment' 90–3; Jones, 'Agricultural labour market', 365.
18. Sir John Sinclair (ed.), *The Statistical Account of Scotland* (Edinburgh, 1790–9), I, 123, V, 571; XIV, 21.
19. Valerie Morgan, 'Agricultural wage rates in eighteenth-century Scotland', *Economic History Review*, 2nd ser., XXIV (1971), 181–201.
20. P. Brodie, 'On green crops', *Prize Essays and Transactions of the Highland Society of Scotland* (here-after called *Trans. H. S.*), I, (1799), 110–11.
21. Malcolm Gray, 'Scottish emigration: the social impact of agrarian change in the rural lowlands, 1775–1875', *Perspectives in American History*, VII (1973), 139–40.
22. 'Agricultural intelligence', *Farmer's Magazine*, XV (1815); XXXIV (1823).
23. See, for example, *Edinburgh Evening Courant*, 8 August 1807. According to a legal judgment of that year reported in the *Courant*, 'it was a mistake in servants, hired by the year or half year, to suppose that, after their ordinary work hours, they are at liberty to dispose of or absent themselves as they please without their master's leave . . .'

24. B.P.P., *Report from her Majesty's Commissioners for Inquiring into the Administration and Practical Operation of the Poor Laws in Scotland*. Appendix, Part III, 1844, XXII (hereafter called *R. C. on the Scottish Poor Laws*, 1844), 28, QQ. 587–8, 69, evidence of William Clugston, Forfar.

25. G. Houston, 'Labour relations in Scottish agriculture before 1870', *Agricultural History Review*, VI (1958).

26. J. Donaldson, *General View of the Agriculture of the County of Kincardine* (1794), 25; B.P.P., *Royal Commission on Labour, The Agricultural Labourer, Scotland, III, part 2, 1893–4, XXXVI* (hereafter called *R. C. on Labour*, 1893, xv, 123.

27. R. P. Newton, 'On the rural management of the Forfarshire part of the western district of Strathmore', *Trans. H.S.*, new ser. IV (1839), 478; *R. C. on Labour*, 1893, xv, 123.

28. B.P.P., *Fourth Report of the Commissioners on the Employment of Children, Young Persons and Women in Agriculture: Appendix, Part II: Evidence from the Assistant Commissioners*, 1870, XIII (hereafter called *Fourth Report on Women in Agriculture*), 56.

29. There is, however, a difficulty about the meaning of 'day-labour'. Such labourers were certainly *paid* on a daily basis but it is by no means clear whether they were hired and fired by the day. There is some evidence that they were taken on for much longer periods. Robert Hope, farmer of Fenton Barns in East Lothian, reckoned in 1836 that his four day-labourers would work on average 48 weeks in the year. For seasonal labour requirements outside the harvest period he could call on six women and boys for three months winter employment and eighteen women and boys for 24 odd weeks in the year for weeding, hoeing and general field labour. See *S.C. on Agricultural Distress*, 1836, 20–1; and for a discussion, Paul F. Docherty, 'The condition of the rural labourer in East Lothian, 1780–1840', B. A. Dissertation, Department of History, University of Strathclyde, 1977, 26–7.

30. Sinclair. *Old Statistical Account*, I, 241; II, 480; VII, 297; VIII, 114–15; IX, 160. There is no evidence of a major increase in the proportion of day-labourers since the compilation of the Statistical Account in the 1790s. According to an inquiry carried out in the counties of Forfar and Kincardine in 1851 only 1483 of a total agricultural labour force of almost 14,000 were day-labourers. See 'Report by a Committee of the Synod of Angus and Mearns as to agricultural labourers', *Journal of Agriculture*, new ser. (1855–7), 398. In 1828, one fifth of the agriculture work force in Kincardine consisted of day-labourers. See G. Robertson, *Rural Recollections* (Irvine, 1829), 420.

31. *S.C. on Agricultural Distress*, 1836, evidence of Robert Hope of Fenton Barns, 21, Q. 9693.

32. E. J. T. Collins, 'Migrant labour in British agriculture in the nineteenth century', *Economic History Review*, 2nd ser. XXIX (1976), 36–59; see above, ch. 10.

33. The Farmer's Magazine gives a coherent series of wage-rates for single male and female servants over the period *c*. 1811–25. The evidence in this source is especially rich for the north-east and south-east zones but much less full for the central districts. Fortunately the *Perthshire Courier*, which began publication in 1809, gives a good coverage of hiring rates for the counties of Perth, Angus, Kinross, Fife and Stirling. The *Courier* evidence formed the basis of Houston, 'Farm wages in central Scotland', 227–8. The better known index of Scottish farm wages compiled by A. L. Bowley has not been used here. (See A. L. Bowley, 'The statistics of wages in the United Kingdom during the last hundred years: Part II, agricultural wages in Scotland', *Journal of the Royal Statistical Society*, LXII (1899), 141–6). Bowley omitted long periods of time since he depended mainly on the Statistical Accounts and the general views of the agriculture of various counties in Scotland. Moreover, he attempted to convert wages in kind into wages in money, an exercise which almost certainly produced imprecise results. An index based on cash wages alone is

preferable; because of its sensitivity it is likely to highlight fluctuations in the labour market more accurately.

34. See Appendix A and B.

35. Only in 1818 did the *Farmer's Magazine* observe: 'manyhinds, or married farm servants, have not found masters', OXX (1818), 239.

36. There is no doubt that the labour market was again buoyant by the early 1830s. *See Report on Agriculture*, 1833, evidence of Adam Murray, land surveyor, 30, QQ. 301–9; evidence of Thomas Oliver, land valuer, Midlothain, 132, QQ. 2755, 2764–5; *S. C. on Agricultural Distress*, 1836, evidence of John Brodie, farmer, Haddington, 56, Q. 10367.

37. *Farmer's Magazine*, XXIII (1822), 238; B. P. P., *Handloom Weavers: Assistant Commissioners Reports from the East of Scotland*, 1839, XLII, 35, 43–4, 187–8, 206–14. Textiles were not the only source of competition for agricultural labour. In 1820, it was reported from Banffshire that, 'owing to the great demand for labour at making roads, harbours and the herring fisheries in this neighbourhood, the wages of farm-servants got up considerably last Whitsunday'. *Farmer's Magazine*, XXI (1820), 366.

38. A. Stewart, 'On the prices of grains from 1647 to 1829 inclusive', *Trans. H. S.* new ser. II, 189.

39. Laurance J. Saunders, *Scottish Democracy 1815–40*, (Edinburgh, 1950), 197.

40. *S. C. on Agricultural Distress*, 1836, 120, Q. 2863; 31, Q. 9932.

41. *Farmer's Magazine*, XXIII (1822), 98; XXII (1821), iii, *Report on Agriculture*, 1833, IX.

42. *S. C. on Agricultural Distress*, 1836, QQ. 11888, 15076, 13599.

43. *Ibid.*, QQ. 9655, 9662, 9975, 10508; Anon., 'On rents convertible into money and limited by a maximum', *Farmer's Magazine*, XVII, (1816), 298–314.

44. *New Statistical Account of Scotland* (Edinburgh, 1845), 205, 364, 956; John Dickson, 'The Agriculture of Perthshire', *Trans. H. S.* II (1868–9), 167–8; *S. C. on Agriculture Distress*, 1836, QQ. 11170, 11173, 10532, 10651–60, 11840.

46. *Farmer's Magazine*, XI (1810)- XXVI (1825), *passim; Farmer's Register and Monthly Magazine*, 1827–8; S. C. on Agricultural Distress, 1836, Q. 13640.

47. *Ibid.*

48. *Farmer's Magazine*, XVIII (1817), 101; IXX (1818), 106; *Farmer's Register and Monthly Magazine*, II (1828), 229, 231.

49. Hobsbawm and Rudé, *op. cit.*, 22–3.

50. The increase in Scottish migration from country to town between 1801 and 1861 is demonstrated in detail in Gray, 'Scottish emigration', 102–6.

55. This paragraph is based on Gray, 'Scottish emigration', 165.

56. 'Report by a Committee of the Directors on Hiring Markets', *Trans. H. S. (1849–51)*, II; J. F. Duncan, 'Scottish farm labour', *Scottish Journal of Agriculture*, II (1919), 499–502.

57. D. S. Macmillan, *Scotland and Australia, 1788–1850* (Oxford, 1967), 14, 295; *Farmer's Magazine, xx* (1819), 358. The proverbially high standards of literacy and general education which prevailed among the 'hind' class may also have contributed to mobility. They were unlikely to be ignorant of opportunities abroad. Again, since the married servant normally owned a cow and had had the opportunity to save during the war years, he was perhaps more able to afford the expenses of emigration.

14

WOMEN ON THE LAND, 1850–1914

An important characteristic of the Scottish agricultural labour force in the nineteenth century was the widespread employment of women in the daily and seasonal routine of lowland farms. Of the 165,096 persons enumerated as farm grieves (or bailliffs), agricultural labourers, shepherds and farm servants (indoor) in 1871, 42,796, or 26 per cent of the total, were women.[1] This, however, was an underestimate of the entire female contribution because the census figure did not include the army of seasonal labourers who came during the spring, summer and autumn months to sow, harvest and gather Scotland's grain, green and fruit crops. Moreover, since the census total referred only to 'number employed', it took no account of the wives and daughters of smaller farmers and crofters who were a vital, though normally unpaid, component of the work force of the dairying districts of the south-west and of the north-east counties of Aberdeen, Banff and Kincardine.[2] In relation to the employment structure in the English countryside, the general engagement of women in Scotland was distinctive. As defined by the classes mentioned above, female wage earners in agriculture in England and Wales formed 5.8 per cent of the total number employed, and only one county, Northumberland, where 25 per cent of wage earners were female, approached the Scottish average.[3] As George Culley, the agricultural reporter for south-east Scotland, noted in 1870, 'The Scotch practice differs from the English in the much more extensive employment of women. Throughout the whole of my district women are employed in all the lighter and in not a few of the heavier operations of farm labour'.[4]

Here Culley was merely echoing the comment of Henry Stephens thirty years before: 'field workers consist mainly of young women in Scotland but mainly of men and boys in England'.[5] Women carried out virtually every task on the farm except those which directly involved the management of horses. Their duties were to perform all the 'normal operations' of the fields and those concerned with the use of 'smaller implements' not worked by horses. The former included sowing potatoes, gathering weeds, picking stones, collecting potatoes and filling drains with stones; the latter embraced such varied jobs as pulling turnips and preparing them for feeding stock, barn-work, carrying seed corn, spreading manure on the land, hoeing potatoes and turnips, and weeding and reaping corn-crops. In addition, they had a monopoly of milking and cheese-making. Thus in 1812 it could be said, 'there are few operations in husbandry in which women are not employed, except those of ploughing and threshing'.[6] The purpose of this essay is to survey the reasons for this characteristic pattern of female employment in Scotland, then to attempt to categorise and describe the varied types of female work-groups, and finally to examine why regular farm employment for women was becoming increasingly unpopular in the later nineteenth century.

I

Before the late eighteenth century some farm tasks had, by custom and tradition, become accepted as the special province of women, and their role in these areas survived throughout the nineteenth century. It was, for example, the invariable custom in Scotland that women attended to the cows. In Ayrshire, 'unlike England, every process connected with the milk, the butter or the cheese is conducted by women and rightly too'.[7] Moreover, in the smaller farms of the era before the 'Agricultural Revolution', wives and daughters had inevitably formed an important part of the family work team. Between 1750 and 1830, this small farm sector did not disappear but survived strongly in modified form in the south-west and north-east lowlands. The women of the family continued to make a major contribution to its labour needs.[8] Also, in the old world, wives of married ploughmen were regarded by farmers on larger units as a useful source of additional labour at the grain harvest. The wives of Berwickshire hinds were obliged to work during the harvest without wages as part of their husband's labour contract in lieu of payment for the rent of the family cottage.[9] This system prevailed throughout the south-eastern district of arable farming and reflected its particular needs for extra labour at harvest time. Over the centuries the sickle was the tool for cutting cereal crops and it was employed chiefly but not exclusively by women. The stalks were cut low down, and 'for this reason it was especially used by women, who are said to be physiologically better adapted to bending than men'.[10] These social attitudes on what constituted male or female tasks continued to influence the labour market for women workers throughout the period covered by this essay.

Demand for female labour was also powerfully affected by the changing economic and social structure of Scottish farming between 1780 and 1830. It was in that period that specialist horsemen emerged on the medium and larger farms. Ploughmen were increasingly withdrawn from the range of farm tasks and instead devoted their time to working with a particular pair of animals in ploughing, carting and related activities.[11] As George Robertson noted in his *Rural Recollections*, it was 'employing professional men to professional objects'.[12] The tendency was already apparent in the Lothians in the middle decades of the eighteenth century. Ploughmen were no longer used directly in the harvesting process but instead worked with their horses 'directly behind the shearers as fast as they could get their way, tilling the ridges that were in the intervals betwixt the rows of stalks'.[13] The result of this new specialisation was to enhance the status of the male farm servant, contribute to the development of his skills and to a sense of pride in the job and, in the long run, increase labour productivity. Necessarily, however, it also meant the recruitment of other regular employees. The extensive employment of female outworkers was one response to this growing differentiation of labour within the new farm structure. In essence, the old blurred distinction between male and female tasks was preserved and strengthened within the new agriculture. Thus in the north-east lowlands in the second half of the nineteenth century 'the cultural prescription against women working with horses was absolute', while before the First World War 'a Lothian ploughman would feel insulted if asked to pull turnips and most ploughmen would refuse to do byre work'.[14]

The employment of female labour reflected other economic and social trends in the late eighteenth century. In that period sub-tenancy was under widespread attack throughout the rural lowlands. The small plots of land which cottagers and sub-tenants had held in return for labour services on adjacent larger farms were now increasingly absorbed within bigger and more compact units. Sub-tenancies were more valuable after c. 1770 to main tenants as food prices rose in the final decades of the eighteenth century, while the achievement of higher levels of labour productivity required the recruitment of full-time workers over whom farmers could exert more discipline and control.[15] Yet the sub-tenant class had been a crucial source of seasonal labour and, as their ranks were thinned, farmers in some areas consolidated the family system of hiring by which married male servants were employed on condition that they could produce a woman to work whenever needed. Seasonal migrants from towns and villages, from the Highlands and Ireland but also members of the families of the married ploughman class, were seen as a reserve army of labour which remained vital in the new farming.[16] Tied female labour, available for seasonal tasks, was especially crucial in the south-east because that area was thinly peopled, with large, isolated farms and limited access to town labour because of the poorly developed industrial structure of the region. Inevitably, farmers were forced to depend on the female dependents of their married workers if for no other reason than that it was difficult to obtain an alternative supply which was both cheap and reliable: 'the practice is good, because it enables the farmer to command a certain number of hands at all times, and also to accomplish his ends by his own resources, independent of extraneous aid. It is no answer to say that women may be hired out of villages when their services are required, because many large farms are situated far from any village and when trade is brisk women are encouraged to desert the fields. ..'.[17]

The problem was not simply or directly associated with the traditional grain harvest, because that lasted for only three to four weeks and its labour requirements, though great, were essentially of short duration. The difficulty was the needs of the new agriculture differed radically from those of the old. More land was absorbed into production and the existing arable was worked more intensively. The development of new field systems, based on turnips and sown grasses, and the cultivation of new crops such as potatoes, stretched the farmer's busy time both backwards and forwards in the year. It therefore became necessary to recruit labour for the new cycle of tasks of weeding, sowing, thinning and gathering which endured from spring to early winter.[18]

Female labour had considerable attractions for those farmers who were developing the new rotations. These systems were highly labour-intensive. Root crops were the most demanding of labour, requiring as many as ten to fifteen worker-days per acre, compared with between four to five worker-days in corn harvesting with the sickle.[19] Robert Hope of Fenton Barns, near Haddington, employed thirteen ploughmen in the early 1830s, a further six seasonal workers in winter but an additional eighteen over a period of 24 weeks for weeding and hoeing turnips. There was, therefore, an incentive to exploit cheap sources of labour if at all possible.[20] Valerie Morgan has shown that female cash wages in Scottish agriculture in the 1790s were approximately half the pay of men.[21] Society regarded women as dependents, whether as wives or daughters, who were not entitled to the same rate for the job as their male counterparts. These differentials were strongly influenced by custom and by what was deemed an acceptable proportion of the male rate.[22] Despite the growing shortage of female labour after 1870, in many areas, these traditional distinctions were preserved with only partial erosion. The advantage of hiring women was obvious. One observer in 1867 put it bluntly: 'Farmers employ women because their wages are about half *what is expected* by men'.[23] There were significant economic benefits in a hiring policy which combined in an effective working partnership, a corps of skilled ploughmen and large numbers of low-paid women. As the Royal Commission on Employment of Women in Agriculture put it in 1870: 'It is no doubt owing to the comparatively lower wages at which female labour can be obtained that Scotch farming in an economical point of view owes a considerable portion of its success'.[24]

It was also recognised that women often gave better service than men. They were regarded as particularly adept at hand-weeding, reaping with the sickle and, when the scythe, a man's tool, was widely adopted, gathering at the grain harvest. In the early nineteenth century, when the sickle was still the most important hand-tool at harvest, several commentators acknowledged the special skill of women and asserted that when work was done by the piece, they regularly earned more than men.[25] Their expertise in turnip-picking was a tribute to their manual dexterity: 'for a woman, though not so *strong is more alert*, and generally, *more neat* in picking the young turnips with her fingers, when they are so close that the hoe cannot separate them'.[26] Early training maximised these physical advantages, as the young daughters of farm servants were reared from their earliest years in the handling of the hoe and other tools.

It would be wrong, on the other hand, to conclude that the widespread employment of women in Scottish agriculture was only conditioned by the nature of the farming system itself. Of considerable additional significance was the nature of industrial demand for rural labour. Scottish farmers had to compete with industrial employers to a much greater extent than their fellows in most parts of England, outside the northern region. Industrial and urban development, though most rapid and vigorous in west-central Scotland, occurred widely throughout the lowland zone. Few rural areas were remote from the pull of alternative employment in towns, cities and industrial villages.[27] Yet, after c. 1830, Scottish economic expansion depended on the growth of the heavy industries of coal, iron, steel, engineering and shipbuilding. Overwhelmingly, therefore, the manufacturing sector had most need of adult male labour, and the evidence suggests that the bulk of its requirement were satisfied by male migrants from the lowland countryside.[28] This sexual bias in the industrial labour market helps to explain why cash wages for men in agriculture were rising in the 1830s and 1840s when female rates were stagnant.[29] Farmers were having to bid higher to retain their male workers as competition from industry increased. In some areas, this may have provided a further incentive to hire women. Thus, in the industrialised country of Lanarkshire, young men were drawn to coalmining in the 1870s and 1880s, a trend which caused heavy reliance on female labour.[30]

Yet, the point, though relevant, should be kept in perspective. Women were widely employed on Scottish farms long before the major expansion of the heavy industries. Some areas, such as East Lothian and the counties of Berwick and Roxburgh, were among the most significant employers of women in agriculture though they experienced only limited industrial development. Moreover, as the economy expanded on the basis of investment in manufacturing and mining, it generated a larger service sector in which women found employment in increasing numbers. By the final three decades of the nineteenth century, then, urban areas were attracting *both* men and women from the land at a faster rate, and this was reflected in a secular increase in female agricultural wages.[31] To fully explain, therefore, why women were such an important part of the farm labour force in Scotland, due attention must be paid to the influence of custom and agrarian structure, already discussed, as well as to the effect of industrial demand for male workers.

II

It is exceedingly difficult to place female workers in precise classifications which have enduring validity both over time and space. However, between 1850 and 1914 roughly four broad groups can be identified: (a) regular and full-time employees, mainly outworkers in the south-east and dairymaids and byrewomen in the dairying districts of the south-west; (b) family workers; (c) 'in-and-out' girls whose work was partly domestic but also involved field labour; (d) part-time, seasonal or casual workers.

(a) Regular workers

Two sub-groups can be discerned here. First, there were women servants employed in the dairying districts of Dumbarton, Lanarkshire, Renfrewshire, Ayrshire and Wigtownshire. They were unmarried and hired to carry out all the dairying work of the farm. Normally they were boarded and lodged by the farmers. They were among the highest-paid group of women workers because of the long hours and hard labour associated with dairying. Byre women were also kept to clean the stalls and tend cattle. The position, however, was complicated because only large and medium-sized farms could afford to hire specialist dairywomen.[32] Often, the work was done by female members of the farmer's family, and when extra labour was hired, the girls were expected to do field work and domestic chores as well as help in milking. Such women were exposed to a particularly arduous regime. One dairy woman in Dunbartonshire in the early 1890s described a typical day: '. . . we start at 5 a.m. and then we milk till 7. We have breakfast, porridge at 7 and a further breakfast at 8. In the house we start at once to work after meal, which occupies scarcely half an hour. Dinner is at 12; start as soon as finished to go and feed the cows; we work away with straw, turnips and other jobs till 4, when we have tea. Then feed cows again; rest from 5–30 to 7, then milk till 8; then fodder cows which takes half an hour'.[33] Perhaps, not surprisingly, skilled dairy workers, despite their high wages, were in short supply in many districts by 1900.[34]

The second group were full-time regular outworkers principally employed in the south-eastern counties of Fife, the Lothians, Berwick and Roxburgh and to a much lesser extent elsewhere. According to the census of 1871, females classed as whole-time agricultural labourers comprised 33 per cent of females employed in Haddington, 32 per cent in Berwick, 30 per cent in Roxburgh, 28 per cent in the county of Edinburgh and 24 per cent in Fife.[35] These ratios can be compared with the north-east counties where, in Aberdeen, only 3 per cent of females employed were full-time agricultural labourers, in Banff 5 per cent and in Kincardine 6 per cent. In the farms of the south-east, therefore, there was very heavy use of regular female workers. In Linlithgow, women were reckoned to be employed to the extent of four to every 100 acres of cultivated land, while in Berwick and Roxburgh in the 1860s, about half the adult labourers and farm servants were women.[36] Table 1 demonstrates the extensive employment of women in the Lothians.

Table: 1 Particulars of Horses and Labourers to Acres in 25 Farms in Mid and East Lothian, 1893

	Per 100 acres	Per 100 acres arable	Per 100 acres under crops
No. of horses			
Labourers (regular)	2.27	2.8	3.57
Men and strong lads	2.33	2.9	3.67
Women and young boys	1.75	2.21	2.76
	4.08	5.11	6.44

Source: R. C. *on Labour, 1893*, Part II, p. 131.

This dependence on women was partly associated with the cropping structure of these areas, with their great emphasis on the cultivation of green crops within the rotation systems. As Table 2 illustrates, the south-eastern counties had the largest proportion of land laid down to these crops of any in Scotland. Turnips were the ones most demanding of female labour. Just as significant was the larger average size of farm in the region: 'a farm of less than 100 acres would not afford constant employment for women'.[37] Regular outworkers were hardly used at all in the small farm districts of the south-west and north-east.

The nature of the supply of female labour in the area varied over time. In the later eighteenth century married ploughmen were hired on condition that they could supply a woman worker when required. Originally this was probably the ploughman's wife, at least in some districts. Thus in Berwickshire, 'wives of hinds are generally bound to shear in harvest without wages, but with full harvest food, and must work at all outdoor labour especially sowing and hay harvest, for the customary wages of the country'.[38] However, the new farming demanded more regular work throughout the year, and this inevitably conflicted with a wife's domestic responsibilities. In addition, it was usual for the hind's wife in the Lothians to keep a cow whose milk and butter were not only an important element in family diet, but which, when sold in local markets, provided a vital source of cash income for households mainly rewarded through payment in kind to the father. Significantly, therefore, the extent to which *married* women worked regularly in the fields in the south-east tended to vary according to the local custom of keeping a cow. So in Linlithgow, 'because the hind's cow is absent, the proportion of married women employed is greater than further south'.[39] The labour returns from 10 farms in that county for the spring and winter quarters of 1867 indicate that 55 married and 99 single women worked during spring and 35 married and 74 single were hired during winter. On the other hand, in Haddington, a 'cow county', on 12 farms, 5 married and 150 single women were employed in spring and only 2 married and 149 single in winter.[40]

It followed, therefore, that except in Linlithgow and also in Fife, increased demand for female labour in the south-east could only be satisfied through the recruitment of single women. Married ploughmen were obliged to supply a female worker whenever called upon. Normally this would be a daughter or sister, but when none was available a 'bondager' was hired from outside. The ploughman was required to board and lodge her and received from the farmer an allowance in money for every day she was employed on the farm: 'The hind is obliged to pay whatever wage the woman can command, according to the current wages of the season, besides finding her lodging, food and washing; from the farmer she receives only so much a day for every day she works, and the number of days she works depends on the will of the farmer'.[41]

Table 2 Percentage of Total Area of Land in Lowland Scottish Counties under Green Crops, 1891

Aberdeen	8.0	Kincardine	8.8
Ayr	2.2	Kinross	6.2
Banff	6.7	Kirkcudbright	2.9
Berwick	*10.8*	Lanark	2.7
Clackmannan	3.8	*Linlithgow*	*7.8*
Dumbarton	2.3	Nairn	3.8
Dumfries	3.7	Peebles	2.3
Edinburgh	*8.2*	Perth	2.8
Elgin	6.0	Renfrew	3.6
Fife	*13.4*	*Roxburgh*	*6.0*
Forfar	8.8	Selkirk	2.0
Haddington	*14.0*	Stirling	2.8
		Wigtown	5.8

Source: Board of Agriculture, Agricultural Statistics for Great Britain for 1891, Parliamentary Papers 1890–1, (c.6524), LCI. South-eastern counties in italics.

By the 1850s there was open resentment of the bondage system throughout the south-eastern lowlands, and a major campaign began to force its abolition.[42] The ploughman had to hire and feed the bondager, but he was only paid when her services were required. The hind therefore preferred to recruit labour from his own family than employ a stranger, and this was an obvious constraint on family freedom and opportunity. One critic of the system pointed out in the 1850s: '. . . rather than be teased with them, hinds often kept their own daughters at home as bondagers, when either they ought to have been earning better wages as principal servants, or at some other occupation'.[43] This was perhaps the crux of the matter. Hostility to bondage was an integral part of a wider change in attitude among farm servants in the south-east. Expectations were rising after 1860 as wage levels increased; the development of more attractive town occupations made it all the more difficult to keep daughters at home working in the fields; migration from the countryside served to increase the bargaining power of the labouring classes. Significantly, the campaign against bondage in the 1860s was the central element in a general attempt to raise wage rates and improve conditions.[44]

Bondage in its original form was therefore in decline in the 1860s, but it did not disappear everywhere at the same pace, and some aspects of it survived down to 1914 even when the formal requirement to hire a stranger 'to work the bondage' fell into abeyance. The system had practically disappeared from the Lothians by 1870 but persisted in Berwick and Roxburgh.[45] Farmers throughout the region, however, still required female labour and responded in a variety of ways to the decay of bondage. Increasingly men who could supply women from within their own families were given preference at the hiring fairs.[46] This gave an advantage to older workers but penalised the younger ploughmen. Another result was the maintenance of the family as the working unit in Berwick and Roxburgh long after the disappearance of formal bondage. As late as the 1920s in these counties women workers were still normally the daughters of men employed on the farms, their engagements were made through their father and they were 'bound' to work for the usual period of engagement of a year. The weekly wage was not paid to each individual separately but in a lump sum to the father or mother. In this way, the dependent position of female labour was perpetuated.[47] Elsewhere in the south-east, notably in the counties of Haddington and Linlithgow, the decay of bondage was accompanied by an increase in the migration of hinds' daughters to seek positions in domestic service in Edinburgh.[48] Farmers in these districts reacted by building bothies for women and boarding in them girls from the Highlands and Ireland. Cottages were also let to single women or to widows with daughters in return for providing work when required at day's wages.[49] Employers sought to maintain a reliable supply of cheap labour which did not have to be paid or maintained when climate deteriorated or seasonal work slackened. Once again, there was a certain continuity between the old days of the bondage system and the new era of 'free' labour.

(b) Female labour in family farms

The large farms of 300 acres and above were only dominant in a few areas, such as the Lothians. Each region, however, particularly outside the south-east, had its share of small holdings mainly or entirely worked by family labour. Table 3 provides an insight into the scale of this small farm sector. The figures are derived from the published censuses where occupiers of land were asked to state the acreage of their farms. The totals in each period have been reduced to 1000 to indicate the relative number of farms of different size in each decade.

The majority of those farmers working 100 acres or less relied heavily on the labour of their own families. One informed contemporary estimate suggested that in 1913 there were about 167,000 full-time and casual workers in Scottish agriculture. About 78,000 of this grand total were considered members of the occupier's family.[50] The importance of female labour within the family system varied both with the size of the enterprise and the emphasis of production. On the small farms of the north-east, 'the success of the holding depends as much upon the skill and industry of the housewife as upon that of the holder'.[51] The female members of the family were especially important in the operation of the crofts in Aberdeen and Banff. Sons apparently went to service on neighbouring larger farms almost as soon as they could, leaving their sisters and mothers to help run the croft. Thus, in 1911, even when wives are not included in the total, women comprised 54 per cent of the labour teams in crofts in Aberdeenshire, 49 per cent in Banff and 57 per cent in Nairn.[52] Similar patterns existed in the dairy farming districts in the south-western counties of Renfrew, Lanark and Ayr. In Ayrshire in the 1860s, 'most of the cheesemakers were the wives and daughters of the farmers, only a few of the larger farms engage dairy-women'.[53] Again, along the southern parishes of Lanarkshire, 'farms are generally about 100 acres in size, many of them are worked entirely by the farmer and his family, the farmer himself handling the plough and the wife making the cheese'.[54]

Table 3 Size of Farms in Scotland, 1851–1881

Size of Farm	1851	1871	1881
Under 10 acres	345	120	160
From 10–50 acres	297	299	288
From 50–100 acres	149	192	174
From 100–200 acres	125	195	188
From 200–300 acres	39	76	71
From 300–400 acres	17	38	39
From 400–500 acres	9	18	18
From 500–600 acres	5	13	13
Over 600 acres	14	49	49
	1000	1000	1000

Source: John W. Paterson, 'Rural Depopulation in Scotland: Being an Analysis of its Causes and Consequences', *Trans Highland and Agricultural Society of Scotland*, 5th ser., IX (1897), p. 261.

When a farm was worked in this way there was normally no wage exchange. The son might aspire one day to succeed to the farm but there was no such hope for the daughters. Yet it was recognised that theirs was a life of drudgery and toil, what one commentator called 'the slavery of family work'.[55] Dairying near centres of population involved very early rising, at about 2 to 3 a.m., because of a popular prejudice in favour of warm milk. Similarly, dairy women in upland farms needed to milk early to ensure that milk could be sent to town by early morning trains. In other cases the milk was manufactured into cheese, which entailed 'an enormous amount of continuous labouring, seven days a week during six to seven months in the year . . . I have seen the women-folk on such farms at 3 o'clock in the afternoon in the same garb they had hurriedly donned between 3 and 4 o'clock in the morning, having been constantly toiling, one duty succeeding another—milking, preparing breakfast, cheese-making, calf and pig-feeding, preparing dinner etc. It is usual for women on dairy farms to work sixteen hours per day, time for meals only being allowed for'.[56]

The widespread use of family labour attracted both apologists and critics.[57] Some contended that it had obvious advantages from the point of view of both costs and productivity: a family working together as a productive unit, each individual feeling that he or she had a direct personal interest in the work and its result, was likely to be an efficient instrument of production. When farm prices declined in the last quarter of the nineteenth century, these farms, particularly in the south-west, met the challenge at least partly because of their minimal cost of labour. Others suggested that family labour was one cause of the general low wage-rates for women in agriculture. As one critic put it: 'a fundamental condition of the employment of paid female labour is that it competes with family labour employed without regular wages and actually as sweated or parasite labour'. There was also growing concern in the early twentieth century that the exploitation of young women inherent in the family system was causing labour scarcity in some sectors of Scottish farming by 1900. Carter, for example, has argued that the first group to leave the peasant agriculture of the north-east after 1880 were young women 'for whom there was no hope of ever replacing domestic servitude with the independence of the peasant farmer'.[58]

(c) 'In-and-out' Girls

According to the census of 1871, of the 42,789 females regularly employed for wages in Scottish agriculture, 52 per cent were described as 'agricultural labourers', by which was probably implied regular, full-time field workers, and the remaining 48 per cent as 'farm servants' (indoor). This latter group was most numerous in Lanark, Dumfries, Stirling, Dumbarton, Aberdeen, Banff, Kincardine and Ayr and least common in the south-eastern counties of Haddington, Fife, Berwick and Roxburgh.[59] They were therefore rare in districts where large farms were the norm and more significant in areas of small and medium-sized holdings. On these farms the female worker had to be versatile because no single task could absorb labour on a continuous basis in the fashion characteristic of the regime in the Lothians. The 'in-and-out' girls, as their name implied, did housework, milked cows, helped in the fields and generally turned their hand to any task in the steading. They had no fixed hours nor, as late as 1914, any generally recognised holiday customs.[60] But it is difficult to generalise about their conditions because much depended on the attitude of the individual employer and local custom. So, in the larger farms of the south-west dairying counties, they tended to spend most of their time in milking and tending the cows. On the smaller farms, they worked alongside the family, doing anything required.[61] In Aberdeenshire and Banffshire, however, the special function of the 'in-

and-out' girl was to work in the kitchen, as most farm employees in the north-east were single males who took their meals in the farmhouse.[62] However, their outside duties also included milking, attending to poultry and occasional help in the fields.

It was generally agreed that the 'in-and-out' girl, especially if she was the only hired servant on the farm, worked longer and harder than any other female employee in agriculture. They became increasingly difficult to obtain in the years before 1914, and contemporaries attributed this to their poor working conditions: 'this state of matters must be attributed to the nature of the employment of these girls and chiefly to the length of their working day and the lack of fixed and regular leisure time'.[63]

(d) Seasonal, casual and part-time workers

The cycle of sowing, growth, maturity and harvesting in agriculture inevitably meant that demand for labour fluctuated throughout the year. There were different work-peaks associated with grain crops, turnips, potatoes and with the new soft fruit industry in Clydeside and the Carse of Gowrie. An indication of the seasonal movement in demand for labour comes from the example of a 'large cropping farm of 250 acres near Glasgow' in the 1880s.[64] The regular staff consisted of three to four ploughmen and two women servants. In winter only a few additional workers were needed about the threshing-machine or for filling sacks with potatoes. For the earliest spring work, planting potatoes in April, more women were hired. Weeding potatoes at the end of May required 30 to 40 women, as did thinning turnips in late May and June. In September and October three major seasonal tasks followed in seqence: grain harvesting, potato lifting and turnip pulling. The gathering of the turnip crop was the most demanding of extra labour on this particular farm and required the hiring of between 60 and 70 extra women workers.

Mechanisation did have a significant impact on the market for grain harvest labour, firstly with the development of the machine reaper and then as a result of the adoption of the reaper-binder in the 1890s. But not all farmers could afford these services and they tended to be most common in regions of larger holdings which could sustain the capital costs involved. The other seasonal tasks remained labour-intensive in the later nineteenth century.[65] Indeed, it is possible to argue that there was an increased need for seasonal workers between 1880 and 1914. Rising wages among regular employees and a growing scarcity of certain grades of full-time labour, as a result of migration, forced farmers in some areas, notably the Lothians, to recruit more workers on short-term contracts.[66] Moreover, in the last three decades of the century, the heavy emphasis in the western parished of Ayrshire on early potato cultivations and the developments of market gardening in Lanarkshire and Perthshire boosted demand for seasonal labour in these districts.[67]

Scottish farmers maintained their supplies of seasonal workers from three main sources. First, there was increasing dependence on Irish male and female labour, recruited either from permanent migrants, resident in the Scottish towns, or from Ireland itself. The Irish were extensively used in the Lothians for both the potato harvest and turnip thinning, filling the gap left by the ploughmen's daughters who sought opportunities elsewhere. The early potato crop in Ayrshire was gathered by gangs of Irish women who came over from Ireland from June to November, and move from farm to farm as the work required.[68] Second, outside the Lothians, wives of ploughmen were extensively employed as additional sources of casual labour. Farmers in areas as far apart as Aberdeenshire and Dumfries often engaged a man on condition that his wife would milk or do seasonal work as required. In the dairying district of the south-west 'a large number of women' were employed in part-time work on the basis of these informal contracts.[69] Thirdly, there was often heavy reliance on workers recruited for the season from neighbouring towns and villages. Casual workers from the towns, the urban unemployed and the wives and daughters of men working in industry were all represented. Women from Aberdeen and Edinburgh were hired to hoe turnips on adjacent farms.[70] In parts of Lanarkshire in the 1860s, 'women do nearly all the working of potatoes and turnips . . . they come to work from towns and villages'.[71] This reflected the industrial structure of the county as wives and daughters of miners and steelworkers sought work in the fields to supplement family income: 'These farms with the exception of the ploughman and an occasional extra hand worked almost entirely by women taken on as extra hands from the mining villages around'.[72] A similar pattern prevailed in the mining areas of Ayrshire and the industrial parts of Fife. Women employed in Dunbar at the herring curing laboured at other times on neighbouring farms.[73] So also around Paisley, the wives and daughters of industrial workers were important components of the seasonal labour force.[74] Ironically, the growth of the towns, which helped to increase the movement of regular employees from the land, also provided a pool of underemployed labour which could be used to carry out the vital tasks of the farming year. This advantage, of course, applied only to those areas close to urban locations.

III

The inadequacies in the census data make it difficult to carry out a precise analysis of the extent of female participation in lowland agriculture between 1850 and 1914. There was a persistent tendency for enumerators to exclude relatives assisting in agriculture, thus virtually ignoring the important contribution made by female family labour. In the 1871 census all children, even those under the age of five, were counted as part of the farm work force, but in 1881 and 1891 only male relatives of fifteen and above were included. This omission of wives, daughters, grand-daughters and nieces helps to explain the apparently massive fall in 'females engaged in agriculture' from 128,500 in 1871 to 51,657 a decade later. Furthermore, there was little uniformity over time or between different regions for some categories of women workers. 'In-and-out' girls were classed in the censuses of 1891, 1901 and 1911 as 'domestic servants' rather than 'workers engaged in agriculture'. This was probably more likely to happen in the north-east counties where outdoor employment was subsidiary to domestic service, but there is no way of knowing this for certain.[75] Finally, the census catagories cannot provide any guidance about seasonal, casual and part-time women workers, a group which impressionistic evidence suggests was assuming an even greater importance in some rural areas in the later nineteenth century.

The main result of these weaknesses is that the census cannot supply even a rough indication of the total numbers of women engaged in agriculture over time. The massive fluctuation in the female labour supply from census to census is to be explained in large part by changes in the census modes of enumeration rather than by any fundamental alteration in numbers in real terms. Reliance on the crude census data obscures more than it reveals. Necessarily, therefore, the historian is compelled to employ only those parts of the census which are least deficient and complement this material with more qualitative evidence in order to gain an insight into female labour supply in the period of study.

While it is impossible to chart the movement of total numbers over time it is still feasible to survey the experience of particular groups of female workers. One such category is that of 'female wage earners in agriculture', i.e. women engaged as full-time regular labour on Scottish farms. Even this class is subject to the distortion caused by the ambiguous status of the 'in-and-out' girl, but that problem is probably mainly confined to the counties of Aberdeen, Banff and Kincardine, where there was undercounting, and, to a lesser extent, the south-west region. Table 4 presents census figures for 'female wage earners' in agriculture, 1861–1911. Table 5 provides a more refined view of regional conditions over the shorter period, 1871–1891. No confidence can be placed in these data either as precise measurements of reality or as indicators of short-run movement between census years. As the Royal Commission on Labour of 1893 commented of the very heavy drop in female wage earners between 1881 and 1891: 'These results are so extraordinary as to suggest that there must have been some difference in the system of enumeration at the two periods'. Nevertheless, the overall, long-term pattern of decline which they reveal is confirmed by other evidence. In the 1890s, in Ayrshire and Renfrewshire, there was a shortage of full-time dairy-women.[76] In the north-east counties of Moray, Banff and Nairn 'women are hardly known as labourers now at all, unless at harvest'. Increasingly, young men were being employed in tasks formerly the preserve of women.[77] Regular female labour was more plentiful in the south-east, notably in Berwick and Roxburgh, but deficiencies were

226

complained of in the Lothians.[78] After its exhaustive enquiries, the Royal Commission of 1893 reported: 'There were few, if any, places where women were available in sufficient numbers for field work, and where the rare instance of their being sufficient occurred, the supply was largely from the neighbouring villages, and not entirely from the staff of the farm or their families'.[79]

Table 4 Female Wage Earners in Agriculture in Scotland, 1861–1911

Year	Total
1861	40,653
1871	42,773
1881	44,172
1891	22,055
1901	19,810
1911	15,037

Table 5 Female Wage Earners in Agriculture in each Civil Division of Scotland, 1871–1891

Civil Divisions	Wage Earners in Agriculture					
	Numbers			Increase(+) or Rate of Decrease(−)		
	1871	1881	1891	1871–1881	1881–1891	1871–1891
Northern	3184	3555	1221	+11.6	−65.7	−61.6
North & Western	4655	5742	3004	+23.3	−47.7	−35.5
North & Eastern	7642	5689	826	−25.5	−85.5	−89.2
East Midland	6186	7346	3292	+18.7	−55.2	−46.8
West Midland	3889	3941	1676	+1.3	−57.5	−56.9
South Western	5952	6373	3884	+18.5	−39.0	−32.8
South Eastern	5781	6850	4935	+18.5	−28.0	−14.6
Southern	5501	4676	3217	−15.0	−31.2	−41.5
Scotland, Total	42790	44172	22055	+3.2	−50.2	−48.4

Source: Census of Scotland, 1861, 1871, 1881, 1891, 1901, 1911.

In fact, as the Commission's statement implied, while there was a general problem of scarcity, it varied between localities and different grades of worker. In the 1890s in the eastern parishes of Fife, there was a broad balance of supply and demand for women as the county's industrial towns and villages normally produced an adequate flow of seasonal labour when required.[80] Similarly, there was no serious problem in Selkirk, Peebles and Dumfries, because their concentration on pastoral husbandry created little demand for much regular field labour.[81] These areas apart, however, the shortage of women workers was virtually a universal complaint throughout lowland Scotland in the last decade of the nineteenth century. It was the growing scarcity of *regular* female labour which caused particular concern: the supply of seasonal workers was deemed adequate in some localities and plentiful in others which had access to town labour.[82] However, in the south-west 'the cry of the dairying districts is loud, that dairy-women were difficult to get at all and fully qualified dairy-women are very rare indeed'.[83] 'In-and-out' girls were becoming scarce in the years before 1914, and in the Lothian counties daughters of the hinds were increasingly seeking employment off the land as early as the 1850s and 1860s; thus, in the 1890s 'women are scarce in Haddington and in Clackmannan they are almost unprocurable'.[84]

The problem stimulated a considerable contemporary debate, and a number of theories were advanced in the later nineteenth century to explain why it was more difficult to obtain women for regular agricultural employment.[85] Some saw it as the inevitable consequence of improving technology displacing unskilled female labour. Others saw a connection with the depression in agricultural prices in the 1880s and 1890s which, in their view, reduced demand for all categories of agricultural labour. A further opinion suggested that conditions of employment for women in agriculture were bad and it was scarcely surprising that they were deserting the land and seeking better opportunities in the towns.

The pace of mechanisation did accelerate in the second half of the nineteenth century. The number of agricultural implement makers in Scotland rose from an estimated 58 in 1861 to 222 in 1891.[86] By 1900, on larger farms, the mechanical reaper-builder had much reduced the old labour requirements of the grain harvest. Even the reaping-machine, introduced into general practice from the later 1860s, in one estimate 'enabled the farmer to harvest his corn crop with half the number of hands'.[87] The horse-rake gave a similar advantage with the hay crop, and the grubber, the chain-harrow, the horse-hoe and the steam threshing-machine all contributed to a reduction in manual labour. But the adoption of these devices was irregular and patchy, and the traditional female tasks of milking, potato picking, turnip harvesting and fruit picking remained, for the most part, unmechanised until 1914 and later.[88] Moreover, was no evidence of a general fall in demand for women as a consequence of improved technology; on the contrary, there were indications that innovation in labour-saving devices derived from labour shortages and rising labour costs caused by migration of workers.[89] As late as 1920, the Committee on Women in Agriculture in Scotland concluded: '. . . in nearly all districts the agricultural industry could still employ more women if women with country experience were willing to do the work.[90] In addition, most of the improved technology before 1914 saved on seasonal labour: the more widespread use of machinery could not in itself explain why *regular* women workers were leaving agriculture. The problem was apparently not one of a major reduction in demand for female services but rather one where supply was not being maintained at the level required by employers.

There are similar difficulties associated with any attempt to explain the scarcity of women workers in terms of 'Agricultural Depression'. C. S. Orwin and E. H. Whetham have argued that 'the main reason' for the decline in rural population after 1870 was 'the restricted opportunity for employment, as farmers cut down their labour force during the depression.[91] But this is hardly a convincing explanation in the Scottish context. Prices did fall for all the major cash crops between 1870 and 1990.

Table 6 *Acreage under different crops in Scotland, 1867–1892*

	1867	1872	1882	1892
Total area under crops, bare-fallow and grass	4,379,000	4,537,000	4,784,000	4,896,928
bean crops	1,364,000	1,435,000	1,425,000	1,297,231
green crops	668,000	701,000	687,000	638,794
bare-fallow	83,000	28,000	21,000	8,584
rotation grass	1,211,000	1,320,000	2,467,000	1,614,070
permanent pasture	1,053,000	1,053,000	1,184,000	1,338,249
horses (farm only)		177,000	191,000	200,109
cattle	979,000	1,121,000	1,081,000	1,221,726
sheep	6,894,000	7,141,000	6,854,000	7,543,447

Table 7 *Acreage under different crops in Scotland, 1867–1892. Calculated on the basis that the Returns for 1867 equal 100*

	1867	1872	1882	1892
Total area under crops, bare-fallow and grass	100	103	109	112
bean crops	100	105	104	96
green crops	100	105	103	98
bare-fallow	100	34	25	19
rotation grass	100	109	121	133
permanent pasture	100	100	112	127
horses (farm only)	100	100	108	113
cattle	100	114	110	125
sheep	100	103	99	109

Source: Paterson, 'Rural Depopulation', p. 268.

Table 8 *Demand for Labour in the Lothians, 1872–1892*

Class of Labourer	Type of Land		
	Purely Arable Per Cent	Mixed Husbandry Per Cent	Hill and Arable Per Cent
Hinds	No Change	−20	−35 to 40
Orra Men	−20		
Regular Women	No Change	−5 to 10	−30
Casual or Day Labourers (Male and Female)	+30	+5 to 15	No Change

Source: R.C. *on Labour, 1893*, Part II, Report by R. H. Pringle on Edinburgh and Haddington (the Lothians), p. 97.

However, as Tables 6 and 7 demonstrate, this led to alterations in balance of the farming system but no drastic reduction in grain or green crop acreage on a scale which would have caused widespread redundancy of labour. Overall, Scottish grain acreage declined by about 15 per cent between 1870 and 1914, but much of the fall was concentrated in that 'cold, infertile plateau' from Midlothian in the east to Dumbarton in the western lowlands.[92] Even in the arable Lothians, as Table 8 illustrates, decline in the demand for regular female labour was confined to areas. fringing the hills and was partly compensated for by an increasing need for seasonal female workers elsewhere in the district.

The impression that demand for female workers was maintained or only fell marginally in most localities throughout the 'Agricultural Depression' is confirmed by the wage data presented in Tables 9 and 10. These suggest a buoyant market for women in general between 1860 and 1890 and indicate, as earlier discussion implied, that only at the grain-harvest, because of improved technology, was there a significant reduction in the need for female services.

The detailed series from Aberdeenshire reveals a rise of about 60 per cent in spring wages between 1870 and 1876. This was then follwed by a fall almost as rapid down to 1881 but, even at the lowest figure, the rate was still above that of 1870. The years 1881 to 1888 were a phase of relatively stable wages, culminating in a significant increase between 1887–88 and 1891–2 and from that point on a general rise to 1900. In brief, spring cash wages paid to women workers increased two to three times over the period 1870 to 1900. It is doubtful if rises of the same order occurred in other areas because, as noted earlier, there was particular difficulty in recruiting female labour in the north-east region. Nonetheless, both the evidence collected by R. H. Pringle (presented in Table 9), and contemporary comment, suggest that farmers in most areas were forced to bid higher in the long run for regular women labourers. Certainly there is no indication that shortage of employment was a factor causing women to leave the land.

It is more likely that the nature of pay and conditions in farming and the pull of alternative employments and opportunities elsewhere were decisive in explaining the migration of female agricultural servants. Some commentators stressed that the central factor was low wages, that women were paid much less than the male rate for doing the same work: 'At many branches of farm labour, a good girl will do more than an average man, yet she had to be content with half his wages. No doubt women's wages have doubled within the last 40 years, but the fact remains that often when working side by side with the orra men and hinds she is doing as much as a man, and yet only getting half a man's wages'.[93] The differential in rates was preserved, despite the difficulty of recruiting women workers, because by custom women's wages were measured as a traditional proportion of the male wage. An additional factor was that many farmers were able to recruit low-paid seasonal workers to replace regular employees, and this reserve may have

Table 9 Average weekly wage of a Woman-Worker (regularly employed) in Scottish Counties, 1867, 1879, 1893

N.R.=No Returns; N.C.=No Change

	Rate of Wage Per Week					
County	1867		1879		1893	
	Ordinary	Harvest	Ordinary	Harvest	Ordinary	Harvest
	s. d.	s. d.	s. d.	s. d.	s. d.	s. d.
Aberdeen	6 0	20 0	7 6	22 6	9 0	N.R.
Ayr	6 0	15 0	7 6	15 0	9 0	N.R.
Banff	6 0	20 0	7 6	15 0	7 6	22 0
Berwick	7 0	20 0	9 0	20 0	10 0	15 0
Clackmannan	N.R.	N.R.	N.R.	N.R.	9 0	21 0
Dumbarton	N.R.	N.R.	N.R.	N.R.	9 0	21 0
Dumfries	6 6	15 0	9 0	18 0	9 0	18 0
Edinburgh	7 0	21 0	8 6	15 0	8 6	13 6
Elgin	5 0	N.R.	7 6	15 0	7 6	22 0
Fife	6 0	18 0	N.R.	N.R.	8 3	18 0
Forfar	6 0	18 0	N.R.	N.R.	8 3	24 0
Haddington	6 0	15 0	9 0	13 6	9 0	16 0
Kincardine	N.R.	N.R.	7 6	20 0	9 0	N.R.
Kinross	N.R.	N.R.	N.R.	N.R.	7 0	18 0
Kirkcudbright	N.R.	N.R.	N.R.	N.R.	8 0	15 0
Lanark	7 6	15 0	9 0	N.R.	9 0	18 0
Linlithgow	7 0	21 0	7 6	15 0	8 0	14 0
Nairn	5 0	9 0	7 6	15 0	7 6	22 0
Peebles	7 6	N.R.	10 0	N.R.	N.R.	N.R.
Perth	6 0	15 0	7 6	18 0	8 0	24 0
Renfrew	8 0	N.R.	9 0	18 0	12 0	21 0
Roxburgh	7 0	20 0	9 0	20 0	10 0	15 0
Selkirk	N.R.	N.R.	9 0	16 0	N.R.	N.R.
Stirling	7 6	15 0	N.R.	N.R.	9 0	21 0
Wigtown	N.R.	N.R.	7 6	15 0	8 0	15 0

helped to depress rates for full-time servants. Female labour was often hired through the father, who undertook to ensure that his women relatives would work when called upon. Joseph Duncan, the Secretary of the Scottish Farm Servants' Union, argued that in Berwick and Roxburgh, '. . . the men have used their women-folk as a lever, for getting better wages for themselves and the women's wages have in consequence suffered'.[94] On the other hand, there had always been a traditional difference between male and female wages. What is significant in the later nineteenth century was not so much the survival of low pay but the fact that it was attracting comment and criticism from women themselves.[95] The controversy over low pay for female labourers, therefore, reflected rising expectations and a growing hostility to farm work which was probably much wider than the problem of inadequate rewards.

Increasingly, agriculture was seen as an 'unwomanlike' occupation.

Table 9 continued

| | Increase or Decrease Per Cent | | | | | |
| | 1867–79 | | 1879–93 | | 1867–1893 | |
Remarks	Ord.	Harv.	Ord.	Harv.	Ord.	Harv.
A 1893 No harvest wage stated	+25	+12.5	+20	...	+50	...
A 1879 Potato-lifting 2s per day	+25	N.C.	+20	...	+50	...
B 1893 £1 for harvest food	+25	−25	N.C	+46.6	+25	+10
B ...	+28.5	N.C.	+11.1	−25	+42.8	−25
C 1893 Potato-lifting 12s per week	...	...	...	...		
D 1893 Potato-lifting 12s per week	...	...	...	...	...	...
D ...	+38.4	+20	N.C.	...	+38.4	+20
E 1893 Potato-lifting 12s per week	+21.4	−28.5	N.C.	−10	+21.4	−35.7
E ...	+50.0	...	N.C.	+46.6	+50.0	...
F 1893 Potato-lifting 12s per week	...	...	...	...	+37.5	N.C.
F 1893 Potato-lifting 12s per week	...	...	...	...	+37.5	+33.3
H 1893 Potato-lifting 12s per week	+50.0	−10.0	N.C.	+18.5	+50.0	+6.6
K ...	...	...	+20.0	...	...	...
K 1893 Potato-lifting 12s per week	...	...	...	...	...	
K ...	+20.0	...	N.C.	...	+20.0	+20.0
L ...	+7.1	−28.5	+6.6	−6.6	+14.2	−33.3
L ...	+50.0	+66.6	N.C.	+46.6	+50.0	+144.4
N ...	+33.3	...	...	...	...	...
P 1867 Turnip-singling 9s	+25.0	+20.0	+6.6	+33.3	+33.3	+60.0
P 1893 Potato-lifting 12s per week						
R 1879 Near towns a higher wage	+12.5	...	+33.3	+16.6	+50.0	...
R 1893 Hay-making 2s 6d per day						
S ...	+28.5	N.C.	+11.1	−25.0	+42.8	−25.0
S ...	...	...	...	...	+20.0	+40.0
W ...	...	...	+6.6	N.C.	...	...

Source: R. H. Pringle, 'The Agricultural Labourer of Scotland: Then and Now', *Trans. Highland and Agricultural Society*, 5th ser. VI (1894) p. 31, based on returns from Royal Commissions, 1867, 1881 and 1893.

Domestic service in the towns, whether or not it offered higher pay, was regarded as more genteel than labouring on a farm. Life on the farm was regarded as 'dirty and rough' compared to some town occupations and was widely criticised for its long and irregular hours, lack of holidays and absence of social attractions.[96] What contributed to these changing attitudes cannot be examined in detail here. Contemporaries explained it in terms of the

Table 10 *Average Female Cash Wages Offered At Spring Hiring Fairs, Aberdeenshire, 1870–1900*

Year Average	Cash Wage
1871	4.9
1872	5.9
1873	6.6
1874	6.8
1875	8.7
1876	8.8
1877	7.8
1878	7.4
1879	6.1
1880	6.1
1881	5.8
1882	6.2
1883	6.6
1884	7.4
1885	6.9
1886	6.6
1888	5.9
1889	6.3
1890	6.1
1891	7.1
1893	7.5
1894	7.3
1895	7.1
1896	7.6
1897	6.9
1898	7.3
1899	8.0
1900	10.0

Source: R. Molland and G. Evans, 'Scottish Farm Wages from 1870 to 1900', *Journal Royal Statistical Society*, Series A (general), CXIII (1950), p. 226.

wider availability of education from 1872, the impact of the railway in forging closer connections with the towns and the rise in earnings of the married farm-servant class, contributing to higher social expectations both for themselves and their families.[97] Whatever the reason, the movement from agriculture was sustained by the development of alternative opportunities outside the farm. As R. H. Pringle argued cogently in 1894: 'Forty years ago, women working on farms had to take what they could get or go idle, for other employment was scarce and factory life was in its infancy. Now the scene is changed, and no educated country girl with a spark of ambition and pride about her need toil among the 'tatties' for lack of opportunities to better herself in a different branch of employment'.[98] The structural change of the Scottish economy ensured that farmers in the later nineteenth century faced greater competition than ever before from urban and industrial employers for women workers. The days of cheap and abundant supplies of women, eager to labour in the countryside for paltry earnings, were gone for ever.

NOTES

1. *Census of Scotland, 1871. Report and Tables Vol. II*, Parliamentary Papers, 1873 (C841), LXXII (hereafter, *Census of Scotland, 1871*).
2. *Ibid.*
3. *Census of Scotland, 1871*.
4. *Royal Commission on the Employment of Children, Young Persons and Women in Agriculture. Fourth Report. Appendix. Part I and II. Parliamentary Papers*, 1870 (C221), XIII (hereafter *Fourth Report on Women in Agriculture*, 1870), p. 227.
5. Henry Stephens, *The Book of the Farm* (Edinburgh, 1844), I, p. 227.
6. Patrick Graham, *General View of the Agriculture of Stirlingshire* (Edinburgh, 1812), p. 313.
7. Archibald Sturrock, 'Report of the Agriculture of Ayrshire', *Prize Essays and Transactions of the Highland Society of Scotland (T.H.A.S.)*, 4th series, I (1866–67), p. 89.
8. *Board of Agriculture for Scotland: Report of the Committee on Women in Agriculture* (1920) (hereafter *Report of Committee on Women in Agriculture*, (1920), p. 19. See below, pp. 107–9.
9. Robert Kerr, *General View of the Agriculture of the County of Berwick* (London, 1809), pp. 414–415.
10. Alexander Fenton, *Scottish Country Life* (Edinburgh, 1977), p. 54.
11. James Headrick, *General View of the Agriculture of the County of Angus* (Edinburgh, 1813), p. 492.
12. G. Robertson, *Rural Recollections* (Irvine, 1829), p. 239.
13. *Ibid.*
14. Ian Carter, *Farm Life in Northeast Scotland, 1840–1914* (Edinburgh, 1979), p. 101; D. T. Jones, Joseph S. Duncan *et al.*, *Rural Scotland during the War* (London, 1926), pp. 194–5.
15. T. M. Devine, ed., *Lairds and Improvement in the Scotland of the Enlightenment* (Dundee, 1979), p. 60.
16. Kerr, *Agriculture in the County of Berwick*, p. 415.
17. Stephens, *Book of the Farm*, II, p. 386.
18. Cunninghame, 'On the Cultivation of Lucerne', *T.H.A.S.*, new series, II, p. 115.
19. E. J. T. Collins, 'The Age of Machinery', in G. E. Mingay, ed., *The Victorian Countryside* (London, 1981), I, p. 201.
20. *Third Report from the Select Committee appointed to inquire into the State of Agriculture and into the Causes and Extent of the Distress which still presses on some Important Branches, Parliamentary Papers*, VIII (1836), Evidence of Robert Hope, pp. 20–21, QQ 9693–4.
21. Valerie Morgan, 'Agricultural Wage Rates in late Eighteenth-Century Scotland', *Economic History Review*, 2nd ser., 24 (1971), pp. 181–201.
22. E. H. Hunt, *Regional Wage Variations in Britain, 1850–1914* (Oxford, 1973), pp. 117–118; E. Richards, 'Women in the British Economy since about 1700', *History*, 59 (1974), p. 353.
23. *Fourth Report on Women in Agriculture, 1870*, Appendix C, p. 121.
24. *Ibid.*
25. Rev. J. Farquharson, 'On Cutting Grain-Crops with the Common Scythe as practised in Aberdeenshire', *T.H.A.S.*, IV (1835), pp. 189–193; Andrew Whyte and Duncan Macfarlane, *General View of the Agriculture of the County of Dumbarton* (Glasgow, 1811), p. 247; Headrick, *Agriculture of Angus*, p. 495.
26. George Skene Smith, *A General View of the Agriculture of Aberdeenshire* (Aberdeen, 1811), p. 521.
27. Malcolm Gray, 'Migration in the Rural Lowlands of Scotland, 1750–1850', in T.

M. Devine and David Dickson, eds., *Ireland and Scotland, 1600–1850* (Edinburgh, 1983), pp. 104–117.

28. *Ibid.*
29. *Ibid.*
30. James Tait, 'The Agriculture of Lanarkshire', *T.H.A.S.*, 4th series (1885), p. 77.
31. *Ibid.*
32. Sturrock, 'Agriculture of Ayrshire', pp. 81–89; *Royal Commission on Labour: the Agricultural Labourer, vol. III, Scotland, Part I. Parliamentary Papers, 1893–4* (C6894–XV), XXXVI (hereafter *R. C. on Labour, 1893, Part I*), pp. 53, 68.
33. *R. C. on Labour, 1893, Part I*, p. 68.
34. *Ibid.*
35. *Census of Scotland, 1871.*
36. *Fourth Report on Women in Agriculture, 1870*, p. 52.
37. *Ibid.*, p. 34.
38. Kerr, *Agriculture of Berwick*, pp. 414–15.
39. *Fourth Report on Women in Agriculture, 1870*, p. 52.
40. *Ibid.*, Appendix F, pp. 185–6.
41. *Ibid.*, p. 53; *New Statistical Account of Scotland* (Edinburgh, 1845), I, p. 78.
42. Anon., 'Social Condition of Our Agricultural Labourers', *Journal of Agriculture*, new ser., 1853–55, p. 152; *New Statistical Account of Scotland*, III, p. 453; Rev. Harry Stuart, *Agricultural Labourers as they Were, Are and Should Be* (2nd ed., Edinburgh, 1854), p. 23.
43. Stuart, *Agricultural Labourers*, p. 23.
44. J. P. D. Dunbabin, *Rural Discontent in Nineteenth Century Britain* (London, 1974), pp. 137–142.
45. *Ibid*; B. W. Robertson, 'The Border Farm Worker, 1871–1971', *Journal of Agricultural Labour Science* (1973), II, pp. 65–93.
46. *R. C. on Labour, 1893, Part II*, p. 196.
47. *Report of Committee on Women in Agriculture, 1920*, p. 13.
48. *Fourth Report on Women in Agriculture, 1870*, pp. 52–3, 102, 105.
49. R. S. Gibb, *A Farmer's Fifty years in Lauderdale* (Edinburgh, 1927), p. 30; James Robb, *The Cottage, the Bothy and the Kitchen* (Edinburgh, 1861), p. 15; T. M. Devine, 'Temporary Migration and the Scottish Highlands in the Nineteenth Century', *Economic History Review*, 2nd ser., XXXII, No. 3., pp. 344–59.
50. Jones, Duncan *et al.*, *Rural Scotland during the War*, p. 197.
51. *Report of Committee on Women in Agriculture, 1920*, p. 19.
52. *Census in Scotland, 1911. Report and Tables, Parliamentary Papers*, 1912–13 (Cd. 6097), CXIX–CXX; Carter, *Farm Life*, p. 106.
53. Sturrock, 'Agriculture of Ayrshire', p. 89.
54. *Fourth Report on Women in Agriculture, 1870*, Appendix F, p. 237.
55. *Report of Committee on Women in Agriculture, 1920*, p. 59.
56. *Ibid.*, Evidence of John Drysdale, Scottish Agricultural Compensation Society, p. 59.
57. The debate can be followed in the *Report of Committee on Women in Agriculture, 1920*.
58. Carter, *Farm Life*, p. 95.
59. *Census of Scotland, 1871.*
60. *Report of Committee of Women in Agriculture, 1920*, pp. 15–16.
61. *R.C. on Labour, 1893, Part II*, pp. 11, 14.
62. *Fourth Report of Women in Agriculture, 1870*, p. 34; A. Macdonald, 'On the Agriculture of the Counties of Elgin and Nairn', *T.H.A.S.*, 4th ser., XVI (1884), p. 119.
63. *Report of the Committee of Women in Agriculture, 1920*, p. 94.

64. James Tait, 'The Agriculture of Lanarkshire', *T.H.A.S.*, 4th ser., XVII (1885), p. 79.
65. Sturrock, 'Agriculture of Ayrshire', p. 59; John Speir, 'Changes in Farm Implements since 1890', *T.H.A.S.*, 5th ser., XVIII (1906), pp. 47–62; *Royal Commission on Agricultural Interests, Reports of Assistant Commissioners, Parliamentary Papers*, 1881 (C2778-II), XVI (hereafter *R.C. on Agricultural Interests*), pp. 567–8; John Wilson, 'Half a Century as a Border Farmer', *T.H.A.S.*, 5th ser., XIV (1902), pp. 39–40; C. S. Orwin and Edith H. Whetham, *History of British Agriculture, 1846–1914* (Newton Abbot, 1971), pp. 256–7.
66. *R.C. on Labour, 1893, Part II*, pp. 9, 49, 51, 89–90.
67. Jones, Duncan *et al.*, *Rural Scotland during the War*, p. 200; *Fourth Report on Women in Agriculture, 1870*, p. 95.
68. *Fourth Report on Women in Agriculture, 1870*, pp. 50–53; *R.C. on Labour, 1893, Part II*, pp. 64, 112, 134–5; *R.C. on Agricultural Interests, 1881, Minutes of Evidence, Part II, Parliamentary Papers*, 1881 (C3096), XVII, p. 318.
69. *Report of Committee on Women in Agriculture, 1920*, pp. 16–17.
70. *Fourth Report on Women in Agriculture, 1870*, pp. 34, 53.
71. *Ibid.*, Appendix C, p. 225.
72. *Ibid.*, p. 107.
73. *R.C. on Labour, 1893, Part II*, p. 209.
74. *Fourth Report on Women in Agriculture, 1870*, Appendix C, p. 250.
75. *Census of Scotland, 1911. Report and Tables: the Counties in Alphabetical Order, Parliamentary Papers*, 1912–13 (Cd. 6097).
76. Archibald McNeilage, 'Farming Methods in Ayrshire', *T.H.A.S.*, 5th ser., XVIII (1906), pp. 11–15.
77. *R.C. on Labour, 1893, Part I*, p. 109. See also *Royal Commission on Agricultural Depression, Minutes of Evidence, III, Parliamentary Papers*, 1896 (C7400), XVII, Q.51, 696, IV, *Parliamentary Papers*, 1896 (C8021), XVII, Q. 51, 829.
78. *Report by Mr. Wilson Fox on the Wages, Earnings and Conditions of Employment of Agricultural Labourers in the United Kingdom, Parliamentary Papers*, 1900 (Cd. 346), LXXXII (hereafter *Wilson Fox's Report on Agricultural Labourers*), p. 68.
79. *R.C. on Labour, 1893 Part I*, p. 52.
80. *Ibid., Part II*, p. 52.
81. *Ibid.*, p. 190.
82. *Wilson Fox's Report on Agricultural Labourers*, pp. 68–69.
83. *R.C. on Labour, 1893, Part I*, p. 52.
84. *Ibid., Part II*, p. 9; *Fourth Report on Women in Agriculture, 1870*, p. 53; *Report of Committee on Women in Agriculture, 1920*, pp. 17–18; *Wilson Fox's Report on Agricultural Labourers*, p. 68.
85. The debate is summarised in Paterson, 'Rural Depopulation', pp. 237–279, but can also be followed in the comments of witnesses to the various Royal Commissions, 1867, 1881 and 1893 mentioned in earlier references in this essay.
86. Paterson, 'Rural Depopulation', p. 265.
87. *R.C. on Agricultural Interests, 1881, Part II*, pp. 567–8; Wilson, 'Half a Century as a Border Farmer', pp. 39–40; Speir, 'Changes in Farm Implements since 1890', pp. 47–62.
88. Orwin and Whetham, *British Agriculture*, pp. 257, 346–8.
89. *R.C. on Labour, 1893, Part I*, pp. 96–7.
90. *Committee on Women in Agriculture in Scotland, 1920*, p. 8.
91. Orwin and Whetham, *British Agriculture*, p. 317.
92. J. A. Symon, *Scottish Farming, Past and Present* (Edinburgh, 1959), p. 197.
93. *R.C. on Labour, 1893, Part II*, p. 117
94. *Committee on Women in Agriculture in Scotland, 1920*, p. 60.

95. *R.C. on Labour, 1893, Part II*, pp. 9, 32, 117.
96. *Fourth Report on Women in Agriculture, 1870*, p. 53, Appendix B, p. 98; *R.C. on Labour, 1893, Part II*, pp. 99–110, 117, 197; *Committee on Women in Agriculture, 1920*, pp. 38, 61, 75, 110.
97. *Ibid.*
98. Pringle, 'The Agricultural Labourer of Scotland', p. 248.

15

THE PARADOX OF SCOTTISH EMIGRATION

European emigration to overseas destinations in the nineteenth and early decades of the twentieth centuries was both extensive and widespread. One authoritative estimate suggests that between 1821 and 1915 about forty-four million emigrated from Europe or about a quarter of the natural population increase on the continent over this period.[1] Scottish emigration was one part of this broader movement and shared many of its features but also possessed certain distinctive characteristics. Most importantly, Scotland lost a much higher proportion of her population than most other European countries through outward movement. In the eight decades before the First World War, M.W. Flinn estimated that somewhat more than half of the natural increase of population in Scotland left the country of their birth.[2] In addition, within the United Kingdom, the Scottish rate of population growth in the later nineteenth and early twentieth centuries was significantly lower than in England and Wales and this can be largely attributed to a rate of emigration about one and a half times that of the two other countries.[3] What is more, the Scottish haemorrhage persisted longer. When UK emigration in general was decelerating, outward movement from Scotland remained very high. Indeed, over the whole period 1861 to 1930, net Scottish emigration reached its greatest ever levels in the decades between the two world wars.[4]

The scale of the exodus from Scotland also stands out in an international context. Dudley Baines has compiled a table of comparative emigrations from European countries between 1861 and 1913.[5] Of sixteen western and central European countries, three, Ireland, Norway and Scotland, in most years consistently headed the league table as the source areas of proportionately most emigrants. Ireland, not unexpectedly, led the list over most of the period. Norway and Scotland fluctuated in their relative positions. However, in no less than three decades, 1851–60, 1871–80, and 1901–10, Scotland was second only to Ireland in this 'unenviable championship' and in 1913 had an even higher rate of emigration than either Ireland or Norway.[6] It should also be noted that these rankings specifically exclude Scottish migration to England.

This comparative context brings into particularly sharp focus the essential paradox of Scottish emigration. Almost all the European countries with significant losses were agricultural economies surprisingly, they included in addition to Norway and Ireland, Spain and Portugal. But in the nineteenth and early twentieth centuries, Scotland's industrial pre-eminence was well established. Already by the census of 1841, only a quarter of her workforce were still occupied in agricultural or related employment. By 1910 it had fallen to just over 10 per cent. From an existing base in linen, cotton and woollen textiles, massive diversification had occurred from c. 1830 into iron, coal, engineering, steel, and shipbuilding. Undeniably by 1900 the heart of the economic system in the west of Scotland deserved the designation 'Workshop of the British Empire'. With industrialisation had come rapid urbanisation. By the end of the nineteenth century, the typical Scot had become a town dweller. In 1911, almost 60 per cent of the population lived in concentrated settlements of more than 5,000 people, while, in a 'Rank Order of European Urbanisation' for 1910–11, covering fifteen countries, Scotland was second only to England and Wales.[7]

Herein lies the puzzle of Scottish emigration. Heavy outward movement from backward and poor rural societies such as Ireland and Italy was not unexpected. As their populations rose in the nineteenth century, these agrarian economies remained relatively sluggish, transatlantic transportation improved, and opportunities increased in North America. Accelerating emigration from these countries could therefore be anticipated. Yet the economic circumstances were entirely different in Scotland. Emigration did already exist in the early nineteenth century but it expanded rapidly just as indigenous employment opportunities became more available and standards of living rose moderately in the later nineteenth century. The transformation of the economy enabled additional numbers to be fed, clothed and employed. Scottish population as a result rose from 1,265,380 in 1755 to 4,472,103 in 1901. But it was precisely in this period that more and more decided to leave. Between 1825 and 1938, 2,332,608 people departed Scotland for overseas destinations.[8] No other industrial society in Europe experienced such a haemorrhage.

Three further aspects deepen the puzzle. First, as the Scots were moving out in larger numbers, so migration into Scotland was on the increase. This was a clear and unambiguous sign that opportunities were not only available in the Scottish economy but were also expanding at a considerable rate. The number of Irish-born had reached 7.2 per cent of the population in 1851 and was still 5.9 per cent as late as 1881.[9] Second, a sampling of Scottish immigrants to the USA in the later nineteenth century indicates that some 77 per cent came from towns rather than from rural areas, a significantly higher proportion than that of the urban proportion within the total Scottish population. Charlotte Erickson has also shown from her examination of American passenger lists that 58.9 per cent of Scottish male emigrants were from 'industrial' counties while, by 1885–8, this ratio had risen to 80 per cent.[10] Jeanette Brock confirms these results.[11] These are significant findings. Even allowing for the possibility of inmigration from rural areas to towns and industrial centres being concealed within the data, they strongly suggest that increasingly after 1860 most emigrants came from the new manufacturing and urban economy and not from distressed or declining country districts in the Highlands or rural Lowlands.

Third, many Scottish migrants in the later nineteenth century and thereafter were possessed of marketable skills. Brinley Thomas has produced figures which show that over the period 1875 to 1914 some 50 per cent of Scottish male emigrants to the United States were 'skilled' and that Scotland also provided the highest proportion of professional or entrepreneurial emigrants from the four UK countries.[12] Interestingly this finding ties in with Isabel Lindsay's conclusions about Scottish graduate emigration in the later twentieth century. Similarly, as many as 55 per cent of adult men leaving Scotland in the early 1920s had skilled trades while in 1912–3 no less than 21 per cent came from the middle-class category of 'commerce, finance, insurance, professional and students'. Only 29 per cent in these years were labourers.[13] Throughout the decades from the mid-nineteenth century, then, a significant number of those who left Scotland were members of the new 'aristocracy of labour' and the business and professional classes. This was again a pattern which was distinctively Scottish. Inevitably the social composition of emigration from most other European societies where agricultural activity remained dominant differed considerably. But the Scottish variant also contrasted with the occupational structure of English emigrants in which common labourers predominated and relatively few were skilled craftsmen.[14] The fact that a substantial number of those who left Scotland had marketable skills helps to account for the remarkable success of many in the New World. Such skills were at a premium in these developing societies and the Scots were often among the minority who possessed them. This is the essential background to Ian Donnachie's survey of Scottish business and economic success in Australia.[15]

Recent research has helped to identify, describe and clarify the distinctive features of emigration from Scotland. Yet, as the inherent paradox becomes clearer, its resolution remains difficult and challenging.[16] Essentially two linked problems come into focus: the reasons why more people left Scotland as the country became increasingly prosperous and the related issue of the forces which lay behind the sheer scale of Scottish emigration which placed it close to the top of the European emigration league. In the state of current knowledge no definitive or entirely convincing answers can be given to these major questions. The purpose of the remainder of this essay is to advance a general interim interpretation of the issues by trying to identify those key features of Scottish society which may help to explain the volume of the exodus. It should be stressed that the exercise is basically speculative and suggestive, an agenda for future research and discussion rather than the setting out of any final thesis.

There is no doubt that the nineteenth- and twentieth-century movement of Scots was very great. However, this fact has tended to obscure the scale of emigration in preceding periods. One of the most important features of modern Scottish emigration was that it was built upon an extensive exodus in earlier times. Inevitably statistics for the pre-1800 phase are even more elusive and less precise than those for later periods. But a recent survey has confirmed that Scotland was then alread a society with very high levels of emigration.[17] Between 1600 and 1650 the net emigration outflow may have been between 85,000 and 115,000 in the second half of the seventeenth century between 78,000 and 127,000. The emigration of mercenary soldiers was very significant but most movement even in this period consisted of civilians. The Scottish colony in Ulster absorbed about 30,000 from the south-west counties in particular by the 1640s. A further 50,000 may have moved across the Irish Sea during the terrible harvest failures of the 1690s.[18] Until the middle decades of the seventeenth century probably more Scots moved to Poland than any other European location but Scandinavia was also a significant point of attraction. Overwhelmingly, Scots emigrants to these destinations were small merchants, pedlars and soldiers while Ulster drew farmers and servants.[19]

Before 1700 there was much greater emigration from Scotland than from England and the country was already losing considerably greater numbers than most European societies.[20] The trend continued in the eighteenth century. Bernard Bailyn's analysis of movement to the thirteen American colonies from Great Britain in the 1770s confirms that proportionately more Scots than English were likely to emigrate.[21] What is also striking is that relative to England, Scotland before 1800 produced a disproportionate number of skilled and educated emigrants: doctors, teachers, ministers, and merchants. As Ned Landsman has succinctly commented:

> In commerce, Scots formed prominent commercial cliques in the Chesapeake, the port cities of New York, Philadelphia, and Charleston, and throughout the backcountry, extending into Canada. In medicine, more than 150 Scottish doctors emigrated to America during the eighteenth century, and almost the whole of the colonial medical profession was Scottish émigré or Scottish trained. In religion, Scots and Scottish trained ministers dominated both the Presbyterian and Episcopal Churches in America. So did Scottish educators, not only at Princeton, under Witherspoon, but at the College of Philadelphia, the many Presbyterian academies in the middle and southern states, and as tutors in Carolina and the Chesapeake.[22]

The professional and entrepreneurial emigration of the nineteenth and twentieth centuries was therefore nothing new. The so-called 'brain drain' has been a feature of Scottish emigration from at least medieval times. Many talented and gifted people left the country even in the eighteenth century which was the great age of Scottish intellectual achievement and remarkable economic improvement. Those critics who see the haemorrhage of indigenous ability as an obstacle to Scottish progress in more modern times need to consider this historical record. The exodus of the able has been a constant theme in Scottish history, even in the most dynamic phases of the nation's development.

This brief survey of the period before 1800 has several implications for an analysis of nineteenth-century movement. It is clear that mass emigration was a continuum; the great diaspora of the Victorian and Edwardian decades was a further stage in a process which had been going on for centuries. The extent of early modern emigration may also have established or extended a 'culture of mobility' in Scottish society. The nineteenth century did, of course, differ from earlier times in one crucial respect. Most Scots in the modern period emigrated to North America and, to a lesser extent, Australasia and South Africa. Before 1700 Ireland, England and Europe were the common destinations. There was therefore little scope for the continuation of 'chain migration' over the centuries. However, in the eighteenth century, important linkages were indeed established between the Highlands and parts of Canada.[23] These became conduits of continuing emigration in subsequent decades. One reason why movement was later so extensive from the western Highlands was the attractive power of these eighteenth-century Gaelic settlements.[24] They provided information and assistance on arrival for new emigrants and so helped to lower the threshold of risk for those contemplating the hazards of the transatlantic journey. Scotland's long record of heavy emigration, however, does still leave the paradox unresolved. In one sense the early modern movements are easily explicable. Scotland before 1700 was undeniably a poor country on the periphery of the European trading system with a climate and topography which were not well suited to the regular production of food surpluses. Recurrent phases of heavy emigration were just as likely in such a society as the harvest crises and failures which punctuated the agrarian economy. In the second half of the sixteenth century, there was grain shortage in some areas of the country in about one-third of the years of the period.[25] But when material conditions measurably improved in the eighteenth century emigration did not recede. On the contrary, it not only persisted after 1750 but accelerated in the second half of the nineteenth century when, by the common consent of historians, standards of life for the majority of people were manifestly becoming better. To understand why this was, a closer focus on this later period is necessary.

To a significant extent the very nature of Scottish economic transformation in the period after c. 1780 became the vital context for extensive emigration. Far from restraining outward movement by providing new employment and material improvement, industrialisation actually stimulated a continuing exodus of people. Basic to the Industrial Revolution in Scotland was profound change in rural social and economic structure. In the Lowlands, farms were consolidated, subtenancies removed and the terms of access to land became more rigid and regulated.[26] Over time fewer and fewer had legal rights to farms as consolidation accelerated and subdivision of holdings was outlawed. As numbers rose through natural increase, mobility of people became inevitable. Peasant proprietorship in Scotland was unknown and by 1840 most Lowland rural Scots were non-inheriting children of farmers, farm servants, country tradesmen, textile weavers or day labourers. The Scottish Poor Law before 1843 was notoriously hostile to the provision of relief for the able-bodied unemployed though, in practice, modest doles were often given. In this context, the majority of the population of the Lowland countryside relied mainly on selling their labour power in the market to survive. The ebb and flow of demand for labour inevitably enforced movement upon them. Before 1800 such domestic mobility was already present and probably gave Scotland a higher incidence of internal migration than most areas of such countries as France the German states.[27]

In the nineteenth century this certainly intensified. There were at least five reasons for this. First, population was rising while both agricultural and industrial opportunities in rural areas were stagnant or, especially after c. 1840, contracting rapidly. In consequence the proportion of natural population employed in agriculture declined markedly from 24 per cent in 1841 to 10 per cent in 1911. Second, most permanent agricultural workers on Scottish farms were 'servants' hired on annual or half-yearly contracts who received accommodation as part of their labour contract. The unemployed farm worker who inevitably had lost his home, had no choice but to move to seek a job.[28] Third, Scottish urbanisation was notable for its speed and scale.[29] The proportion of Scots living in settlements of over 5,000 rose from 31 per cent in 1831 to almost 60 per cent in 1911. The vast majority of the new urban populations were from the farms, villages and small towns of the Lowland countryside.[30] Fourth, the first phase of industrialisation down to c. 1830 had extended manufacturing employment, especially in textiles, in rural areas. During the coal, iron and steel phase, production concentrated more intensively in the central Lowlands, the Border woollen towns, Dundee, Fife and Midlothian. Indeed one of the most striking features of Scottish industrial capitalism was its extraordinary concentration. This process ensured a rapid shedding of population from areas of crumbling employment to the regions of rapid growth in the Forth-Clyde valley.[31] Fifth, in the last quarter of the nineteenth century, clear evidence emerged of a growing rejection by the younger generation of the drudgery, social constraints and isolation of country life. The towns had always had an attraction but now they seduced the youth of rural society as never before.[32]

The interaction of all these influences produced an unprecedented level of mobility. The 1851 census shows that no less than a third of the Scottish population had crossed a county boundary. Recent demographic research has demonstrated also that in the 1860s the vast majority of parishes in all areas were experiencing net outmovement of population.[33] Heavy losses in the Lowlands were especially pronounced in the south-west region and in many parts of the east from Berwick to Moray. The only areas attracting people were in the central zone and the textile towns of the Borders: 'The conclusion must be that almost the whole of rural Scotland (and many of the more industrial and commercial areas also) were throughout our period, unable to provide enough opportunities at home to absorb even quite modest rates of population increase.'[34]

This demographic pattern is crucial to an understanding of the roots of Scottish emigration. The Scots were mobile abroad partly because they were increasingly very mobile at home.[35] No comparative index exists of national rates of European internal migration. If it did, it would probably put the Scots near the top. Emigration, then, was but an extension of migration within Scotland, which was much less painful after 1860 with the revolution in transatlantic travel associated with the steamship. Such a suggestion is entirely consistent with the point made earlier that most emigrants in the later nineteenth century were urban in origin. Almost certainly concealed within this category are many who had been born into an agricultural or industrial background in the countryside and moved to the towns before emigrating. At the same time, one must be careful not to see the process of internal movement as a simple relationship between rural and urban society. After 1860 there was much greater migration between cities and towns of varying size, prosperity and occupational structure than there was between urban areas and country districts.[36]

The direct and indirect links between Scottish emigration and Lowland mobility helps to place the well-known contribution of the Highlands in perspective. But the significance of Highland emigration as an important part of the Scottish exodus as a whole should not be underestimated. Until the middle decades of the nineteenth century the region contributed disproportionately to the total outflow. In more precise terms the western Highlands and Islands did so; most of those who left the parishes of the southern, central and eastern fringes in the first instance made for the Lowland towns.[37] The factors explaining the Highland exodus are far from simple. The far west was a poor, conservative peasant society where, through subdivision, access to land, albeit in minute holdings, was still possible for the majority. The regional society most closely comparable within the British Isles was the west of Ireland which was broadly similar in its poverty, peasant social system and tenacious attachment to peasant values. For these very reasons, however, emigration from this area was limited compared to Ulster and the eastern districts of Ireland.[38]

In part what made the western Highlands different was the incidence of soldier emigration from the region. This not only established a tradition of mobility and spread knowledge of overseas destination but the military settlements created after the Seven Years' War the American War also acted as foci of attraction for successive waves of Highland emigrations.[39] Scottish Gaeldom was also much more subject to intense levels of commercialisation than the communities of the west of Ireland. The rent inflation of the post-1760 period, the 'modernisation' of the social system through the destruction of the old joint tenancies, the imposition of the croft system and the clearances is for sheep all represented the powerful impact of 'improving' ideology and Lowland market forces on traditional society. Up to c.1820, the Highland emigrations can be regarded as attempts to resist the forces which were transforming the old ways so painfully and rapidly. Internal protest was muted but emigration was extensive and was preferred to migration to the south because of the independence which came from holding land and because the preservation of traditional values could be more easily ensured.[40]

But the mass outward movement of Highlanders only occurred after 1820 and especially in the famine of the 1840s and 1850s.[41] Essentially that can be seen once again as a process intimately associated with Scottish industrialisation. This is a connection which reinforces the thesis under discussion: the economic transformation itself was in the final analysis a major influence on emigration. It was the stimuli of southern industry which produced buoyant demand for Highland cattle and kelp and encouraged landlords to subdivide land among the population to boost output of these commodities. But this inevitably led to an imbalance between the number of inhabitants and existing resources which was rendered even more acute after 1820 when Lowland textile and chemical industries found cheaper alternatives to Highland kelp. At the same time the now 'redundant' population in the north-west was further squeezed by clearances designed to extend sheep farming, which because of changing external demand remained the only significantly profitable specialisation.[42]

The emigration of the Highland population therefore indicates how a society can experience very heavy outward movement despite the growth of a modern economic system. Industrialisation brings increased wealth but its benefits are usually spread unevenly. Growing poverty in one region is entirely compatible with plenty in another, especially as the dynamic industrial growth ensures the destruction of formerly viable subsistence and semi-subsistence economies in peripheral areas. As manufacturing concentrated ever more in the central zone the mass exodus from the poorer rural areas of the south-west and the north became inevitable.

Yet, as indicated earlier, specifically 'rural' factors cannot explain the later nineteenth-century emigration which derived predominantly from the industrial and urban regions and eventually mainly comprised those with industrial skills. The dynamism of the manufacturing economy had for some time created stresses and tensions which squeezed out certain groups of worker. The classic example was the impact of changing technology on the handloom weavers.[43] One of their responses was the formation of emigration societies which gave support to those in declining crafts to seek a new life overseas. This phase in Scottish emigration forms the background to Michael Vance's study.[44] But the movement of the handloom weavers was never numerically significant and was over in large part by 1850. The large-scale emigration of craft and industrial workers after that date cannot be explained in terms of technological unemployment. If many emigrants were 'victims' of Scottish industrial society their condition was dictated by more subtle forces than this.

Two features of Scottish industrialism may have promoted significant levels of emigration. First, for much of the period, Scotland was a low-wage economy. Indeed, it was generally recognised that Scottish industrial success in large part rested on low labour costs, the result in part of mass inward migration from the rural areas and Ireland to the industrial centres. There was considerable variation between areas and occupations but in 1860 Scottish wages were often up to 20 per cent lower than for equivalent English trades.[45] Scholarly debate continues over the extent of convergence thereafter but when real wages are considered the most recent estimate suggests that Scottish manufacturing earnings were still 10 to 12 per cent less than in the industrial areas of England on the eve of the First World War.[46]

There is no inevitable correlation between low wages and emigration. What is crucial is the relative differential between opportunities at home and overseas. In the second half of the nineteenth and early twentieth centuries that differential between western Europe and the New World became greater. Wages and opportunities were increasing at home but they were doing so with even greater speed overseas because the American economies were very rich in resources but grossly underpopulated. Those with industrial skills and experience were especially in demand.[47] The scenario for mass emigration from societies such as Scotland was clearly emerging as the previous constraints on movement crumbled. Ignorance of conditions across the Atlantic and in Australasia diminished as information was disseminated more widely through the press, government sources, emigration societies and previous emigrants. Emigration therefore became available to many more as income levels rose in the later nineteenth century. The sheer cost had been a significant obstacle to many in previous times. Detailed analysis of migration in Scottish rural society after 1870 has suggested a marked increase in social expectations, a change partly related to higher wages but also to expansion in educational opportunities after 1872.[48] It would seem likely that there were similar attitudinal changes among many urban and industrial workers and these may have intensified their awareness of greater opportunities overseas.

Above all, the transport revolution was critical.[49] The steamship did not so much lower the costs of transatlantic travel as radically increase its speed, comfort and safety. In the 1850s it took six weeks to cross the Atlantic. By 1914 this had fallen to a week. In 1863 45 per cent of transatlantic emigrants left in sailing ships. By 1870 only a tiny number travelled in this way.[50] By drastically cutting voyage times the steamship removed one of the major costs of emigration, the time between embarkation and settlement, during which there was no possibility of earning. In North America itself the unprecedented expansion of the railway from the 1850s further facilitated rapid movement. All in all, what was being created for the first time was a truly efficient international transport system. The essential infrastructure for the formation of a transatlantic labour market was evolving.

That the Scottish labour market had now become internationalised was apparent in three ways. First, it is shown in the way that heavy phases of emigration were very closely related to boom conditions in the North American economy.[51] Second, it is illustrated by the seasonal emigration across the Atlantic of particular groups of workers, such as Aberdeen granite tradesmen, who were recruited in Scotland by agents for American companies.[52] Third, and most importantly of all, the process can be seen in the increasing frequency of return emigration. Transport constraints in the era of the sailing ship ensured that emigration was virtually permanent exile for most. The steamship made return not only more possible but very common. One (probably) conservative estimate suggests that by the later nineteenth century around one-third of those who left, sooner or later returned.[53]

In this period, then, the habitual and historic internal mobility of the Scots could be translated fully into international movement. In the same way as they had compared wages and employment within Scotland, it was now easier than ever before to evaluate opportunities in New York, Toronto and Chicago in relation to Glasgow and Edinburgh. The income differentials were often so enormous and the skills shortage in the New World so acute that many thousands could not resist the lure, especially since, in the event of failure, the return journey home was the price of a steamship ticket. The temptation was also there, of course, for the skilled of that other advanced economy, England. But it is hardly surprising that the Scots found it more irresistible. Scotland was still a poorer society than England and the difference between opportunities at home and abroad was greater for the Scots. Quite simply, they had more to gain by emigration. The proof of this was the enormous migration from Scotland to England before 1900. For the period 1841 to 1911, according to one estimate, about 600,000 Scots-born persons moved to England and Wales.[54] This was around half of the total net emigration from Scotland in the nineteenth century and was not paralleled by any similar significant movement from the south to the north. This was eloquent testimony of the perceived differences in standards of life between the two socities, especially when it is remembered that from the 1870s many Scots who moved to England were skilled and increasingly settled in the mining and heavy industrial areas of England and Wales.

But it was not simply because the rewards of industry could not compete with those abroad or in England. Scottish emigration also attained such high levels *because* of the peculiar economic structure of the society. It had a higher proportion of its inhabitants employed in industrial work by 1871 than any other country in western Europe apart from England. But unlike England, the majority of the employed male population in Scotland was heavily concentrated in the capital goods sector of shipbuilding,coal, metals and engineering. In addition, to an unusual extent, many of these activities were heavily dependent on the export market. The Scottish economy lacked the cushion of a strong service sector and a range of industries catering for the domestic market.[55] After 1830 the British economy as a whole became subject to more extreme fluctuations in the trade cycle but in Scotland the amplitude and duration of cyclical change was more violent because of the tight interrelationships within the heavy industrial structure, the bias towards foreign markets, which were inherently fickle, and the relative weakness of domestic demand. This economic insecurity was basic to emigration. Violent fluctuations in employment were integral to Scottish industrial 'prosperity' even in the heyday of Victorian and Edwardian expansion. Their scale and frequency can be seen in the building industry which employed about 7 per cent of the occupied male labour force in the 1880s. Between 1881 and 1891 the numbers employed fell by 5.1 per cent, rose by 43.4 per cent during 1891 to 1901 and contracted again by a massive 21.4 per cent over the years 1901–11.[56] Not surprisingly emigration was at its height at the bottom of these cycles. Because fluctuations were probably more savage and longer lasting in Scotland it is reasonable to assume that the volume of outward movement would be greater than south of the Border. The dramatic peaks in Scottish emigration, the later 1840s and early 1850s, the mid–1880s and 1906 to 1913 all took place in periods of serious industrial depression at home.

Similarly, the continuation of heavy outmigration from Scotland in the 1920s and 1930s at a time when it was decelerating elsewhere in the United Kingdom is itself largely attributable to her characteristic industrial structure. Because of the peculiar mix of heavy, export-orientated industries, Scotland's most populated areas were a good deal worse off than elsewhere. At the bottom of the slump in 1931–3 more than a quarter of the Scottish workforce was without a job compared to a little over a fifth in the UK as a whole.[57] The Scots suffered disproportionately and not surprisingly tended to emigrate when they could in greater numbers. *Plus ça change, plus c'est la même chose.*

NOTES

1. I. Ferenczi and W. F. Willcox, *International Migrations* (New York, 1929–31), pp. 236–88.
2. M. W. Flinn (ed.), *Scottish Population History from the Seventeenth Century to the 1930s* (Cambridge, 1977), p. 448.
3. M. Anderson and D. J. Morse, 'The People' in W. H. Fraser and R. J. Morris (eds.), *People and Society in Scotland, 1830–1914* (Edinburgh, 1990), pp. 12–14.
4. Flinn (ed.), *Scottish Population History*, p. 449.

5. Dudley Baines, *Migration in a Mature Economy* (Cambridge, 1985), p. 10.
6. Flinn (ed.), *Scottish Population History*, p. 448.
7. R. J. Morris, 'Urbanisation and Scotland' in Fraser and Morris (eds.), *People and Society in Scotland*, p. 74.
8. Flinn (ed.), *Scottish Population History*, pp. 441–2.
9. R. H. Campbell, 'Scotland', in R. A. Cage (ed.), *The Scots Abroad* (London, 1985), p. 13.
10. Charlotte J. Erickson, 'Who were the English and Scots Emigrants to the United States in the Late Nineteenth Century?' in D. V. Glass and R. Revelle (eds.), *Population and Social Change* (London, 1972), pp. 360–2.
11. Jeanette M. Brock, 'The Importance of Emigration in Scottish Regional Population Movement 1861–1911', in T. M. Devine (ed.), *Scottish Emigration and Scottish Society* (Edinburgh, 1992).
12. B. Thomas, *Migration and Economic Growth: A Study of Great Britain and the Atlantic Economy* (Cambridge, 1973), p. 62.
13. Isobel Lindsay. 'Migration and Motivation: A Twentieth-Century Perspective' in Devine ed. *Scottish Emigration.*
14. Baines, *Migration*, p. 51.
15. Ian L. Domachie, 'The Making of "Scots on the make": Scottish settlement and enterprise in Australia, 1830–1900', in Devine ed., *Scottish Emigration.*
16. R. H. Campbell was one of the first to indicate the paradox in print. See Campbell, 'Scotland', pp. 29–45.
17. T. C. Smout, N. C. Landsman and T. M. Devine, 'Scottish Emigration in the Seventeenth and Eighteenth Centuries' (forthcoming).
18. M. Perceval-Maxwell, *The Scottish Migration to Ulster in the Reign of James I* (London, 1973), pp. 311–14; L. M. Cullen, 'Population Trends in Seventeenth-Century Ireland', *Economic and Social Review*, 6 (1975), pp. 154–7.
19. A. Bieganska, 'A Note on the Scots in Poland, 1550–1880', in T. C. Smout (ed.), *Scotland and Europe, 1200–1850* (Edinburgh, 1986), pp. 157–161.
20. Smout, Landsman and Devine, 'Scottish Emigration'.
21. B. Bailyn, *Voyagers to the West* (London, 1986).
22. Smout, Landsman and Devine, 'Scottish Emigration'.
23. J. M. Bumsted, *The People's Clearance: Highland Emigration to British North America, 1770–1815* (Edinburgh, 1982).
24. *Ibid.*
25. S. G. E. Lythe, *The Economy of Scotland in its European Setting, 1550–1625* (Edinburgh, 1960), ch. 1.
26. The most recent examination of this process is by M. Gray, 'The Social Impact of Agrarian Change in the Rural Lowlands' in T. M. Devine and R. Mitchison (eds.), *People and Society in Scotland, 1760–1830* (Edinburgh, 1988), pp. 53–69.
27. R. A. Houston, 'The Demographic Regime' in Devine and Mitchison (eds.), *People and Society in Scotland*, p. 20.
28. T. M. Devine (ed.), *Farm Servants and Labour in Lowland Scotland, 1770–1914* (Edinburgh, 1984), *passim.*
29. T. M. Devine, 'Urbanisation' in Devine and Mitchison (eds.), *People and Society in Scotland*, pp. 27–9.
30. *Ibid*, pp. 41–7.
31. Malcolm Gray, *Scots on the Move: Scots Migrants, 1750–1914* (Dundee, 1990), pp. 14–23.
32. T. C. Smout, *A Century of the Scottish People, 1830–1950* (London, 1986), pp. 81–4; Devine (ed.), *Farm Servants and Labour*, pp. 251–3.
33. Anderson and Morse, 'The People', pp. 19.
34. *Ibid*, p. 22.

35. Campbell, 'Scotland', p. 10.
36. J. M. Brock, 'Scottish Migration and Emigration, 1861–1911', unpublished PhD thesis, University of Strathclyde, 1990.
37. T. M. Devine, 'Highland Migration to Lowland Scotland, 1760–1860', *Scottish Historical Review*, lxii (1983).
38. C. O'Grada, 'Irish Emigration to the United States in the nineteenth century', in D. N. Doyle and O. D. Edwards (eds.), *America and Ireland, 1776–1976* (London, 1980).
39. Bumsted, *The People's Clearance*, pp. 67–9.
40. T. M. Devine, 'Landlordism and Highland Emigration', in T. M. Devine (ed.), *Scottish Emigration and Scottish Society* (Edinburgh, 1992), pp. 92–5.
41. T. M. Devine, *The Great Highland Famine: Hunger, Emigration and the Scottish Highlands in the Nineteenth Century* (Edinburgh, 1988).
42. *Ibid.*
43. N. Murray, *The Scottish Handloom Weavers, 1790–1850: A Social History* (Edinburgh, 1978), pp. 142–7.
44. Michael E. Vance, 'The Politics of Emigration: Scotland and Assisted Emigration to Upper Canada, 1815–26', in T. M. Devine (ed.), *Scottish Emigration and Scottish Society*, (Edinburgh, 1992).
45. Smout, *A Century of the Scottish People*, 112; R. H. Campbell, *The Rise and Fall of Scottish Industry, 1707–1939* (Edinburgh, 1980), pp. 76–101.
46. R. G. Rodger, 'The Invisible Hand: Market Forces, Housing and the Urban Form in Victorian Cities', in D. Fraser and A. Sutcliffe (eds.), *The Pursuit of Urban History* (London, 1980), pp. 190–211.
47. J. D. Gould, 'European Intercontinental Emigration, 1815–1914: patterns and causes', *Journal of European Economic History*, 8 (1979).
48. Devine (ed.), *Farm Servants and Labour*, pp. 119–20, 251–3.
49. Baines, *Migration*, p. 279.
50. M. Harper, *Emigration from North-East Scotland* (Aberdeen, 1988), I, p. 96.
51. Brock, 'Scottish Migration', p. 410.
52. Harper, *Emigration from North-East Scotland*, pp. 254–9.
53. Anderson and Morse, 'The People', p. 16.
54. Flinn (ed.), *Scottish Population History*, p. 442.
55. Clive Lee, 'Modern Economic Growth and Structural Change in Scotland: the Service Sector Reconsidered', *Scottish Economic and Social History*, 3 (1983), pp. 5–35.
56. J. H. Treble, 'The Occupied Male Labour Force' in Fraser and Morris (eds.), *People and Society in Scotland*, pp. 195–6.
57. Smout, *Century of the Scottish People*, p. 114.

INDEX